KARMA AND GRACE

RELIGION, CULTURE, AND PUBLIC LIFE

RELIGION, CULTURE, AND PUBLIC LIFE

Series Editor: Matthew Engelke

The Religion, Culture, and Public Life series is devoted to the study of religion in relation to social, cultural, and political dynamics, both contemporary and historical. It features work by scholars from a variety of disciplinary and methodological perspectives, including religious studies, anthropology, history, philosophy, political science, and sociology. The series is committed to deepening our critical understandings of the empirical and conceptual dimensions of religious thought and practice, as well as such related topics as secularism, pluralism, and political theology. The Religion, Culture, and Public Life series is sponsored by Columbia University's Institute for Religion, Culture, and Public Life.

For a complete list of books in the series, please see the Columbia University Press website.

KARMA AND GRACE

Religious Difference
in Millennial Sri Lanka

NEENA MAHADEV

Columbia University Press

New York

Winner of the 2021 Claremont Prize
Institute for Religion, Culture, and Public Life at Columbia University
Publication of this book was made possible in part by funding from the
Institute for Religion, Culture, and Public Life at Columbia University.

Columbia University Press
Publishers Since 1893
New York   Chichester, West Sussex
cup.columbia.edu
Copyright © 2023 Columbia University Press

Library of Congress Cataloging-in-Publication Data
Names: Mahadev, Neena, author.
Title: Karma and grace : religious difference in millennial Sri Lanka / Neena Mahadev.
Description: New York : Columbia University Press, 2023. | Series: Religion, culture, and
    public life | Includes bibliographical references and index.
Identifiers: LCCN 2023016673 (print) | LCCN 2023016674 (ebook) | ISBN 9780231205283
    (hardback) | ISBN 9780231205290 (trade paperback) | ISBN 9780231555937 (ebook)
Subjects: LCSH: Christianity and other religions—Buddhism. | Buddhism—Relations—
    Christianity. | Sri Lanka—Religion—21st century.
Classification: LCC BR128.B8 M325 2023 (print) | LCC BR128.B8 (ebook) |
    DDC 261.2/43—dc23/eng/20230530
LC record available at https://lccn.loc.gov/2023016673
LC ebook record available at https://lccn.loc.gov/2023016674

Printed in the United States of America
Variations upon chapter 1 and chapter 5 have appeared in *Current Anthropology* and
in the *Journal of the Royal Anthropological Institute*, respectively.
Cover design: Elliott S. Cairns
Cover image: J. C. Rathnayake, painting of Athurugiriya, Sri Lanka

In loving memory of my dear brother, Kishore Mahadev.

And in memory of my friend Blayne Grenfell, a consummate pluralist.

Contents

Acknowledgments

At the core of this book is a layered set of debts to interlocutors, teachers, mentors, and friends. The gifts they have offered me as I undertook this work can never fully be repaid.

My gratitude goes to the interlocutors and friends in Sri Lanka that I have met over the twenty odd years since my very first visit. I thank Thushari Dinusha Sunnadeniyage for her friendship, care, and intrepid assistance. Suneel DeSilva, my "Amma," and the late J. Chandra DeSilva, my "Thaththa," and Chandima Weerasuriya and Chanaka Lokuge and their families have nourished my curiosity with their intelligence, friendship, hospitality, and care. Noel Arokiam, Piumi Ederage, Ramesh Mendis, and the Francisco family offered support, interpretation, clarification, and companionship as I carried out my research. Herath Bandara has been a most generous Sinhala *guruwarayak*. Numerous other friends and interlocutors feature in the pages of this book. Many of them I cannot name directly, so I have used pseudonyms for reasons of agreed upon anonymity and prudence. I wish to convey to all of them, named and unnamed here, an abundance of merit and love. This book would not have been possible without their warmth and graciousness.

Several generous readers ensured that I became more meticulous in my craft of ethnographic writing and argument. Matthew Engelke, Maria José de Abreu, and Sudipta Kaviraj, all participated in a discussion of this manuscript in the Claremont Prize workshop sponsored by the Institute for Religion, Culture, and Public Life (IRCPL) at Columbia University in December 2022. Suggestions they offered during the final phases of my writing have substantively improved the work. I especially thank Matthew for engaging this project as the series editor and for giving me the opportunity to work on the manuscript as an affiliate of IRCPL in 2022. Additional thanks to Zé too; since we have known each other, the conversations I have had with her have never ceased to spark my imagination.

The research that animates this book began at Johns Hopkins University. Veena Das, Naveeda Khan, and Jane Guyer were exemplary mentors as I began to develop this ethnography. Each one of them gave me incisive comments that inspired me to deepen and refine my inquiry. Although I have sometimes articulated it subtly, they have each left invaluable imprints upon my thinking. I also had the privilege of studying with Deborah Poole, Fenella Cannell, Bill Connolly, Jane Bennett, Niloofar Haeri, John D. Kelly, and Hent de Vries, who additionally stimulated the directions of my thought. Amrita Ibrahim, Andrew Bush, Hester Betlem, Aaron Goodfellow, Sylvain Perdigon, Andrew Brandel, and Thomas Cousins have variously engaged and encouraged my work for many years. It is because of Amrita's intellectual generosity that I eventually came around to reconceptualize my work through the lens of religion, media, and mediation.

During my time in Sri Lanka, discussions with Gananath Obeyesekere, Shanta Premawardhana, Tudor Silva, the late S. H. Hasbullah, Sunil Bastian, the late Malathi de Alwis, Jayadeva Uyangoda, and Sudharshan Seneviratne helped to guide my observations. Many thanks also to Father Aloysius Pieris, the late Father Tissa Balasuriya, Venerable Reverend R. Assagi Thero, Father Jayasiri Pieris, Reverend Keerthisiri Fernando, Sister Noel Christine Fernando, Father Sarath Iddamagolla, Sandamali Karunarathna, and Angel Kotelawala. The late Ponnuthurai Thambirajah, librarian of the International Centre for Ethnic Studies, and Chandini Perera, librarian at the Center for Society and Religion, were also immensely helpful to me during my time in Sri Lanka.

Jonathan Spencer, Charlie Hallisey, Farzana Haniffa, Jon Bialecki, Cecilia van Hollen, Jean Comaroff, and Stuart Strange each read and offered astute comments on an earlier iteration of the full manuscript. They encouraged me to allow my ethnographic writing to perform more of the work—and the book is all the better for their suggestions. Yale-NUS College generously sponsored workshops in Edinburgh and in Singapore that allowed me to be in conversation with them.

A cohort of colleagues whose paths crossed mine during research in Sri Lanka have also been formative in my thinking—namely Nalika Gajaweera, Ben Schonthal, Mythri Jegathesan, Nimanthi Rajasingham, Bart Klem, Vivian Choi, and Eva Ambos. Conversations with them continue to excite my thinking.

At the Max Planck Institute, Peter van der Veer became a source of support, insightful conversation, and good advice. At the University of Göttingen, Patrick Eisenlohr, Srirupa Roy, Rupa Viswanath, and Nate Roberts gave counsel. Since our time in Göttingen, I have enjoyed conversations with Jeremy F. Walton, a generative and generous thinker and friend.

I thank Valentina Napolitano, Filippo Ossella, Anne Blackburn, Sidharthan Maunaguru, Mark Whitaker, Paul Sorrentino, Anderson Blanton, Rob Blunt, Elliott Prasse-Freeman, Leilah Vevaina, Girish Daswani, Liana Chua, Radhika Gupta, Aparna Nair, Saikat Maitra, and again Naveeda Khan and Andrew Bush. They each engaged pieces of this work when I shared it with them in early stages. Two anonymous reviewers also provided immensely helpful feedback on the manuscript.

Additionally deserving mention for conversations that have inspired my thought are Bénédicte Brac de la Perrière, Patrice Ladwig, Nicolas Sihlé, Atreyee Sen, Carola Lorea, Roshan de Silva-Wijeyaratne, Harini Amarasuriya, Tam Ngo, Vineeta Sinha, Sian Lazar, Kenneth Dean, Webb Keane, Michael Lambek, Anne Hansen, Michael Puett, Ananda Abeysekera, Balasingham Skanthakumar, Sasanka Perera, Michael Edwards, Méadhbh McIvor, Gerard McCarthy, Lauren Leve, Lucinda Ramberg, Kathy Ewing, Simon Coleman, Michiel Baas, Céline Coderey, Catherine Scheer, Justin Henry, Chitra Venkataramani, Amanda Lucia, Laura-Zoë Humphreys, Alan Strathern, Matthew Walton, Dominik Müller, Jock Stirrat, Tom Widger, Scott MacLochlainn, Dan Bass, Bernardo Brown, Luke Heslop, and Rukmini Barua. I have had the opportunity to present my research at University of Toronto, Cornell University, Columbia University, New York University, Jawaharlal Nehru University, Oxford University, National University of Singapore, Johns Hopkins, the University of California–Riverside, Augustana College, the Open University of Sri Lanka, University of Utrecht, Durham University, the Society for Buddhist-Christian Studies, and the Centre d'Études Interdisciplinaires sur le Bouddhisme in Paris. I am grateful for the excellent audience questions and comments at those venues, many of which have facilitated the development of this book.

A number of scholars associated with the American Institute for Sri Lankan Studies have been encouraging sources of support, namely John Rogers, Sharika Thiranagama, Dennis McGilvray, and Jeanne Marecek, along with others already named. I am also grateful for the ISLE Program for sparking my fascination with and love for Sri Lanka.

In Singapore, my colleagues at Yale-NUS College have been tremendously supportive. I am grateful particularly to Zach Howlett, Ting Hui Lau, Amali Ibrahim, Gabriele Koch, Rohan Mukherjee, Ben Schupman, Larry Ypil, Christina Tarnopolsky, Nirmali Fenn, Erik Harms, Marcia Inhorn, Jane Jacobs, Chris Howell, and David Jacks. At the National University of Singapore, I would like to thank colleagues of the Asia Research Institute, the Sociology and Anthropology Department, and the South Asian Studies Program. Conversations with a wonderful set of students at Yale-NUS have also shaped the thinking that has crystallized in this book.

Wendy Lochner at Columbia University Press has done exceptional editorial work to help see *Karma and Grace* through to publication. Lowell Frye also deserves special mention for his editorial acumen. My sincere thanks to them, and also to Leslie Kriesel and Gregory McNamee, for their consistent care and attention to this project.

Utmost thanks to my friends, relatives, and parents who sustain me. In Singapore, Sri Lanka, and the U.S., I thank Dany Inthaxoum, Dona Inthaxoum, Magda Magiera, David Teh, Kane Cunico, Dhivya Sivanesan, the Tholandis, the Nagarajans, and the Brayaks. In Tamilnadu and beyond, thanks to the Krishnamoorthys, the Natarajans, the Soundarapandians, the Rajarams, the Dhanapals, the Geethagiris, and the Thiagarajans. Kiku, who has sprawled across laptop keys and printed pages, has gained osmotic familiarity with the contents of this book. He helped me survive a pandemic-era sabbatical in Singapore, and provides joy on the daily. In Geneva, Illinois, I am grateful to Kelly, Blake, and Jackson Mahadev for their presence in my life. The untimely passing of my brother, Kishore, is unspeakably sad. But together with them, and my parents, we celebrate his life. This work would not have come to be without my Mom and Dad, Shashi and Vennar Alagappan Mahadev. For their wisdom, guidance, and brave and unstinting support of me, my meanderings and travels—and of this labor of love of a book that took ever so long to write—they have my eternal gratitude.

———————————◆———————————

The field research \that this book is built upon was generously supported by the Wenner Gren Foundation for Anthropological Research, the National Science

Foundation Graduate Research Fellowship Program, the Philanthropic Educational Organization, the Yap Kim Hao Memorial Fund, the J. William Fulbright Foundation, the Johns Hopkins University Department of Anthropology, and the Max Planck Institute. I was afforded time to finalize the manuscript at Yale-NUS College and at the Institute for Religion, Culture, and Public Life at Columbia University.

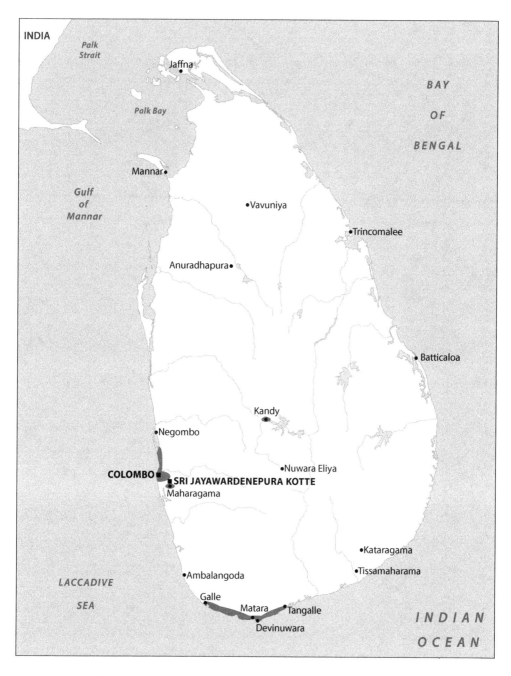

0.1 Map of Sri Lanka, and the Ethnographer's Itineraries
Rainer Lesniewski/Shutterstock.com, modified by the author

KARMA AND GRACE

Introduction

Inter-Religion in Sri Lanka

Heretics will converge on the center of Dambadiva *from the periphery and sur-round it. Like the waves of an ocean, they will inundate the land. [The kingdom] will come under siege and fall into the hands of these frightful heretics.*

    —The Carpenter Heretic (1762), trans. Richard Fox Young and G. S. B. Senanayake

The modern nation as an imagined community is always mediated through con-structed images. . . . For the media are not simply the means through which indi-viduals simultaneously imagine their national community; they mediate that imagination, construct the sensibilities that underpin it.

    —Talal Asad, Formations of the Secular

Although the sky hadn't yet turned toward dusk, small terracotta oil lamps flickered along the pathway from the road to the gather-ing hall at Maharagama temple-monastery, a center famed for training many of Sri Lanka's most eminent, politically engaged, and socially con-servative Theravadin monks.[1] As planned, I met Nimesh at the front gate, and we walked that path solemnly alongside many others who donned the white garb of Buddhist devotion to attend the seventh year death memorialization of Rev-erend Soma Thera in December 2010.[2] Nimesh and his family were devotees of the monk until his "mysterious" death brought him to an early demise. The ven-erable had garnered the adoration of a large subset of Sri Lankan Buddhists. Many of my interlocutors conveyed that it was Soma Thera who had introduced them to "real Buddhism" (*āthatama Buddhāgama*). They expressed an affinity for

Soma Thera's preaching of Sinhala language sermons (*bana*) that were regularly broadcast on television and for his writings circulated in print. In the cities of Colombo and Kandy, and in towns and villages in the southern coastal stretches of Sri Lanka, I often found that Sinhala Buddhist families had enshrined a full-color photograph of the late monk, sometimes clipped from the newspaper, prominently within their homes. Devotees typically placed a single photo of Soma Thera below a statue (*pilimeya*) of the Buddha, alongside incense, oil lamps, and *araliya* flowers. During the 1990s and early 2000s, the monk had become a central figure in the revival and reform of Buddhism in Sri Lanka (Berkwitz 2008). In the course of his eloquent discourses on Buddhist thought and practice, Soma Thera warned Sri Lankan Buddhists of the rise of "unethical" conversions to Christianity, and of the encroachment of Islam in their country (Deegalle 2004; Uyangoda 2007). The events associated with Soma Thera's passing reached me as I perused the international news from my desk in Baltimore in early 2004. In the months following his death, BBC News headlines announced that a contingent of Sri Lankan monks formed a political party to gather public support for a legislative ban to curb "unethical" conversions. The monks were spurred to action by Soma Thera's sudden death, which a contingent of his devoted followers claimed was the result of machinations that corresponded to a broader Christian conspiracy to destroy Buddhism.

As that late afternoon in 2010 turned to evening, nearly two thousand Buddhists crowded the grounds of Soma Thera's home temple in Maharagama for the yearly memorial service.[3] Sinhala Buddhist *dāyakayo* (lay patrons) reverently sat on the floor facing several rows of monks donning their saffron, tangerine, and burgundy colored robes. Among the clergy, I recognized a bespectacled Dhammadutta Thera, a monk whose name means "messenger of the Dhamma," and who made remarkable efforts to engage in charitable works in hospitals, orphanages, and preschools around Sri Lanka (a life's work that I discuss at length in chapter 2). I knew him to insist that by providing provisions to the poor, Buddhists could actively thwart conversions among those who may otherwise be swayed by Christian charity. As the *bhikkhu* and *dāyakayo* orated their reminiscences over Soma Thera's life and "mysterious death," many of those seated near us were moved to tears. A dignitary, a temple *dāyaka*, took the microphone to eulogize the monk. As the orator commemorated Soma Thera's legacy, he implored the lay Buddhist audience to vindicate his death by working to put a stop to unethical conversions.

In his rousing speech delivered in Sinhala, the *dāyaka* blamed foreign funding for the growth of new churches in predominantly Buddhist areas. He provided testimony on how one young Sinhala Buddhist woman approached the priest of a local Catholic parish in hopes that he could help her secure employment abroad. Purportedly, the priest agreed to help the Buddhist girl find employment in Italy, but, allegedly, only on the condition of her conversion. The young woman, we were told, accepted a lucrative job offer in exchange for her adoption of Catholicism. Pacing in front of the assembly hall, the *dāyaka* continued, expounding how upon the woman's return to Sri Lanka she possessed a clothing garment that dishonored the Lord Buddha. With dramatic pause, the *dāyaka* pulled the offending garment out of his bag. In a clenched fist, he raised the black garment above his head and unfurled the material to reveal a pair of trousers embossed with golden images of the Buddha. Shaking the garment overhead, he exclaimed into the microphone, *"Balanna!"* (look!), gesturing at how the consumption of Christianity leads Sinhala people to desecrate the image of the Lord Buddha. Two women seated in front of us clicked their tongues and shook their heads with disdain. The orator explained that some neighbors who had found the article of clothing in the young woman's possession assaulted her and confiscated the offending garment. They then turned her in to the police for disciplining. The *dāyaka* revealed that he had become privy to this incident through his amicable ties with his local police force. The young woman's act of desecrating the Buddha's image was just one of ways in which Christians "insult Buddhism" and "make a business out of conversion."

We listened to lay orators and monks discourse on Sinhala Buddhists' obligations to protect the *sāsana* (Buddha's dispensation and legacy), first in the space of the assembly hall and then outside under the sacred Bodhi tree. After nearly three hours, Nimesh *malli* tapped my shoulder. "Shall we make a move, *Akki?* he asked quietly. (*Malli* is a kin term for younger brother, while *akki* is an affectionate variation on *akka*, older sister, used for kin and kinlike friends.) "It's getting late." I hesitated, wanting to know what more I might learn from being present at the event. The *dāyakayo* around us remained firmly planted under the Bo tree, listening attentively to a sermon. The commemoration event for Venerable Soma Thera did not seem to be ending anytime soon, but, feeling both exhausted and obliged to remain under Nimesh's care during the journey back to Colombo, I nodded with hesitant affirmation. I joined Nimesh in bowing in the direction of the Bo tree and the monks seated underneath it, and we respectfully took our

Figure int.1 Soma Thera's seventh-year death anniversary, memorialized in the outer Colombo suburb of Maharagama in 2010.

leave of the gathering, exiting through the temple's front gate to the main road. Lucky in our timing, we managed to quickly catch a slow-rolling government bus back to Colombo from the satellite town of Maharagama. Still thinking of all that I heard in Sinhala, I asked Nimesh to expound upon some of the terms used in the religious leaders' rhetoric. Over the clank and clamor of the bus's deteriorating metal carriage and the deep hum of its engine, Nimesh tucked his chin toward his chest and whispered a few words of reply in English. "What? I can't hear you, *Malli*. Can you say again?" I strained to hear but spoke quietly to respect his posture of discretion as he whispered in my ear. The bus was less than a quarter full, and I surmised that our conversation was inaudible even to those nearest to us. Yet Nimesh replied in hushed tones, "I'll tell you later, *Akki*. These are sensitive things," and ultimately demurred from speaking further on it for fear of offending or agitating overhearers. Attached though he was to the venerable monk whose passing triggered antipathies among Sinhala Buddhists toward "Christian fundamentalists," with his silence Nimesh seemed to temper the transmission of the vengefully politicized religious discourses that we had heard that evening.

NEW RELIGIOSITIES AND ESTABLISHED INHERITANCES

With new intensity in the new millennium, majoritarian Sinhala Buddhist discourses in Sri Lanka have actively thrown the material and moral persuasions of religious others into question. During the 1990s, several South Asian states saw a rise in majoritarian nationalist agitations against conversions to minority religions. Pentecostalism represents one of the newest frontiers of rivalrous religious entanglement with majoritarian nationalists in the region. During the lead-up to the new millennium, after the 2004 Indian Ocean tsunami, and in the late stages of Sri Lanka's civil war, Sinhala Buddhist nationalists were vigilantly attentive to the apparent changes in the country's religious landscape. The advent of new churches, prayer halls, pastors, converts, and charismatic prayer styles—all of which signify the growing presence of Pentecostal Christianity in pockets throughout the country—has captured the ire of Buddhist revivalists. Long established mainline Christian entities too have been swept up into these anti-conversion antipathies, as evident in the orator's discourse profiling Catholic clerics as proselytizers among Buddhists. Buddhist revivalism in Sri Lanka includes ordinary commitments to learning and practicing the *Dhamma* (Pāli: Buddha's teachings). It also involves a range of temperate and intemperate nationalistic political rhetoric, which is magnified through mass mediation. Sri Lankan Buddhist nationalists overtly leverage state news media in the Sinhala vernacular, and to some extent in English, to interrupt local and translocal Christian ministerial efforts to publicize their miracle work and to advance the evangelical mission. At peaks of hostility, small but vociferous contingents of Sinhala Buddhist nationalists episodically carry out vigilante violence against Christian persons and properties. *Karma and Grace* examines the nationalist anxieties that have grown alongside intensifying millennial urgencies as Theravāda Buddhist revivalists seek to retain and Christian evangelists express hopes to newly carve out sovereign religious domains. The ethnography explores these competing aspirations, techniques of political mobilization, and the tangles of perspectivism, in the war and postwar eras—a time when various religious agents were embroiled in efforts to redraw the lines of conflict and belonging in Sri Lanka.

Complex historical associations between European colonialism and Christian expansionary missions partly shape the majoritarian discourses concerning Christian conversion in Sri Lanka. Having long asserted the necessity of reclaiming the nation from the colonial past, in recent decades Sinhala Buddhist nationalists began to assert that the renewed growth of Christian "fundamentalism" (*Cristiyāni muladharmaya*) is a force for "recolonization." While the growth of new forms of Christianity has largely gone unregistered in Sri Lanka's wartime and postwar census, Sinhala Buddhists have sought to curb the evangelical project of Christian ascendance. As charismatic and evangelical Christian Sri Lankans feel called to publicize "the Good News," this book asks: What happens to this "news" when it is propagated amid subsets of a population that sharply resists it? What happens when the collective undulations of pneumatic praise and worship reverberates and seeks establishment, but is released to an outside milieu that rejects its territorialization as an affront to long established inheritances? In pursuing these questions, *Karma and Grace* sets out to contribute to scholarly literature on nationalism and evangelism, rupture and cultural continuity, religious media and mediation, and the negotiated nature of pluralism in a multireligious context. To do so, the ethnography examines the nexus of significations that links conversion and anti-conversion politics to theological concepts, to practices and ideologies of material mediation, and to transformations in the political economy.

The initial chapters of this work interrogate how "prosperity gospel" Christianity stands at odds with the ethos of "the middle-path" and modulated, modernist styles of Buddhist renunciation and monastic patronage in Sri Lanka. Distinctive orientations to the political economy find resonance with the differential logics of moral personhood that inhere within Pentecostal Christianity and Theravāda Buddhism. In chapter 1, I show how these tensions are intensified in the way they have been lodged in popular perception and in partisan politics in Sri Lanka. Second, the ethnography and analysis illuminate how aspects of Buddhist-Christian difference associated with mediation and media—the press, money, charity, secular aid, political-economic ideologies, miracles, gods, and "demons"—are not only vehicles for religious transmission. But they also serve as nodes of recurrent conflict, as well as dialogical sites of religious innovation. In the tense interplay of religious difference in millennial Sri Lanka, Buddhist and Christian rivals exploit old and new forms of mass media to challenge the grounding of one another's doctrinal premises, ethical practices, and intercessional efficacy.

Karma and Grace queries how Pentecostal Christian evangelists publicize their faith and explores how "the Good News" (Sinhala: *Subha Aranchiya*) that promises the immediacy of Christ's gift of grace is received among Buddhist skeptics who conceive of the attainment of *nibbāna* (Pāli; *nirvāṇa* in Sanskrit) as requiring many, many lifetimes of deep moral labor, or meritorious karma. On an elemental level then, *Karma and Grace* addresses Buddhists', Pentecostals', Protestants', and Roman Catholics' vastly different soteriological (salvational) premises of intercessory presence, absence, and temporalities of the eschaton. To examine the entanglement over matters of immediacy, deferment, media(tion), and modalities of religious persuasion that are at the heart of the revival of Sri Lanka's Buddhist inheritances and the expansionary efforts of born-again Christians, this book builds upon the anthropological literature on "religion and the media turn." This body of scholarship underscores how powerful principles of divine presence differently inhere in particular religious traditions and doctrines, which lend to specific ritual mediations of that presence (Engelke, "Religion"; Meyer 2010; Eisenlohr 2012; Hirschkind 2006; Heo 2018). In attending to the doctrinal sensibilities and "semiotic ideologies" (Keane 2007) that animate rituals of prayer and embodied forms of ethical cultivation (Hirschkind 2006) and that shape the sensorial field and "sensational forms" engaged by the devout (Meyer 2009), anthropologists have deftly advanced scholarship on religious publics (Hirschkind, de Abreu, and Caduff 2017). They have done so by interrogating how it is that technologies— ranging from text, to television, to embodied comportments of the prayerful self—allow the devotee to mediate the vast gap entailed by communing with the divine. In a similar vein, in ethnographically documenting the contestations over conversion within the Sri Lankan public sphere, *Karma and Grace* theorizes the presences and liveliness entailed by Buddhism and Christianity as rival forms of religiosity. Illuminating the interplay of the competing soteriological presences, and the distinctive modalities that are intrinsic to Buddhist and Christian forms and styles of mediation, this book addresses the conditions of possibility for religious pluralism in postwar and millennial Sri Lanka.

Pentecostal-charismatic Christian miracles of deliverance and sanctification entail an especially pronounced promise of intercessional immediacy through the Holy Spirit (*Śuddha Ātmaya*), which anthropologists have richly examined to address the allure of this relatively recent arrival on the scene of global Christianity. In contrast, Theravāda Buddhist scriptures extol the Lord Buddha as the *Tathāgata*, or "The Thus-Gone One" who holds no immediate intercessory capacity in the world. In Sri Lanka, like throughout much of Asia, the exemplary figure of the historical Gotama Buddha and his dispensation and legacy (*sāsana*) animate profound and often nationalistic commitments to uphold established religious inheritances. Christians' and Buddhists' disparate orientations to the end-times, and to presence, absence, continuity, rupture, sovereignty, and the moral and material forces of religious persuasion, are matters of mediating soteriological gaps. I demonstrate how these soteriological concerns, embedded as they are in contemporary material and political-economic realities, also produce trenchant disputes over the ontological depth and the semiotic surfaces of religious personhood.

Taking the doctrinal, practical, and material affordances of these rival religions seriously, I take what I call a "multicameral" approach to interrogate the conversion disputes in millennial Sri Lanka. Through ethnographic multicameralism, I dually hold in view the resistances and receptivity to new charismatic forms of Christianity in Sri Lanka. Situated among modernist and traditionalist Theravāda Buddhists, Pentecostal Christian "newcomers," established Christian denominations, and innovators of revival, *Karma and Grace* engages perspectives of Christian believers (*adhahiliwāntayo*) and Buddhist skeptics, as well as those who pivot in between. In doing so this book reveals some of the distinctive forms of persuasion that are at the heart of these mutual consternations over conversion. Yet, too, by exploring the maneuvering political negotiations concerning religion, exclusion, and belonging within the postwar nation, and by examining the revivalist innovations and everyday efforts to navigate interreligious sociality, this book serves to elucidate the vicissitudes of pluralism in a multireligious public.

Karma and Grace offers the caveat that despite overarching intensifications of anti-pluralistic religious politics, centrifugal forces and simple ambivalences episodically emerge, to orient accommodations of difference. Even as revivalist and evangelical interchanges between Buddhist and Christian rivals episodically resurge as hostile politicization, the ethnography illuminates how Buddhists and Christians—even those who are interpellated by exclusivist forms of religiosity—nevertheless manage to mitigate interreligious antagonisms. Sometimes it is simply a matter of showing leniency and forbearance, or, as with the case of Nimesh, quietly refraining from recounting incendiary discourses. Several chapters demonstrate how interreligious competition creates a field that is generative not only of antagonism but also of possibilities for diversification of religious movements and forms, and for agonistic deflection, religious leniency, and identitarian ambiguation—features of a religious public that allow plurality to flourish even in the face of ever-rearticulating conflicts.

SKEPTICS, BELIEVERS, AND RELIGIOUS MEDIA

Scholarship on religion since Weber's thesis on the *Protestant Ethnic and the Spirit of Capitalism* has elucidated how vernacularization and modernization of religious forms prototypically generated new avenues of religious access, which at the same time propelled interiorized quests for authentic religious commitments among lay practitioners (Weber [1905] 2001; Anderson 1983; Keane 2007; Engelke 2013). These traits are fairly consistent throughout Protestant Christianity. These features are also evident in Buddhist modernism, which Gananath Obeyesekere (1970) observed to be taking place through middle-class and nationalist transformations that, to an extent, engage Buddhist laity in practices that were formerly reserved for ordained monks—a phenomenon he famously and somewhat controversially characterized as "Protestant Buddhism" (see also Gombrich and Obeyesekere 1988). Even as technologies and vernacular texts produced interiorized religious compulsions and commitments, print capitalism spurred a new kind of mediation that made new types of imagining possible, as Benedict Anderson argued (1983, 188). Thus, while religious modernization placed a premium upon interiorized authenticity, modernist religious forms have also been liable to reach new intensities as public religions. As with Sri Lanka, public religion has been critical to the construction of the modern nation. This dual phenomenon of enacting Buddhist "philosophy" as individuated interiorized practice and outward propagation has been amply evident during the Buddhist revival that was first sparked in Ceylon's colonial era.[4]

Buddhist monks first negotiated for access to Protestant missionaries' printing presses; and then, when roundly denied, they competitively acquired those very presses, enabling their access to printing capacities by the 1860s (Malalgoda 1973, 191–92). The "biblification" of Buddhism in Ceylon generated a Buddhist scripturalism (Seneviratne 1999, 3). In that era, learned Theravādin monks in

Asia undertook a self-conscious effort at "purification" of the Pāli Buddhist *Tipiṭaka*, removing any space for hermeneutical inconsistency, since Buddhists felt a heightened need to "defend the integrity of the Pali texts" in the face of Christian missionization (Blackburn 2010, 6). At roughly the same time Christians and Buddhists translated Pāli Buddhism into European languages. The shaping of the Theravādin canon of Buddhism through Pāli coincided with the intensified vernacularization of Buddhism, creating simultaneous international flows of westward Buddhist orientalism, even as Pāli Buddhism became more intensively accessible and locally emplaced among lay Buddhists in South and Southeast Asia (Kemper 2015; Blackburn 2010).

Quite differently from entextualized and interiorized Protestant modernities, though, Pentecostalism animates ostensibly olden, apostolic styles of outward religiosity anew. The charismatic Christian form sparks the palpable exuberance of charismatic tongues, and corporeal spiritual battles between the Holy Spirit (*Śuddha Ātmaya*) and various maleficent spirits (*Yakśa Ātmaya*). Typically in ministerial discourses, *Yakśa Ātmaya* signify the malign "demons" of religious difference. Anthropologists have suggested that charismatic Pentecostalism can best be classified as a postmodern aesthetic form rather than a modernist one. Csordas (1997) points to how the prime characteristic of the Pentecostal form is glossolalia, a semantically incoherent speech form. Talking in tongues is taken as a sign of charismatic Christian communion, which Csordas argues serves to processually reintegrate the person who is fragmented by the forces of modernity and places the person into a "reconciled" social body.[5] Such a utopic Christian image of the future kingdom, in theory, immanently bears the signs and sensations of promised transcendence.

Throughout Asia, modernist forms of Buddhism grew up through a long era of contending with Roman Catholic and Protestant Christian missionization, and colonial supremacy, spurring the emergence of a nativist ethnoreligious supremacy of its own. In the era of postcolonial nationalism, Buddhists have tended to perceive Christianity as inherently supremacist even when some subsets and strands of Christianity recoiled from its originary supremacist conceits and were reshaped into pluralistic, nationally grounded, ecumenical forms. In some cases, these ecumenical and pluralistic religious forms have even become postnationalist in their political orientation (Mahadev 2022). At the same time, other kinds of believers take prosperity-oriented evangelical Christian forms to signify embodied cosmopolitan social distinction. These distinctions are taken to run deep into the ontological core of the person, and are apparent as *habitus* in the Bourdieusian sense. In many corners of the world, strands of cosmopolitan habit might appear outwardly secular while being inwardly pious. Or, as I demonstrate in chapter 2, dedicated Sinhala Buddhists might read, and often misread, outward signs of Western-style cosmopolitanism—as evinced by secular NGO workers, for instance—as attached to the seductions of Christian proselytizers' gifts.

Rather than interiorization, Pentecostalism takes inspiration from biblical passages of Acts 2 to validate engagement in a highly exteriorized aesthetic form—an "apostolic" one that involves glossolalia and other theatrical performances of divine presence. In the Sri Lankan Catholic archbishop's denunciation (chapter 4), Pentecostalism is impolitic because of the way that it involves people in a "cacophonous exuberance" that offends the quietist sensibilities of Sri Lanka's established religious communities. In their exteriorized, material theatrics of deliverance, Pentecostal ministerial practices take very seriously the spirits whose actions misfire (*prēta* or karmically clinging "hungry ghosts"), together with the "devils" (*yakśa*) whose bad karma manifests as plagues against the living. Pentecostal ministers do so by uttering maledictions to performatively damn those spirits and vanquish them from their earthly grounding once and for all.

Prompted in part by the rationalizations of Protestant missionaries' critiques, the modernist orientations to Buddhism that emerged in an earlier era had tended to "civilize" the fears of spirits, and the ill health and impediments to upward mobility that the spirits are locally believed to inflict, by classifying them as immaterial fears, fetters, and mere figments of the imagination. For Buddhist modernists, in accord with the *dhamma*, the spirits are just matters for the mind to contend with—through mindful compassion and the moral currency of sharing gifts of merit, such that the mind and body that can be fortified ("buffered" in the Taylorian sense) to endure hardship. For the ideal-typical modernist, cultivating good thoughts and moral action can karmically strengthen the conditions of one's present life, and future rebirths, while the spirit cults are to be condemned as false "superstitions." Yet, as I show, it is primarily within traditionalist Sinhala Buddhist forms that ritual specialists engage the spirits—and thus take the spirits to be as materially real as Pentecostals do.

While Christian evangelicalism is inherently oriented to publicizing and "sharing the Good News" (*Subha Aranchiya paturanawa*), I illustrate how certain charismatic schools of Christian discourse treat Theravāda Buddhist cosmologies as manifesting "absence." Since the colonial era, Protestant missionaries have alleged that the Buddha was absent of all divinity and blamed that "lack" of divinity for Sinhala Buddhists' persistent efforts to beseech an array of tutelary deities and spirits (Harris 2006; Scott 1994). Pentecostal charismatics today, like their Protestant predecessors during the colonial era, tend to treat these spiritual agents as diabolical excesses that are materialized in the landscape, implying that Sinhala Buddhists are given to dedicating themselves to "heathen" religious agents. The doctrinally embedded differentials relating to pentecostalist sensibilities of divine presence, and the "Thus-Gone" Buddha's ostensible "absence," I contend, shapes the contemporary Buddhist-Christian disputes over what forms and modalities of attracting and persuading devotees are deemed to be "ethical" or not.

Emergent, more mediatically attuned and stylized forms of Buddhism, growing up alongside heightened awareness of charismatic Christian practices, promise Sinhala Buddhists certain alternatives. A new Buddhist movement that I detail in chapter 5 promises to accelerate the Dharmic subject's capacity to achieve eschatological goals, rearticulating the kinds of moral effort, ritual practice, and dedication to the *dhamma* as a way of being that is in keeping with the commitments of one's own karma. It is one of the manifold ways in which Buddhists address the obligation to fulfill what is written as one's samsaric destiny. This particularly inventive pathway that I attribute to a maverick monk is slated to quicken the pace of Buddhist futurity to actuate the potentials of the self and society. Viewing the contentious social processes of religious propagation in this way, these religiosities are undergoing various mediational shifts. To be sure, the persistent endeavor to keep pace with new rivals creates a religious field that is ripe for new innovations.

MEDIATING ANXIETY, URGENCY, AND "SMALL NUMBERS"

A variety of conduits have propelled these tense religious entanglements forward in the Sri Lankan public sphere during an era of ebbing and flowing neoliberal transformations. Far from unfolding as an unilinear phenomenon, as detailed in chapter 1 the advance of neoliberalism has been channeled through oscillating closings and openings of the Sri Lankan economy since the 1970s. Structural adjustment and open economy policies introduced in 1977 in association with Sri Lanka's center-right postindependence political party created renewed growth of translocal consumer markets that also deepened the sense of exclusion and alienation among rural communities and the urban poor. As well documented by political scientists, transformations in Sri Lanka's political economy in the late 1970s were also conducive to the intensification of ethnic-based exclusions, that in turn led to the formation of Tamil minority parties that went on to make separatist political demands (Bastian 2009; Lakshman 1985; DeVotta 1998; Venugopal 2018). These sustained tensions ultimately led to the outbreak of a brutal civil war between the Sri Lankan state and Tamil nationalist LTTE secessionists that lasted for more than twenty-six years (1983–2009). Broadly speaking, the neoliberal era is also known to have given rise to what is known as "Third-Wave" Pentecostalism in the postcolonial Global South, representing a new era in global Christianity (Freston 1995; Coleman 2000). On the tail of the Sinhala-Tamil ethnic conflict, what has come into view through analysis of majoritarian nationalist and evangelical Christian rhetorics is the perceived religious character of these neoliberal transformations. Chapter 1 articulates how it is that the personae of two kinds of converts—one to Christianity, and one to Buddhism—have become emblematic of a divided postcolonial polity.

In an era of neoliberal transformation, mass media platforms have extended the consumptive habits of religious revival. Despite the reach of global televangelism and online platforms for Christian mass mediation, the postcolonial Sri Lankan state has as its mandate to protect and promote Buddhism. This mandate is partly carried out through vernacular media. Sri Lanka's first homegrown television broadcasting network was launched in 1979, and since then, private and state-backed channels have existed alongside one another (Karunanayake 2008). Mainstream television programmers are compelled to abide by Sinhala Buddhist majoritarian interests or to produce secular content. Sinhala television news media segments often spotlight episodes of Buddhist-Christian conflict. As I detail in chapter 3, telecasters narrate vernacular news segments on these altercations in a way that intentionally undercuts the possibility that Sinhala Buddhists might become positively attuned to the Christian "Good News."

In comparison to the context of India, television viewership also proliferated by the 1980s, inaugurating a new era that scholars argue contributed to the rise of muscular religious ideologies and the sharpening of anti-minority sentiment (Mankekar 1999; Rajagopal 2001; Ghassem-Fachandi 2012).[6] Arvind Rajagopal (2001) has shown that the televised *Ramayana* series that was broadcast widely in the late 1980s sought to produce a "unified visual field" to consolidate a Hindu nationalist self-conception among viewers and voters, indicating a clear move away from the secular ethos of Nehruvian politics in India. However, drawing upon Stuart Hall's theorization of disparate processes of encoding and decoding, Rajagopal shows that despite the effort to build unified messaging, the broadcast was launched to a "split public"—a public fractured by not only religion but also language, regional and class-based interests, and especially caste, which ultimately broke the Hindutva vote apart (2001, 151). In other words, politically inflected public religion not only consolidated a hardline majoritarian nationalist movement in India, but diverse audience interpretations of the televised serial also generated other variegated political and religious sentiments. Sri Lanka is also deeply fractured along ethnoreligious, class, and linguistic lines, and these fractures are variously perpetuated amid neoliberal transformations—and not least through mass media. Rather than offer a systematic study of religious media however, in this ethnography I address television, printed news and religious tracts, SMS advertisements, CD and DVD circulations, online videos, and large, live, in-person, recorded, and amplified religious ceremonies and sermons as they appear by way of the disputes and innovations that are stirred in a multireligious public.

Inter-religion entails the complex dynamics that emerge from adjacent and intertwined religious publics. This dynamic relationality bears not only upon theology and ritual practice but also upon sociocultural and political-economic processes and perceptions. What becomes clear through this present study of inter-religion in Sri Lanka is how fractured, albeit adjacent and intertwined Buddhist and Christian publics are found to be in competitive, agonistic, and, less commonly, cooperative relation to one another. This social adjacency ensures that Sinhala Buddhists and Sri Lankan Christians are conversant with one another's theological premises and are mutually aware of one another's ritual practices and, generally too, of the social and political profiles of religious adherents. In their social proximity, Buddhist and Christian revivalist formations are dialogically responsive to one another (Mahadev 2016). This responsiveness can be seen, for instance, in emergent Catholic liturgical remediations and messianic Buddhist innovations, respectively detailed in chapters 4 and 5.

This responsiveness can also be seen in the way that religious programming arrived to televisual audiences in Sri Lanka over the last two decades. For example, in 2007 the state-backed vernacular religious television channel called The Buddhist was launched from studios headquartered at the Sri Sambodhi Vihara

Buddhist temple in central Colombo.[7] Endorsing the endeavor, then-President Mahinda Rajapaksa extolled the channel's efforts to propagate the *dhamma* through modern mass media by likening it to the work of the meritorious monk, Mahinda Thera, the singular emissary from the Mauryan Empire who introduced Buddhism to what is now Sri Lanka by converting King Devanampiyatissa during the 3rd century BCE. At the launch event, Rajapaksa reported that under his guidance, the Ministry of Religious Affairs had allocated a great sum of money to finance the endeavor, to "nurture the nation's spiritual development" in concert with economic development.[8] The monks who led The Buddhist channel's mass media initiative in turn overtly endorsed Rajapaksa's agenda for economic development, and implicitly too, his broader promises to end the civil war.

That same year, cable providers in Sri Lanka introduced the GOD TV televangelical network as an opt-in channel available to subscribers.[9] A Sunday sermon broadcast on the GOD TV satellite television channel reached the Colombo home where Nirmali was employed as a domestic worker. Nirmali appeared to be transfixed by the broadcast, the songs and sermon emanating from the high-definition screen capturing her full attention. Since the family who employed her was out that morning in 2010, Nirmali had been tasked with opening the door to the neighboring apartment for a showing, facilitating my hunt for an apartment. She did so and promptly returned to her station in front of the TV, ignoring our lingering presence. The camera panned in on the face of the Indian televangelist as he extolled in English how in advancing the word of God, embracing one's own persecution will allow one to attain "higher levels of heaven." To my ears, the evangelist's languaging invoked a sense of fantasy fashioned for a generation that finds itself easily engrossed in playing videogames. The preacher went on, naming several pioneering Korean "martyrs." In a performative eulogy of these martyrs, the televangelist proclaimed that those exemplary Koreans achieved such "higher levels of heaven" when, some fifty years earlier, "they worked tirelessly to bring Korea to Christ while boldly staring death in the face!" Beaming as the sermon turned to song, Nirmali raised her hands toward the screen to receive the Holy Spirit. Closing her eyes, she quietly sang along.

In the Sri Lankan economic hub of Colombo such visions of South Korea's receptivity to the evangelical message have loomed large on the horizon during the first two decades of the millennium. The reality of South Korean religious

demographics is a great deal more complex than what is signified by this caricature of Christianity's overwhelming growth in the country.[10] Yet for Sri Lankans
who hold dedicated religious commitments, the caricature serves as a significant
reference point. The projection bears an aspirational resonance for born-again
Sri Lankans. Among Sinhala Buddhists, however, the thought that the "island of
the *Dhamma*" (*Dhammadipa*) might be transformed into a Christian one, touches
off profound anxieties.[11] The 2009 *Buddhist Commission Report on Conversion by
Fraudulent Strategies* published in Sinhala by the All-Ceylon Buddhist Congress—a
Colombo-based organization that has been central to the Buddhist revival in Sri
Lanka for many decades—evokes this very worry about transregional religious
propagation. The report alleges that American-influenced "Christian fundamentalists" encourage converts to "smash idols of the Lord Buddha" as a sign of
their allegiance to a new god. It also asserts that without concerted efforts to
curb "unethical conversions" by criminalizing the activities of proselytizers, Sri
Lanka too will wind up like the "small Buddhist isle of [South] Korea," which
made a demographic transition to become "a predominantly Christian nation
within half a century." The projections of a demographic shift that will reduce
the established religious traditions to little more than a discreet minority are
inflected by translocal and especially inter-Asian imaginaries. Sri Lankan devotees variously receive these forecasts of the religious future as a fantastical dream,
or a dreadful nightmare, depending upon one's perspective.

Anxious that minority religions could overwrite the country's heritage with
their growing demographics, Sinhala Buddhist discourse reflects a nativist inclination to vilify minorities that is laden in a "fear of small numbers" (Appadurai
2006). This affective tenor concerning conversions to Christianity is fortified by
demographic uncertainties. The quantitative (and for that matter, qualitative)
uncertainty over conversion in Sri Lanka allows both Buddhists and Christians
to engage in demographic understatement, or embellishment of numbers, as and
when it is convenient to do so (Mahadev 2018). Uncertainty, paired with the
sense of the smallness of an "insular" land that could be flooded out such that
minorities, like "heretics" from the outside (per the epigraph), could potentially
become the majority exacerbates this sense of alarm. Those old anxieties evident
in that early era of colonialism bears a striking resemblance to millenarian discourses of a "tsunami of religious change" that was projected to beset the island
and wreak havoc upon the country's Sinhala Buddhist inheritances in the aftermath of the 2004 disaster.[12]

Actual changes documented in the census appear to provide but a partial view of the extent of conversions in Sri Lanka. The two most recent full census counts from Sri Lanka in 1981 and in 2012 suggest that the Buddhist population of Sri Lanka has seen a marginal increase from 69.3 percent to 70.1 percent. The Roman Catholic population declined from 6.9 percent to 6.2 percent, while the "Other Christian" category (Protestants and Pentecostals) has increased from .7 percent to 1.4 percent. The Muslim population has increased from 7.6 percent to 9.7 percent. The Hindu population decreased from 15.5 to 12.6 percent, a decline attributable to emigration and casualty deaths over the course of the civil war.[13] The government suspended its census operations during the war years. Given the complexities of population enumeration as it pertains to religious and ethnic identity in the context of militarized conflict and the transition to peace, the numbers must be viewed with care (Mahadev 2018, 687). While Pentecostal-charismatic Christianity is growing in pockets and evangelical activity is evident in certain areas of Sri Lanka, the real demographics remain a major unknown.

According to the National Christian Evangelical Alliance of Sri Lanka (NCEASL), there were ninety-four incidents of violence, intimidation, and property destruction against Christians in 2019 alone.[14] This figure includes the three churches that were decimated in the suicide bomb attacks alleged to be the work of a Sri Lankan Islamist cell linked to the Islamic State (Daesh) movement on Easter Sunday 2019. But in the main, vigilante Buddhist groups, rather than Islamist groups, have commonly carried out violence, albeit on a much smaller scale, on churches, pastors, and Christian congregants in Sri Lanka. In fact, Buddhist protectionist vigilantism has taken aim at Muslims, especially since 2011—well before the bombings. The Buddhist-Christian disputes over conversion that peaked earlier, in the late 1990s through the late 2000s, documented here, have generally been perceived as being displaced and eclipsed by Islamophobia and Buddhist-Muslim conflict that spectacularly came into the foreground by 2011. After this turn toward majoritarian nationalist Islamophobia in Sri Lanka, the international evangelical organization Open Doors dropped Sri Lanka from its World Watch List of top fifty countries where it is "most dangerous to follow Jesus." In a written response, the NCEASL cautioned, "Sri Lanka's problem of Christian persecution should not be forgotten." In subsequent statements, the organization explicitly expressed solidarity with Muslims under threat in Sri Lanka.[15] Conversely, Buddhist public intellectuals who associate the advance of

Christianity with colonialism and neocolonial political and economic formations address these narratives of religious persecution by attempting to undermine minority fears. One such nationalist figure accuses Sri Lankan Christians
of melodramatically performing a "fear psychosis" over their minority status
(Ivan 2009). This book demonstrates that these impasses over religious conversion are symptomatic of the ingraining of a public divide along lines of religious
and ethnolinguistic sentiments, and aspirations and experiences of social mobility and relative immobility, which have intensified in the era of decolonization,
political economic transformation, and new varieties of mass mediation.

HISTORICAL VALENCES OF RELIGIOUS
AND POLITICAL-ECONOMIC CHANGE

The Sinhala Buddhist revival first emerged as a movement in the late colonial
era with the aim of recuperating the nation's inheritances against the intrusion
of European colonialism and Christian missionization. The European colonial
presence in Ceylon lasted for over four hundred years.[16] Recent scholarship
points out that Christian missionization during the colonial era was hardly a
unilinear process, and that interreligious relations and the uptake of conversion
among local Ceylonese varied greatly during that time.[17] But the overarching
thrust of the popular nationalistic historiography that circulates in the contemporary Sri Lankan public sphere contends that the imperial regimes and missionaries of European provenance who arrived in Ceylon acted strictly, brutally,
and uniformly in accord with supremacist and supercessionist attitudes. This
overarching sensibility has shaped majoritarian political imaginaries concerning
religion and the stakes of nationalism, decolonization, sovereignty, and revival
in contemporary Sri Lanka.

In nuanced historical accounts, K. M. de Silva (1965) and other scholars have
documented the pivotal moment in 1815 when imperial British forces deposed
the king of Kandy to take over Ceylon. These accounts reveal that Buddhist clerics had allowed the takeover in exchange for firm guarantees that the British
would protect Buddhism and the promise of Buddhist sovereignty (de Silva
1965; Malalgoda 1978; Seneviratne 1999). British agents of the Crown were con-
tractually required to serve as custodians over the Buddha's Sacred Tooth Relic.
Throughout the Buddhist world, the Buddha's relics are believed to carry a

substantive trace of the historical Buddha's animating power and thus are considered founts of sacred, sovereign rule. As scholars have noted, the British administrators sought to instrumentalize the relic for its political agenda and thus acquiesced to the clerics' demands to protect the Buddhist faith.[18] However, some influential Protestant missionaries objected to the premise of the Crown's "secular" rule in Ceylon because it appeared that colonial administrators were saluting and hence venerating the relic as an article of Buddhist faith. These missionaries sought to appeal to exclusivist Protestant moral sensibilities of the British public and ardently petitioned the British Colonial Office to "disestablish" Buddhism in Ceylon (de Silva 1965). Largely as a result of the influence of these prominent evangelists, the Crown officially severed its connections with Buddhism in Ceylon in 1844 (de Silva 1965, 83; Malalgoda 1978; Seneviratne 1999).[19]

In response to such early Christian shows of religious exclusivism in Ceylon, by the late nineteenth century a majoritarian nationalist movement began to crystalize around a conjoined set of ethnic and religious heritage principles. This nationalistic Sinhala Buddhist self-conception hinged upon a monolithic image of precolonial civilizational heritage (Spencer 1990; Rogers 1990). During the post-independence era, and especially in the electoral politics of the 1950s, majoritarian nationalist sensibilities tended to predominate, adding ethnolinguistic and religious majoritarianism to the operations of state and civil society (DeVotta 2004; Schonthal 2016).[20] When Ceylon was finally released from Dominion rule by the British Crown in 1972, the establishment principles of Sinhala Buddhist majoritarianism were made manifest in the new constitution. The constitution of 1978, which stands today, treats the state as the guarantor which ensures that Buddhism receives the "foremost place." Ultimately, the theocratic efforts to singularly recuperate the nation's heritage became detrimental to a wide array of minority groups and created a crucible of violence (Tambiah 1992; Seneviratne 1999; Spencer 2007).

Within the repoliticization of conversion in Sri Lanka since the late 1990s, majoritarian discourses tended to cast variegated forms of Christianity as unequivocally unified under the sign of the cross, as a "foreign" religion that bears sinister neocolonial inflections. As seen in the lay Buddhist orator's speech vilifying Christians documented earlier, it was a Catholic priest to whom a Sinhala Buddhist girl allegedly "fell prey" to the material accoutrements of conversion. Yet, despite this Catholic profiling, it is primarily Pentecostal and born-again evangelical forms of Christianity that have experienced visible growth over the last few decades in Sri Lanka. Nowadays it is Sri Lankan charismatic ministerial discourses that tend to most audibly evince the drive to expand the Christian faith with exclusivist verve. Further addressing the terms of religious expansion as I use them throughout the book, please see "A Note on Terms: Defining "Evangelical," which immediately follows this introduction.

During the era of missions enabled through European colonialism, Pentecostalism remained a very minor presence in comparison to Catholic and Protestant church missions. Distinct from the Catholic and Protestant Christian forms that were fostered under colonialism, relatively new kinds of Pentecostal expression promised that charismatic miracle work would empower a "revival" capable of renewing and expanding the Christian faith. Yet, when Pentecostalism first arrived in Ceylon in the early twentieth century, shortly after the 1906 Azusa Street Revival in Los Angeles, California, that first sparked the movement, it had largely remained confined to insular covenant communities (Somaratna 1996). Later, in a second wave, denominational Pentecostal churches, including Assemblies of God (1914) and the Ceylon Pentecostal Mission (1923), gradually took root.[21] But during the era of decolonization, a global "Third-Wave" intensification seeded nondenominational Pentecostal ministries in various parts of the world beginning in the 1970s, coinciding with the dawn of neoliberal transformations of the global economy (Coleman 2000; Comaroff and Comaroff 2001; Freeman 2012; Bialecki 2015). Particularly in the Global South, Third-Wave Pentecostalism has tended to thrive through nondenominational ministries that emotively deliver believers (*ädahiliwantayo*) from "demons," in ways that rhetorically coalesce with ideologies of Christian Dominionism. Pentecostalism's Third Wave reached Ceylon in the era when it was renamed as "Sri Lanka"—coinciding roughly with the time frame of neoliberalism's intensification there too. By the 1990s denominational and especially nondenominational "free churches" of the Third Wave gained greater visibility and audibility in the Sri Lankan public sphere, sparking controversies due to the apparent growth of conversions and the voluble aesthetics of Pentecostal deliverance practices. This renewed growth of Christianity through the Pentecostal-charismatic form moves against the nativist grain to recuperate the nation's Sinhala Buddhist heritage.

With some important exceptions, Christian groups tend to express expansionary ambitions. After the war, Christian leaders sermonized to their congregations that Sri Lankans must build a "bridge of peace" to mend the wounds of war and to reunify the nation. Evangelical and charismatic discourses implored believers to pray for the revitalization of Christianity, so that their faith could serve as that bridge. Born-again preachers effusively characterized the postwar moment as a time optimal for bringing the country to Christ. For Sinhalas dedicated to Buddhism, this expansionary rhetoric concerning Christianity spurred anxieties analogous to those that had been triggered in the colonial era. Under colonialism, Sinhala speakers posited that the English language represents a "*kaduwa*" or a double-edged "sword" by which one could be cut or could be wielded to cut others—signifying the power of socioeconomic mobility and cultural capital associated with one's capacity to fluently speak English (Rajasingham-Sennanayake 1997). From the vantagepoint of nationalistic Sinhala Buddhists, Christianity, like the English language, may well be a force for an individual's social mobility, but it also nefariously serves to ontologically break Sinhala people from their natal inheritances. In this complex milieu, I take a multicameral perspective to address the constructions of what might transpire if Christian belief were to become further moored among the citizenry, and within the soil of the nation.

POSTWAR THEOPOLITICS

Interreligious hostilities were further complicated as a result of the culmination in 2009 of twenty-six years of ethnic-based civil war between the majoritarian nationalist state and the minority LTTE insurgents, also known as the "Tamil Tigers". This book argues that a nexus of significations reconfigured majoritarian perceptions in such a way that Sinhala Buddhist nationalists understood the Western humanitarian censure against Sri Lanka's conduct in war in much the same way that they conceived of Christians' efforts to secure new conversions: that is, as corresponding to a foreign and "anti-national" political agenda that is liable to undermine Sri Lankan sovereignty. During the war, the LTTE themselves had raised insurgent forms of sovereignty in the northern and eastern territories, which challenged the sovereignty of the majoritarian state by mimicking the muscular state form (Klem and Maunaguru 2017; Klem 2018). Civilians from ethnic Tamil backgrounds (including Hindus, Catholics, and Protestants), and also Muslims and Sinhalas, were left vulnerable to the violence between the two entities that were locked into a fight for sovereignty and self-determination (Thiranagama 2011). During the war years in Sri Lanka, the ubiquitous mode of private and commercial transportation was a white Toyota Hiace passenger van. In the final years and months of civil war though, in the parlance of local human rights activists, the term "white vans" came to stand as a metonym for the Sri Lankan state's unmarked perpetration of abductions and extrajudicial killings of journalists and activists and the suppression of rights and of the free press. At the same time, humanitarian aid organizations and foreign states did also condemn the LTTE's conscription of child soldiers and horrific suicide attacks upon civilian targets. However, from the point of view of the Sri Lankan state and majoritarian nationalist civilians, Western humanitarian critics appeared to be unfairly siding with the insurgents and unevenly castigating the state for atrocities in war.

With the end of the illiberal war brutally won by state forces in 2009, Sri Lanka was suddenly cast into the global spotlight. International humanitarian organizations reported that Sri Lankan armed forces killed thousands without discerning between civilians and combatants during the final weeks of battle. Remarking upon Sri Lanka's "illiberal peace," scholars have outlined the consequences of failing to enable thorough reckoning, justice and reconciliation (Rajasingham-Senanayake 2009; Stokke and Uyangoda 2011; Goodhand, Spencer, and Korf 2010). Sri Lankan scholars, peace activists, international observers, and civilians feared that the postwar conflagrations, still left unmitigated, could cause a resurgence of civil strife. To humanitarian organizations and donor states located in the West, Sri Lanka's "final solution" appeared to be an ethnic pogrom on a massive scale. But U.S. conservatives fighting their own "War on Terror" viewed Sri Lanka as a harbinger of how to successfully carry out a war of counterinsurgency. For Sri Lankans of various minority communities, the lived reality was that the violence of the war did not end in 2009 (Thiranagama 2013; Choi 2015; Klem 2018).

Yet within Sri Lanka, triumphalist state pageantry and postwar political discourses placed majoritarianism on full display, with only gestural tones of reconciliation through assimilation into the reunified state. Facing the onslaught of humanitarian criticism, Sri Lankan state discourses oscillated between triumphalism and sovereign defensiveness (Goodhand, Spencer, and Korf 2010; Thiranagama 2013; Klem and Maunaguru 2017). Majoritarian nationalists of Sri Lanka rhetorically held up a mirror to deflect U.S. "hypocrisy." Sinhala Buddhist critics defensively castigated "Western Christian modernity" writ large for its arrogant "refusal(s) to respect the sovereignty of other nations" (see chapter 1). With Christianity appearing to connote a vector of localized Western influence at a time when Sinhala majoritarian nationalists felt especially given to pride associated with being custodians to their "small Buddhist island," the initial chapters of this book address the politics of perception concerning Sri Lankan Christians' national belonging. In 2022, yet another contingency shifted the tenor of what it means to belong to the nation in Sri Lanka: an unprecedented sovereign debt crisis—the direct result of government mismanagement, corruption, excessive borrowing, and predatory lending by international entities—has turned the people against the Rajapaksa regime (reelected in 2019). The Sri Lankan people, including among them members of the Sinhala Buddhist majority, ousted the band of brothers—once symbolic sovereigns—from office in 2022. The country's leadership subsequently resumed business as usual through a proxy who has enabled the deepening of structural adjustment via an IMF loan granted in 2023. The crisis is yet unresolved. While these late-breaking events are largely out of the scope of this book, I briefly touch upon the implications of this crisis for public religion in the epilogue.

PERSECUTION AS COMPLEX

The political mission to advance "religious freedom" has been conceptually underwritten by entities within the United States that bear an evangelical Christian inflection, as amply demonstrated by scholars (Castelli 2007; Hurd 2017; Mahmood 2015; Sullivan et al. 2015). Sri Lankan Christian evangelical organizations too advocate for prayer to "equip the National church" and emphasize the imperative to "Pray for the Persecuted Church." The pairing of ambitious evangelism with discourses that Christians must pray for the "universal persecuted Church," is undergirded by apologetical accounts that situate persecution in olden legends of early Christian martyrs (Castelli 2007; see also Girard, Antonello, and de Castro Rocha 2008; Moss 2013). The iconic conversion of the Apostle Paul particularly animates the expansionary and sovereign ambitions that persist in the Dominion theology promoted by evangelicals in the modern day.[22] In the contemporary context of global evangelical advocacy and proselytism, early apocryphal legends of conversion and martyrdom animate Christian "persecution complexes" (Castelli 2007). The biblical trope of Christian persecution, as well as "invented" and embellished depictions of early Christian martyrs, ideologically reinforces contemporary ambitions and the praxis of born-again Christians (Moss 2013).

In expressions of principled concern for freedom of conscience, liberal Western advocacy groups promulgate religious freedom as a universal human right. Particularly in regions where Christianity is at once established and emergent as a minority religion, as in South Asia, as well as in the predominantly Muslim regions of the Middle East and Asia, such politicization is geopolitically contentious. Yet, however much these logics of religious freedom are laden in a theological structure that might give rise to Christian "persecution complexes" and performative calls for contemporary martyrdom, great care must be taken with the rhetorical implication that evangelicals invite their persecution, particularly in these thorny zones where reactionary violence is physical and all too real. In both directions, the implications of such logics are dangerous in contexts like Sri Lanka where nativist and dominionist religious supremacies mutually compete and clash with one another. Both religious forms bear potentials to stoke and perpetuate interreligious violence.

MILLENNIAL CONVERSION DISPUTES:
"MAKING A BUSINESS OUT OF CONVERSION"

We have already seen that during the tumult of the British colonial era, some influential Protestant missionaries called for the Crown to "disestablish" Buddhism by severing the link between Buddhism and the colonial state. As studies of secularism have amply shown, a heterogeneous set of liberal democratic polities—ones that are primarily Christian and Protestant—globally extended their reach during the colonial era and asserted democratic political goals through a secular ethos. Talal Asad has emphasized how secularism as a doctrine is premised upon a mission of keeping peace between people of different backgrounds, and secular ideologies thrive because capitalist nation states exert their power through them (2003, 7). In contrast to the modern liberalism through which the concepts of freedom and of religion are procedurally engaged, delimited, and definitionally inflected by Protestant Christianity (Asad 2003; Sullivan 2005; Sullivan et al. 2015; Keane 2015), the debates on religious freedom in

Sri Lanka are rather different. The country constitutionally gives primacy of place to Buddhism while allowing lesser provisions for religious minorities. As Spencer and colleagues observe, "Sri Lankans seem—unlike Asad and his followers—to be quite relaxed about detaching the category "religion" from the bigger package of post-Enlightenment liberalism in which it is supposedly embedded" (2015, 9).

In postwar and millennial Sri Lanka, what is especially remarkable is how Sinhala Buddhist nationalists contest the intervening "powers of the secular modern" which are proffered via the West's humanitarian rebukes.[23] They do so by attempting to expose how the Western humanitarian missions retain the biases of an implicit Christian ethos, as evident in chapters 1 and 2. Related to majoritarian nationalists' concerns that social and material capital (or "soft power") is a potent medium for "anti-national" influence, Buddhists accuse Christians of "making a business out of conversion." This follows from Buddhist revivalists' perceptions that from the colonial era until the present day, Western capital flows, Christian charity, and prosperity gospels are directly linked to church expansion and "encroachment" upon Buddhists' sovereign grounds.

Elsewhere in Asia, the clash between capitalism and socialism had been marked in "Cold" War battles that ran very hot (Kwon 2008). Throughout Southeast Asia during the era of decolonization, historical associations between capitalism and Christianity on the one side, and socialism, anti-colonialism and Buddhism on the other, are evident. Responding to a sense of threat by Christian missionaries who sought the "disestablishment" of Theravāda Buddhism in Southeast Asia and Sri Lanka, reactive (and sometimes reactionary) forms of revivalism and Buddhist millennialism arose in several late colonial and decolonizing states. Although Maoist and other left movements in Asia were overtly atheistic, episodically, communist aspirations inhered in Buddhist-inflected millenarian logics in Theravādin South and Southeast Asia (Keyes 1977; Salter 2000; Ladwig 2014; Hansen 2019; Patton 2020). Indeed, Buddhist millenarianism coalesced with visions of ousting of European rule as well as Christian missionaries and other wayward detractors.[24] At the same time, Western nations' ostensibly secular Cold War military interventions against communism in Southeast Asia were embedded implicitly within the ethos of "Judeo-Christian religion" and broader political and moral imperatives that Robert Bellah (1967) famously characterized as "American civil religion."[25] Beyond the longstanding links between southern Buddhist monasticism and ideologies of statecraft that unite

Sri Lanka and Southeast Asia, wider patterns of affinity between these regions may be observed through consideration of modern Buddhist–Christian disputes and how these figure into today's contentions over the righteous trajectory of the political economy.

KARMA AND GRACE: RELIGIOUS CONTINUITY AND RELIGIOUS CHANGE

As discussed earlier, Sri Lanka does not have an entirely secular constitution, although it does leave minor provisions for religious choice. What is especially striking in this legally inscribed religious protectionism is how Sinhala Buddhists perpetually feel compelled to challenge secularist rights-based terms of "freedom," "conscience," and "religion" through Buddhist grammars of what it is that constitutes "a free conscience" (Schonthal 2016, 243).[26] This is also evident ethnographically, in the way that Buddhists and Christians spar in the vernacular over conceptions of religious freedom. Such sparring is symptomatic of how these rival forms of life are embedded in a broader economy of social and spiritual influence.[27] Sinhala Buddhists rhetorically condemn Christian conversions as "unethical" because they rely on material "allurements" and "inducements" proffered by proselytizers (Mahadev 2014; Hertzberg 2016). This sensibility coheres with doctrinal views in Theravāda Buddhism whereby material life is but a "fetter" (Pāli *saññyojana*, Sinhala *wilangu* [lit. "shackles"]) that impinges upon the mind. Considering the Western formulation of the right to "freedom of conscience" from a Pāli Buddhist perspective, then, a mind that is swayed by the material accoutrements of (Christian) charity is a mind that is rendered as infirm and thus as unfree. Sinhala Buddhist anti-conversion discourses are implicitly attuned to this common doctrinal sensibility of the imperative to overcome *saññyojana* (material fetters) by relinquishing wealth through material patronage (*dāna* or almsgiving) of the *sangha* (monastic order) in order to actuate the fullness of one's karmic potential. In this contested milieu, these distinctive Buddhist and Christian epistemologies animate a differential set of ideas concerning religious freedom, thus presenting a political impasse situated in definitional disputes over what constitutes the ethics of conversion.

Observing how the theopolitical disputes concerning Sri Lanka's religious inheritances and religious future intensified in public discourses on conversion over the last several decades, a primary intervention that this book makes is to lay bare the correspondences between Pentecostal Christian grace and the rupture of religious conversion on the one side and karma as an eschatology of continuity on the other. Karma and grace are recognized as logics that relate to one's ontological standing within the wider cosmos. At the same time, in the entanglement of these religious forms, their logics are rendered political. While Buddhist revivalists call upon Sri Lankans to abide by the karmic inheritances of the self and the nation, Sri Lankan Christian evangelists project the possibility of forging a new future "through the grace of God."

Within the doctrine of karma, actions carried out in an individual's past lives produce their present life's conditions. Karma thus equips the individual with aptitudes and ethical dispositions that are appropriate to their station in life. Meritorious action (*puñña karmaya*) from one's past enables one to deftly navigate one's own present life conditions. As such, this eschatological and ontological sensibility posits that capacities for individuated and collective moral ascendance require one to abide by the inheritances given in life. Karmic outcomes rely on unseen and unscripted cosmic temporalities, which are ordinarily not unilinear. Thus, the shape of one's past, present, or future trajectory is something that humans can rarely discern.[28] Nevertheless, a "karmic eschatology" implies a kind of continuity for Buddhists, whereby staying true to one's religious inheritances by following the *dhamma* will enable the fruits of merit to ripen over the course of many lifetimes (Obeyesekere 1963, 2002; Mahadev 2019). In this Buddhist rendering of moral logic, one's karmic inheritances are righteously in line with the *dhamma* (nature of the cosmos), as well as with a trajectory toward heightened capacities for moral discernment of which the historical Buddha was exemplary. Accordingly, Buddhist scriptures suggest that obedience to the "Middle Path" (*madhayma pratipadāwa*) ultimately comes to fruition in worldly signs of the ontological capacity for heightened moral attainments.

In contrast to this Buddhist *doxa*, for believing Christians conversion is premised upon the idea of God's gifts of grace. Born-again conversion prototypically involves a rupture whereby ministerial discourse implores believers to "make a complete break from the past" (Meyer 1998; also Robbins 2007). In the case of Ghanaian Pentecostalism, Birgit Meyer (1998) has suggested that even as ministers insist upon remembering and discerning the occult and ancestral sources of their ailments, this discursive call for rupture has the potential to facilitate processes of urbanization, modernization, and individualization, with the implication that mass conversion *may* serve to transform complex corporate webs of kin obligation into atomized nuclear families. Among my interlocutors in Sri Lanka, to become "born-again" (Sinhala: "*näwatha ipadīma*") entails not only a change of belief but is also conceived of as involving a change in the very constitution of the person. As Pentecostal-charismatic Christians are inclined to see it, conversion is a matter of the miraculous reception of grace through the inflowing of the Holy Spirit (*Suddha Ātmaya*). The flowing ease and immediacy through which grace is conveyed and transduced through the Holy Spirit are believed to manifest as one's readiness to receive God's grace. In turn, Pentecostals credit the presence of the Holy Spirit for producing indelible conviction within believers, individually, and en masse.

By this logic, Pentecostal Christianity's fervent expansionism is believed to coincide with how easily and effectively the pentecostalist *charism* can move, diffuse, and sanctify, so as to generate conversions "miraculously." From the born-again vantage point, conversion is structured along the lines of God's grace: conversions come about not only as a matter of the will of the proselytizer or of the convert. Pentecostals avow that they experience a spirited conversion that is shaped by the will of God, rather than by a decision that resides solely in one's own mind. Born-again converts in Sri Lanka insist that they undertake faith commitments out of one's own volition, because their volition coordinates with their God's salvific will. Accordingly, from the vantage point of born-again Christians, Buddhists' contentions that proselytizers engage new recruits in ways that facilitate conversions "unethically" out of strictly pragmatic motivations are invalid. These distinctive soteriological premises and their attendant messianic temporalities can generate tense entanglements in the Sri Lankan public sphere.

Addressing how within Sri Lankan religious discourses Buddhism corresponds to concepts of karmic continuity while born-again Christianity corresponds to grace-based orientations to discontinuity, this book intervenes in major debates within the anthropology of religion. Several thinkers have worked with the dichotomous concepts of continuity and discontinuity to address the local attributes associated with the global emplacements of Christianity, sparking an important set of theoretical debates grounded in ethnographic work. To carve out space and set a scholarly agenda for the nascent subdiscipline of the anthropology of Christianity, Joel Robbins (2004, 2007) and Fenella Cannell (2006) have each argued that anthropologists had paid insufficient attention to

Christianity up to that point. Each suggested that anthropologists who did encounter Christianity and Christians in their field sites had tended to approach them in their analysis with inattention to epistemological and ritual changes and dramatic narratives of conversion.[29] Robbins attributed this to anthropologists' inclinations to engage in "continuity thinking," which resulted from the overarching disciplinary endeavor to understand, value, and to "salvage" diverse cultural forms in the face of globalization and colonization.[30] He called for anthropologists to develop an attunement to discontinuity as an essential feature of Christian culture.

A number of productive critiques of this provocation emerged, based upon studies of varied global Christian forms. For one, the sharply enunciated imperative to "break with the past" stems primarily from Pentecostalist discourse, which does not necessarily apply to other denominations and sects of Christianity (Engelke, "Past Pentecostalism"; Chua 2012). Second, anthropologists have emphasized that the totalizing rhetoric of evangelical and Pentecostal Christian discontinuity does not necessarily match the lived experience of conversion (Daswani 2013; D. Premawardhana 2018). Matthew Engelke illustrates how various forms of Christianity exist coevally alongside of Pentecostalism, thus challenging the postulate that Pentecostal Christianity—like an ideal-typical telos of modernity—supplants and supersedes preexisting religious and cultural forms. Based on fieldwork among an apostolic Christian community (classified as an "African Independent Church") in Zimbabwe that rejects the use of biblical texts, the Friday Masowe instead seek to ensure that they receive the "live and direct" word of God. Rather than representing a unilinear break toward modernity, Engelke argues that the Friday Masowe's quest for God's presence engages Christian cultural scripts in ways that inscribe other kinds of pasts—including an ancient Apostolic age, as well as a golden age envisioned as the precolonial African past.[31] In a similar vein, Liana Chua (2012) addresses denominational plurality in her work among Anglican and Catholic Bidayuhs of Malaysian Borneo, where large-scale conversions took place in the 1970s. She demonstrates that in a context of state policies of inculturation and multiculturalism, paired with the cultural imperatives to maintain *adat*, or customary practices that emphasize harmony and social "coolness," Biduyah Christians consistently approach the "old ways" amiably. She argues that in the culture of Bidayuh Anglican and Catholic Christianity, conversions were rarely marked by rupture but rather were piecemeal, rarely remarked upon, and ensured social harmony. At bottom, these anthropologists attend to the ways that the lived experience of conversion often differs from the discursive framing of wholesale conversion and discontinuity, particularly when it comes to abiding by obligations to kin, neighbors, and ancestors who sustain the integrity of village society in these contexts of the Global South.

Karma and Grace adds to these debates on continuity and discontinuity in several respects. First, rather than stem from the anthropologist's own predilections, in the case at hand Sinhala Buddhists themselves contend or imply that it is vital to abide by one's karmic self-constitution and that karmic eschatology itself signifies moral continuities and potentials for meritorious progress that must be carried out over many, many lifetimes. Among my interlocutors, dedicated Buddhists emphasized the importance of not deviating from the religion of their birth (*upathinma āgama wenas keranna epā*). They often implied that forsaking one's karma in favor of Christian grace deprives one of the well-calibrated moral compass that is attuned according to the merits of one's prior actions, and thus, that abiding by one's own karma is most appropriate to propel them forward along the path. In essence, karma, I argue, informs an ideology of religious continuity that adds a sense of moral force to nativist and nationalistic religious commitments.

Although attaining *nibbāna* and receiving salvation are incommensurable eschatological goals, in their proximity, the born-again Christian idea of salvational *immediacy* chafes against the far-distant potentialities for Buddhists to attain their eschatological goals of better future lifetimes, and ultimately, *nibbāna*. This is not to say that Buddhism and Christianity are inherently at odds at one another. However, when undergirded by political-economic disputes that are borne out through the particularities of Sri Lanka's postcolonial, millennial, and postwar circumstances, these distinctive orientations to karmic continuity and grace-filled discontinuity bear the potential to materialize as mutual hostility. Querying the politicized impasses between nationalistic and nativist calls for religious continuity on the one side, and evangelical appeals favoring the rupture of conversion on the other, the chapters of this book explore how these soteriological differences are discursively and materially mediated and mitigated.

Further to the point of anthropologists who have suggested that there is an overdetermining thrust to the call to set one's sights upon analyzing discontinuity, neither majoritarian Buddhists' rhetorical work of vilifying evangelizing Christians nor Christian ministers' stated ambitions to expand the faith produce the fullest picture of interreligious pluralism in contemporary Sri Lanka. In lived practice, Sri Lankan Christians' expansionary ambitions are necessarily enacted in fragmentary ways. Particularly when enraptured in charismatic states, some of my Pentecostal interlocutors evidently absorbed authoritative ministerial discourses in fragments. Otherwise stated, exclusionary discourses, even those propagated within a church, may well fall upon ears made deaf by the enchantments of the *charism*. Or, as discussed earlier, they may be heard but not enacted as rupture either because of reticence to shirk the spiritual and material obligations to one's kin and ancestors or because another deity appears to wield exceptional powers. Additionally, despite the stated ministerial appeals to proselytize, Sri Lankan Christians from most social and denominational backgrounds—including charismatics and evangelicals—are careful not to stir up conflict with Buddhists, in part because of the threat they pose.

Take for instance the kinds of tensions that stem from mutual derogations of "selfishness" that Sri Lankan Buddhists and Christians hurl at one another's traditions, which I explain in chapter 2 in terms of the long-standing disagreement over the moral economies of Christian charity and the Buddhist almsgiving (*dāna*) that is directed from laity to monks. While there is no absolute resolution to the kinds of disagreements over these differences, in chapter 6 we learn how one Pentecostal convert named Dhanika remembered the anti-Christian violence that took place in her village two decades earlier. Dhanika, for her part, took pains to make peace with the village Buddhists, in part by ensuring that her household continued to contribute *dāna* for the care of the monks of her local temple. Neither absolute exclusivity nor radical pluralism are evident within these socially proximate interchanges. Between wives and husbands, parents and children, siblings and in-laws, friends and neighbors, macro-level political antipathies are managed and mitigated through quotidian negotiations.

Prudence and pragmatism are not the sole reasons that Sri Lankan Christians and Buddhists strive not to agitate conflict. A subset of Sinhala Buddhists is made up of conscientious objectors who reject the violence carried out in the name of Buddhist protectionism. Not all of them hail from elite and cosmopolitan backgrounds, but they assert their influence and make their mark on the Sri Lankan public sphere nonetheless. Likewise, some Sri Lankan Christians who identify as evangelical, Pentecostal, or born-again are dual belongers in practice, or otherwise may act as progressives, and open-minded friends toward Buddhists and other minority communities. Despite the diabolizing character of sermonic discourses, and despite authoritative, nationalistic calls to be vigilant against Christianization, what is made plain through ethnographic attention to interreligious relationships is that occasionally, Christians and Buddhists undertake complex negotiations to ensure social peace across religious divides.

PLURALITY AND "MULTICAMERALISM"

To capture the nature of Buddhist and Christian relationality and the plurality of the Sri Lankan milieu, my ethnographic fieldwork method is multisited. It is also what I call "multicameral." This multicameral ethnographic approach involved tacking between a variety of Sri Lankan Buddhist and Christian communities to understand conversion as a situation of identitarian conflict that was exacerbated through the contingencies of the illiberal postwar and millennial context, and channeled through old and new conduits for religious expression. Multicameralism is a mode of ethnographic inquiry whereby one is situated not only within but also at the interstices between distinctive religious communities. This approach was crucial for examining the conflictual and conciliatory quotidian realities and intimacies expressed by Buddhists and Christians who are proximal rivals.

In terming my approach as hinging upon a "multicameral" perspective, I riff upon political theorist William E. Connolly's idea of a "bicameral orientation"—a duality in one's own perspective that he suggests is essential for one to develop an engaged "ethos of pluralism" (2005). While drawing on his generative notion of a personal ethos to examine and theorize an empirical reality would ordinarily trouble the divide between prescriptive and descriptive approaches to pluralism (Klassen and Bender 2010, 8), my ethnographic project remains deeply empirical.[32] In Connolly's theorization of an "ethos of pluralization," it is attitudes and aspirations through which political actors concertedly orient themselves toward pluralism (1995, 2005). Rather differently, throughout this ethnography, it is apparent that many of my interlocutors are not necessarily motivated by an "ethos" and sentiment of pluralization, in large part because the ideological and material affordances for such sentiments are not easily forthcoming within the Sri Lankan public sphere. This is not to discount the political efforts of those Sri Lankans, for example, artists, intellectuals, and scholar-monks raised in the tradition of Sinhala Buddhism who conscientiously object to majoritarian nationalist political violence either by aligning themselves with "unBuddhism" (Chandrasekera 2021), who refer to themselves as "thinking people" and critics (Weerasinghe 2009), or who exceptionally work toward interreligious dialogue (Dhammananda 2013). But what is most apparent throughout this ethnography is that it is quotidian moral negotiations—which arise perhaps before any clearly articulated and prefigured formation of an ethos—that subtly challenge dominant strands of antagonism that are in circulation. With respect to method, I argue that using a multicameral ethnographic approach to query inter-religion is conducive to seeing the nondialectical aspects of religiosity, evident in the ordinary leniencies and experimentations, and in the ways that religionists may practically fall outside of bounded categories of identitarian belonging (see especially chapter 6).[33]

Such indeterminacy is a valuable facet of religious life. This book touches upon dialectical and nondialectical forms of relationality to grapple with plurality beyond the bounds of exclusivist identitarian belonging. A fine theoretical picture of this nondialectical indeterminacy and how it may be conducive to pluralism can be seen in Theodor Adorno's critical inquiry into the dialectics of identitarian conflict. Reckoning with genocidal violence in the aftermath of the Holocaust, the German philosopher and Frankfurt School theorist implored his readers to consider persistent human proclivities toward identitarian violence, in its material and ideational manifestations. In his treatise on *Negative Dialectics* ([1966] 2004), Adorno discerned that violence was a constituent part thinking itself. To put an end to it, paradoxically, humanity had to think itself out of the inclination toward violence. His point is premised upon the way that thinking involves a dialectical process of concept creation. To think is to produce a thesis and its contrapuntal antithesis. In turn, he argued, that the act of category creation does violence to remainders—that is, thinking violently cordons off what lies outside of concepts, in the negative space of the dialectic. Such violence is mirrored in identity-based conflicts, and practically in the Holocaust, insofar as violence hinged upon categorical determinations of who was to be sent to the camps and who was to be free from a violent end. While the genocidal scenario is an extreme case of bureaucratized violence, my point is to draw an analogy between the nondialectical dwelling in the negative space, which Adorno extols, and identitarian indeterminacy, experimentation, noncommitments and ambivalences of belonging, and the conditions of possibility for abiding plurality. It is in the immanent conditions of life and in the negative space between concepts that humanity can think itself out of identitarian violence.

MULTICAMERALISM AS METHOD:
NOTES ON CONTEXT AND FIELDWORK

My field research took place intensively over the course of twenty-eight months from 2009 to 2011 and builds from longer-standing engagements carried out over prior stints of living in Sri Lanka that span back to 1998. The work began with interviews and participant observation among leaders from established "mainline" Protestant and Catholic Churches in Colombo, legal advocates, and evangelical civil society groups. I involved myself in dialogue forums with interreligious organizations led by Christians as well as by Buddhists. These learned priests and lay organizers make heartening grassroots efforts to teach pluralistic values and engage in dialogue and learning.

Following initial fieldwork in the hub of economic and political authority that is Colombo, I commenced research on the outskirts of the city and in rural southern coastal stretches of the country. Buddhist monks and lay leaders, some engaged in ordinary work of sustaining Buddhism and others who were more active in their revivalist praxis, were among my interlocutors. Beyond Colombo to the north, one finds suburbs and a string of small towns and villages constituted by a mixed demographic and small enclaves of Pentecostals. But one also finds some of the largest concentrations of Sri Lankan Catholics there, too. Charismatic Christian churches, of varying size and stature—included megachurches, smaller storefront style urban churches, house-churches, and nondenominational (Third-Wave Pentecostal) deliverance ministries, are found in pockets throughout Colombo, in periurban areas, and occasionally too on rural terrain. Distinct from Pentecostal denominational franchise churches (e.g. Assemblies of God), deliverance ministries are often housed impermanently in weak infrastructures or are hosted on large privately owned grounds where congregants are shielded from the scorching sun and monsoon rains by corrugated tin roofing. These makeshift spaces often draw one to two thousand congregants for any one "praise and worship" session, in the course of which one finds spectacular practices of Pentecostal deliverance (chapter 3). In comparison to the urban denominational Pentecostal churches where one finds relatively elite and upwardly mobile Christians in Colombo city, the deliverance ministries in the suburbs are quite different both in terms of class demographics, aesthetics, and ritual practice (chapters 3 and 6).

Roughly half of the ethnography in this book was carried out in villages located in a part of the country commonly referred to as the "Sinhala south." The south coast was a particularly important area for this research because it had been badly devastated by the 2004 Indian Ocean tsunami a few years before, and as a result the area had been subject to much secular humanitarian aid, Christian charity, and occasional church planting activity and thereby became a locus of alarm over "unethical" conversions. I concentrated my energies within several villages on the coast, and one in particular that I refer to by the pseudonym "Weligoda."

A multicameral approach involves more than a "multisited" ethnography. It is different from classical anthropological studies which are prototypically carried out whilst being situated snuggly and exclusively within a firmly demarcated social milieu, in order to settle one's focus upon a single identity-based "community," or subsets of a community. Rather, to capture the nature of interreligious conflict, I discuss the emic perspectives of religionists, while also focusing etically on points of contention between communities. The upshot is that book "takes religion seriously" by situating both religious skepticism and sincerity, continuity and discontinuity, from the vantage points of Sinhala Buddhists as well as different communities and denominations of Christians.

It is often said that the anthropologist's craft involves knowledge production that makes the strange familiar. Yet, just as often, anthropologists tend to circle back home to topics that ring familiar. When the 2004 BBC headline on Sri Lankan Buddhist monks lobbying for a ban against unethical conversions came through to me as I browsed the news from my desk in Baltimore, elements of the story hit close to home for two reasons. Via distant relatives in the southern Indian town of Sivakasi, some of my closer relatives, mainly my maternal aunts in India, converted to Pentecostalism. The network of my mother's kin, which had formerly been concentrated in my mother's hometown in southern India, had been mainly sanguine. But throughout the 1990s conversion from Hinduism to born-again Christianity had sparked episodes of kin trouble among my family members living in southern India and in the United States. After some years of episodic intrafamily quarrels between those who put primacy of place upon heritage and the southern Indian politics of "self-respect" and those who embraced new orientations to Christian salvation, the "affliction" of religious multiplicity gradually softened into a kind of "mutuality of being" and belonging, between sisters, brothers, mothers, daughters, sons, in-laws, and cousins.

Second, conversion and resistances to it mattered in my childhood and youth in the 1980s and 1990s, in another very different locale too. In the rural and not especially ethnically diverse regions of the United States where I grew up as a second-generation Indian American, my mother and I had dabbled in occasional churchgoing roughly from the time I was six until the age of twelve. In our search for friendship and belonging in the upper reaches of northern Michigan, we were partially incorporated, like fictive kin, into an evangelical Baptist family with whom we spent Christmas and other holidays in intensive commensality, rituals of gift exchange, and familial warmth. For me, a pair of sisters near to my own age were my core link to this family. Together the sisters and I constructed heavily blanketed forts, had Saturday sleepovers followed by breakfast and Sunday School at their church, and on one occasion we spent a summer week together at church camp. But the occasional churchgoing came to a hard stop for my mother and me when certain members of their extended kin network began to express the view that those who hadn't accepted Jesus Christ as their "one and only Lord and Savior" were bound to go to hell. The hard stop on churchgoing didn't necessitate a totalizing end to all of those friendships, but for a time those friendships were strained. Geographical and affective separation grew between us, particularly when I continued my studies while they proceeded to expand their families and recommit themselves to their church and began new practices such as homeschooling. Today, although difference remains, through our mutual efforts to refrain from speaking of religion or politics, our shared sadness over one aunt's prolonged illness, the loss of my dear brother, and occasional joys of childhood reminiscence, those tensions too have softened, and relations warmed.

It is this familiar-strangeness of disputes over conversion to born-again Christianity and of countervailing nativist tendencies toward religious exclusivity, of ideologies that promote discontinuity and continuity of religious practices and relations, that has called me to examine inter-religion from a multicameral perspective when controversies over conversion took hold in Sri Lanka—a country I had come to love since my first visit as a college student in 1998. Approaching the multireligious field in such a fashion, I suggest, is requisite for understanding these dense and dynamic religious and political tensions, and to discover the socially embedded ways in which people work to ensure that those tensions might dissolve, or be ameliorated, or are simply lived, agonistically, together.[34]

In an altogether other context from Sri Lanka, Steven Wasserstrom remarked that "all religion is inter-religion" (Wasserstrom 2019).[35] The point is relevant to the situation of social proximity between Buddhists and Christians in Sri Lanka too, wherein one finds a densely relational multireligious field. *Karma and Grace* is structured to first examine the overarching political impasses of conversion in Sri Lanka, and how the economies of religious difference add fuel to the fires of interreligious hostility. In the later chapters of this book I trace out the persuasive forces of Buddhist and Christian logics of aspirational religious sovereignty in Sri Lanka. In doing so, I elucidate forms of religious change that result not only from the radical discontinuities entailed by conversion but also from the innovations and adaptations that are required to keep pace with new rivals. Innovations in charismatic personality politics, liturgy, practical institutional maneuvering, media usage, and rituals that bridge temporal and ontological gaps and hasten messianic arrivals allow Christians and Buddhists to respectively ensure the continued flourishing of the Church and the *Dhamma*. Simply put, even as antipathies arise between Christian believers and Buddhist nationalist skeptics, so too do religious innovations and accommodations appear at the newest frontiers of rivalry. The ethnography reveals how even in times when antipathies are running hot, dedicated practitioners of religion sometimes manage to partake in leniency and ambiguation—like Nimesh's cautious silence—in ways that enhance capacities to dwell together amid difference. In various quotidian ways, religious practitioners manage to draw and redraw the lines of conflict and belonging.

A NOTE ON TERMS: DEFINING "EVANGELICAL"

Throughout this book I use the term "evangelical" in lowercase to connote the expansionary ambitions that are common to many but not all varieties of Christianity. The lowercase "evangelical" can modify an array of sectarian or denominational forms of Christianity. In this way, it can be applied not only to Protestantism but also to Roman Catholicism and Pentecostalism—inasmuch as ambitious expansion is taken as central to the credo. Yet some Sri Lankans do not define the term as such. This was evident for example, when my interlocutor and friend Samanthi, a well-educated, left-of-center Sinhala Protestant woman in her late sixties, accepted the definition reported to her by her American Baptist pastor. The visiting pastor had explained to her that "evangelical simply means 'Bible-based.'" Given that "Bible-based" can correspond also with classic Christian conceptions of love—*agape*, *philia*, and fraternal love—for Christians like Samanthi who hold a social justice orientation to the faith, such a general definition may well warm the heart—especially in the face of pernicious and exclusionary forms of majoritarian nationalism. Thus, like Samanthi, Sri Lankan Christians who might self-identify as "evangelical" may express a range of political and social sentiments. However, I use the term "evangelical" specifically to designate Christians who hold to the imperative to spread the gospel, to witness, and to proselytize.

In the main, Sri Lankan Christians are relatively "liberal" in the political sense. Compared to nationalistic Sinhala Buddhists who oppose the growth of minority religions in Sri Lanka, not surprisingly, at the ballot box Christian minorities in general tend to support rights paradigms that (in theory) equitably allow minoritized people to equally flourish. Samanthi, a dedicated Christian, was politically left-of-center, a Sinhala married to a Tamil Christian man. For her part, she adamantly characterized herself as a "nationalist," a label she embraced notwithstanding its application to the hardline majoritarian nationalists who tended to vilify Christians as "anti-nationals" as a matter of political stereotype. In fact, Samanthi embraced the label "nationalist" precisely as a matter of rejecting the allegations of anyone who might accuse her—as a Christian, and as a Sinhala married to an ethnic Tamil—of doing anything other than loyally adoring her nation.

More often than not, Sri Lankan evangelicals' tendency to embrace political liberalism converges with a neoliberalist political-economic bent—a phenomenon that congeals as a matter of political stereotype, as I detail in chapter 1. It has been widely documented in the anthropological literatures on evangelical economics that the prosperity gospel and "millennial capital" are highly portable phenomena (Coleman 2000; Comaroff and Comaroff 2001; Csordas 2009). The orientation to the prosperity gospel is not uniform among evangelicals in Sri Lanka or otherwise, but it is commonplace in Pentecostal-charismatic discourse (Haynes 2014). As an example, in a small, well-to-do urban Assemblies of God church that I observed in the outskirts of Colombo, the Pentecostal minister would regularly cajole his Saturday afternoon congregation to tithe and make seed offerings generously, with an exuberant call to "Give *excellently* to Jesus, and He will give *excellently* to you!" Analyzing such a premise in her ethnography of Pentecostalism in the Zambian Copperbelt, Naomi Haynes explains that seed offerings are attached to "positive confessions," such that Christians' hopes are articulated as subjunctive truths; in other words, a layperson's hopes are uttered *as if* they are already reality—or a reality in the making. Haynes writes, "As with seed offerings, when God is confronted with a believer's faith, he will—indeed, must—respond by giving the thing they have confessed. Here again, scripture affords these claims. The Pentecostal notion of positive confession follows from the observations that humans are created in the image of a God who created the world through speech, that a mountain will move if one tells it to, and that 'the tongue has the power of life and death' " (Haynes 2014, 360).

As one can ascertain from Haynes's work, Pentecostal discourse is a form of prophetic speech that is felt to bring specific hopes to fruition. Otherwise put, charismatic Christian discourses discipline believers into experiencing charismatic speech as infused with perlocutionary force—force that is propelled by "the grace of God." Evangelical and charismatic styles of faith in God are archetypically secured through the discipline of abiding by grace, as well as by taking individual responsibility for one's personal faith. "Surrender" and patience are said to bring health and wealth efficaciously into fruition.

Inasmuch as evangelical and Pentecostal forms of Christianity converge with the "gospel of prosperity," then, these discursive practices generally do not incline Christians toward a politics of redistribution—even as they pray that all who are suffering will come to Christ and reap the same paradisiacal rewards that they will, as Believers. Thus, the evangelical Christian form stands in contrast to "ecumenical" Christianity. Ecumenical Christianity, as it is defined especially throughout Asia and the Global South, orients believers to interreligious dialogue, social justice, and redistributive politics. My Sri Lankan ecumenical Christian interlocutors are insistent upon *not* proselytizing their Christian faith, and instead they strive to "indigenize" Christianity within Asia (Balasuriya 1976 Pieris 1995; Premawardhana 2004; Mahadev 2022). In addition to the denominational pluralism that is evident in Sri Lanka, the distinction between "evangelical" and "ecumenical" runs throughout this book; but I offer the caveat that some Sri Lankan Christians, like Samanthi, may not entirely concur with my characterization.

CHAPTER 1

Tangles of Religious Perspectivism

Economies of Conversion and Ontologies of Difference

As in sacrifice, dispossession converts having into being; the struggle for achievement is over, material possessions are traded for grace.

—J. G. Peristiany and Julian Pitt-Rivers, *Honor & Grace in Anthropology*

Of all the disgrace deservedly reaped by theology, the worst is positive religions' howl of rejoicing at the unbelievers' despair.

—Theodor Adorno, *Negative Dialectics*

On December 12, 2003, news reached members of the Buddhist sangha in Maharagama and Colombo that the Sri Lankan revivalist monk Gangodawila Soma Thera died unexpectedly while visiting St. Petersburg, Russia. With the news of his passing, his devoted Sinhala Buddhist followers were overcome with shock and sadness. The sentiments of those who were moved by his teachings quickly turned to anger when after intense scrutiny the monk's inner circle deemed his death to be untimely and the cause suspect. During the last decade of his life the reformist monk had preached and written himself into the center of a new wave of Sinhala Buddhist revivalism. As Soma Thera's body was transported from St. Petersburg back to Colombo, rumors of conspiracy circulated in the Sinhala- and English-language news media. Prominent monks and lay activists proclaimed that his "mysterious" death was the result of the sinister machinations of "Christian fundamentalists" (*Cristiyāni muladharma wādiyo*). These champions of Buddhism used the tragedy of his death to stand as a warning to Sinhala people about the treachery of Christians. Monastic authorities from Soma Thera's home temple in Maharagama scheduled his funeral for Christmas Eve in Colombo. For Christian city-dwellers, the events cast an air of disquiet on their holy day as massive crowds of lay Buddhist devotees clad in white and monastics clad in orange walked in procession through the city streets to Soma Thera's funeral pyre.

Soma Thera's life, and the critical event of his death, has been significant in the galvanization of a new phase of politicized Buddhism in Sri Lanka, since the lead-up to the millennium. The monk's incitements to revive and reform Buddhism, beginning in the 1990s, can be seen as being in line with the work of a long succession of Buddhist revivalists in Sri Lanka, many of whom promoted exclusivist views of the nation's heritage (Berkwitz 2008). In his sermons Soma Thera had warned his followers that Buddhists would become a demographic minority in Sri Lanka by 2025 if they did not resolutely work to protect their religion against the expansionist agendas of Christians and Muslims (Uyangoda 2007, 169). Seizing upon the Sinhala Buddhist public's outrage over Soma Thera's death, a contingent of nationalistic monks formed a political party, Jathika Hela Urumaya (Sinhala Heritage Party), to generate popular support for a legislative bill that would criminalize proselytism and Christianization in the country (Deegalle 2004).[1] Although the legislative bill to ban "unethical conversions" was never passed into law, the publicly articulated allegation that Christians have sinister designs to destroy Buddhism had a salient afterlife in Sri Lanka.

What undergirds the anti-conversion narrative enunciated in majoritarian nationalist discourses? Despite the minority status of Christians, Sinhala Buddhist revivalists perceive Christianity to be in direct competition with Buddhism. Hence, powerful revivalists like Soma Thera are believed to attract the jealous attention of Christians. Rumors circulated in urban Buddhist circles in Sri Lanka claiming that the esteemed monk had been led to his tragic demise by a "fraudulent" Sinhala convert to Christianity. The revivalist monk and the Christian business mogul who was said to be culpable for his death have served as the *dramatis personae* of Buddhist-Christian enmity that fomented in Sri Lanka in recent decades. Specifically, the rumors held that the culprit was a high-profile businessman named Lalith Kotelawala, who, upon his conversion from Buddhism to Christianity in the 1970s, allegedly became involved in machinations to "destroy Buddhism." For dedicated Sinhala Buddhists, especially those in the urban milieus of Colombo and Maharagama, the story of the alleged culprit's conversion is the prototype of Christian "fundamentalism" that inflamed anti-conversion politics. By what chain of associations did Sinhala Buddhist discourses construe this affluent Christian convert as a fraudulent *disgrace*? Analyzing this and other iconic Sri Lankan conversion narratives makes evident how nationalistic Sinhala Buddhists tended to conceive of conversion to Christianity as a fraudulent and ill-advised investment—in both the material and moral senses. Doing so also makes evident how Sinhala Buddhists and Christians regard conversion as having a profound effect upon the constitution of the self, and ultimately, upon the nation too.

BUDDHIST VIRTUOSITY AND CHRISTIAN "FRAUDULENCE"

Ahead of Soma Thera's funeral, posters scripted in Sinhala appeared in public spaces throughout Colombo. They alleged that the executive director of Ceylinco, Sri Lanka's largest private corporation, was involved in "leading the monk to his demise."[2] The Sinhala-language press put forth cryptic allegations of the businessman's culpability for many years afterward. As detailed in the introduction, several years later at the commemoration of Soma Thera in 2010, lay Buddhist orators contended that Christian "fundamentalists" persist in making a business out of conversion. Amid thousands of lay Buddhist devotees, they invoked the allegations implicitly held against Kotelawala, and beyond the specific event of Soma Thera's death they extended their references to the connivance of Christians in general.

As rumor had it, Kotelawala had concocted a plan to lure Soma Thera away from Sri Lanka with the offer of an honorary degree of questionable merit from a university in St. Petersburg. Soma Thera's Russian trip was said to have been arranged by an accomplice, another Christian, whose brother surreptitiously gained employment on one of Soma Thera's main projects as the newspaper editor for the Janavijaya Foundation, an organization founded by Soma Thera and other monks of the Maharagama temple monastery. The Janavijaya Foundation is charged with the task of "the propagation and revival of Buddhism." Rumors had it that this accomplice was a Sinhala Christian minister posing as a Buddhist to carry out the plot against Soma Thera. The two accomplices were rumored to have arranged Soma Thera's invitation, his travel, and the awards ceremony, while Kotelawala was alleged to have paid the expenses.

Soma Thera's supporters demanded that the Sri Lankan government investigate his death. When autopsy reports indicated that he had died of natural causes, anti-conversion activists offered a slew of justifications to corroborate the guilt of Christians. They insisted that the government investigators falsified the autopsy report to prevent civil disturbance. In variations on the narrative, different degrees of culpability were imputed to Kotelawala and his accomplice: at most, the culprits were alleged to have committed premeditated murder. At the very least, the invitation to Russia was believed to have been intended to publicly humiliate Venerable Soma Thera, since it appeared implausible that any legitimate Russian institution could have had genuine intentions to bestow an honorary degree upon a monk whose entire body of work had been written in Sinhala (Berkwitz 2008).

I learned of the Christian businessman's supposed culpability for the death of Soma Thera in public whispers over sips of Nescafé in Colombo bakeries, at dinner tables and in sitting rooms in the city and suburban Colombo homes, and less commonly while walking along back roads in southern coastal villages of Sri Lanka. Piumi, a devoted Buddhist woman in her thirties, expressed her conviction about Kotelawala's culpability for Soma Thera's death and the broader problem of Christian "fundamentalism," telling me the story from the comfort of her home in Piliyandala, a Colombo suburb. Books in Sinhala by Soma Thera had changed her life. As she put it, "his teachings have given me the true understanding of the religion of my birth." A glint of pain appeared in her eyes as we spoke of his death. After a day of teaching she had changed out of her sari, and she sat with me in her living room sipping tea in shorts and a T-shirt as a dialogue from a Sinhala teledrama droned on in the background. When her husband came home, we paused our conversation. She offered him a peck on the cheek and some tea before returning to her place on the sofa. With her voice lowered, she continued the story. She told me with relish how the conniving Christian businessman who had killed Soma Thera was ultimately imprisoned for fraud and thus had gotten his karmic just deserts. She told me as we sat just out of earshot of her husband—a born-again Christian who she evidently adored very much.

Lalith Kotelawala's conversion narrative and its uptake in popular majoritarian-nationalist lore reveals that what is at stake in anti-conversion politics are not merely the anxieties of a demographic shift that is projected to reduce Sinhala Buddhists to a discrete minority. Following Soma Thera's death, anti-conversion activists retrospectively treated Kotelwala's conversion as signifying how his adoption of Christianity was pivotal to his transformation into an enemy of Buddhism, and moreover, into a figure who harbored seditious sentiments. For Sinhala Buddhists who are alarmed by the apparent growth of born-again Christianity, Kotelawala's "fallen" character came to stand as the archetypical upshot of Christian conversion: the narrative of the "fraudulent" Christian businessman epitomizes perceptions about the dangerous effects of conversion on the character of a person who turns to Christianity in the struggle to succeed in a modernizing economy.

Kotelawala's iconic biography illuminates the material and ideological grounds upon which Sinhala Buddhist nationalists have come to read negative significations into the persuasions of Christians. Here I consider "persuasion" in its double sense. First, it connotes the act or the process of convincing and coaxing another person to believe or to act. Second, it connotes the essentialized character and inclinations of a person who engages in unseemly, even villainous activities. With the apparent growth of born-again Christianity in pockets throughout Sri Lanka, negative construals of Christians' persuasions thickly resonated with many devout Buddhist laity, and especially those who were inspired by Soma Thera's teachings. The public secret concerning the Christian business mogul who Sinhala Buddhists hold culpable for the death of the monk makes evident that at the heart of anti-conversion politics in South Asia is the nativist contention that conversion to Christianity appears as an insidious socialization process that transforms citizens into subjects who are hostile to the majoritarian ethos of the nation.

Lalith Kotelawala was a public figure at the helm of Sri Lanka's largest and most successful corporation. The story of his conversion was relatively well known and gossiped about, particularly among elite and urban middle-class circles. The tale of his conversion shows how the adversarial politics of Buddhist nationalist perception pivots upon polarities between political-economic ideologies in Sri Lanka. These polarities have been inscribed in Sri Lanka's modern political history and are marked in Buddhist nationalists' discourses on the perceived character of Christian philanthropists, businesspeople, and charismatic "peddlers" of the prosperity gospel.

The language of "fraudulence" in anti-conversion discourse indexes the economic accoutrements and political affinities that Sinhala Buddhists understand as leading people to be persuaded to become Christian. Iterations of the draft legislative bill of 2004 that sought to prohibit "unethical" and "forcible" conversions borrowed language from legislation that had been ratified in several Indian states. The bill held that "force, allurement, and other *fraudulent* means" (my emphasis) were tactics that proselytizers use to "induce" conversions "unethically." Buddhist protectionists insisted that passing the measures into law would preserve the conditions of possibility for religious freedom by allowing vulnerable Buddhist "innocents" to be free of the impositions of proselytizers. Anti-conversion discourses cast "Christian fundamentalists" as culprits who tempt conversions among Buddhists by demanding that newcomers "smash 'idols'" of the Buddha, among a host of other rituals of initiation that serve to denigrate Buddhism. The "plot" against Soma Thera stood out as the most sinister of ways in which Christians were alleged to conspire to destroy Buddhism. The language militating against "fraudulence" and "unethical conversions" that is crystallized in the draft legislation has had a profound resonance among Sri Lankan Buddhists who remain alarmed and decidedly vigilant against the expansionary ambitions of Christians.

The fact that the concept of "fraud" inscribed in the proposed legislative bill connotes a type of deceitfulness that is an expressly economic crime is significant. The entrepreneurial profile, conversion narrative, and allegations against Lalith Kotelawala underscore why Buddhist anti-conversion activists suspect that fraud is a common feature of the moral economy of Christianity. The sense that fraudulence is prevalent in the very constitution of Christian persons particularly chimed with Sinhala Buddhist anti-conversion activists. Concerns about Christian fraudulence point to some of Sinhala Buddhists' most cynical contentions against Christians today. How did this politics of anti-Christian perception, for a time, gain such immense traction among dedicated Buddhists in Sri Lanka?

In studies of religion and political economy, anthropologists have observed how certain structural openings allow for the advance of Christianity, with its prosperity gospels, "millennial capitalism" (Comaroff and Comaroff 2001), and anxieties about moral accountancy and reckoning in the "near future" (Guyer 2007). These approaches often bear the mark of skepticism or of Marxian atheism, which have both troubled and enlivened new ethnographic approaches to Christianity. In recent years, scholars within the subfield of the anthropology of Christianity have emphasized the importance of ethnographically accounting for Christian ways of knowing, being, and valuation that "takes religion seriously" in Christians' own terms (Robbins 2007). One of the foremost concerns among scholars involved in this vein of research on Christianity is to take care not to reduce Christian religiosity to epiphenomena of the political economy (Coleman 2000, 2004; Haynes 2017). Yet, scholars must necessarily query the ways in which notions of Christian salvation are connected to poverty and prosperity, possession and dispossession (Mahadev, "Karma"). The question of how possession and dispossession "converts having into being," and thus how it relates to "states of grace"—and I would add *disgrace*—is of particular relevance here (Peristiany and Pitt-Rivers 1992, 12). I contend that the lines of Buddhist-Christian enmity have been drawn along points of political-economic and religious convergence. Conversion in Sri Lanka and the implications of Lalith Kotelawala's conversion in particular must be understood in relation to the historical trends and through discourses about politically and economically expedient conversions that took place during colonialism and decolonization.

Karma entails a kind of religious continuity that stands opposed to the ruptures entailed by the convert's experience of Christian grace. What are the implications of these disparate religious sensibilities concerning the moral economy of the person? How do these sensibilities track within Sri Lanka's political economy? To pursue these questions of the imbrications of religion, personhood, and the political economy, I first discuss how conversion relates to the formative era of partisan politics in Sri Lanka. By reconstructing Kotelawala's personal biography—as well as the iconic conversion narrative of another prominent Sri Lankan, from Christianity "back" to Buddhism—it becomes clear how conversion trends are lodged within perceptible political-economic trajectories of national belonging.

CONVERSION, COSMOPOLITANISM, AND
THE RELIGIOUS VICISSITUDES OF POWER

Both in popular and historical terms, conversions among the rising elite in modern Sri Lanka are typically characterized as being undertaken for pragmatic and disingenuous reasons. As popular critiques have it, conversion is a matter that is less commonly determined by personal conviction, than by economic and political expediency. What shapes this perception can be seen in the way that distinct waves of Christian conversion are charted out with respect to key points within Sri Lanka's modern political and economic history. Sri Lanka's economy has long been intensely subject to fluctuations in the global commodities market (the 2022 sovereign debt crisis, which is ongoing, is a dire case in point). Policies to manage the economy have created sharp and long-standing partisan divisions (Venugopal 2018). Historically in Sri Lanka, this economic polarization along party lines roughly correlates with distinct sets of religio-economic ideologies. This is evident in the way that a dialectics of derogation and embrace of conversion articulate with political-economic events, which in turn contribute to the hostile politicization concerning the moral inclinations of converts.

In the modern religious history of Sri Lanka, two distinct phases of conversions from Buddhism to Christianity sandwich a wave of conversions from Christianity to Buddhism. The first wave of conversions from Buddhism to Christianity coincided with colonial-era missionary influence. A second wave, from Christianity to Buddhism in the era of nationalization, followed from Sinhala Buddhists' aspirations to reverse European colonial and Christian inflections upon their country's character. These first two waves are associated with colonialism and nationalization respectively and crucially relate to social, political, and economic structures of religious belonging. The relevance of a third wave of conversions, and the growth of charismatic varieties of Christianity since the post-1970s postcolonial era, will become evident later, in a discussion of Kotelawala's conversion.

The first wave of conversions to Christianity emerged out of the work of European missionaries in Ceylon's colonial period. At that time the rising political and economic elite converted to Christianity, as did some segments of lower caste and class groups. During the period of British colonialism converts to Christianity generally became proficient in English. The Ceylonese elite took on "Anglicized" modes of dress, and their acquired skills and cultural capital enabled them to enter the ranks as civil servants (Jayawardena 2002). European Christians who proselytized to pursue conversion as a civilizing mission, and who held broader ambitions to "disestablish" Buddhism in Ceylon and Southeast Asia, of course responded to the conversions of the local elite favorably (Tambiah 1973; Malalgoda 1976).

In the later phases of British rule, Sinhala Buddhist lay and monastic leaders increasingly sought to preserve their heritage and thus became increasingly hostile to the apparent growth of Christianity. In turn, a second phase of conversions occurred in the lead-up to decolonization, wherein political elites made "return" conversions from Christianity to Buddhism. A growing set of Ceylonese nationalists began agitating against Anglicization in the late nineteenth and early twentieth centuries; these agitations accompanied a surge of Buddhist revivalism (Gombrich and Obeyesekere 1988; Jayawardena 2002). In turn, broader anti-minority sentiments began to frame decolonization and nationalization in Ceylon. This exclusivist form of nationalism consolidated in response to rapid transformations in the political economy (Moore 1997, Venugopal 2018).[3] Sinhala Buddhists perceived that various anglicized and cosmopolitan minorities—including Tamils, Muslims, and Sinhala converts to Christianity—became markedly privileged in their ability to land careers in civil service and to prosper via entrepreneurial opportunities. In turn, during the postindependence period, including while Ceylon officially remained under the dominion of the British Crown (1948-1972), majoritarian nationalists agitated for a cultural decolonization to recuperate the nation's heritage. The dominant strand of Ceylonese nationalist recuperations of heritage during the postindependence era advocated stripping privilege away from the anglicized and Christianized elite. These majoritarian nationalists criticized members of the United National Party (UNP) who took the lead in postindependence electoral politics, for being elitist anglophiles and Christians. In sum, postcolonial aspirations towards democratic socialism narrowed and became increasingly populist and exclusionary in nature.

Given this majoritarian nationalist contempt for the ruling elite, during the late colonial era the vast majority of the Sinhala political elite converted from Christianity "back" to Theravāda Buddhism. They converted to Buddhism in anticipation of universal franchise and the democratization of electoral politics, foreseeing that with independence they would need to appeal to a predominantly Buddhist and Sinhala-speaking electorate (Ashton 1999). Prior to independence there had been limited agitation for self-rule in Ceylon. As a result, upon finding their political voice Sinhala Buddhist nationalists channeled their anticolonial sentiments against Ceylonese cosmopolitans. Those critical of the tendency characterized the elites who pragmatically embraced conversion to Buddhism in the period of nationalization pejoratively as "Donoughmore Buddhists," named after the interim constitution drafted by the British in 1931 that introduced universal suffrage (Ashton 1999; de Silva 1982). This late colonial political trend also oriented aspiring politicians to use Buddhist styles of moral engagement and persuasive oratory in vernacular Sinhala to attract the majority vote (Manor 1989; Rambukwella 2018). One by one, those ethnically Sinhala Ceylonese who held political aspirations became Christian apostates, for "returning" to Buddhism was practically required of them.

Members of the political party that had initially taken the reins of independent Ceylon's political machinery in the 1940s, the United National Party (UNP), had converted from Christianity "back" to Buddhism. However, in the initial decade after independence the UNP led Ceylon while it remained a British dominion. The UNP thus maintained its reputation for its liberal economic policies and for retaining ties to the British with the aim of sustaining Ceylon in the global economy. In turn, by the early 1950s Ceylonese populists—that is, those dedicated to the vernacularization of politics—disparaged UNP premiers for maintaining the status quo via policies inherited from the British. Such majoritarian nationalists have long criticized the UNP platform, seeing it as unfavorable to ordinary citizens, and as counter to nativist ideals. They commonly accused UNP leaders of being only nominally Buddhist crypto-Christians who were insufficiently dedicated to the nation. The UNP's reputation as a pro-business and pro-minority party rests upon the overlap between the constituencies (Venugopal 2018).

With the sweeping victory of S. W. R. D. Bandaranaike of the Sri Lanka Freedom Party (SLFP) over the UNP in the parliamentary election of 1956, there was a sea-change. A nationalism that was populist came to prevail in the Ceylonese

1.1 "Mara Yuddhaya" ("War with Mara"), ca. 1955. The political cartoon depicts Sir John Kotelawala, prime minister of Sri Lanka and uncle of Lalith Kotelawala, donning a cross, sitting atop an elephant, the UNP's party symbol, and being courted by Uncle Sam, the country's elite, and all manner of undisciplined followers.

Artist unknown, circulated by Eksath Bhikku Perumuna (United Monks' Front)

political arena. Sinhala Buddhist nationalists tended to see Bandaranaike's victory as rectifying the liberal, Anglicized, implicitly "Christian" political agenda carried out by the UNP in the immediate postindependence years. Solomon West Ridgeway Dias Bandaranaike was Oxford-educated, had been a chief interpreter for the Crown, and was a dedicated Anglican through the early years of his career (Manor 1989). But with the wave of nationalist populism that emerged during the late stages of British colonialism that introduced universal suffrage to Ceylon in the early 1930s, Bandaranaike converted to Buddhism. Thus, Bandaranaike too was technically a "Donoughmore Buddhist" in that he converted from Christianity to Buddhism in the era of decolonization, swayed to reclaim a native disposition in order to achieve resonance with majority Sinhala Buddhist voters. He had once represented the very "Anglicized" traits that Sinhala Buddhists so criticized in their nationalistic and populist rhetoric. However, whereas Sinhala Buddhists generally regard UNP politicians as disingenuous in their embrace of Buddhism, they tended to regard the SLFP leader's conversion, if opportunistic, as nevertheless constructive insofar as he promised to use his position to overwrite the political, economic, religious, and cultural interests installed by the British.

Bandaranaike campaigned with the promise of restoring the Sinhala Buddhist heritage of the island. He wore austere, white vestments signifying the piety of a lay Buddhist (Manor 1989). Following local nativist demands, he strived for proficiency in Sinhala and to reinhabit a Sinhala Buddhist social *habitus* after he came to power. These moves were central to his self-fashioning as an authentically dedicated nationalist (Rambukwella 2018). Although the language of his upbringing was English, Bandaranaike unequivocally introduced the "Sinhala-only Act" (Spencer, *Sri Lanka: History*; DeVotta 2004). In essence, he and his elite Sinhala supporters worked to reverse colonial-era missionary efforts to "disestablish" Buddhism by intensifying the independent state's patronage of the sangha. Years after Bandaranaike's death, in the 1970s, the privileged position for Buddhism was ultimately codified under SLFP leadership in the Sri Lankan Constitution's Buddhism Chapter, which rendered the state as the guarantor that Buddhism and the Buddha *sāsana* (doctrine, legacy) retain "the foremost place" in the country.

Bandaranaike and his SLFP strived for sociopolitical decolonization by taking the first steps toward "nationalizing" the Ceylonese economy and reversing liberal UNP economic policies that had remained friendly to the Crown (Winslow and Woost 2004). As Premier, he became a central contributor to the

Non-Aligned Movement, which sought alliances with other decolonizing "Third World" nations in lieu of following the dictates of either the former colonial powers or the Soviets. His economic ideology promised support for the working class, and to fundamentally alter the Ceylonese political economy. In short, Bandaranaike, and most subsequent SLFP party leaders, promised to move Ceylon toward a center-left economic model (Shastri 2004; Moore 1997). Alongside SLFP's efforts to nationalize the economy, various minority communities (including Christians, Tamils, European and Anglicized contingents of elite Ceylonese society) were stripped of certain institutional privileges previously afforded to them.[4]

In essence, the majoritarian political ideology that emerged had it that Christian conversion generated "denationalized" and deracinated subjects. But ironically, the Sinhala-only Act that was intended to recuperate this majoritarian heritage disallowed a generation of Sinhala people from studying in the English medium. The ruling, inaugurated by S. W. R. D. Bandaranaike, had the unfortunate effect of further aggravating their sense of disadvantage in the global economy, which in turn exacerbated communalism and anti-minority sentiment in Ceylon. The significance of Bandaranaike and his SLFP's victory for the furtherance of populist nationalism and nativism cannot be underestimated—though the implementation of his ideals fueled ethnic chauvinism inadvertently, and much to his regret.[5]

To summarize, important linkages between religious affiliation, political-economic sensibility, and party alignments contributed to the entrenchment of Buddhist-Christian antagonisms in Sri Lanka. Since independence, two core parties, the UNP and the SLFP, which represent a bifurcation of the polity along economic and religious lines, have dominated politics. As a matter of political stereotype, the UNP tends to support economic liberalism and pursue Western aid. During certain intervening years the UNP lost its reputation as a pro-minority party in the 1960s, 1970s, and 1980s, but by the 1990s the party actively sought to reconsolidate a reputation for cosmopolitan inclusiveness, liberal economic policies, and liberal privileging of minorities' concerns.[6] During the war years, nationalistic Sinhala Buddhist revivalist politicians and public intellectuals, the prototypical supporters of the SLFP, intensified their derision toward UNP politicians. The former accused the latter of being anti-Buddhist crypto-Christians inclined to cater to the neocolonial interests of the West as a result of their adopted Christian values.

As will become apparent, majoritarian nationalist political adversaries frequently malign the UNP for being guided by a Christian ethos. On the other hand, through the 1990s and early 2000s Sinhala Buddhists would often describe the SLFP to be "with the people" on socialistic premises of promoting local economic growth and supporting the nation, insofar as the nation is defined by that majority (Spencer 1990). Aesthetically, SLFP leaders tend to performatively embody lay Buddhist asceticism. In reality, the SLFP too has pursued interests of foreign investment by especially looking toward Sinhala diaspora and East Asian sources of support, which are imagined to be unfettered by Christianity and neocolonial agendas (Abeyesekera 2002). These stereotypes perdured within political affiliations until recently, despite the tendency of ministers who make superficial changes of party affiliation (much like the "pragmatic" conversions discussed earlier), and however much history adds layers to complicate the correlations between political, economic, and religious persuasions that constituted the core of the UNP-SLFP polarity. Today, these party-based polarities have shifted dramatically and have apparently begun to dissolve in the intervening years.[7] Nevertheless, the identitarian stereotypes that were historically ingrained through these polarities provided fodder for the enmity between Buddhists and Christians as it has played out in Sri Lanka over the last several decades.

THIRD-WAVE ECONOMIES OF CONVERSION

Through this historical sketch of these waves of religious conversions in Sri Lanka, what is evident is that political, economic, and religious affinities have been linked together in practice, as well as in popular perception. If the earlier two waves of conversion to Christianity and to Buddhism can be characterized as "political" in motivation, this third phase of conversions to Christianity that began in the 1970s may be seen as more squarely economic in nature. Indeed, charismatic and born-again Christian emergences coincide with global economic fluctuations against which Sri Lanka attempted to shield itself via stiff economic regulations under the socialistic SLFP.

Shanta Premawardhana, a Baptist minister, theologian, and scholar-activist working to promote interreligious peace and mutual understanding through the World Council of Churches, was generous with his time when I met him in Colombo in 2009. He told me a joke that he had first heard in circulation in

Ceylon in the 1960s, telling it with his characteristic good humor and without betraying his Christian faith: "How do you know when you've been saved?" I told him I didn't know, and he answered with a smile, "You suddenly begin to speak with an American accent!" I laughed, and he detailed how the punchline had shifted in the 1970s. "Nowadays, the punchline goes: 'You know you've been saved when you suddenly get the taste for Coca-Cola!'" The shifting punchline expressed a critical awareness of how the expansion of Christianity had been enabled globally via political and economic modalities. As he explained to me: "Initially, Christianity gained its influence through political colonialism. . . . Nowadays, Christianity extends its reach through economic colonialism." He critiqued evangelicalism and the "gospel of prosperity," which he saw as standing opposed to the orientations of dialogue, ecumenism, and social justice to which he had become attuned while coming of age as a Christian in Ceylon (see also Premawardhana 2004, 2015).

The jokes imply that with the adoption of Christianity a person experiences a shift in disposition, of linguistic attunement, and of taste. In a sociological rendering, linguistic attunement and taste are elements of *habitus* or embodied dispositions, which in Bourdieu's (1980) terms are inculcated with time and social station. The joke that Premawardhana conveyed thus indexes continuities between secularized, sociological notions of habitus, Christian theology, and contemporary charismatic convictions that radical shifts in disposition stand as miraculous signs of God's grace. Bourdieu's secularized concept of habitus is derived from moral philosophy, which had taken its inspiration from Augustine's theology to connote "an acquired disposition to cooperate with the will of God" (Peristiany and Pitt-Rivers 1992, 429). Put otherwise, the joke relates to how charismatic and global forms of born-again Christianity rouse cosmopolitan forms of social distinction. What becomes evident through the reconstruction of Lalith Kotelawala's conversion narrative is how a story of deep conviction articulates with broader economy of religious conversion.

A CONVERT'S TALE

It is in the 1970s—coinciding with Ceylon's transition from dominion status under Britain to full independence as the Democratic Socialist Republic of Sri Lanka—that the story of Lalith Kotelawala's conversion begins. The Ceylonese businessman and philanthropist converted in 1976 from Buddhism to a vernacular form of Catholicism. This variety of Catholicism featured exorcism and deliverance rituals that charismatic priests carried out for congregants en masse, thus rendering it a highly popular folk-charismatic Catholic form. In becoming a Christian in the era of decolonization and nationalization in the new republic, Kotelawala's conversion went against the grain of majoritarian efforts to recuperate the Buddhist heritage of the nation.

The uptake of Kotelawala's conversion narrative within nationalistic discourses in Sri Lanka is illustrative of how conversion to Christianity becomes overdetermined within majoritarian nationalist logics. The businessman's conversion took place during a time of acute "crisis" for large Sri Lankan corporations, a crisis that was set in motion by the introduction of socialistic financial regulations that were envisioned by its Sri Lankan formulators as steeling the country against the ravages of a neoliberal economy. The ontological dimensions of Christian conversion, (neo)liberal economics, and liberal peacemaking and humanitarian action, all come together to crystallize in the iconic figure of Lalith Kotelawala. His narrative of receiving God's grace coordinates with the orientation to the prosperity gospel, charitability, neutrality, and forgiveness. At the same time, Sinhala Buddhists—especially those at the center of the anti-conversion movement—interpreted these aspects of his conversion narrative as confirming broad stereotypes that, at bottom, Christianity habituates converts into acting upon an "anti-national" ethos.

Lalith Kotelawala was born and raised in an affluent Sinhala Buddhist family, and he remained a Buddhist as a young adult. His grandfather served in the ranks of the Ceylonese police and military, and his uncle, Sir John Kotelawala, served as the third prime minister of Sri Lanka. As a young Buddhist man, Lalith Kotelawala married an Anglican Protestant Sinhala woman from a wealthy family. According to sympathetic accounts of his life story, their happy marriage was widely praised as a testament to the positive relations between Buddhists and Christians in postcolonial Ceylon.[8] With his father's death in 1973, Lalith Kotelawala inherited the executive role at the Ceylon Insurance Company, or "Ceylinco."

But the early 1970s inaugurated a time of crisis for large businesses in the postcolony, which had a profound effect upon Lalith Kotelawala's performance in his role as CEO at Ceylinco. The SLFP center-left ruling government had "nationalized" the economy by regulating private corporate holdings and

promoting policies of import substitution. The effect upon the insurance industry was acute. The financial pressures resulting from the socialistic initiative had
"broken and disillusioned" his father, about whom, writing hagiographically,
his biographer stated had "died in 1973 . . . branded a profit-making capitalist
whereas he was an indigenous pioneering businessman who placed a solid foundation stone for free enterprise in the not yet politically independent Ceylon."[9]

Fearing that his newly inherited company would fail due to being sequestered
behind closed economic doors, Kotelawala became anxiety-ridden by his new
responsibilities. Recognizing his distress, his brother-in-law introduced him to a
Catholic shrine in the village of Kudagama, which at the time was a major site
for pilgrimage. At the spiritual helm of the shrine was a Catholic priest, Father
Camillus Jayamanne, who was famed for his abilities to deliver supplicants from
demonic spirits and to unblock channels for spiritual and worldly success. Kotelawala marked his conversion in 1976 and became one of the faith-healing priest's
primary devotees and patrons.[10] The Catholic priest-healer was a "surrogate suf-
ferer" who carries the burden of supplicants' sin, through the ritual work of
shouldering a heavy wooden cross through the grounds of his shrine (Stirrat
1992, 118). For his devotees, Jayamanne's austere, Christic display at the Stations
of the Cross, along with his public performances of exorcism and potent ability
to channel *charismata* (gifts of god's grace), enabled their healing, prosperity, and
happiness. This rustic strand of Catholicism at Kudagama first came to prominence in the 1970s, roughly around the start of the "Third Wave" arrival of charismatic Pentecostal deliverance to Ceylon.[11] (The vernacular Catholic deliverance rituals once found at Kudagama and elsewhere within this Catholic belt of
Sri Lanka, as captured in R. L. Stirrat's deft account, have since been supplanted
by Pentecostal deliverance practices that remain prevalent today.)

Despite economic hardships during nationalization, Kotelawala managed to
achieve astonishing financial success on behalf of his company. He ultimately
expanded Ceylinco, turning it into the most successful set of capitalist enterprises in the country. In a 2006 interview Kotelawala reflected upon the hardships created by the SLFP's economic nationalization and import substitution
policies in the 1970s and offered testimony of his conversion, described in a Sri
Lankan business journal:

> "[Ceylinco] had no money to pay a host of claims. I had hundreds of people at
> my doorstep asking for their money—accusing, threatening and scolding me.

It was probably the darkest time of my life," he remembers. A trip to and blessing in the miraculous precincts of Kudagama was a turning point, he testifies. "It was then that I saw Jesus; and even though I was a Buddhist, I know I was saved by him. Even now, whenever I have wanted funds for my charitable ventures, for instance—or had problems—I have felt his presence," Kotelawala says. He also defied the government many a time, especially when he felt injustice being meted out. His first such act of defiance was when he dismantled and relocated an entire printing press that was to be taken over due to nationalisation policies, at a time when businesses were nationalised by merely posting a notice on a tree.[12]

As extolled in life histories that circulated in the Sri Lankan public, Kotelawala believed that Father Jayamanne's benedictions divinely enabled him to propel Ceylinco forward despite the stagnation of a highly regulated economy. Having survived the trying times, Kotelawala became one of the faith-healing priest's most eminent and dedicated patrons.

Kotelawala expanded his company, building it into the most successful set of enterprises in independent Sri Lanka. Ceylinco's success was later facilitated by the UNP's restoration of economic liberalization policies in 1977, after returning to power in its electoral victory over the SLFP. The UNP enabled a period of open economy that lasted until the mid-1990s when the party was again voted out of power. In that time, the Ceylinco conglomerate grew to consist of more than three hundred subsidiaries. Having transformed Ceylinco into a fiscal pow-erhouse that so greatly benefited the national economy, Kotelawala was revered by upwardly mobile Sri Lankans for his business acumen. In the early 1990s, the UNP government bestowed Kotelawala with one of the country's highest civil-ian honors—the title "Deshamanaya"—which distinguished him as a "national treasure."

AN EPIPHANY AND A TURN TO PHILANTHROPY

A second notable moment of Kotelawala's biography as a Christian occurred during the 1996 bombing of Sri Lanka's Central Bank. The Central Bank bomb-ing was an atrocity acknowledged by the LTTE to have been the work of one of its suicide cadres. Ninety-one people were killed in the act of domestic

1.2 An LTTE suicide cadre bombed the Central Bank in 1996. There were many casualties, and it devastated the financial district of Colombo. The Ceylinco tower was damaged in the attack, and Lalith Kotelawala, Ceylinco's CEO, was injured. The *Daily News* is Sri Lanka's government-run paper.

Daily News, http://archives.dailynews.lk/2009/08/06/fea10.asp

terrorism. Kotelawala was one among more than 1,500 people who were severely injured: he lost an eye in the fallout. Once recovered, Kotelawala shared in a public statement that during his convalescence he had had a vision of an angel. The epiphany signified a second pivot in his life as a Christian, which inspired him to deepen his religious commitments and to invest his time and money in philanthropic work.

The Sri Lankan business community expressed admiration for Kotelawala's entrepreneurial achievements and altruistic spirit. However, eventually his pursuits as a capitalist and philanthropist produced equally many detractors, particularly after the death of Soma Thera in 2003. Convinced of Kotelawala's Christian brand of villainy, Buddhist anti-conversion activists conceived of his turn to philanthropy to be motivated by a desire to attract underprivileged Sri

Lankans to Christianity. Suspicions of Kotelawala's extra-altruistic motives coincided with accusations that Christians in general are in the practice of "unethically" using charity as an instrument to attract converts from among vulnerable segments of the population.

Apropos of this stereotyping, the narrative of Kotelawala's philanthropic turn further consolidated majoritarian populist perceptions of his elite, Christian brand of villainy. His economic persona has analogically followed the party lines of the UNP, which promoted economic liberalization and typically advocated for a negotiated peace settlement in accord with stipulations of the international aid community. Emphasizing his commitment to his adopted religion, Kotelawala made his support of the UNP public in the lead-up to the 2005 presidential election. In so doing, he gained even more adversaries among SLFP supporters who tended to subscribe to majoritarian-populist nationalist ideology. Specifically, Kotelawala, alongside the archbishop of the Colombo Catholic diocese, publicly entreated Christians to vote against Mahinda Rajapaksa, who at the time had been campaigning for the presidential bid on the SLFP ticket. Kotelawala did so under the auspices of the Society for Love and Understanding (SOLO-U), a business-based lobby he founded to enjoin the Sri Lankan government to ease back on the counterinsurgency against the LTTE secessionists.[13] Kotelawala sponsored a full-page political statement in Sri Lankan newspapers, with images of Kotelawala and Catholic Archbishop Oswald Gomis, flanking text that beseeched Christians to "Awaken!" The statement warned Sri Lanka's Christian minority that if Rajapaksa were to be elected he would allow ethnoreligious chauvinism to flourish. His censure of Rajapaksa served as an implicit endorsement of the UNP opposition candidate.

Kotelawala, along with Archbishop Gomis, addressed Sri Lanka's Christians in order to persuade them to vote in favor of a peaceful resolution to the ethnic conflict. Rajapaksa's hawkish campaign platform and Sri Lanka's political history itself had given Christian leaders reason to believe that the SLFP candidate's stance would impinge not only upon ethnic minorities but also upon the country's religious minorities. The SOLO-U campaign also intimated that if elected, Rajapaksa would allow majoritarian nationalists to advance their anti-conversion legislation. The premonitions were partly correct: after he was elected, Rajapaksa pursued an unstinting military battle against the Tamil insurgents, putting a brutal end to the war in 2009 that at once resulted in humanitarian disaster and majoritarian triumphalism. Kotelawala's 2001 campaign to undermine the SLFP candidate outraged Rajapaksa's supporters and added to Sinhala Buddhists' convictions that the Christian business mogul was an adversary inclined to use religion and party politics to conspire against their efforts to defend the nation.[14]

Up until 2005, while President Chandrika Kumaratunga Bandaranaike (SLFP) had been in power, Kotelawala used his SOLO-U to encourage the president's bipartisan efforts to negotiate with the LTTE, to resume peace talks, and to enable a devolution of power that would give the secessionists a reason to put down their arms and return to the Sri Lankan fold.[15] In 2006 Kotelawala shocked Sinhala nationalists when he described his diplomatic manifesto. He stated in the international press that the LTTE should put down their arms. But he also went on record as having said:

> In all fairness, the LTTE has been pushed into [taking up arms]. They have done great service to their people and you can't brand them as pure terrorists as they are genuine freedom fighters. . . . The current policy of the government is a hit-back policy. . . . I don't think it's right. Mahatma Gandhi said that the eye-for-an-eye, a-tooth-for-a-tooth policy makes the world blind and toothless. . . . We can't ask (the LTTE) to disarm in order to sit down and talk while we hold onto our arms. Things must be left as they are and we must talk about devolution, federal state or autonomy.[16]

Kotelawala emphasized that a negotiated peace between the government and the LTTE would be good for Sri Lanka's economic growth. His political stance was consonant with a post–Cold War ethos whereby international development agencies promoted "peace and stability" with the agenda of enabling markets to flourish, with an eye toward capacitating neoliberalism in the "developing" world (Bastian 2007; Kelly et al. 2010). The post–Cold War development agenda affected Sri Lankan politics along partisan lines (Bastian 2007). Sinhala nationalists, adamantly opposed to proposals to negotiate with the rebel group, perceived Kotelawala, with his UNP political orientation and adopted Christian faith, to be dangerously acquiescent to "terrorist demands."

Condemning Kotelawala for taking a stance in the international press against Sri Lanka's pursuit of war, the Ministry of Defense issued a rejoinder on their website:

A person who is being philanthropic but spends ten times more of his philanthropic budget to get public attention may be alleviating some deep mental agony.... Further, people who support a terrorist organization by way of
humanitarian activities ... to express their violent motives or hatred of society stems from some mental disorder. Mr. Kotelawala, who claims to be a
morally superior being, a compassionate and forgiving Christian, has a moral
responsibility to express his views honestly and openly without distorting
the facts. Any ordinary person who reads the article ... will not be able to get
the correct picture of the LTTE and most dangerously, will be left with a
totally distorted picture of Buddhism.[17]

Because of the perverse tactics undertaken by the LTTE secessionists, and because
of Sinhala Buddhists' wartime discourses that roundly vilified Tamils in general
as potential insurgents and as unrepentant enemies of the Sri Lankan state,
Kotelawala became further mired in controversy as he sought to speak from a
position of neutrality. Majoritarian populists and representatives of the state
condemned the Christian entrepreneur for his religious inclinations. On top of
allegations that he had been responsible for the 2003 death of Soma Thera, the
Ministry of Defense considered his 2006 statement as evidence that he harbored
unwarranted sympathies toward the ethnic-minority secessionists. In the eyes of
Sinhala Buddhist nationalists, Kotelawala's expression of "LTTE sympathy"
served to incriminate him further as an anti-nationalist.

In sum, Kotelawala's visionary experience during his recovery from the 1996
Central Bank bombing was a critical event that he characterized as heightening
his commitment to Christianity. In his account, the epiphany inspired his charitable ethic and impelled him to become exceptionally forgiving. In the populist
imaginary, however, Kotelawala's Christian moral trajectory, his philanthropic
spirit, and forgiving Christian nature were not rendered as virtues. Rather,
majoritarian nationalists cast his charitable endeavors as efforts to "bribe" poor
Sri Lankans into converting, and they apprehended his generous view of the
LTTE as causing him to imprudently think that the insurgents could be engaged
diplomatically. The businessman's forgiving nature was deemed to be not simply
foolhardy, however. Within a Sinhala Buddhist nationalist imaginary, Kotelawala's conversion was also understood as having initiated the businessman
into immorality, an anti-national ethos, and a sinister agenda to destroy Buddhism. In this politics of majoritarian-populist perception, Kotelawala's political

inclinations, like his misguided charitable spirit, appeared as malignant attributes of his adopted religion.

KARMIC JUST DESERTS

The rumors of the malevolent character of Lalith Kotelawala have had an interesting afterlife that exceeds the scandal of his alleged involvement in Soma Thera's death. By 2009, the tabled legislation to ban "unethical conversions" was stalled, and ultimately was never passed. This left Sinhala Buddhists incensed that Kotelawala, in their view, was getting away with the murder of the monk feeling unrequited in their demands for justice. However, when in June 2009 new events implicated Kotelawala and Ceylinco Consolidated in financial fraud, the belief that karmic justice was on their side reinvigorated anti-conversion activists and followers of Soma Thera. Independently of prior accusations against Kotelawala, one of the many subsidiaries under the Ceylinco Consolidated Group fell into disrepute. The 2008 global financial crisis destabilized the system of global high finance, and the Sri Lankan economy began to experience tremors. This prompted the Central Bank of Sri Lanka to newly enforce capital requirements and to investigate corporations that appeared to have been skirting the requirements. Having offered remarkably attractive rates of return, thousands of Sri Lankans had invested their life savings in Ceylinco's Golden Key Credit Card Company (Ltd). The Central Bank's investigation revealed corporate dishonesty in the subsidiary, and the press described the Golden Key investment as a "scam" akin to a Ponzi scheme.[18] Specifically, the Central Bank charged Ceylinco with having maintained insufficient capital to support the Golden Key Company. When the Central Bank revealed this fact, investors ran to retrieve their finances, and a liquidity crisis ensued. In turn, Kotelawala was accused of defrauding Sri Lankan investors. Seylan Bank, another subsidiary within the Ceylinco group, divested stakes to settle investor accounts, and it too faced a liquidity crisis.[19] The state-owned Bank of Ceylon was ultimately put in charge of bailing out the insolvent bank.[20]

In his own defense, Kotelawala claimed he had not had direct oversight over the Golden Key Company and was unaware of any malfeasance. He pleaded ignorance of the scheme that "defrauded" Sri Lankan investors of 26 billion Sri Lankan rupees, roughly equivalent to $230 million U.S. dollars. However, the court considered his defense insufficient, and issued a guilty verdict. Sri Lankan authorities apprehended Lalith Kotelawala, and he was imprisoned in July 2011. The Supreme Court ordered a seizure of his assets and offshore accounts. His wife, Sicille Kotelawala, was reported to have fled the country with some of the ill-begotten riches. Exiled, she was portrayed in the press as a selfish hoarder. Interpol apprehended her in England in March 2012.

For the many Buddhists who felt embittered that Lalith Kotelawala had plotted and gotten away with the murder of Soma Thera, the new round of accusations against his fraudulent character felt like poetic justice. Several of my urban Sinhala Buddhist interlocutors expressed great satisfaction at the thought that with Kotelawala's arrest and eventual conviction, there was at least some vindication for Soma Thera's untimely loss. The rhetoric of one Sinhala Buddhist blogger exemplifies the comparative theodicy invoked as penalty for Kotelawala's moral failure:

> Let us sincerely hope that Dr. Kotelawala, even though he no longer believes in The Buddha word, [at least still believes] there is a thing called "*Ditta Dhamma Vedaneeya Karma*" (retribution within this life) unlike in Christianity where a mere "confession" can cancel all one's misdeeds. Even as did Jesus Christ express loudly on the Crucifix "*Eli, Eli, Lema, Sabachthani?*"—"My God! My God! Why Hast Thou Forsaken Me?" These words may be ringing in the ears of Dr. Kotelawala as well. Let us be merciful and hope that this drama will be resolved quickly—personal credibility and reputation is another issue altogether. [blogger's translation][21]

The Buddhist blogger's satirical statement against the fallen businessman enunciates a major quarrel with Christian and especially Catholic theology. It suggests that even as Catholics may consider confession and expiation to restore a "state of grace," Sinhala Buddhist opponents of the business mogul reckon that karmic inheritances which reside at the core of one's being prevail over Christian grace. The blogger's derisive statement condemning the entrepreneur was subsequently reproduced in news editorials after Kotelawala's conviction, including in Sri Lanka's state newspaper.[22]

Given the dense vernacular interchanges in the Sri Lankan public sphere, it is not uncommon for Buddhists to appropriate Christian theological concepts satirically and cynically in this fashion, and vice versa. The didactic nature of karma is prevalent in Sinhala Buddhist material culture, from wall paintings to children's books that portray specific sins and punishments, acts of merit and resulting rewards. From doctrine to popular tales, in Theravāda Buddhism there are multitudinous depictions of what happens to a person in the hell realms (*apāya*) if one defies the prohibition against taking a life, and especially the prohibition against killing an ordained monk. For the Sinhala Buddhist protectionists who routinely accuse Christians of preying upon vulnerable people, of conspiring to destroy Buddhism, and of being attracted to false and fleeting economic advantages, Kotelawala's disgrace was a public validation of their suspicions. *This was karmic retribution.*

SPECULATIVE RELIGIOUS FUTURES

Around the turn of the millennium, Sinhala Buddhists' consternation over the possibility that ambitiously proselytizing Christian groups might supplant the existing Buddhist heritage of the nation ran especially deep. The links between capitalism and Christianity are ramified through the particularities of the religious profile of the entrepreneur and the material forms that his success took. This conjuncture is tangibly linked to what may be called "speculative religious futures."[23] The fact that Kotelawala's affluence was built through Ceylon's nascent insurance industry and hinged on an actuarial conception of the future and speculations of risk is significant for understanding the resonances of the expansionary project of evangelical Christianity, and the majoritarian anxieties that it triggered in the postcolony.

Kotelawala's successful expansion of the insurance industry in the "developing" postcolonial economy formed an integral part of his conversion narrative. These features of his biography relate to how the making of the Sri Lankan middle and upper classes stemmed from the shift from a feudal economy to a plantation and industrial capitalist economy.[24] The times might be described as "an actuarial age," as Rosalind Morris (2010) has characterized the intensification of bodily risk amid economic change in a very different context.[25] Where does insurance, speculation, and actuarial futures fit into these cosmologics? Whereas in rural and premodern economies there are countless "risk-sharing arrangements" (Coate and Ravallion 1994), in developing nations entrepreneurs must carve out a market for insurance through "a supply-leading approach"

(Outreville 1994).[26] Put otherwise, urbanization and the creation of the insurance market may chip away at rural forms of risk-sharing and interdependency in ways that impel "a break from the past."[27] In present day urban Sri Lanka, the industry speculatively creates demand for insurance provisioning through advertising, using generic languaging like "Stay ahead, or get Left Behind" and "Ceylinco: Breathing New Life into Insurance Space."[28] These pliable referents might at first blush appear utterly secular, yet the referents to premillennial anxieties associated with the rapture and to pneumatic affinities to a "new life" resonate perfectly well with evangelical Christian ambitions.

The implicit religious referents within insurance marketeering are apparent to attentive Sri Lankan observers too. In the Sri Lanka–based *Journal of Business Management*, one analyst critically observed how advertisers are aggressive in their campaigns to overcome low levels of market penetration: one ad suggests that Buddhist monks might do well to purchase insurance so that they can pursue their path without worry of material shortfalls (Jeyaseelan 2020). The ad implies that by buying insurance, Buddhist monks will gain an "extra piece of mind" during times of economic and political uncertainty. Analyzing this actuarial discourse, Gnanaseelan Jeyaseelan remarks on the offensive implication that Sri Lankan society may not have the wherewithal to materially support the Buddhist sangha. Jeyaseelan maintains that the advertisements insinuate a "despiritualization" is underway in Sri Lanka and that insurance marketing subtly "belittles" the established religion of the country even as it pretends to "safeguard" the tradition.

If one extrapolates from Jeyaseelan's observations about insurance marketeering in his country, the relevance for religious disputation under neoliberalization in Sri Lanka is striking. One implication of this actuarial imagination could be that in a punishing economic system, lay Buddhist devotees (*dāyakayo*) may be prone to hardships that would destabilize efforts to sustain the sangha with provisions of *dāna* (alms). If one were to take the implications of Jeyaseelan's discourse analysis further, the advertisement campaign might suggest that insurance profiteering hinges on the anticipation that laypeople might break ties with Buddhism—by joining another religion, for instance—and that in turn there may be an insufficient base to sustain the monks. As I detail in the next chapter, lay provisioning of *dāna* to sustain the sangha is an essential component of Buddhism; yet Sri Lankan evangelists' rhetoric criticizes *dāna* as taxing to lay Buddhists. My point here is not intended to corroborate majoritarian suspicions about Christian minorities or about Kotelawala in particular. Rather, my focus on these materializations is intended to address the structural and symbolic ramifications of capitalism, Christianity, and speculative religious futures, which have tacitly informed the adversarial profiling of Christians in Sri Lanka.

BUDDHIST KARMA, CHRISTIAN GRACE, AND COMPETING ECONOMIES OF BELIEF

Observers of the "developing world" tend to assume that Christianity in the postcolony is growing primarily among the poor. So too do majoritarian nationalists in South Asia suggest that the poor become "rice Christians," "induced" to convert through the allure of charity. However, the story of Lalith Kotelawala is indicative of how prosperity and poverty are linked within Christianity in postcolonial Sri Lanka and how sets of economic, political, and religious affinities are perceived through cosmologically informed ideologies of being and belonging. Kotelawala is exemplary of this phenomenon insofar as many Sri Lankan Buddhists interpreted his conversion and his supposed culpability for Soma Thera's death to be reflective of a set of propensities among Christians in general. The story of Kotelawala's financial success, believed to be enabled through God's sanctifying grace and deliverance from demons in a heterodox variety of Catholicism, is reminiscent of pentecostalist prosperity gospels which have enlivened Christian piety in various world locales, particularly since the 1970s. Such an economy of religious persuasion contributes to skeptics' contentions that Christianity shallowly plays to "consumers" of religion.

These elements of identitarian enmity in Sri Lanka are associated with the political economy of transnational Christian arrival and localized charismatic Christian revival. In completely different historical circumstances of medieval Europe, Christians' economic relations with Jewish merchants became entrenched as anti-Semitism, a phenomenon that Max Weber characterized as "pariah capitalism" ([1922] 1993). Catholic mercantile expansionism relied upon the "wanderings" of disenfranchised Jewish moneylenders (Simmel 1950). European Christians found themselves in economic competition with Jews and as a result rendered Jews as "economic enemies," dramatized by Shakespeare's Shylock (Anidjar 2005, 2014).

Comparing Eucharistic transubstantiation to Marx's observations on the transformation of use value into currency, Gil Anidjar argues that "economic theology is the history of religion as political economy" (2005, 501). *The Merchant of Venice* offers commentary upon how Jews came to be considered impure by blood, condemned as irredeemable sinners through the charge of usury. The conversion by elopement of Shylock's daughter, Jessica, is a point of comment, when Shylock laments that his "own flesh and blood" disavowed him along with her religion. Salarino responds, "There is more difference between thy flesh and hers than between jet and ivory; *more between your bloods* than there is between red wine and rhenish" (498, Anidjar's emphasis). The problem transcends economics, Anidjar compellingly argues. Within the paradigms of race and religion in Europe, to drink from the communion chalice is to alter one's own blood, producing ontological difference. From the perspective of the Catholic merchants of Venice, conversion inaugurates Jessica into a superior sociality and morality that breaks vital bonds with her father (498). Conversion to Catholicism in this Venetian lifeworld had a fundamentally deracinating effect that penetrates as far as the nature of being. Christian-Jewish enmity in that time hinged upon differences that became racialized within discourses that equivocated between of the purity of blood and righteous use of money (Anidjar 2005).

My digression is not intended to equate the historical persecution of Jews to what evangelical Christians describe as persecution, however much the contemporary global evangelical movement may like to insist there is such an equivalence. For indeed, given that the Sri Lankan elite, to some degree, inherited vestiges of British infrastructures, the type of capital historically leveraged by them cannot be classified as the so-called pariah capitalism by which Max Weber characterized the social segregation, political disadvantage, and economic distinctiveness of European Jews (1922, 493). Rather, my point is to shed light on how the political perceptions that congeal into interreligious enmity follows patterns of these religious communities' relations to the economy during colonialism and decolonization, and how conjunctures between religion and political economy are embodied as traits perceived to be constitutive of being.

In the Sri Lankan context, religious subjectivity is not as heavily racially intoned as in Renaissance Europe. Rather, as a result of his conversion, Buddhists considered Lalith Kotelawala to have become estranged from righteous and inborn religious and nationalist sentiments. This skeptic's view of conversion as estrangement bears a relation to George Simmel's concept of stranger-sociality. Christianity first arrived in Sri Lanka from beyond the bounds of the country's littoral contours, and it appears to Sinhala Buddhists that Christianity inappropriately inducts foreign values among Sri Lankan people. The itinerant Simmelian "stranger" chooses to lay down roots and thus embodies a "synthesis of nearness and distance." For those most agitated by the introduction of these forms of difference that dilute the singular constitution of the Sri Lankan nation as Sinhala and Buddhist, so too is "nearness and distance" perceived to be characteristic of Sri Lankan converts to Christianity. However, this sociality emerges not as a result of strangers who enter from the outside but rather through conversion that inaugurates estrangement. For Simmel, the subjectivity of the stranger stems from being simultaneously insider and outsider to the dominant milieu, and this duality imbues the stranger "with the attitude of 'objectivity'" (Simmel 1950). It is precisely this attitude of objectivity and neutrality, evident in Kotelawala's ambivalent and forgiving stance toward the LTTE insurgents, which his Sinhala Buddhist critics found most objectionable: because the Christian businessman did not condemn the militant-secessionists as "terrorists" but instead stood in "sympathetic" relation to (militant) Tamil nationalism, public discourse treated his apparent neutrality as a betrayal of the majoritarian ethos of the nation. His expression of Christian "forgiveness" was rendered as practically seditious. In the popular press, editorials, blogs, and statements from the Ministry of Defense, majoritarian nationalists conceived of the business mogul's loyalty to the nation as having disintegrated in the process of his conversion to Christianity.

Inasmuch as the nation is defined hegemonically by the majority, conversion to Christianity is construed as a process synonymous with estrangement from a nation. However, rather than involve an alteration of blood, from the vantage point of Sinhala Buddhists, Christian conversion and Buddhist apostasy are conceived of through the cosmologically and culturally built ideas of being, morality, and selfhood that are prevalent within the concept of karma. The widely used Sinhala expression that conversion presents a transgression "against the religion of one's birth" (*janmeyen laebu Budhdhāgama athharala*) is partly structured by natalist convictions that one's life conditions are karmically inherited. The sense that conversion reconstitutes being appeared in late colonial-era discourses against Christianity, as is implicit in the rhetoric of one Sinhala critic, a lay Buddhist revivalist, who wrote in the 1940s that "any attempt to make a full-blooded Sinhalese the follower of any religion other than his ancestral faith would be like grafting something alien to the stem of an old oak" (see Stirrat 1992, 21). Indeed, in Sri Lanka, conversion and apostasy does not deracinate *per se*. Rather, in the view of dedicated Sinhala Buddhist nationalists, the promise of grace offered by Christian conversion disrupts the person's capacity to recognize the value of one's karmic inheritances. As this cosmologic has it, disavowing one's karmic inheritances by deflecting sin unto a savior short-circuits the labors of moral learning and self-betterment which are the quintessence of the Buddha's *dhamma*.

THE ECONOMICS OF VILLAINY

Lalith Kotelawala, who converted from Buddhism to Christianity, found financial success and used his wealth for charitable purposes. He stands as an archetype in the majoritarian-nationalist politics of perception, confirming for Sinhala Buddhist anti-conversion activists that adopting and persuading others toward non-native Christian commitments begets immoral dispositions. Kotelawala's persona and politics have acquired almost mythic status, which resonated deeply with the logic of anti-conversion activism. In the view of many believing Christians, however, it is neither a foreign nor an estranged god that enables grace. Rather, Kotelawala's deliverance from demons, acquisition of blessings, and capacities to tap into the gospel of prosperity were signs of God's capacity for presence in Sri Lanka.

The Christocentric calendar, with its eschatological promise that it will arrive at its end in the "near future," produces prophetic reckonings concerning salvation and damnation. This temporal dimension of the moral economy is prevalent in global and local economic ideologies, as Jane Guyer (2007) observes in her studies of structural adjustment in the context of Africa. Under the rubric of "millennial capitalism," a whole host of binary complementarities—from prosperity gospels to Ponzi schemes, deregulation to high levels of regulation—are endemic in neoliberalism and lend themselves to ever more "inscrutable speculations [that] seem to call up fresh specters in their wake," as Jean and John Comaroff have argued (2001, 2). Elsewhere, pastoral fakery and parody challenges the potency of prosperity gospels and Christian sincerity on the margins of Ghanaian Pentecostalism (Shipley-Weaver 2009, 529). In circumstances of stark religious rivalry as those seen in Sri Lanka's present milieu, fakery and deceit serve not only to undermine the potencies of the divine personage in question. Skeptics as adamant as those Sinhala Buddhists who subscribe to the exclusivist rhetorics that I have described here take these attributes as corroborating the invalidity of an unsound creed.

What millennial varieties of Christianity offer, like Ponzi-scheme capitalism, is the allure "of accruing wealth from nothing" (Comaroff and Comaroff 2001, 22). While "nothing" is not what Lalith Kotelawala had at the time of his conversion, the miracle of prosperity enabled by the graceful blessing of a Catholic priest known for extraordinary abilities to vanquish demons and unblock channels to worldly success allowed for abundant acceleration despite the stagnation caused by stringent regulations on the island's economy. The narrative that connects economic felicity and fraudulence to the perceptions of Kotelawala's rise and fall expresses double-sidedness, of rural risk-sharing to urbanistic expansions, of prosperity gospels and Ponzi schemes, and so too of virtue and villainy. Such dualities can be seen as endemic to supernatural power. After all, as the anthropological archive on magic, science, and religion makes clear, success is often just as easily seen to result from the workings of grace, as it may be construed as the work of a sorcerer's magic. In a similar vein, the charitable "objectivity" activated by Kotelawala's estrangement from Buddhism allowed him to proclaim something akin to the idea that "one person's terrorist is another's freedom-fighter." The very lines that rendered Kotelawala as a moral exemplar to his Christian brethren underscored to his critics how his adopted religion led him down a path toward fraudulent anti-nationalism.

ANTHROPOLOGY, LOCALITY, AND SITUATED POLITICS OF PERCEPTION

At Sri Lanka's political and economic center, devoted and politicized Buddhists expressed a troubled sense that conversion to Christianity bears the potential to give rise to anti-nationalism. Sinhala Buddhist anti-conversion activists, and indeed many lay Buddhist followers of Soma Thera, remain convinced that the virtuous revivalist monk was killed by the machinations of a Christian businessman as a part of a larger conspiracy to destroy Buddhism. The anxiety about what conversion does to one's character, proliferated easily through coded and overt expressions in English- and Sinhala-language media and rumor precisely because of resonances that track with partisan politics, and endemic political-economic polarities in modern Sri Lanka. The growth of millennial Christian urgencies and ambitions, paired with Christian accoutrements, contributed to politicized views that conversion is a process that alters the ontological and moral constitutions of people in economic ways, which added to the incitement of interreligious tensions in Sri Lanka.

The political entailments of Buddhist nationalism and Christian evangelism persist and become rearticulated with the contingencies of history from decolonization to the closings and reopenings of the economy, the rise of charismatic luminaries, and the global economic forces that began to destabilize high-finance and provoked new regulations in this small, proud country. The political corollaries of conversion are evident in the iconic conversion of Bandaranaiake, who Sinhala Buddhists consider as instrumental in recuperating Sri Lanka's heritage during the era of decolonization. Kotelawala's conversion flowed in an opposite direction than the conversions undertaken by the independence-era political elite of Ceylon. The economic corollaries of his Christian faith are abundantly evident in his biography. From the vantage point of Sinhala Buddhist nationalists, his conversion to Christianity initiated him into political and economic subjectivities that supposedly inclined him to commit fraud and to forgive more vicious enemies of the Sri Lankan state. In turn, majoritarian nationalists considered his Christian persuasions as forming the core of his anti-national character.

While devout Sinhala Buddhists strive to uphold Buddhist continuities and karmic inheritances, for Sri Lankan Christians, Kotelawala's story of deliverance from demons, acquisition of blessings, and capacities to tap into the gospel of prosperity remained as signs of God's capacity to be present for Sri Lankans in the here and now. For believing Christians, it is not a foreign and estranged god that enables grace; rather, as they tended to see it, grace touched Kotelawala, even if only for a time.

ELECTIVE AFFINITIES OF THE RELIGIOUS ECONOMY

The "elective affinities" between religion and the economy, and capitalism and Christianity in particular, are abundantly clear here. Max Weber characterized the ways in which capitalism and Christianity are imbricated as a durable chemical bond (Weber [1905] 2001; McKinnon 2010). Although there are rearticulations and varied kinds of uptakes of this coupling in different contexts, it is arguably a pairing that is practically impossible to break. The neoliberalization of the economy began to unfold in 1971 when the dollar was fully unhitched from the gold standard. Among other things, the event triggered a misalignment between the economy and politics, wherein the economy became globalized even as politics remained rooted in national concerns (Hart 2015). In Sri Lanka, anxieties about the global forces intervening within locally established forms of life consistently reinforced majoritarian nationalism. (The 2022 debt crisis has apparently created an exceptional state of exception in that it has brought together mass protests that cuts across all ethnic and religious identities.) The deregulated workings of global high finance create onerous conditions and impoverishment that demand the formulation of ever "new justifications for belonging and abandonment" (Povinelli 2011, 19). Indeed, in this era, the political

1.3 Millennial Christianity and the neoliberal economy: some will be elevated, while others are left behind.
Shutterstock

economy constantly promises to elevate some, even as it threatens to leave others behind. This contemporary condition resonates with the eschatological image of the Rapture.

For Sri Lanka, the 1970s was an era when economic doors were closed in the hope of sheltering the tiny island economy from the waves to come. Well before that, competing styles of political work to engage the economy took root within religious difference, and antipathies resurged therein. While the 1970s coincided with the growth of evangelistic prosperity gospels globally, Sri Lankan Buddhists responded with a majoritarian populism that doubled down and matched the exclusivist tendencies of born-again evangelism. They sought to guard the nation against those they deemed as heretics, frauds, and anti-nationals. In part due to these forms of resistance, historically, conversion in Sri Lanka has not taken a strictly unilinear trajectory that bears the potential to bring about wholesale religious change—even as such ambitions might inspire the recurrence of millennial urgencies and anxieties that mutually deepen religious hostilities.

Given popular usage, the logic of karma may appear at first blush as shallow rhetoric that only serves to cast ethical judgement upon others with respect to the self. However, in Sri Lanka, the concept of karma is used commonly, didactically, and with much seriousness, to express causal logics for personal joy, lament, and *muditā* (sympathetic joy), as well as moments of *Schadenfreude* such as that which appeared when anti-conversion activists learned of Kotelawala's charge of guilt. In this contested milieu, Buddhists and Christians put their ontologies of karma and grace to use in ways that undergird antipathies between nativism and evangelism.

Tangles of religious perspective in Sri Lanka are sharply articulated around material nodes of conflict. This is clear in the course of Lalith Kotelawala's conversion narrative and both the implicit resonances (e.g. of insurance, speculation and the actuarial economy) and the highly publicized retrospective upon his conversion. In Sri Lanka, Buddhism and Christianity are rooted in economies of persuasion that link up with distinctive ethical orientations concerning material life. Attraction to—and indeed, a *persuasion* toward—Buddhism and Christianity are mediated by different local and global configurations of material culture.

For Sri Lankan Buddhists, several features of the businessman's conversion signified how, well after decolonization, Christianity has stood as a competitive threat to their heritage. Reinvigorated by the apparent growth of Pentecostalism in Sri Lanka by the mid-1990s, Buddhists castigated Christian evangelists for launching an expansion through material allure and social capital. Oriented as they are to a speculative religious future, certain material features of Kotelawala's conversion narrative became integral to the charismatic force of his persona. For Buddhists, these attributes were cause for moral panic.

Two ontological features of grace materialized in his conversion narrative are especially remarkable: his philanthropic spirit and his "miraculous" capacities to exude charisma and material acumen in a modernizing economy. These two gifts, of charity and of miracles, are salient material and spiritual modalities for religious attraction and thus are nodes of competition and conflict. In the following two chapters, I elaborate how and why the Christian gifts of charity (chapter 2) and of charismatic miracles (chapter 3) became substantive bones of interreligious contention.

CHAPTER 2

Charity and Dāna

The Selfish Gift?

The proper idea of sin cannot enter into the mind of the Buddhist. His system knows nothing of a supreme intelligent Ruler of the universe. The priest is to consider, "I am the result of karmma [sic]; this forms my inheritance, my state of birth, my relatives, my support: I shall be heir of all of the actions I perform, whether they be good or evil." There is no law, because there is no lawgiver, no authority from which law can proceed. Buddha is superior in honor and wisdom to all other beings; but he claims no right to impose restrictions on other men. He points out the course to be taken, if merit is to be gained; but he who refuses to heed his words, does the Thathágato no wrong. Religion is a mere code of proprieties, a mental opiate, a plan for being free from discomfort, a system of personal profit, a traffic in merit, a venal process. In addressing itself to the individual man, apart from its honied words, it is a principle of selfishness; and yet, though his is its beginning, center, and end, it seeks to hide its selfishness by denying there is any self.

—Robert Spence Hardy, *Legends and Theories of the Buddhists* (1866)

At the corner of Baudhaloka Mawatha and Sarana Road, a major intersection in the heart of Colombo, one finds a set of institutions that are well-known founts for the promotion of Buddhism. An international Vipassana meditation center, attached to the Sri Sambodhi Viharaya (temple), attracts many visitors. On a near corner, the Buddhist Media Network broadcasts throughout Sri Lanka. The All-Ceylon Buddhist Congress, an approved charity that was first established in 1919, is also situated on that corner.[1] It was at the All-Ceylon Buddhist Congress that the former president, Mahinda Rajapaksa, bidding for election as prime minister in March 2020, launched his campaign promise to Buddhist constituents that he would entertain their efforts to resurrect legislation to criminalize unethical conversions.[2] Although foreign embassies, a church, and a swimming club also flank this urban junction, the Buddhist institutions clustered on this corner are veritable centers of nationalist activism, advocacy, and revivalist mediations within the country.

On a July afternoon in 2009, just over a month after the official close of the civil war, I walked down to this corner and entered the All-Ceylon Buddhist Congress Bookshop. I asked the shopkeeper in Sinhala if he could direct me to specific tracts on Buddhist revival by learned monks. He helpfully pointed to a number of books, including those written by Buddhists who were thinking with but more often against Christianity. The shelves held an array of Sinhala books by the revivalists Madihe Pannasiha Thera and Gangodawila Soma Thera, whose life and death I discussed in chapter 1. Several short volumes by an up-and-coming figure, a maverick monk named Pitiduwe Siridhamma Thero, who figures prominently in chapter 5, were evidently also gaining popular readership among urban Sinhala Buddhists. Worn paperback copies of Bertrand Russell's *Why I Am Not a Christian*, printed in eye-catching green and black English-language script, sat pointedly on the crowded shelves alongside Sinhala translations. Other English-language authors included Ajahn Brahm, an internationally famous British-Australian Theravāda Buddhist monk of Thai ordination who garners a wide following throughout Asia. For English-speaking Sri Lankans and for Singaporean and Malaysian Buddhists as well, Brahms's teachings on the Dharma have proven compelling, and even humorous after a fashion. Sinhala Buddhist mothers and grandmothers typically send copies of Brahms's books to their émigré children and grandchildren in Australia, Britain, and the United States, in hopes that his writings might persuade their English-educated kin to stay within the Buddhist fold. The ACBC Bookshop shelves also held the popular English text, *What Buddhists Believe*, by Venerable Sri K. Dhammananda, a Sri Lankan monk famed among *Dhamma* followers throughout Asia for establishing international missions in Malaysia and Singapore in the 1940s (Blackburn 2012). Still celebrated in Asian Buddhist circles, Dhammananda's writings and sermons have been transformative for anglophone ethnic-Chinese Singaporeans who avow new or renewed commitments to Dhamma following and who travel together to Sri Lanka and other Theravādin regions for pilgrimages and charitable tours (Mahadev, "Secularism").

I had come in search of a report produced by the All-Ceylon Buddhist Congress, which had been commissioned to carry out investigations and develop testimony on the problem of unethical conversions. The kindly shopkeeper directed me to copies of a thick tome, its heft secured together with a plastic ring binding, offering testimonies in Sinhala that conversions to Christianity were taking place "by fraudulent strategies." The beige cardstock cover noted the publication year as 2009, and alongside the Gregorian year was "2552," signifying alignment with the Buddhist calendar. The All-Ceylon Buddhist Congress produced the report in collaboration with a Buddhist women's organization Jayagrahanaya (known also by the name "Success")—a project undertaken at the cost of nearly 4 million rupees (roughly $20,000) (Deegalle 2012). The shopkeeper explained to me that in addition to the Sinhala edition, the ACBC intended to undertake a translation of the Commission Report into English too.

As the shopkeeper further guided me through the rows of books, I elaborated upon what I was looking for, code-switching between Sinhala and English as we went. A Sri Lankan woman who had been browsing nearby turned a curious ear my way. She asked about my research. "I am a student of anthropology, based in the United States. I'm doing my PhD research," I began. "Oh. My daughter is also studying anthropology," she said. "She's also doing her degree in the United States." Mutually intrigued, the woman proceeded to ask more about my research. "I'm studying about Buddhism . . . and also Christianity," I said, with anticipatory stammer. "I am studying about the religions of Sri Lanka," I awkwardly resorted to saying. Looking me squarely in the eyes, she responded, "Christianity is such a selfish religion. Christians believe that only humans can be saved. In Buddhism, all beings—the animals, and even the insects—*all* will be saved." Before I had a chance to converse with her further, the woman turned on her heel and proceeded to the checkout, leaving the bookshop without giving me a second look.

The Buddhist woman's indignation that her religious philosophy and practice might be judged and compared to Christianity was striking in its discursive force, as was her further insistence upon the negative moral character of "selfishness" that Christianity engenders. Her view that selfishness is a problem intrinsic to Christianity is indicative of a more generalized nativist hostility toward the premises of Christian moral superiority, which has long been riled in the course of the Buddhist-Christian encounter in Sri Lanka and other southern (Theravādin) Buddhist contexts (see Seneviratne 1999, 110). Her indignant response was an implicit rejoinder to a long-standing point of contention between Christians and Buddhists over comparative soteriology (notions of salvation and *nibbāna*), generosity, and moral action. On a philosophical and metaphysical register, the woman's point of derision targeted Christianity's humanistic conceits and exclusivist ontologies of salvation. Her exposition points to how the idea of Christian salvation chafes against the Buddhist doctrine of *kamma* (action) and the transmigratory principles entailed by *saṃsāra* (cycles of death and rebirth), *nibbāna*, and *anattā* or "nonself."

As is clear from the epigraph and its ostensibly learned ruminations of Robert Spence Hardy (1866), a British Wesleyan missionary who undertook study of Buddhist thought and practice in Ceylon in the mid–nineteenth century, the monotheistic orientation of European Christianity commonly gave rise to orientalists' negative appraisals of Theravāda Buddhist soteriology. In their invectives against the Buddhist character, British orientalists deemed that "selfishness" inheres in persons guided by Buddhist principles. They alleged that atheistic pragmatism concerning "merit" inclined Buddhists toward "selfish" and self-interested action. Hardy reckoned that the moral failings of Buddhists stemmed from the absence of a "supreme intelligent Ruler of the universe," which in turn lent to the "absence" of fear of divinity who casts judgment against and forgives sin (Harris 2006; Schlieter 2013). Hardy was not unlike the British Protestant Christian missionaries of his time who were stationed in Ceylon and Burma in the mid-nineteenth century, who thought Buddhists performed righteous actions only because doing so would eventually occasion return through the karmic favor of the accrual of "merit." These Protestant missionaries disparaged Buddhist logics of meritorious action as involving pragmatic accountancy, and thus as morally disingenuous (Schlieter 2013). They deemed Buddhism to be a "fatalistic faith" that inclined Buddhists toward moral depravity and that at best hobbled people's capacities for ethical discernment (Harris 2006). As with Hardy's condemnation, orientalists and missionaries commonly traced these logics of Buddhist practice to the atheistic doctrine of *anattā* or "nonself," deriding it as a permissive cover for "selfishness."

In my encounter in the bookshop, the Sinhala woman appeared to preemptively deflect and reverse the kinds of allegations that Western thinkers have long lodged against Buddhists' moral practices. In condemning Christianity for failing to offer salvation to all beings, she implicitly invoked the concept of *anattā*, the substancelessness and the transience of persons, coupled with the transmigratory principle of samsaric *kamma* (Pāli, action) that makes possible the upward ontological trajectory of "lesser" sentient life forms over the course of many, many lifetimes. In so doing, she insisted that Christianity narrowly precludes the possibility of salvation for nonhumans. She intimated that for Buddhists, *all* beings may attain *nibbāna*—whereby "*nibbāna*" is imprecisely translated as a kind of "salvation." The point is consonant with Jim Sykes's observation that the arrival of European Christian epistemology in Ceylon marked a sharp distinction between nature and culture, which impelled Europeans to characterize the nonhuman wild as barbarous beings incapable of gaining salvation, whereas Sinhala Buddhist "zoopolitics" entailed an inclusive ontology in which nonhuman beings can karmically ascend toward *nibbāna* (Sykes 2019, 218).[3] Such commensurations of incommensurate soteriological concepts, articulated in the vernacular, are commonplace in the Buddhist-Christian encounter (see Mahadev 2016; Edwards 2021). Given their distinctively different systems of moral value and repertoires of giving, Christians and Buddhists engage very different criteria for judging and reckoning what it is that constitutes generosity (Mahadev 2014, 2019; Sihlé 2015; Brac de la Perrière 2015).

GIFTS OF RELIGIOUS SOVEREIGNTY

Buddhist nationalists and Christian evangelists consider the question of whether the sovereignty of their religion can be secured to be contingent on the extent to which their tradition is recognized as offering an apt moral compass to orient people and the nation. Much of this consternation centers on the traditions of religious giving and the scrutiny to which these traditions were subject in peak moments of publicity. As demonstrated in the previous chapter, Sinhala Buddhists perceived Christianity to be specially albeit unfairly equipped with a material force capable of drawing in new converts: that is, capital, coupled with the injunction to give to charity. I showed through the iconic conversion of the businessman-cum-philanthropist, how contemporary Christian (Catholic, as much as Protestant and Pentecostal) concepts of salvation are connected to prosperity and poverty, possession and dispossession.[4]

Giving and gifting, both religious and secular, constitutes a substantive node of interreligious conflict in Sri Lanka. This is evident in the ways in which millennial Christian urgency and Buddhist nationalist anxiety played out with new intensity in the conjunction of the tsunami disaster (2004) and the end of the civil war (2009). Sinhala Buddhist revivalists disputed the moral grounds of Christian charity and even secular humanitarianism, treating them as ever-ready instruments in the production of Christian converts and anti-national subjects. Suspicious of the surge of humanitarian aid and charity, they perceived these seductive and moralistic "foreign" pathways as a political affront to Sinhala Buddhism. To understand the amplification of interreligious conflict that stemmed from these kinds of gifts and transactional forms, in the remainder of this chapter I explore Christian charity in comparison to Buddhists' repertoires of almsgiving (*dāna*) and other acts of care. The history of the Buddhist-Christian encounter in Theravādin contexts reveals that tensions arose around the practices of *dāna* (almsgiving) and charity, specifically concerning the seductions of material gifts, the problem of indebtedness, and the implicit obligations that stemmed from receiving gifts. Scholars commonly link such perceptions concerning the unspoken obligations to donors—including religious patronage and conversion—to classical anthropological theories of the gift, reciprocity, and debt (Bowie 1998; Korf et al. 2010; Sihlé 2015; Brac de la Perrière 2015).

At its foundations, the ethical sanction for Buddhist almsgiving is quite different from that of Christianity. As such, what it means for a Buddhist and for a Christian to be a generous moral agent are different as well (Sihlé 2015). Christian charity and Buddhist *dāna* are distinct kinds of gifts that differently mediate people's religious affinities and their obligations to religious community. Sinhala Buddhists identify a slant in Western media that wittingly or unwittingly mischaracterizes dharmic practices and sensibilities concerning generosity. As the ethnography in this chapter illustrates, Buddhist acts of care are often undertaken unceremoniously and are seemingly so ordinary that they are invisible to the international media's eyes. At the same time, in their competition with rivals and adversaries, Sinhala Buddhist revivalists take great pride in rendering Buddhist forms of generosity legible for the world stage.

Dāna is archetypically the donation of provisions to the Buddha and mendicant monks who follow the Buddhist path. In return for their care and material provisioning for monastics, lay donors are karmically rewarded with merit (*puñña karmaya*). Under certain conditions, Theravāda Buddhists also transform their conceptions of *dāna* in ways that reinforce the ethic of compassion toward all who are suffering (Bowie 1998; see also Hallisey, "Challenges"). By the mid-nineteenth century, Sri Lankan Buddhist revivalists deepened pan-Buddhist solidarities internationally, and simultaneously propelled practices of philanthropy, altruism, and "socially engaged Buddhism" (Jayawardena 2000; Bond 2004).

The influxes of humanitarian and charitable aid in the new millennium, paired with the majoritarian nationalist anxieties that were triggered by the growth of new styles of Christian influence, have provoked and inspired a new era of Buddhist charitable and social service work in Sri Lanka. Extending earlier phases of revival, Buddhist *dāyaka* (laity) and some mendicant monks renewed the practice of *shramadāna* (social service) and giving charitably to the poor as means to undercut the competitive materialist edge that Christianity appears to have over Buddhism. Because of the priority to stave off conversions to Christianity, in some domains Sinhala Buddhists dedicated to social service have redefined the idea of "*dāna*" to also include the act of giving to the indigent poor (Mahadev 2014; Gajaweera 2020). Some rare mendicant monks, as we will see, reinvented their vocations by involving themselves in projects of giving to materially deprived and disaster-struck Sri Lankans. Since primacy of place has traditionally been given to lay patronage that channels provisions toward the sangha, orthodox circles of Sri Lankan Buddhists occasionally take these transformations of meritorious practice as a paradox with respect to their duties to uphold the *Vinaya* or monastic rules. Considering the established hierarchies in these repertoires of giving and the present contingencies that shape the entanglements of charity and *dāna* illuminates the nature of the derogations of "selfishness" that Buddhist nationalists and Christian evangelists lodge against one another's religious goals.

2.1 *Poya* day offerings arranged by lay *dāyaka* for the Buddha, Weligoda village.

2.2 Offerings of flowers, oil lamps, incense, and water on *Poya* day, presented with pious care, and accompanied by intensive beating of the *beravā* drum, in Weligoda.

2.3 Preparing oil lamps for devotions on Binara Poya day.

2.4 Sated village monks departing from an almsgiving hosted by a family in the rural south.

INSTITUTIONS AND CONTINGENCIES OF RELIGIOUS GIVING

A version of the draft legislative bill on the "Prohibition of Unethical Conversions" that had been disseminated throughout Sri Lanka by Gazette Notification in 2004 decries conversions that took place through "force, *allurement*, and other fraudulent means." The All-Ceylon Buddhist Congress's Buddhist Commission Report (2009) details numerous incidents in which Christian NGOs were said to have given material "inducements" to tsunami-affected people with an agenda to recruit new converts. In the report, two organizations that operated in Sri Lanka after the tsunami, World Vision and Samaritan's Purse, came under fire for opportunistically evangelizing in Sri Lanka.[5] Some proselytizing groups purportedly rescinded charitable aid if the recipients rejected Bible offerings and invitations to come to church (89, sections 352–53). The report quotes a woman from Kandy who remarked upon her neighbor's conversion, stating that "this is a business conversion"—"*meeka bisnas convert ekak*" (88, section 343). The exasperation conveyed by the Sinhala woman, as it is portrayed in the report, suggests that what belies the persuasions to and persuasiveness of Christianity is something suspiciously transactional and disingenuous.

Despite the alleged pragmatics of the "business" of conversion, both in theory and praxis Christians see grace as attached to pastoral care and to charity. In

India, care of the subaltern who seek escape from indigent poverty as well as Brahmanical caste denigration, discrimination, and anti-Dalit atrocities often conceive of conversion away from Hinduism as an avenue to free themselves from oppression. Indian Dalits have historically converted to Buddhism under B. R. Ambedkar, to atheism under E. V. Ramaswamy Naiyakar (Periyar), to Islam, and frequently to Christianity. Tacit claims of karmic continuity underpin Hindutva ideologues' attempts to dissuade conversion to other religions, and thus the ideology of karma can play out perniciously in India given the cruel derogations against those of putatively "low" caste (Wadley 1994; Cotterill et al. 2014). Dalit oppression is a direct result of typically intransigent hierarchies in the religious establishment, and moreover historical subjugation within agrarian servitude and slavery, endemic in precolonial southern India (Viswanath 2014; Mohan 2015). Anti-caste activism centers around Dalit self-respect. As such, anti-Brahmanism has been a substantial course of political action and coalesced with the work of itinerant Protestant missionaries during the era of British colonialism. Indeed, Christianization was part and parcel of Dalits' resistance to caste strictures especially in southern India (Mosse 2012, 11). As such, historically, anticolonialism has not found much resonance among Dalits in India. From the perspective of Dalits, no nationalistic form of religiosity could alleviate entrenched forms of caste discrimination (Rao 2009). Thus, too, in India where Buddhism is rare and is delinked from majoritarian nationalism, Ambedkar and his followers considered conversion to Buddhism to be an appropriate avenue to throw off the yoke of caste. Nowadays, the disruptive and liberatory aspects of Pentecostal conversion, arguably more than Catholicism or Protestantism, have also served as an especially fecund vehicle for Dalits' rejection of caste as the basis for sociality in India (Bergunder 2008; Roberts 2016).

Very differently to the case of Hinduism in India, among Sinhala Buddhists of contemporary Sri Lanka, caste does not feature quite as prominently nor as perniciously (Simpson 1997, Seneviratne 2000).[6] Yet in several sectors, caste does persist as a form of social channeling among Sinhala Buddhists and draws subtle lines of belonging and exclusion. In certain realms caste can constrain kin relations and affinal partnerships. Historically in Ceylon, caste has been prominent in intra-sangha disputes, and it gave shape to the formation of sangha lineages (*nikaya*) and affiliation. Even as there is a good deal of mutability of Sinhala caste confinements in comparison to contemporary India, to some degree caste can affect political clout and occupational mobility. In chapter 6 I offer a small glimpse of how poverty, more than caste, intersects with Christianity and the conditions of possibility and constraint of socioeconomic mobility in a village setting where caste holds social relevance.[7] In short, in Sri Lanka various factors contribute to why people feel impelled to convert or feel categorically dissuaded from changing their religion. While caste may not be a primary factor in contemporary Sri Lanka, it can inflect social disadvantage and put latent limits upon social mobility.

Material provisioning of social care is certainly one reason for attraction to Christianity. Flows of giving are cause for anxiety among Sinhala Buddhists, and Christians occasionally attribute this to "jealousy" over the social and economic capital that Christians wield. One Sinhala Colombo-based mainline Protestant minister attributed the rise of Christianity in Sri Lanka to the attractiveness of Christians' generosity. In our 2009 interview, he held that lay Buddhists become "put off" by all of the obligations to maintain the monks. He explained the economic logic for this resentment: "You see, the Buddhist monks take alms on a daily basis from the laypeople. When Buddhist laypeople see all that the Christian pastors do for their people, they get attracted to Christianity. So when the people convert, the monks get upset. *Conversion hits the monks in the stomach, you see?*" he said, while emphatically poking at his own stomach, gesturing to how the Buddhist sangha loses its constituents to Christianity and thus how conversion materially strangles the monks' livelihoods. The point is consonant with the linkage identified in chapter 1 whereby entrepreneurs pitched insurance as a social and economic protection to be directed toward Buddhist clergy who may face a declining base for material support due to economic modernization. The differential affects of Buddhist and Christian forms of obligation, need, and desire are central to the interreligious antipathies in this context.

During the war, the surge of Western humanitarianism, paired with local Tamil Catholic and Protestant pastoral care and conflict mediation, intensified majoritarian accusations against those bearing malignant wartime "sympathies" and seditious sentiments. Sinhala Buddhists received this onslaught of humanitarian critique and charitable intervention as a political affront that they regarded to be tied up with a Christian ethos. These majoritarian nationalist anxieties became hegemonic in the Sri Lankan public sphere. With the eventful contingencies of the new millennium, Sinhala Buddhists became reanimated in their worries over Christian and secular gifts of care, the obligations that they spark, and what these debts and obligations might do to negatively alter the moral and political compass of those who are drawn into the orbit of their purveyors' influence.

In the post-tsunami and postwar conjuncture, Sri Lankan Buddhists and their international Asian Buddhist allies intensified their engagements in charitable work (Mahadev 2014; Mahadev, "Secularism"). They did so while expressly underscoring the Buddhist ethic of generosity and the need to stave off conversions to Christianity and to Islam. In her insightful ethnographic study Nalika Gajaweera (2020) demonstrates how elite Sinhala women of the Buddhist organization Jayagrahanaya (a.k.a. Success), mentioned earlier, engage in social service and charitable activities and purvey anti-conversion discourses in rural areas to dissuade Sinhala people from leaving the Buddhist path. They called upon Sinhala "mother warriors" to serve as culture bearers amid the postwar anxiety concerning the growth of Christianity. Gajaweera captures the didactic speech of these Sinhala women activists, in this case, in a medical doctor's address to villagers in war-torn regions of the country: "Do not lose the victory that your sons have secured.... If they (Christian evangelists) come to your house, show them the door, chase them out with a broomstick! Tell them our (*apē*) ancestors preserved this tradition, and that we will not sacrifice it. When we convert like this, they want us, the Sinhala Buddhists, to lose our force (*apē balaya naethi karanna*)" (2020, 197–98). As Gajaweera demonstrates, the Jayagrahanaya women activists include doctors, academics, lawyers, and other professionals who engage idioms of domesticity and enclosure to fend off the advance of Christianity among Sinhala people in rural contexts.

CHARITY, ALMS, GIFTS, AND TRANSACTIONS: ECONOMIES OF RELIGIOUS ATTRACTION

Colonial missionary endeavors took place in, and engendered, an age of highly differentiated geographies of affluence and poverty.[8] As a result, European Christians viewed generosity and altruism as a virtue critical to their sense of religio-moral accomplishment in the colonies (Haskell 1985; Parry 1986; Calhoun 2010; Fassin 2012). The missionaries who arrived in Ceylon early on during the British colonial era viewed Buddhist monks as wittingly depriving themselves for the sake of their own spiritual release. Seeing that many Ceylonese were perceptibly "poor," the European expatriates of the colonial era understood this condition to be the result of the moral failing of the local elite to treat them charitably. As the Europeans' Christian logic had it, poor Ceylonese were languishing due to Buddhists' lack of generosity. Even as there were preexisting conditions of drought in the region, colonial-era critics ignored the fact that new inequities and environmental degradation were inaugurated via the predacious colonial economy.[9] Their judgments followed from the modernist expansion of empire that coincided with Christian moral imperatives to extend care and compassion to soften the pernicious effects of poverty. In viewing the *dāna* (alms) that sustained the Buddhist sangha from that Eurocentric perspective, the early missionaries in Ceylon pronounced Christian charity as morally superior to Buddhist *dāna*.

In her account of the missionary archive, Elizabeth Harris (2006) finds that by the later years of the British colonial era, British and American missionary-theologians in Ceylon began softening their negative assessments of Pāli Buddhism. Some Western missionaries, orientalists, Theosophists, and scholars eventually turned sympathetically toward Pāli Buddhist philosophy, ethics, and practice to develop a more inclusivist, ecumenical Christianity, Harris demonstrates. Some of these itinerants in Ceylon even joined the Buddhist revival and were inspired to write with ecumenical appreciation, advocating for the advance of Pāli Buddhist thought and practice.[10]

Despite of the emergence of ecumenical interest in Buddhism during the latter days of the British colonial era, in the main, Christian missionaries were hard in their judgments of Buddhism. For example, one early British-era missionary, Anglican minister Reverend James Selkirk, complained that "one of the worst parts of the native Singhalese character is their neglect of the poor, sick and destitute" (1844, 265; see Harris 2006, 57). He wrote polemically to inspire Christian missionary action among Ceylonese Buddhists: "Does this not prove that the tender mercies of the wicked are cruel and that those who have no love to God have little disinterested love to their neighbors?" The imperious missionary critiques faulted Buddhism's atheistic karmic doctrine for destroying compassion, since others' misfortunes were conceived of as "payments" for past misdeeds (Schlieter 2013).

By the early twentieth century, upwardly mobile Ceylonese Buddhist *dāyakayo* (laypeople) responded to colonial-era missionary provocations against Buddhism by directing their profits to Buddhist charities and educational institutions in order to compete with missionary schools, orphanages, and other institutions through which Christians exerted their influence (Jayawardena 2000, 267).[11] By the mid-1900s the Buddhist revival was in full swing. Carrying out altruistic work among relatively impoverished people became a vital part of ethical self-formation known as *shramadāna* (Gombrich and Obeyesekere 1988; Bond 2004; Gajaweera 2020). The practice of *shramadāna* has tended to remain steady among lay Buddhists, whereas social service work by Buddhist monks has periodically gained and lost currency.

BUDDHIST EXTENSIONS OF CARE

In the aftermath of the December 2004 tsunami, when international news teams came to Sri Lanka to cover the devastation wrought by the catastrophe, insinuations of ostensible Sinhala Buddhist selfishness especially touched a nerve. The coastal village of Athuluwatta was one place where I had found this to be starkly evident. Athuluwatta was home to a temple-monastery and *pirivena* (monastic school) where novice monks follow the practices and precepts to embody Buddhist monastic life, study the Pāli scriptures, and receive the foundations of secular education, too. The temple-monastery was a major *rajamahavihara*, a temple renowned for its royal commission and the kings' patronage during pre-colonial times. The abbot there, a grandfatherly man known as Sumangala Thero, was one of my most generous interlocutors. During various stints between late 2009 and early 2011 I spent many an afternoon at the temple sitting on the veranda in casual discussion getting to know the shy young novice monks, the lay and clerical *pirivena* teachers, and the daytime streams of lay visitors.

After the monks had eaten their final morning meal, the last of the day, Sumangala Thero would serve me lunch alongside the lay Buddhist family that had come to offer the day's provisions, and the teachers and other visitors and well-wishers. He would serve us with an almost maternal style of care that resembled the way that Sinhala aunties served excessive quantities of rice and curry to guests. He would fondly search out the best remaining piece of fish from the serving bowl and place it on my plate. On one occasion when I traveled to the temple with my landlord and his family, by happenstance we arrived just in time and were invited to partake in the post-*dāna* meal. The family was unacquainted with the abbot, and so while accepting Sumangala Thero's kind offer, my host "uncle" emphatically commented that much merit would come my way on this occasion: *"Oyata godāk pin labēwī!"* He and his wife explained to me that I would receive merit because I was the conduit for this serendipitous meal at the temple shared in the sanctifying presence of the monks. Hearing this, Sumangala Thero beamed his warm, cherubic smile. This generous sharing of food and the proliferation of merit calls to mind Wendy Doniger's elegant turn of phrase expressing that Buddhism merit transfer entails a spiritualization of karma and that "somehow, the more you give, the more you have, as with love or cell-division" (1980, xix).

Over the course of many conversations with Sumangala Thero I learned that when Athuluwatta village saw the devastation of the tsunami, survivors fled inland beyond the train tracks to the monastery. With his permission, traumatized survivors carried the bodies of the dead to the temple premises, keeping them on the temple grounds for mourning until the bereaved community could arrange proper burials. It was an extraordinary thing for the body of a layperson to be sheltered on temple premises. Traditionally oriented Sinhala Buddhists often express fear of *killa* or inauspicious impurity associated with a corpse, and particularly a layperson's corpse that had not been prepared through mortuary rites. Ordinarily, fear of miasmatic impurity would bar such an occurrence. But Sumangala Thero was called to action by the extraordinary circumstances, and he responded with his characteristic generosity. What is more, survivors of the tsunami were without question given space to rest and recover in the large hall connected to the monastic quarters. With the temple's resources and donations of food brought by villagers who had been out of harm's way when the tsunami hit, the village monks and laity fed and calmed the traumatized survivors and offered them space to grieve and rest in the safe haven offered by the temple.

For several days, up until tsunami shelters were opened, monks and laypeople cared for those who were left bereft and homeless. Before the flow of external humanitarian relief supplies had reached the area, a BBC News team showed up, looking to cover the people's plight in places where tsunami victims had taken shelter. However, Sumangala Thero refused to admit the international news team onto the temple premises. He explained to me in Sinhala why he shooed the foreign media away, some five years after the event:

The newscasts showed images of our Sinhala people taking refuge in the temples after the tsunami hit us. But BBC News reporters were stating that our people had not been provided with food to eat, or even water to drink. Even after our people had just eaten what we had given to them, and were sitting in the safety of the temples with full stomachs, the reporters said that they were without food and water! I had heard that BBC was in the habit of portraying the situation this way from monks in neighboring temples, and from laypeople [*dāyakayo*] who met the news teams filming the wreckage. I didn't want this to happen at my temple, so I sent them away and refused to let them film here. They have given the world wrong ideas about our country.

Sumangala Thero also turned away World Vision, denying its offer to distribute aid on the temple grounds. Sri Lankan Buddhists have long suspected World Vision of facilitating "unethical conversions" by the pull of their charitable provisions.

Despite Sumangala Thero's adamant refusal to allow international media coverage in his temple in the immediate aftermath of the 2004 tsunami, he coordinated with certain other international NGOs in distributing aid and cooperated with Rotary International to rebuild the village school that was wiped out by the tsunami. The Buddhist *dāyakayo* who were responsible for the temporal affairs of the monastery and *pirivena* advised him to preserve the temple lands exclusively for monastic activities. The lay council's advice accords with traditional cultural taboos against laity's appropriation of temple lands (Seneviratne 1999, 321). Defying their objections, Sumanagala Thero generously allocated temple lands for the construction of the new village school. He was pleased with these international partnerships and gave the foreign NGOs due credit for their contributions. In several respects, Sumangala Thero was very moderate in his political inclinations, oriented more toward civic forms of nationalism than to anti-pluralistic currents of Buddhist nationalism. Still, like most Sri Lankan Buddhists, he was apprehensive about the negative spin and extractive nature of foreign media. He carefully drew a distinction between conversions that were undertaken by an individual's own volition and those that were induced "unethically" by manipulating vulnerable individuals' socioeconomic situations.[12]

For Sumangala Thero the issue was that the international media had depicted Sri Lankan Buddhists as unable—or worse, unwilling—to feed and care for survivors of the tsunami. A network of Buddhist monks and laity in the tsunami-affected areas held that the foreign media was intentionally misconstruing the situation as well as the character of Sinhala Buddhists in a neocolonial fashion.

It is possible that BBC News was simply trying to raise awareness around the world about the ecological travesty and the urgency of relief operations and the need for donor assistance, and in turn described an absence or insufficiency of local relief efforts. It may have been the case that these local forms of care were so quotidian and unremarkable by the standards of the international media that the foreign newscasters did not have the eyes to see them amid the spectacularly despairing scene of the tsunami catastrophe. Although the work of publicizing the impact of the disaster to encourage aid relief to flow from transnational sources was primarily a secular endeavor, Sinhala Buddhists perceived the BBC portrayal as a failure by Westerners to acknowledge Buddhists' care and generosity. They considered these secular incidents to be consonant with broader Christian tendencies to denigrate Buddhism. Through this filter of an antagonistic past, the pairing of Western media and humanitarian agendas was seen as predictably undermining Sri Lankans' sense of national pride and sovereign self-sufficiency.

In many respects Sinhala Buddhists' interactions with international aid entities felt to them not so unlike how they imagined their predecessors experienced missionaries who came to Ceylon bearing goodwill coupled with evangelical zeal. This point finds resonance in anthropologists' observations that in the development discourses of our age, the secular notion of "empowerment" is an epistemological cognate of Christian conversion (Stirrat and Henkel 1997, 68). Both religious conversion and developmentalist notions of empowerment signify how sovereign self-composure can be installed in the person or community through the adoption of new moral and economic techniques. In a time of disaster, the traumatized individual's self-composure might radically fall away. But in the case at hand, Sinhala Buddhists were emphatic that their networks of kin, neighbors, and clergy pulled together to assist one another. That the BBC news—a media network they closely associate with the former colonial power—failed to acknowledge local acts of generosity and capability in that time of crisis appeared to Sri Lankan Buddhists as a painful throwback to colonial-era encounters with Christian missionaries.

With the 2004 tsunami, several church organizations reportedly used the disaster as an opportunity to proselytize. A high-profile case in the post-tsunami period involved a church organization based in Waco, Texas, that sent missionaries bearing aid to Sri Lanka (Matthews 2007; Mahadev 2014). The church boasted a number of new mass conversions during a post-tsunami mission trip on its website. The *New York Times* picked up the story in an article published in January 2005, bearing the headline, "Mix of Quake Aid and Preaching Stirs Concern."[13] When this news reached Sinhala Buddhist readers in Colombo, the article heightened their fury against foreign Christian aid organizations in Sri Lanka.

Sinhala Buddhists have long responded to suspicions of evangelical opportunism with various counterefforts to keep "impressionable" and "vulnerable" Sri Lankans within the Buddhist fold. In 2010 I met with a Sri Lanka medical doctor who I will call Dr. Weerasooriya. She described various acts of Western humanitarian condescension during the period of tsunami recovery. In her view, a slew of "quack doctors" arrived in Sri Lanka along with the aid efforts. She also told me of the problem of opportunistic Christian conversions as she drove us to pay a visit to an orphanage that she sponsors in a rural district. Dr. Weerasooriya had founded the children's home with several Buddhist partners in the 1970s. The children's home offers orphans a Buddhist upbringing. Their intent in establishing the home, Dr. Weerasooriya informed me, was to help stave off the possibility that missionary caretakers and adoptive parents from abroad would raise these disadvantaged Sinhala children as Christians.

In a comprehensive ethnographic survey on religious giving in South Asia, Filippo Osella notes that it is tremendously difficult to "disentangle secular from religious motivations in giving and receiving" (2018, 6). Such confusions are reflected in the fact that several nominally religious organizations that arrived during the tsunami operated upon entirely secular principles, yet Sri Lankans assumed that they were opportunistically spreading the Christian gospel. Sri Lankans commonly surmised that the International Committee on the Red Cross (ICRC) and the International Federation of the Red Cross and Red Crescent Societies (LRCS) were serving religious principles, even when from the institutions' and employees' points of view this was not the case. UMCOR, the United Methodist Committee on Relief, came under scrutiny in Sri Lanka because of its Christian name and symbolism. An UMCOR employee who I met in Colombo, a British citizen and self-described atheist, detailed how despite the fact that the organization was avowedly secular in practice and principle, its monies did flow from liberal Christian supporters in the United States and Europe. Although expatriate and local UMCOR employees insisted upon the secularity of their work, ministerial leaders of the Sri Lankan Methodist Church expected provisioning from the organization on religious grounds. UMCOR

staff consistently denied such partisan requests. Despite the organization's secular commitments, as a direct result of anti-Christian hostilities in Sri Lanka,
UMCOR was compelled to remove the image of the cross and a flame from its
logo, keeping to a less conspicuous all-caps acronym. In short, most international charities, including those with Christian origins, were generally pluralistic and willingly abided by mandates to operate on the basis of secular
nonpartisanship.

To Sri Lankan Buddhist nationalist-protectionists, Christian charitability, as
well as Western secular humanitarian aid, appears to be built upon an ulterior
motive: through their charitable work, it appears that Christians and foreigners
(*sudhāyō*) attempt to outshine Buddhists' expressions of generosity. They further
suspect foreign and local evangelists, and Christian converts too, of inaugurating "anti-national" sentiment through postwar paradigms of transitional justice
(see chapter 1). What is more, as I observed, Sinhala Buddhist recipients of aid in
southern tsunami-affected regions of the country commonly assumed that
sudhāyō (white or Western foreigners) are Christian irrespective of their actual
backgrounds, identities, and affinities. This perception only facilitates the moral
panic concerning anti-nationalism.

RELIGIOUS GIVING, HUMANITARIAN CONCERN,
AND SINHALA BUDDHIST SOVEREIGNTY

Within months of the close of the civil war in 2009, Sinhala men and women of
Colombo and other urban areas in Sri Lanka could be found sporting silicone
wristbands resembling those I had seen young evangelical Christians wearing in
the United States. Intrigued by the brightly colored bands, I had first guessed
that they were imprinted with "WWJD?" standing for "What Would Jesus
Do?"—as young American Christians sport to remind themselves to self-
reflexively "walk with Jesus." Nilantha, a young Sinhala man who worked as a
bank teller in Colombo, proudly held out his wrist to let me examine his band
when I asked him about it. "What does it say? WWJD?" "What?" he asked, not
recognizing my assumption. "It says, *'Api Wenawen Api.'*" "We for us?" I asked,
searching his face as I grasped for the meaning. "We for ourselves," he answered.

Nilantha explained that the embossed Sinhala script signified that Sri Lanka
had "won the war and defeated the terrorists without the help of any other

country. We are a small country, no?" Sinhala tuk-tuk drivers and former army "boys" who I encountered after war's end offered the same explanation for their wristbands and the bumper stickers adorning their vehicles.[14] "Now we can live together in peace," several Sinhala men and women averred when I spoke to them in the months following the war. Both cosmopolitan Sinhala Buddhists in Colombo, as well as people in more rural coastal areas, uttered this reconciliatory aspiration with such conviction that it was as if in saying it they believed that they had already made it come true. In the main, the subjunctive tone in which these statements were delivered struck me as absent triumphalism. Proud of Sri Lanka's success in defending the nation from ethnic fractures and secessionist violence, many of the Sinhala Buddhists whom I met appeared unconvinced by or even unaware of international human rights reports of mass civilian deaths, since state authorities had blocked transparent reporting on casualty counts in the final phases of war.[15] Others adamantly stood by the state's justifications for the end of war military operations and saw foreign humanitarian organizations as harboring unwarranted "sympathies" for the vanquished insurgents. They tended to presume these organizations were Christian or held to an implicit Christian ethos, regardless of whether the organizations abided by secular or Christian principles.

One month before the end of the war when international humanitarian concern was reaching its apex, then–Secretary of State Hillary Clinton sharply condemned Sri Lanka's military offensive. In her formal statement, she said: "I think the Sri Lankan government knows that the entire world is very disappointed, that in its efforts to end what it sees as 25 years of conflict, it is causing such untold suffering."[16] Nationalistic Sinhala Buddhists were outraged by the international community's attempts to undermine Sri Lanka's efforts to protect against internal threats to its territorial integrity, especially given that it was the U.S. "War on Terror," launched after September 11, 2001, under the Bush administration, that set the tone for global counterinsurgency. Sri Lanka, under Mahinda Rajapaksa's presidency, took the global War on Terror as a nod to use unstinting military means to fight the Tamil insurgents. While Sinhala Buddhist nationalists were celebrating their military victory over the LTTE secessionists and extolling the win as a "liberation" of Tamil civilians, they countered international human rights criticisms with the charge of Western "hypocrisy."

Exasperation concerning international human rights interventions and local humanitarian NGO activity permeated majoritarian nationalist political discourse.

Sinhala Buddhist public intellectuals, journalists, monks, and lay orators warned that Sri Lankans should "get ready for a humanitarian attack." In a May 2011 editorial a conservative commentator and university professor, Nalin De Silva, excoriated "Western Christian Modernity" ("the WCM") for having "no respect for the sovereignty of the other countries."[17] In an alarmist tone, he wrote,

> The West could even prop up a tiny group of Tamil Christians in Sri Lanka to agitate against the Sri Lankan government so that they could invade Sri Lanka under the guise of protecting various rights of the group, with or without taking economic measures. Whatever the mechanism may be the invasion will not be due to the love of Tamils but in order to destroy the Sinhala Buddhist culture which is a threat to WCM. We have to prepare for this so called "humanitarian" attack from this moment and the government should be ready with a plan to face any eventuality.[18]

In the heavy polarization over the question of whether conduct in war was ultimately just or not, majoritarian nationalist discourses tended to vilify critics of their military success as anti-national "LTTE sympathizers." They classified humanitarian agencies and Christian charities operating within Sri Lanka as "foreign-funded NGOs" and cast them as agents seeking to "recolonize" Sri Lanka.[19]

Sinhala Buddhists' assertions that Western humanitarianism is only putatively secular and carries a strong trace of a clandestine Christian ethos came to a fever pitch in postwar Sri Lanka. A paranoid style of nationalism intensified. The suspicions that local and foreign Christian and secularist sympathies were inclined to be with the Tamil minorities, were further intensified by the fact of religious "peace brokering" during the war (Johnson 2012; Brown 2015). Jesuit priests, mainline Protestant ministers, and lay Christians inhabiting the war zones commonly supported Sri Lankan Tamil human rights activists, who reported injustices committed both by the state and rebel militaries. They acted as brokers who secured the lives of Tamil civilians, and occasionally the lives of conscripted cadres too. This configuration of liberal neutrality associated with Christianity in general exacerbated perceptions of Christians' sympathies toward the insurgents (detailed also in chapter 1). In this fraught context, the ethnic fractures and north-south regionalism of the war resulted in cleavages in the unity of Sri Lankan Christian church denominations, a point that I address with respect to the complex position of the Catholic Church in chapter 6. Buddhists' and Christians' tendencies to both recognize and misrecognize the convergences and conflations between Christian and secular forms of giving, intensified these identitarian consternations. As a result, there was a great deal of misrecognition of the diverse ways that one might embody their religious commitments in Sri Lanka.

THE PROBLEM OF THE GIFT, AND RECIPROCAL OBLIGATION

In post-disaster and postwar Sri Lanka, the "problem of the gift," as it were, is that giving invariably raises questions about what "hidden agendas" are hitched to the gifts of aid and charity. In the moral economy of European Christianity, the emphasis upon altruism and compassion was critical to countering the alienating and impoverishing drives of the free market (Haskell 1985; Parry 1986). Otherwise put, capitalism and colonialism provided the conditions of possibility through which liberal Europeans and Americans could expand their sense of moral responsibility. Secular humanitarianism was built upon older, Christian notions of charity. The Protestant Christian imperative toward "internal rectitude and purity of religious communities" was transformed with expansionary ambitions of evangelicalism, which instead engaged "a new outward orientation" that "addresses the world of strangers as potential converts" (Calhoun 2010, 35-37). Taking the case of the Red Cross, Craig Calhoun points out that the founders endeavored to mitigate the suffering brought about by war through politically "neutral" means. In nineteenth-century Europe the secularity of humanitarian care emerged via the International Committee of the Red Cross, which "provided its care under the flag of neutrality. This flag, of course, appropriated a Christian symbol. Care—charity—was provided not only out of religious motivation, but also on the basis of religious understanding of what common humanity meant beyond national identities" (Calhoun 2010, 37). The Red Cross and other cognate humanitarian organizations became secularized over time. Sinhala Buddhists easily spot this isomorphism within humanitarian practice. They identify continuities between religious and secular material and moral interventions and in turn are sharp critics who consider the neutrality of these organizational endeavors to be putative at best.[20]

Marcel Mauss ([1925] 2016) famously argued that the gift necessarily demands reciprocity, compelling people to connect through webs of mutual obligation. This obligation holds human society together as if it is some unseen supernatural force—in the Māori language, the *hau* or "spirit of the gift"—inherent to sociality and material life. Thus, for Mauss, a "pure gift" is a fiction. Anthropologists of secular development draw upon this Maussian framework, elaborating how, when material reciprocity is to be withheld and a "pure gift" of charity is extended, it will inevitably "wound" the recipient through the sublimation of material debts (Douglas 1966). Sri Lanka's post-tsunami period was rife with complications of aid distribution, dissatisfaction among beneficiaries, and suspicion that humanitarian organizations are a vehicle through which Westerners could instill foreign values. Examining the knotty phenomenon after the catastrophe, Malathi de Alwis recalled Douglas's insight, observing that although charity is on the surface a "salve" to heal the wounds of war and natural disaster, Sri Lankan beneficiaries were also subjects who were "aided and ad(minister)ed and disciplined in additionally wounding ways" (de Alwis 2009, 122).[21]

Beyond the critique of the dependencies that are installed by paradigms of foreign development, the unwritten demands of reciprocity created by charity and aid had implications too for the politics of religious affiliation, as demonstrated earlier. A "patrimonial rationale" in tsunami aid delivery was inescapable (Korf et al. 2010, 506). Even as religious institutions strived to reject partisanship in aid delivery, tsunami-affected people often expected to be the exclusive beneficiaries of religious charity being delivered from their churches, temples, and mosques, as several scholars found in a collaborative study carried out in eastern Sri Lanka.[22] I found a similar phenomenon in southern tsunami-affected villages. My Sinhala interlocutors often wryly commented and sometimes complained that because of the aid offered by churches there were a number of new conversions. But these conversions were often temporary. Buddhists often found it laughable when their neighbors became churchgoers, exclaiming that "once the tsunami aid dried up, they came right back!"—back to Buddhism, including to veneration of a wide spectrum of Sinhala Buddhist deities.

This "patrimonial rationale" affected intra-Christian relationality too. Saman, a matchmaker in Weligoda village, was driven to attend the newest church in the area in accord with the demands of post-tsunami reciprocity. Although he had devotedly traveled sixteen kilometers by bus to the nearest city to attend his Assemblies of God Church on Sundays since the 1990s, Saman felt beholden to a new minister in the area who had come bearing aid after the tsunami. He felt obliged to become a patron of Pastor George, based at a newer ministry located much closer to his home because he had received substantial provisions from him after the tsunami. Saman expressed some sense of remorse about betraying a long-standing connection to his first pastor. With his conflicted feelings on the matter, Saman alternated between the two places of worship, but he felt obligated to be most consistent in attending Pastor George's new ministry—which, at the time I had attended church with them, had a regular attendance consisting only of four or five families. He did so in spite of feeling less than persuaded to attend the new church. Pastor George was adamantly against "speaking gibberish" and admonished Pentecostals for speaking in tongues, as per the injunctions of the Church of Christ.[23] As a result of Pastor George's denial of charismatic practices, the new church was less attractive to Saman than the Pentecostal church located farther from his home. Yet Saman felt compelled to "show his face" occasionally at his new church. Temporary dalliances with newly planted churches are fairly common, as I detail in the ethnography of chapter 6. Evidently it is not only interreligious relations that turn acrimonious due to congregational poaching; intra-Christian relations are also often affected and are further marked by the schismatic splitting characteristic of Protestant denominations (Handman 2014), as well as by the competitive air between individual evangelists who vie to performatively display their charitable capital or their charismatic grace.

Although Marcel Mauss invokes the notion of the *hau*, the *spirit* of the gift, interpreters have regarded *hau* as a "secular" force materialized in the gift that enforces the rule of return. Critically revisiting the Maussian thesis, scholars have begun to take seriously the idea that the *hau* is an actual spiritual force that compels return. Discerning a duality in the thesis on the gift, Simon Coleman argues that the modern gift may well also have the potential to initiate a secular *contract*, but that in the view of evangelical and charismatic Christians the gift rather is seen as inaugurating a *covenant* (2004, 421–22). This "covenantal" spiritual force is consonant with what my Sri Lankan Christian interlocutors insist happens—or ought to happen—in the process of conversion: believers stress that if people feel compelled to convert it is not because of material "inducement" but rather that it results from the sanctifying transmission of the Holy Spirit in the exchange between the donor and the beneficiary of charity. As opposed to a contractual, patrimonial relation to the gift, for the prototypical Christian sincerity is considered to be inherent in a covenantal relationship.

A pair of Sinhala Protestant evangelists whom I met in southern Sri Lanka maintained that advancing a covenantal commitment must be the evangelist's singular objective. I met them at one of a series of visits that I made to the Methodist church in a small southern coastal town. The ministerial head, Pastor Silva, was evidently anxious about the dwindling congregational numbers at his Sunday services. He invited me to dinner with his family, along with a visiting Sinhala minister, Pastor Chandrasooriya, an up-and-coming figure on the international evangelical circuit who had just returned from seminary training in the United States. On his return mission to Sri Lanka he was tasked with conducting sensitivity trainings to help Protestant ministers advance their goals. He advocated for a kind of ecumenism in service of evangelical expansion, as validated by his theological training. Pastor Chandrasooriya emphasized the covenantal aspiration to consolidate authentic commitments to their god and to avert or transform instrumentalist and disingenuous conversions. His influence was reflected in Pastor Silva's account of his association with a Buddhist monk from a nearby temple. The monk befriended him, asking in earnest if the minister would teach him English. Pastor Silva readily accepted the task and invitation. "I of course won't go in for direct conversion. But I hope that that monk sees the God working through me, and that he will gain the conviction to convert." Indeed, a covenantal orientation to Christianity's gifts has a significant place within Sri Lankan evangelists' narratives of conversion.

While the central allegation by Buddhist protectionists is that Christian charity materially "induces" the poor and vulnerable into converting to Christianity, the conversion narratives I collected rarely attributed attraction to Christianity to be the sole result of the gift of charity (see chapters 3 and 6). World Vision does operate their global mission on expansionary, evangelical Christian principles, and Sinhala Buddhists widely alleged that World Vision actively uses the material accoutrements to sway indigent Sri Lankans to convert. Yet in pockets where I carried out my research, it appears that after the tsunami, World Vision employees refrained from proselytizing—a necessary condition to operate in Sri Lanka in light of anti-conversion hostilities. Sinhala beneficiaries of World Vision housing whom I surveyed in 2010 in tsunami village project homes stationed kilometers inland from the southern coast complained about the distance from the main road and the sea (the result of a government-mandated "buffer zone"), and about builders' lack of attention to *vastu* geomantic practices that homeowners believed to be critical for the flow of good fortune and health. But all of the families that I surveyed at World Vision Village reported never having experienced proselytism or any pressure to convert to Christianity from their benefactors. In this wide-ranging survey that I conducted with the help of Thushari Dinusha, my intrepid research assistant, we did ask about individual and family religious affinities and yet diligently took care to avoid asking any leading questions concerning conversion. They evidently all remained devoted Buddhists, despite the material provisioning they had received from the evangelical Christian organization.

In sum, many local informal Buddhist networks and revivalist organizations, as well as established Christian organizations and secular nongovernmental organizations, have done heroic work for communities affected by the tsunami and civil war. Sinhala Buddhists who held strongly onto their natal religion viewed Christian charity as an always-already attractive tool through which Christians—be they foreign or local—work to ensnare new converts. They often classify the Christian gifts of charity and miracles as "inducements" or even bribery. However, studies of evangelical conversions in South Asian contexts indicate that it is often the expressions of care and community generated through pastoral relationships that serve to persuade converts (Perera 1998; Roberts 2016). For recipients of religious charity, patrimonial senses of obligation were practically inevitable. Despite evangelists' latent desires to exert influence through pastoral care and charitable works, many individual Christians and even large-scale NGOs were careful not to set a clear agenda to proselytize in this fraught context.

DĀNA IN THE CANON: MECHANICS OF RECIPROCITY

Considering how ethnocentric critiques of "selfish" Theravādin Buddhist giving have historically fueled interreligious hostility in colonial Ceylon and in contemporary Sri Lanka, it is worth examining the foundational paradigms of *dāna* within the Buddhist tradition. In the regional context, overarching hierarchies of purity and pollution—substantive conditions that were normatively understood in Brahmanical Hinduism to be transmitted through material exchange in ritual and nonritual circumstances—have long enabled caste hierarchies and discrimination. Given the casteist cruelty that stems from anxieties about biomoral impurity which conditions South Asian transactional paradigms, the "Indian gift" entails substantively different principles of exchange than Christian, Māori, or Papua New Guinean spirits of mutual obligation and reciprocity that Marcel Mauss characterized as fueling the moral economy of the gift (Parry 1986). Indic forms of giving classically do not correspond with Mauss's observations on reciprocity, precisely because material gifts are loaded with substantive impurity and karmically inauspicious consequences. Thus, giving is especially contentious in South Asia, entangled in "shame and status hierarchies" (Osella 2018). With this in view, considering how the moral economy of Buddhism accords with classical Buddhist doctrines on *dāna* reveals that far from being a conservative practice the Buddha's approach to materially sustaining the sangha was for its time revolutionary. This point is typically lost when Christian sensibilities of charity and altruism are taken as the benchmark for Buddhist generosity—which is almost inevitably the case in a "global," modernist perspective.

Classically within Hindu *dānadharma* (righteous ritual giving), the objective was to ensure that the pollution transmitted through the gift, ritual offering, or other transacted substance, does not contaminate the purity of the recipient. Brahmanical *dānadharma* then can be spiritually burdensome and perilous to the donor since the gift embodies "the sins of the donor"; donors in turn rid themselves of substantive residues of evil "by transferring the dangerous and demeaning burden of death and impurity to the recipient" (Parry 1986, 459). The paradox in the Brahmanical context is that anyone willing to *receive* a gift to facilitate the expiation of the sins of the donor in turn "is almost by definition unworthy to receive them" (460). As Jonathan Parry illustrates, distinct from the moral orientation of a generous donor, in South Asia giving is an activity that has implications foremost for the moral comportment and status of the *recipient* of the gift, and only secondarily for that of the giver.

Compared to normative Brahmanical soteriologies and karmic scales of purity and impurity, Buddhist *dāna* was a profound amendment to the Brahmanical relationship between ascetics and lay donors (Egge 2002; Findly 2003; Heim 2004). In contrast to the then-dominant Brahmanical paradigm that gave credence to derogatory biomoral evaluations of persons and caste hierarchies, the historical Buddha sought to undo these discriminatory ideologies. This early Buddhist reformism offered an interesting prospect: within the Buddhist ideology of *dāna* there is virtue in *receiving* indiscriminately, with great composure (*muditā*). This feature of the Buddha's discourses was intended to undercut anxieties that receiving defiling substances might result in ontologically damaging effects.[24]

According to the canon that guides the Pāli Buddhist tradition, the onus to remedy the negative psychological effects of receiving the impure substances of the gift or sacrifice is upon the beneficiary of *dāna*—that is, upon the Buddhist monk. A member of the sangha, who in principle could be someone from any caste, is asked to forgo preoccupations with purity and pollution of the donor—to explicitly reject caste hierarchies (Egge 2002, 3–4).[25] In Buddhist exchange, mental comportment is of utmost importance. These Buddhist principles challenged the presumptions that offerings must be ritually purified to ensure that the offering would be acceptable to the gods (26). The Pāli canon suggests that donors were instructed to give liberally, with a happy, calm state of mind. Doing so with a mind that is impervious to the fear of potential for hunger and thirst and to the fear of contamination through the gift received was said to effect the mental and emotional purification required for attainment of *nibbāna* (35). This requires releasing the mind from preconceived notions regarding the status of the donor and expressing indifference to worldly distinctions (Heim 2004). In this cognitive turn, the Buddha refashioned the idea of a successful ascetic as one who attains mental purity as the true "Brahman" (Egge 2002, 26). Otherwise put, the early Buddhic reforms over Brahmanical Hinduism were modernist insofar as they did away with material purification by fire as the ritual modality to transcend *saṃsāra* and reconceived ontological "purity" as an interiorized state of mind.

Radical generosity also had mythic potential to reorient the person toward renunciatory ends in pursuit of *nibbāna*. The exceptional giving of Prince Vessantara—a central story of the *Jātaka* tales concerning the Buddha's past life—exemplifies this virtue of indiscriminate giving. The tale construes a donor's fixation upon the accrual of merit itself as an act of demerit (Cone and Gombrich 1977). The myth highlights how the Prince gave lavishly, indiscriminately, and without regard to the merits of the act (Heim 2004). He gave away his possessions and even his family members to a demon. The Prince undertook extreme renunciation with embodied equanimity, earning him profound merit within the cosmological circuit of karma. So meritorious was his giving that it resulted in the magical return of all of the Prince's possessions and his rebirth in the next lifetime as the Bodhisattva who ultimately became Sakyamuni Buddha, the historical Gotama Buddha.

Whereas these widely circulated Buddhist doctrines validate monastic provisioning as a source of merit, altruistic and compassionate giving to the indigent poor is not classified as *dāna* as such (Heim 2004, 74–75). Although foundational teachings insist that acquisitive fixation upon merit has the opposite effect and serves to create demerit, in practice Theravāda Buddhists do tend to assign maximal value to the practice of giving alms to those who are karmically "worthy" of receiving; thus, giving to Buddhist monastics is typically deemed to be the most meritorious form of giving. Hierarchy endures thereby, and charity to the poor can be seen as producing a certain conundrum according to these classical premises of Theravāda Buddhism (74). Maria Heim writes that "it is not clear how the ethics of esteem could accommodate the ethics of altruism" (75). That tension remains within the categorical difference between giving to the sangha and giving to those in need. Yet there is a certain "alchemy" of charitable practice, evident in Buddhist contexts (Bowie 1998; see also Hallisey 2007).[26] The anthropologist Katherine Bowie observes that an alchemy of Buddhist charity extends (Thai) Theravādin Buddhists' generosity in accord with need, rather than in accord with problematic discursive categories such as "the poor" that tend to create harmful ontologies out of circumstantial suffering.

MIND, MATERIALITY, AND ETHICS IN THERAVĀDA BUDDHISM

The Theravāda Buddhist archetype ascribes liberative qualities to states of mental freedom that are achieved through freedom from attachments. A Theravāda Buddhist adage avers that "suffering is a teacher only second to the Buddha" (Hallisey 2007).[27] Suffering—including but not limited to the suffering of the poor—is rendered in the Sinhala Buddhist tradition of ethical thought as bearing didactic potential.[28] The experience of suffering is posited as a spur to impel an individual to develop the compassionate disposition that is essential to setting oneself on a meritorious path toward *nibbāna*. Ordinarily, Sri Lankans estimate that one's spiritual progress accords with one's apparent lives' conditions, based on the karmic eschatology that instills practices of ethical discernment into the conduct of everyday life. Sri Lankan Buddhists generally consider poverty, emotional difficulty, and other hardships to be karmically governed—that is, to be the result of righteous or sinful actions committed by the person in some past life. Given this theodicy, wherein the moral qualities of one's cumulative actions are believed to dictate the conditions of one's lives, those who apparently experience great suffering are sometimes viewed as if they are in their spiritual infancy, a point from which it requires much moral work to make a spiritual ascent.

Out of this logic it is occasionally with condescension that some upper-class Sri Lankan Buddhists and Hindus contend that charity presents a problem precisely because these external means to alleviate suffering do not allow people to feel their suffering as a karmic effect, thereby causing the poor to lack sufficient inspiration to strive for a better rebirth. Hence, this logic sometimes morphs into a forceful judgment that insists that it is the individual's responsibility to recognize suffering as *guruwarayak* (a teacher) and to meritoriously overcome that suffering. This is not to deny genuine compassion in Sinhala Buddhism. But this sort of karmic neoliberalism takes as given that there is something productive to be mined from the experience of suffering.[29] In an inversion of this elitist articulation of the karmic paradigm that one must assume responsibility for things beyond one's immediate power, the anthropologist Martin Southwold found that a contrary logic exists among Buddhist villagers in Sri Lanka. He showed that relatively disadvantaged village folk were emphatic that it is wealthy and powerful people who are unlikely to attain better rebirths because they could not possibly be suffering enough to impel them to perfect their conduct (1983, 202–12).

Buddhist nationalists who seek to protect their religious heritage often claim that charity serves to unethically "allure" and "induce" vulnerable people to convert. This concern is tightly connected to the ways in which Pāli Buddhist thought and practice are rooted in an ideology of renunciation that problematizes what materiality does to the qualities of the mind. Implied in modern legal and political discourse over religious conversion in Sri Lanka, too, are Theravādin soteriological concerns that translate as a charge against the potentially dangerous effects of charity. Charity, one version of this logic goes, could partially alleviate material suffering, and thus one's life conditions could produce an inadequate spur for individuals to achieve an enlightened state of mind—an ideal that hinges on nonattachment to material life and the acceptance of transience of one's life's conditions. This view of Buddhist philosophy of mind coalesces with and tacitly informs Sinhala Buddhists' nationalistic critiques of Christian charity, as well as of secular human rights conceptions of religious freedom.

BUDDHIST GIVING AS MONASTIC VOCATION

The liquid call of the *koha*, the bird of the Sinhala-Tamil New Year, punctuated my dialogue with Reverend Dhammadutta Thero. We sat opposite from each other in a large sitting room off of the main entrance at the monastic training center in Maharagama. The door ajar behind me, monks in training passing by craned their necks to peer in and hear what the bespectacled monk had to say. Dhammadutta Thero was one of the central figures in the Janavijaya Foundation, a social-service organization founded upon Buddhist revivalist principles by the late Soma Thera. He shared with me his experiences of embarking on a Buddhist mission in Sri Lanka. He subsequently contributed to missions in Singapore and Malaysia, and for a sustained period of time also in Australia. Over the years he has updated me on how he has involved himself in establishing schools, building homes for soldiers and Tamil and Sinhala war victims, distributing scholarships and gifts of support for school children, and equipping Buddhist elders' homes. Entrusted with one of the leadership roles in the Janavijaya Foundation, Dhammadutta Thero fashioned himself as a figure of Buddhist charitable service.

Dhammadutta Thero introduced me to one Janavijaya Foundation initiative to establish a Buddhist school in a tsunami-affected coastal village. Despite the foundation's stated concerns about unethical conversions and inclinations to condemn Christians in general for their expansionary ambitions and exclusivist tendency, a Protestant church in Europe was the primary sponsor supporting the post-tsunami childcare project. The partnership was facilitated through a close friendship between the head minister of a parish in a small German town and Sri Lankan monks based in the United States who are also linked to the Foundation. The preschool was built in dedication to Venerable Madihe Pannasiha Thero, founder of the Bhikkhu Training Center of Maharagama.[30] The late monk was a champion of the Sinhala Buddhist monastic revival, and to that end he emphasized the value of social-service work. Because of his centrality within the Sinhala Buddhist revival, supporters of the foundation found it to be their special preserve to maintain Buddhism as a moral and religious force in Pannasiha Thero's name.

In addition to these various social service projects, Dhammadutta Thero frequently invited Japanese Mahāyāna monks to join him as benefactors of the Foundation's projects and cultivated other important associations abroad.[31]

Although the young monk garnered respect, he pursued social-service work to such an unusual extent that certain other monks at the monastic training center viewed him as failing to abide by the *Vinaya*, the Buddhist monastic code of conduct. This is consistent with the terms of the monastic dispute that had consumed Sinhala Buddhist revivalists and reformers in an earlier era, whereby clergy fixated upon preserving the *Vinaya* rules were pitted against those who advocated for the revival of Buddhism through monastics' turn to social service, as H. L. Seneviratne described in *The Work of Kings* (1999). In the time that I knew him, Dhammadutta Thera was compelled to relocate to a temple-monastery of lesser prestige that could better accommodate his erratic schedule. Lay supporters of Dhammadutta Thero's work suggested that other monks had become jealous of his travels and ease in associating with laypeople and foreigners, whereas other monks felt that the requirements of their monastic life barred them from participating in such temporal activities.

The thirty-five-year old monk's dedication to social service went against the grain of Buddhist monastic conventions. "I feel it is my duty," he said, in halting colloquial English, before remarking upon how he does not fit the mold of a traditional monk, and about what his future retirement might require. "After age fifty or fifty-five, I would like to change my life. I want to leave the house. I would like to meditate. This work that I do is not the monk's duty. Normally the monk's duty is meditation. To be without attachment—*Siha kalpanāwa* [without attachments of the heart/mind]. This is not for me, it's for others."

Dhammadutta Thero implied that his retirement from charitable work as a monk would be akin to leaving behind his role as a householder. "Leaving home" in one's old age to undertake an ascetic lifestyle unto the death (*sannyāsa*) is a classic life trajectory in the Hindu tradition, while the traditional Buddhist monastic trajectory generally entails early mendicancy or "retirement" from the world to pursue the path of *nibbāna*. Dhammadutta Thero left home to join the sangha when he was only eleven, received higher ordination at the age of twenty, and finished his education in Buddhism and Pāli language when he was twenty-two. Despite his higher monastic ordination (*Upasampadā*), Dhammadutta Thero avowed that his true vocation was social service and that he would defer his aspirations toward mendicancy until he reached his age of retirement.

REHABILITATING PERCEPTIONS:
POSTWAR POLITICS OF THE GIFT

As a steward of Buddhist social service, Dhammadutta Thero worked with lay Buddhists in Sri Lanka and abroad to offer gifts of school supplies, shoes, umbrellas, and major provisions such as housing to tsunami-displaced families in the south, as well as to Tamil refugee children being temporarily housed in IDP camps in the Vanni, a primary combat zone during the war. Reverend Dhammadutta emphasized that his mission was "to change the impression held among Tamil people that Buddhist monks are always fighting," a reference to the fact that prominent contingents of the sangha lobbied Sri Lankan political leaders to pursue military means to extinguish Tamil militancy.

The monk maintained that the image of war-mongering Buddhist monks was a misrepresentation by the Tamil militants and foreign media, which he wished to dispel. To do so, Dhammadutta Thero, along with a couple of other service-oriented monks, traveled to the Vanni, a region that had once been held by the LTTE and a major battle site in the final military offensive. Dhammadutta Thero proudly recounted to me how he had gathered ninety Hindu priests who had been internally displaced during the war. He described how he had ceremonially gifted them white cloth, the traditional dress of Hindu *pūcāri* ritual officiants, and held a three-hour discussion with them. In his lecture he admonished the priests for their inaction during the long war. In Sinhala, with a Tamil translator to facilitate understanding, he had rhetorically asked the gathering of Hindu priests, "Why did the war start? You never did your duty . . . Hindu priests should do their duty. If [you] Hindu priests had done your duty well, the war would have never started." Further, he implied that disharmony between Sinhala and Tamil people, and the rise of the LTTE, was the upshot of the Christianization of Tamils. Seamlessly shifting out of reported speech to explanatory mode, he said to me, "Prabhakaran [the leader of the LTTE insurgency], and Tamil children [child soldiers], and Anton Balasingham [LTTE political strategist]—all are not Hindus. All are Catholic. They never attended any Hindu *kovil* (temple). Prabhakaran, Anton Balasingham, and Charles Antony [founding member of the LTTE]—these names are not Hindu names. That war is not a Tamil war. There is something behind it. That's the truth."

I interjected, addressing him with the requisite honorific to address a monk, "but *hamaduruwo*, as I understand, the LTTE, they're not only Catholic … nor Christian. They're mainly Hindu, no?" Reverend Dhammadutta responded:

> Ordinary Tamil people don't know anything [about their religious tradition]—they only learned to fight. They don't know Hinduism. There are not any [real] Hindus [among them]. When I spoke with the Hindu priests, it was clear that they don't know anything—they can't advise their people, they don't speak to them and counsel them. They don't know about Hinduism … *Vēdanta*, the *Vēda* book—they know nothing of it. What do they teach? They don't know how to teach. I advised them, "first you must look after your people." It is very important for them. I tried to discuss with them, rather than preaching to them as in a sermon. I prefer to discuss and also work with children. That way they can learn more from us. Buddhism is very practical. If we work with [Tamil] children or with people, they can understand who is a Buddhist monk [relating to the monk's vocation and good intentions]. Dharma talk is, only talk. They can understand more easily, practically [through practical engagement].

From Dhammadutta Thero's perspective, it was the induction of Christianity in Tamil regions of Sri Lanka that had torn the social fabric and debilitated Sinhala-Tamil and Buddhist-Hindu coexistence. In his view, the two religious traditions are stitched together by shared cultural traditions; it was conversion to Christianity rather than inherent Sinhala-Tamil enmity that had engendered communal conflict in Sri Lanka. While Reverend Dhammadutta suggested that Catholic and Christian clergy are hostile toward Buddhism and Buddhist monks, he would occasionally concede that *some* Catholic and Christian figures, particularly those Sinhala Christians in southern Sri Lanka, are "good" and cooperative. He argued that significant capacities for discernment—of the type that he himself exercised—were necessary to differentiate between those Christians ("Catholics") who were upstanding citizens and those who were oriented by malignant anti-national persuasions.

Other Buddhist monks and lay Buddhist protectionists enunciated similar views. Their statements implied that it was Christianity that had given rise to Tamils' sedition and secessionism. Further, they argued that Tamils' insurgency was sparked by Catholic, Protestant, and other "fundamentalist" Christian practices of distributing charity in the northern and eastern war-torn regions of Sri Lanka. In Sinhala nationalist rhetorics, the Tamil rebel leader, Velupillai Prabhakaran, had become a dissident only after disavowing the "religion of his birth" to become a Catholic (or a Methodist, in other versions of the lore). To the contrary, however, Prabhakaran's biographer insists that the "elusive" rebel leader had been born a Hindu and had never converted to Christianity—that Prabhakaran's only "religion," if his zeal could be characterized as such, was Tamil nationalism.[32] But in the popular majoritarian nationalist imaginary, the LTTE leader had purportedly converted from Hinduism to Christianity, and this renunciation of the religion of his birth was believed to have caused him to become an upstart and to demand far more for the minority than what was commensurate with minority numbers in a majority Sinhala Buddhist nation.[33]

The All-Ceylon Buddhist Congress report on unethical conversions pointed to potentialities for anti-nationalism ignited by the transnational forces of Christian and secular giving. As stated in the report, "We cannot put into figures the enormous monetary help that Sri Lanka received after the tsunami. Problems arose from the aid that was received in dollars and sterling pounds" (158, section 686). It further alleged:

> There were three problems with regard to the monetary aid Sri Lanka received. The first was, that the money and aid was coming in under the guise of humanitarian aid was actually going to the Tamil Tigers. . . . The second was that the Disaster Management Center had spent huge amounts of money to cater to the needs of the NGOs that had arrived to the island. The final one was that Buddhists, Hindu and Muslim people were harassed by the NGOs in their big effort to convert them to Christianity. (158, section 687)

The compounded set of issues concerning foreign humanitarian aid resulted in the perception among Sinhala Buddhists that the seditious, anti-national Tamil Tigers, NGOs' humanitarian operations, and expansionary ambitions of Christians, are all cut from the same poisonous cloth.

Along these lines, Dhammadutta Thero adopted a revisionist "postethnicity" explanation for the Sinhala-Tamil conflict, which appears to have superseded long held nationalistic discourses that there was an inherent "racial" basis for the conflict.[34] Such revisionism is indicative of how Sinhala Buddhist nationalists retrospectively recognized the conflict with Tamils as contingent, rather than a matter of inherent difference. In using this reasoning, a displacement and rearticulation of blame is evident. In postwar discourses, state-run and Sinhala Buddhist civilian-run operations were envisioned as crucial to the process of "reconciliation" by "rehabilitating" internally displaced Tamil people. They construed Tamil IDPs as having been enculturated into Tamil nationalism and anti-Sinhala sentiments under the reign of the LTTE secessionists. As Sinhala anti-conversion activists had it, they had been drawn into the Tamil rebellion under the implicit sway of Christianity.

Statist postwar campaigns projected an image of a polity that eagerly sought to transcend the ethno-religious nationalisms that had divided Sri Lanka. These discourses of reconciliation hinged upon the radical refiguration and reassimilation of Tamils, who rather than being potential traitors and "terrorists" could be rehabilitated and transformed into citizens through moral guidance and care. According to this strand of postwar majoritarian rhetoric, any residual anti-Sinhala Buddhist sentiment among Tamils was treated as a problem fueled from *outside*, by the Tamil diaspora. Sinhala Buddhist nationalists reasoned that the Tamil diaspora had been fostered in the "Christian" West, and those who left during the war were thus enculturated in liberal sensibilities and inclined to act as enemies of the postcolonial Sri Lankan state. Likewise, Dhammadutta Thera held that Sri Lankan Tamil converts to Christianity had been denuded of homegrown, autochthonous Lankan values and that it was their adoption of Christianity, rather than being Tamil, that disposed them toward continued hostility toward Sinhala Buddhists.

———— ◆ ————

Christians' and Western secularists' tendencies to negatively appraise the moral and material value of Buddhism have contributed to Sinhala Buddhists' imperatives to jealously guard their nation's ethnoreligious inheritances and its capacities to wield soft power. Internationalist expressions of generosity, materialized as charity, foreign aid, and humanitarian critique, are instruments of that soft power. One way that majoritarian nationalists concertedly strive to guard Sri Lanka's inheritances amid such uneven geopolitical dynamics is to publicly exhibit the depth of Buddhists' generosity for the world stage. In 2010, Charities Aid Foundation, an international organization, issued a country ranking of the world's most generous givers. According to this World Giving Index, Sri Lanka was ranked eighth, tied with the United Kingdom. Other Theravādin Buddhist countries including Laos and Myanmar also ranked very highly, alongside countries of the Global North. Their high rank gave Sri Lanka and other predominantly Theravādin Buddhist countries reason to celebrate. Nightly newscasts highlighted these soundbites in Sinhala and English as a point of pride from the first instance in 2010, and in each consecutive year that Sri Lanka captured high marks in the index to this day. Receiving acknowledgment of Sri Lankans' superior generosity is remarkably meaningful for Sinhala Buddhists and serves as a resounding source of national pride. As a result of the tensions produced since the colonial missionary encounter, Sinhala Buddhist nationalists have considered Buddhist charitable giving to the poor and vulnerable to be a bulwark against Christian conversion. Public, global acknowledgment of Buddhists' generosity and self-sufficiency shores up their sense of Buddhist sovereignty over the nation.

Religious gifts signify a multitude of things—moral, material, spiritual, and ontological. In this context of stark interreligious competition, giving is a potent modality for religious attraction. For Christians, charity can serve as medium and conduit for grace that establishes and perpetuates covenantal commitments. For Sinhala Buddhists, giving to mendicant monks and others in need is a meritorious practice that can generate merit and karmic rewards for all involved in the transaction, furthering all parties along their samsaric paths. Yet, depending upon the source of the gift, in the view of many Sinhala Buddhists material provisioning might serve to lead a person astray, detracting one from the persons' natal trajectory of moral development. For devoted Sinhala Buddhists, the gifts offered by well-heeled Christians to the poor can be particularly upsetting to that ascent—a view that adds to the ire of anti-conversion activists.

Mauss's classic formulation on the gift emphasized the "total social fact" of giving which would inevitably tie people together in a set of cohesive social bonds and stave off conflict. For European social theorists, the charitable gift economy functioned alongside and extended into what would otherwise be an alienating capitalist economy (see Bloch and Parry 1989). But precisely because religious gifts can be a vehicle for religious attraction, the charitable gift can be a profound source of religious contest. The differences between Christian charity and the Buddhist ethos of *dāna*, which entails care for and patronage of the Buddhist clergy, are an enduring source of interreligious antipathy in Sri Lanka and elsewhere in Theravādin Southeast Asia. From the point of view of Sinhala Buddhists, the Christian genealogies that inform secularized conceptions of religious freedom cannot easily be assimilated to their own conceptions of what it means to have a free conscience. Thus construed, the "negative right" to be free *from* impingements and "allurements" that block the free flourishing of the mind implicitly inflects the political discourse of Sri Lankan anti-conversion activists.

Distinctive paradigms of Buddhist *dāna* and Christianity charity shape conflicting logics of giving and religious propagation. As seen in the mutual derogations of "selfish" forms of religiosity, comparison of incommensurable practices of giving means that both Christians and Buddhists tend to use unfitting criteria in the judgments they foist upon one another. This is particularly evident inasmuch as these traditions are historically situated along variegated gradients of power. The differences in Buddhists' and Christians' religious criteria and repertoires for giving provides substantial fodder for interreligious argument, especially concerning what it means to be a generous social being and concerning who is capable or incapable of freely making discernments with respect to individuated religious commitments. In the conjuncture between post-tsunami and postwar circumstances, humanitarian critiques from the Global North clashed with local imperatives to reinstate majoritarian sovereignty, self-rule, and supremacy over the country. Contests over giving have lent themselves to consternation over conversion and raised questions about where givers' political sympathies lie, and how recipients might be corrupted by the obligations that arise from the seductions of the religious gift.

CHAPTER 3

Mediating Miracles

Buddhism does not hold out worldly advantages or immediate rewards in this life to its votaries, so much as demonism does. Its task is the graver one, of pointing out a way (though an erroneous one) of obtaining salvation for the soul; an object which is to be obtained, only after passing through many transmigrations of the soul, through countless million years—a consummation therefore which, however devoutly wished for by a Buddhist, is still one to be attained only in another state of existence, at some unknown distant period of time. Demonism, on the other hand, deals with the concerns of this life, and of this life alone. This therefore, appeals more to the passions and the feelings, in as much as it relates to things nearer and present. Hence, demonism never lost its hold on men's minds, but, on the contrary, it still continues to be the most popular of all forms of worship prevailing among the Singhalese.

—Dandris de Silva Gooneratne, *On Demonology and Witchcraft in Ceylon*, 1865

As Christianity and polytheism entered into mortal combat, miracles became a major weapon in the arsenal of Christianity.

—Robert Garland, "Miracles in the Greek and Roman World"

For believing Pentecostals, miracles saturate everyday life. Iterated and reiterated in the testimonials that Christian converts enunciate in Pentecostal prayer halls, gospel rallies, and churches in Sri Lanka, conversion itself is a "miracle" (*prātihārya*) enabled by the inflowing of the Holy Spirit (*Śuddha Ātmaya*). Beyond the quotidian platforms for Christian witnessing in and outside of church services where Christians "share the Good News" (*Subha*

Aranchīya paturanawa), escape and survival in the 2004 Indian Ocean tsunami catastrophe was a potent site for testimonies of miraculous intercession. In the course of the extraordinary devastation, miracles were a significant node for religious attraction, and thus for interreligious antagonism too. In littoral cities, towns, and villages of Sri Lanka, discourses of miracles took a sharply competitive tone, anchoring rivalries, and intensifying animosity between religious communities. Buddhists and Christians commonly asserted the superiority of their own tradition over that of the other. Miracles and opinions on the value and efficacy of a given form of religiosity became matters of comparative judgment and religious reckoning (Mahadev, "Karma"). On the basis of their distinctive doctrinal premises, Theravāda Buddhists and Pentecostal Christians are differently enjoined to celebrate miracles. They moreover differently conceive of the sanctifying power of spiritual agents who produce worldly miracles, and in turn their theologies hold distinct ideologies of religious sovereignty.

Christian evangelists aspirationally project growth through their charismatic rhetoric and practice. Ministerial teams strive to consolidate this growth through various media technologies that render their miracles spectacular and amplify the allure of churchgoing. In turn, Sinhala Buddhist anti-conversion activists harness Sinhala news media to warn against Christian proselytizers and against churches that appear to be "springing up like mushrooms" in firmly established Buddhist areas. However, in the charismatic paradigm, Pentecostals conceive of miracles as a sanctifying force that enacts sovereign authority over the self (Marshall 2009).[1] Testimonies within Pentecostal churches extoll how the experience of the Holy Spirit is a "live and direct" modality of Christian power which itself cements conviction (Meyer 2010). According to this reasoning about the inherent persuasiveness of Christian miracles, my Sri Lankan Pentecostal interlocutors argue that born-again conversions are not undertaken unethically. In their view, such conversions cannot be considered "unethical" because they are not undertaken entirely as a matter of the human will. As they see it, it is the will of God that incites conviction and the conversion experience, and therefore they consider conversion to be a "miraculous" event.

Pentecostalist conceptions of miracles and their attendant sense of sovereignty over people and place present a significant departure from conceptions of dharmic sacra within the established tradition of Sri Lankan Buddhism. These disparate theopolitical orientations to miracles produce a profound site of conflict between Sinhala Buddhists and charismatic Christian evangelists. As scholars of Sri Lanka have amply shown, ritual officiants legitimized rule through ceremonial enactments of sovereignty that attached the polity, place, and the Sinhala people to the power vested in the Buddha's Sacred Tooth Relic (Malalgoda 1976; Seneviratne 1999). Heritage-based inscriptions of Buddhist sovereignty geomantically link the seat of dharmic power in the precolonial capital to satellite towns and rural peripheries. Yet, as the following ethnography makes clear, competing rituals of charismatic Christian "anointing" discursively reinforce expansionary evangelical aspirations by sanctifying and thus disciplining the person as well as the social and material environment. As such, charismatic Christian practices are fraught in this context precisely because, as discursive endeavors, they seek to challenge Buddhists' sacralization of the land, people, polity—that is to say, to their hegemonic majoritarian claims over territory. These disputes over conversion implicate rival forms of miracles that imbue distinct religious potencies into the social body. The upshot is that while Sinhala Buddhists take themselves to be "sons of the soil," they consider Christians who proclaim charismatic materialization of the spirit to be participating in religious repertoires that seek to encroach upon this soil. In fostering exclusivist emplacements and commitments of the people, Buddhist revivalists and charismatic Christian evangelists find themselves situated on disputed terrain.

Starting with the theopolitical claims attached to these distinct Buddhist and Christian styles of miracles, I analyze the rival discourses of religious sovereignty and territorial dominion. The ritual mediations that are at the core of charismatic Christian propagation are met with remediated messages put forth by nationalistic Sinhala Buddhist entities. Buddhist protectionists leverage vernacular news media to groom and shape the perceptions of the Sri Lanka public, emphasizing how new Christian forms pose dangers to the vitality, health, and esteem of the nation's heritage.

PENTECOSTALIST SOVEREIGNTY OF MIRACLES

For Pentecostals, the Holy Spirit is the singular modality for divine intercession, a sovereign hand in the "miracle" of conversion. Yet Pentecostalist and evangelical aspirations powerfully exceed the self. Analogously, the Holy Spirit is believed to infuse material life not only to sanctify individual persons but also to infuse and bless Christian place and polity (Marshall 2009; McAlister and

Napolitano 2021). In many contexts this charismatic sovereignty of miracles bears implications for born-again expansion that rest upon a more or less overtly political conception of governance and territorial expansion (Bialecki 2015; de Abreu 2021, Haynes 2021). Rhetorically, Pentecostal-charismatic ministers project hope for wholesale religious change—an ethos of evangelical expansion which, in a fraught context, is not necessarily taken fully on board by otherwise observant Christian converts. These relatively newly arriving styles of dominionist ministerial discourses extol a coming kingdom of God. In doing so in Sri Lanka, these Christians encounter a very different conception of Buddhist sovereignty. The point of interrogating this rival form of Buddhist sovereignty is consonant with anthropologist Robert Blunt's (2019) observation that distinctive, intersecting forms of sovereignty are commonly found within colonial and postcolonial contexts, and thus that the concept of sovereignty requires relativization and theorization beyond what is derived from European political forms.

For majoritarian nationalists, Sinhala Buddhist sovereignty over Sri Lanka is textually validated through the *Mahāvaṃsa* chronicles. The mythohistorical chronicles document the implantation of the first seeds of Sinhala Buddhist sovereignty with the arrival of Prince Vijaya from India in the sixth century BCE, and gradual inhabitation by the "people of the lion" (Kapferer [1988] 2012; Spencer, *Sri Lanka: History*). The *Mahāvaṃsa* tells the legend of how Sinhala settler sovereignty was sown and gradually grew into the dominion of the Sinhala as an ethnolinguistic "race" (*jathīya*). Sinhala place-making was fortified by the rooting of Buddhist kingship, monastic development, the growth of devoted Buddhist laity, and rituals associated with guardian deities, who together upheld the values of the "Triple Gem," the Buddha, the *Dhamma* (teachings), and the Sangha (clerical order). Later, in the centuries when European colonialism was experienced as a threat to sovereignty and pride, nationalists looked to the *Mahāvaṃsa* to validate how the fructification of Buddhist morality had served to civilize the land as the domain of Sinhalas long before the arrival of European colonialism (Smith 1978; Kapferer [1988] 2012; Obeyesekere 1989; Rogers 1990; Spencer, *Sri Lanka: History*). Thus, as I will detail, competing ritual enactments of sovereignty create entanglements over religious presence down to the spiritual and material substance of the people, the soil, and the polity. With the collective conviction of devotees, these identitarian communities seek to build metonymic connections to sovereignty to advance religious presence miraculously and providentially, albeit in accord with very different cosmological timescales.

Animated utterances about the Christian god's vitality reverberate within the space of Pentecostal deliverance ministries. In charismatic prayer—especially in varieties characteristic of Pentecostalism's "Third Wave"—deliverance ministers engage exuberant maledictive speech and gestures to vanquish "demons" and demonic spirits (*Yakśa Ātmaya*) that are enfolded within the unchristened landscape. Within the frame of these deliverance rituals, a common refrain is that the Lord Buddha is "only a statue" (*pilimaya vitharai*) with "no living presence," one that has no bearing on the world today. The refrain is usually followed by a contrasting proclamation that extolls Jesus as a vitalistic presence who actively works in and through the lives of believers. "*Jesu wahansē jiwitta innawa!!* Jesus is ALLLLIVVVE!" Ministerial proclamations of charismatic presence and alleged absence of divine power expressively seek to orient people toward Christian belief, often by highlighting purported deficiencies of Buddhism. When Sinhala Buddhists overhear these diabolizing maledictions, as they occasionally do, they take charismatics' declarations about sanctifying Christian grace to be an encroachment on their religious sovereignty.

Picking up on the murmurs and charismatic shouts, rumors, and contentions that are evinced from charismatic Christian spheres of activity, networks of Sinhala Buddhist nativists and nationalists in turn rebuff these "fundamentalist" Christian assertions of spiritual warfare. One way they do so is by exerting influence over vernacular Sinhala- and English-language news media in the country. From time to time in popular newspapers, nightly television newscasts and radio reporting, and specialized Buddhist publications, anti-conversion activists undermine the profusion of born-again miracle claims by casting the work of Christian ministers in unflattering terms. Buddhists and Christians mutually extend these hostilities, partaking in rivalrous and symbolically violent discourses and rituals of spiritual warfare while standing at a distance from one another. Occasionally, they create the conditions for physical violence. Acts of vigilantism, harassment, and violence against Christians in turn further fuel international evangelical advocacy networks whereby ministers of far-distant Christian congregations transmit their messages locally. Oftentimes via global televangelism they ask believers to "pray for the universal persecuted church" (Castelli 2005).

The consternation over acts of spreading the "Good News" through proselytism hinges upon religious media and mediation in a double sense: the first is the macro matter of religious publicity that draws attention to and renders spectacular sacred power. Second, considering Christian and Buddhist miracles in a comparative frame makes evident the profound differences in the way that sacred power is conceived as being righteously and efficaciously transmitted within these forms of religiosity. These mediating rituals promise practitioners divine communion or the dawning of profound dharmic awareness and insight. Christians comparatively engage Buddhist cosmological concepts, and vice versa, to spar over theology. But more than an engagement with the ideational content of theology, religious practitioners deal in questions of ontological states and materializations of various kinds of spirits that can pass in and out of the human sensorium. The doctrinal premises of Pentecostal-charismatic Christianity and of the Theravādin Dharma produce distinct ideological and liturgical structures that shape how sacred power is and ought to be transduced, engaged, and mediated, to cross gaps in space and time for the realization of soteriological goals. Understanding how these distinctive modalities and mediums of religious transmission are rooted in distinctive Buddhist and Pentecostal theologies provides a clearer picture of the clash of these religiosities as their adherents respectively seek to retain territory and gain new ground.

For anthropologists working at the intersection of religion and media, the "problem of presence" is a central feature of religiosity (Engelke 2007). The problem is this: in any religious formation there is a gap between the self and the ultimate soteriological goal. There is a gap between self and salvation through God, and between self and the goal of *nibbāna* or "awakening" within Buddhism. This gap must be traversed or mediated. How religious practitioners conceive of righteously and effectively bridging this gap—through vision, audition, or through other sensory apparatuses, and by way of specific mediums, such as texts, icons, and various other technologies—is laden in particular sensibilities structured by doctrinally rooted traditions of religious transmission, what Keane (2007) calls "semiotic ideologies." Further, how these semiotic ideologies are expressed in a given religious milieu as well as how these ideologies, and expression itself, may be informed by technological advances are matters central to understanding the production of the "sensational forms" of a tradition or new religious configuration (Meyer 2009, 2012). These concerns have clear consequences for disputes over religious publicity and public religions. To illuminate the competing imperatives to make miracles newsworthy, I now turn to a discussion of the tsunami disaster, and the eschatological meanings that Catholics, Buddhists, and Pentecostals impute to tales of survival amid catastrophic loss.

DISASTER, THE SECOND COMING,
AND DISCORD AMONG NEIGHBORS

In the southern tsunami-afflicted town of Matara, the black waters had devastated large swaths of land, sweeping away the vegetable market, bus depot, and several buildings—including some of the buildings enclosed within the Dutch colonial fort. More than 450 townspeople were counted dead in the tragedy. The buildings of some religious entities remained intact, whereas other nearby buildings were demolished. Farther down the road, the tsunami hit the Catholic church and convent school facing the beach. Several of the parish buildings were left in ruins. When the waves struck the sanctuary, various Eucharistic implements were demolished or were dispersed and lost. The sacred statue of the Virgin Mary was swept away from the sanctorum. But several days later, a Buddhist man found it lying among the rubble on the beach, far away from the church. He returned her to the parish, fully intact and still softly smiling. Parishioners deemed the statue of Mother Mary to be "miraculous," and the Buddhist man who returned her was celebrated as a forever friend to the parish. The miracle was storied to be in continuity with a prior set of miraculous recoveries of this particular statue of the Virgin. For example, during the early 1900s, Church authorities had shipped her by sea back to Belgium for restoration, but her container was mistakenly directed to another European port. She was waylaid for many months and feared missing. But "by the grace of God" and by the powers of Lady Mary herself, she was ultimately restored and returned to the small colonial parish on the southern coast of Ceylon. Sri Lankan Catholics referenced the multiple miraculous recoveries of the Virgin, thereby extending the parish's claim to her divine efficacies.

Catholic and Pentecostal Christians certainly did not have the monopoly over tales of tsunami miracles, however. In the nearby coastal city of Galle, stories of how people miraculously survived by clutching onto an apparently indestructible statue of the Buddha were published in Sri Lankan newspapers and circulated in everyday tellings of survival stories. It was a common point of comment among ethnic Sinhalas that a Muslim man's life had also been spared in this way. In these exceptional circumstances Sinhala Buddhists extolled how the Lord Buddha's *Dhamma* became manifest as a kind of cosmic will, animating a miraculous intercessional presence that intervened in the samsaric life course of survivors. In still another rustic seaside locale some forty kilometers in the other direction of Matara town, one finds a life-size diorama of the Buddha delivering a discourse on the *Dhamma* (*Dhammadesanawa*) to his inner circle of disciples. On ordinary days, the waves lap the white concrete foundation of the diorama. On the day when the vicious tsunami waves hit the shore, the diorama miraculously remained intact whereas several monks living in the nearest inland village monastery were killed. This became a point of comment and critique among lay Buddhists of the area. Some of my interlocutors in surrounding villages pointed to the phenomenon as evidence of the strength manifest in the original presence of the Buddha's *Dhamma*, in contrast to the eroded capacity of modern-day members of the sangha to embody the *Dhamma*. Such reproachful views are not uncommon in popular discourse. Even as respect for the sangha is paramount in Theravādin tradition and practice, many laity reckon that precious few living monks are worthy of high esteem. Of course, the laity's veneration of and in some cases even fandom toward monastic clerics who are deemed worthy of their robes is striking.[2] Nevertheless, the laity's reproachful views of monks are consonant with the overarching premise that only the rarest of monks are capable of embodying the rules of the *Vinaya* (monastic rules) and fully realizing dharmic virtues in these times. These judgments accord with the doctrinal view of the cosmos, which posits that the purest, most lucid iterations of the *Dhamma* exist only in the age of a living, preaching, teaching Buddha.

A dense field of religious judgment was consolidated in the aftermath of the tsunami catastrophe, wherein people of all kinds made thick and thin claims of miraculous exceptionalism. Religious actors consistently framed these fortuitous moments of survival as evidence of how they laid exceptional claim to tap the will of intercessory cosmic agents. This exceptionalism is perhaps most stark within Pentecostalism, where the prolific, quotidian character of miracle discourses, of storied discontinuities and radical Manichean overcoming of adversity, is said to bring to fruition the fullness of an individual's born-again belief. With the tsunami, the circulation of miracle stories among Pentecostals was voluble indeed. Catastrophes remind evangelical Christians of prognostications of end-times. Escaping and overcoming the devastation of the natural disaster powerfully resonates with broader charismatic Christian claims of owning the exceptional ontological capacities to tap into God's grace.

A few years after the tsunami tragedy I made several sustained visits to a Pentecostal church situated along the southern littoral. The church had "miraculously" evaded the grip of the catastrophe. Just a few days after attending the

Christmas Day service at this church in 2010, I waited to meet with the head pastor, Pastor Jayanth. Adorning the walls of the church lobby was a mosaic of posters written in Sinhala and English. One called for the prevention of domestic violence, a glossy one encouraged breastfeeding, and a third poster described the science behind a tsunami. One faded black-and-white photocopy of a poster waxed ominous in English on Christ's Second Coming: "'I will shake heaven and earth, the sea and dry land. And I will shake all nations.' God is shaking the World! Unless you repent, you will Perish! Even now, God is preparing for Judgment Day. Are you?"

After several earlier conversations with Pastor Jayanth, on this occasion I eventually steered my inquiry to gently ask whether he was concerned about persecution. I had come with awareness of the popularity of this church; of the precarity Pentecostals faced, especially in the southern districts of Sri Lanka; and of the resentments held by other Christians and Buddhists that had stacked up against Pastor Jayanth over the years since he had established his ministry. Just as carefully as I had asked, he conveyed that there was nothing controversial in his ministerial work and that thus he was not invested in preparing his congregation for persecution. Rather, Pastor Jayanath insisted, his objective was to prepare members of his church for the End of Days (*Antīyama Kālē*): "At that time Jesus will come to the sky . . . to the clouds actually, and will lift up those who are Saved from the coming destruction. I want my people to be prepared to be with Jesus."

Pastor Jayanth's experience of the 2004 tsunami was well known about the town and had even made headlines internationally in BBC2's special coverage of instances of "religious resilience" in several tsunami-affected countries. The BBC2 news story cast him as a "Miracle Man" who had stopped the waves with the power of his prayers that Sunday. With the characteristic flair of his testimonial style, he reiterated the story of how he had beseeched god to intervene. Pastor Jayanth prayed as he ran from the first wave. He then found himself perched on a high tree branch as the second wave approached. The waves had destroyed neighboring buildings, but in response to his prayers a sinkhole suddenly opened up and funneled the black waters away, sparing his church and his people. The publicity surrounding his eventful survival enhanced Pastor Jayanth's profile as one who could wield profound spiritual gifts through prayer. This news, as well as Pastor Jayanth's preaching, brought several newcomers to his church—and, as I learned from other local pastors, to some of the neighboring mainline

Christian churches. Yet Pastor Jayanth was lavished with attention in the aftermath of the tsunami, stoking skepticism, jealousy, and even quiet condemnation from the clergy of neighboring Catholic and Protestant establishments. One Anglican priest from another church in town recounted how Pastor Jayanth had once asked to borrow his cassock. Half-laughing, the priest explained how the Pentecostal minister had used his priestly cassock as a pattern for his own sartorial designs. The priest alleged that Pastor Jayanth had modeled his ministerial vestments upon his own, so as to give newcomers to the newfangled charismatic church visual cues to indicate his credibility. Local irritations concerning the Pentecostal pastor festered in other corners too. Pastor Jayanth's assertive recruitment efforts, the boisterous sounds of worship that emanate from his church, combined with other generalized resentments toward charismatic propagators of Christianity, had occasionally provoked the monks of a neighboring Buddhist temple to target Pastor Jayanth with complaints and hostility (see also chapter 5).

Considering miracles in the very different context of ancient Athens, the classicist Robert Garland addressed the advance of Christianity, remarking, "As Christianity and polytheism entered into mortal combat, miracles became a major weapon in the arsenal of Christianity" (2011, 87). Similarly, with the increased visibility of neo-Pentecostalism in Sri Lanka over the last few decades, charismatic Christian claims of miracles and "miraculous conversions" became a significant node of interreligious conflict. Yet, however much born-again charismatic Christians share the Good News by seeking to publicize the efficacy of their charismatic miracles, Sri Lankan Buddhists equally engage Sinhala-language news media to directly undercut Christians' claims.

THE ORDINARY AND THE EXTRAORDINARY

The circulating discourses over tsunami miracles lay bare the extent to which the agentive capacities of the deity or karmic destiny itself are believed to manifest in extraordinary times. Religious tensions surfaced therein. In ordinary times, however, it becomes apparent that Christian and Buddhist sensibilities about miracles are really rather different. For Sri Lankan Pentecostals, miracles are said to happen daily. In contrast, by the dictates of Buddhist modernism and conservative approaches to the textual tradition, miracles are a rarity. Although

Pāli Buddhist canonical texts are loaded with tales of Gotama Buddha's superhuman miracles, these "miracles" (*prātihārya*) are not treated as "supernatural" intercession, but rather are "natural" phenomenon associated with the profound mental achievements of the Buddha and a few exceptional disciples (Gethin 2011, 217). *Vinaya* monastic codes bar the use of miracles as a means of attracting followers (Fiordialis 2010). Accordingly, those who have genuinely attained advanced dharmic states of consciousness will not be inclined to showcase miracles theatrically merely to attract disciples.

Nevertheless, Sinhala Buddhists do see miracles in states of emergency and exception, such as those discussed earlier. What is more, within Sinhala Buddhism there is whole pantheon of deities and spirits, hierarchically subsumed under the supermundane (*lōkkōtara*) authority of the Buddha (Obeyesekere 1963, 1981; Holt 1991). Within traditionalist spheres of religiosity, these deities and spirits are treated as having a tangible material and affective bearing upon the world. Sinhala deity mediums channel the power of deities to mediate the worldly (*laukika*) affairs of humans. They are conduits for the magical and miraculous capacities of deities and demigods who positively intercede in the human world, ritually blessing, "cutting" sorcery curses (*sunnīyan*), and allowing supplicants' lives to flourish (Obeyesekere 1981; Scott 1994; Kapferer 1997; de Silva 2000, 2006).

Venerating deities and demigods; transacting in ritual offerings, vows, and boons with them; engaging in divination, geomancy, and astrology; and making bargains with lower spirits for protection and ensorcellment constitute the hierarchical array of traditionalist Sinhala Buddhist popular religion. Ritual officiants leading these practices tend to be gifted laypeople who are often but not exclusively from categorically "lower" status backgrounds. They occupy a position relatively far removed from the ordained monks whose investments are oriented to normative moral teachings and the *lōkkōtara* pursuit of *nibbāna*. For the adepts who practice them, these *laukika* (worldly) ritual arts are deemed to be appropriate to their relatively subaltern and karmically disadvantaged station in life (Simpson 1997).

In Sri Lanka, sanction (*varam*) from the gods grants the lay Buddhist deity mediums capacities for divination, production of *yāntra* (talismans), and performance of apotropaic rituals. In contrast to the magic of lay adepts, within the Theravādin traditions of Thailand and Burma one commonly finds "magical" monks (McDaniel 2011). In contemporary Burmese *Weikza* cults, monks engage in apotropaic rituals, alchemy, talisman creation and *yāntra* diagramming, medicinal practices, and mantras (chanting) (Brac de la Perrière et al. 2014; Patton 2018). Although often diminished as improperly Buddhist, for many Burmese Buddhists *Weikza* is a pathway toward *nibbāna* that engages a more "circuitous route" to *nibbāna* than its counterpart, Vipassana meditation, which coexists alongside of it (Brac de la Perrière et al. 2014, ix). In the case of Sri Lanka, rather than Buddhist monks it is typically a separate class of lay priests, priestesses, and ritual officiants who deal with deities and conduct apotropaic rituals that are considered to be highly efficacious in worldly terms. These practices are considered to be perfectly in sync with Buddhism, even if they engage a meandering karmic pathway toward far-distant soteriological goals.[3]

On Sinhala television programming, an occasional scrolling marquee appears advertising the work of monks who are uniquely adept in miracle work and in the telling of prophecies. Some Sinhala Buddhists are roused to curiosity and interest in magical monks. But in the main, Sinhala Buddhist reformers and revivalists denigrate the practices of magical monks as completely out of step with dharmic teachings. With more media attention given to miracles and to magical monks and gurus in Sri Lanka, certain figures occasionally rise to prominence. But their popularity tends to be greatly circumscribed, since their miraculous capabilities are typically diminished by reformist strands of the Buddhist sangha (see chapter 5). Few Sri Lankan Buddhist monks are lauded for their success in these arts, and those who publicize such skills are typically deemed to be charlatans. The tendency among upper- and middle-class Sinhala Buddhists and reformist monks to disparage the use of miracles as gimmicks that do not achieve true depth of the practice necessary to realize the *Dhamma* inheres in doctrine as well as in the purifying ideologies of Buddhist modernism (Gombrich and Obeyesekere 1988). Buddhist modernists tend to disavow deity veneration, reductively characterizing them as "Hindu" or "pre-Buddhist" gods. This is ironic given that four guardian deities serve as spiritual and material protectors of the Tooth Relic and by extension of Sinhala Buddhist sovereignty. In the forms of Sinhala Buddhism typically practiced among the middle class and elite of Sri Lanka, the modernist approach of a positivistic and rather disenchanted orientation to the world is quite strong (Obeyeskere 1970; Gombrich and Obeyeskere 1988). It is important to note, though, that the modernization of Buddhism is not a totalizing phenomenon, insofar as middle- and upper-class Buddhists sometimes involve themselves in experimentation, seeking out deities, gurus, and spirits to intervene in their mundane affairs according to the vagaries of life.[4]

The drift from "traditional" Sinhala Buddhism deepened along class lines largely as a response to colonial and Protestant Christian critiques of localized "superstition." Rather differently from mainline Protestantism though, Pentecostal Christianity "takes the devil seriously" as a force for sin and evil in the world. Pentecostalist discourses contentiously render local spiritual practices and presences as diabolical agents of Satan and seek to root those demonic agents out of the established religious landscape through charismatic ritual means.

THE SOVEREIGNTY OF MIRACLES

The Good News Calvary Church was always brimming with people during my Sunday morning visits. Situated in the outskirts of Colombo, the deliverance ministry occupied the fourth floor of a building that was partially still in use as a factory. On other days noise from the machinery was overpowering, giving Pastor Milton and his ministerial team much to complain about even as they had an abundance of gratitude for their God. But on Sunday mornings it was the charismatic Christian soundscape that reverberated within the old building's walls and wafted outward into the large suburban factory yard.

The refrain that the Lord Buddha is "only a statue" crossfaded into the pastor's bellowing exclamation that "Jesus is ALIVVEEEEEE!" Maxed-out amplifiers transmitted the pronouncement of Christ's vitality with heavy reverb. Pastor Milton's punctuated remarks were underlaid by the congregation's glossolalic utterances, which added further density to the soundscape. The layers of sound yielded a mesmerizing dissonance. Miracles of sanctification, healing, and prosperity are embodied, felt, and transduced through the touch of the Holy Spirit. Members of the congregation seek to access Christ's charism or gift of grace through the ineffable material trace of the Spirit. These charismatic healing practices are prominent in Sunday services where hundreds of devotees present themselves at Good News Calvary Church and various other nondenominational deliverance ministries to haptically receive the Holy Spirit. Most of those who gather there are propelled into varyingly exuberant states of praise and worship.

Assertions over the vitality and abiding presence of the Christian God are common within Pentecostal-charismatic practices of witnessing and evangelizing. Theologically, the possibility of miraculous conversion is shored up by the New Testament story of the Apostle Paul. Anthropologists of Pentecostalism identify a "neo-Pauline" turn in Christianity (Bialecki 2010; Robbins 2010). Pauline expressions of grace arrive spontaneously from on high via the Holy Spirit to interrupt the flow of historical and quotidian continuity. Saint Paul is considered to be an exception among exceptions. Unlike the other Apostles, he was not present at the Last Supper and did not receive a substantive, corporeal transmission from the living Jesus. Rather, Paul became inducted as a "believing servant" of Christ well after Christ's ascension. Charismatic ministers in Sri Lanka commonly emphasize the story of the conversion of Paul in their sermons. Based upon the Pauline Epistles, they tell of the dramatic sequence that preceded his conversion. One such iteration of the story was shared at a praise and worship service in Colombo I attended with Crystal, a born-again Christian, along with her religiously experimental husband and her Buddhist father-in-law, who had recently been diagnosed with cancer. To the congregation of several hundreds who had gathered at his church on a Tuesday night, the pastor exuberantly recalled the Damascene scene:

> The Jew named Saul was a *harsh* persecutor of Christians. But on the road to Damascus, he was struck down from his horse with a blinding vision! With his momentary blindness Saul heard the voice of God. God spoke to him, and he was graced with a *charism* direct from the heavens. Saul immediately turned toward the voice of God! This epiphany turned Saul away from his terrible persecution of Christians, towards firm belief in Christ as the Savior and Son of God! With that glorious vision, Saul the Persecutor of Christians, became Paul the Apostle of Christ! Halleluiah, Halleluiah, Halleluiah!! *Saul became Paul, you see? You too must experience such a Pauline conversion!*

He exhorted his congregation to evince dramatic certitude in their faith. The instantaneous and miraculous epiphany of Saint Paul, coupled with the "apostolic" experience of the Pentecost wherein the disciples received grace through the Holy Spirit and experienced "tongues of fire" well after Christ's ascension to heaven (Acts 2), are theologically paramount in Pentecostalism. The Pauline model of post-ascension charismatic experience validates the notion that even at a far remove from the corporeal Jesus Christ, charismata (Sinhala: *anu hās* or miraculous presence) are capable of democratically gracing even nonbelievers and turning around the thickest of Christ's adversaries.

Recipients of the "grace-filled touch" of the Holy Spirit are miraculously sanctified and "spontaneously converted." This Pauline theology validates an "acephalous," rhizomatic rather than rooted, profusion of Pentecostal belief (Bialecki 2010, 2017). The experience of the Holy Spirit sanctification is emotionally, corporeally, and spiritually cathartic for those who experience it. The catharsis can be seen in the rises and falls of the charismatic soundscape and the wide-ranging emotive shifts—anguished streams of tears that turn to joyful smiles, exuberance that turns to serenity—in the course of Pentecostal praise sessions. What is more, the universalizing orientation to the evangelical spread of Christianity is validated in Pentecostalism's illiberal political theology (Marshall 2009, 2014). In Marshall's critique, this political theology hinges upon "the absolute transcendent power of the Father [which] takes the form of a horizontal, spectral, and immanent dissemination of the Spirit through language and diaspora—a tongue of fire on every head" (Marshall 2014, 352).

The portable, global charismatic Christian aesthetic form is identifiable in Sri Lanka, with Pentecostal ministers offering praise of god with comparable style and exuberance. In Sinhala, and also in Tamil and English, charismatic ministers' assertions of the vitalistic presence of God are pronounced and punctuated. The Holy Spirit is extolled as sacred, pneumatic breath—the modality for divine presence, which is at the same time synonymous with that presence. Deliverance ministers extol the infusion of the Holy Spirit into the body of a person and the unfurling of glossolalic tongues as signs of sanctification that are tantamount to "being anointed by the Holy Spirit" (*Śuddha Ātmayen ālēpāya*). The spiritual force is said to directly sanctify individuals, producing a communion that is palpably experienced as ontologically transforming the individual into a Christian.

The affective tenor of these deliverance rituals and the promise of Christ's enduring vitality hang thick in the air of these praise and worship sessions. Yet the supersessionist inflection upon the Christian gospels that is prevalent within evangelical and charismatic exegesis produces discourses that are hostile to existing forms of religiosity. Deliverance healing hinges simultaneously upon discourses of Christ's enduring love and symbolic gestures and violent metonyms of freeing newcomers from demonic affliction through "spiritual warfare." In the dramatic rhetoric of spiritual warfare, what is to be expunged are all non-Christian influences in the lives of believers. Whether made explicit or left implicit, the metaphor of expulsion includes expelling the "demons" of religious difference. For Pentecostals who become fully interpellated into belief through these discourses, their God is "alive." This vitality, instantiated through the haptic energetics and "miraculous gifts" of the Holy Spirit, stands to reveal to supplicants the ostensible deficiencies of Buddhism.

THE PROBLEM OF PRESENCE: THE "LIVING GOD" AND THE "THUS-GONE" BUDDHA

From where, when, and how did the notions of Christ's abiding presence and the Lord Buddha's absence enter Sri Lankan Christian iterations of theology? Like the contemporary born-again Pentecostal characterizations of Buddhism, Protestant missionaries writing in the nineteenth and early twentieth centuries expressed similar disdain for Theravāda Buddhism. The missionaries from that era surmised that the Buddha "idol" was "empty" of all divinity, and this "emptiness" in turn oriented Sinhala Buddhists to embrace "false" deities and engage in "devil worship" (Harris 2006, 54–55). In their assertions, the empty space of the idol allowed the devil to seep in, and "usurp the place of God." This is consonant with the idea of "demonism" as detailed in the writings of the Sinhala colonial administrator and convert to Christianity, Dandris de Silva Gooneratne, in the mid–nineteenth century, quoted at length in the epigraph to this chapter.[5] Christian missionaries, colonial administrators, and Sinhala Christian *Mudliyars* such as Gooneratne acted as early rapporteurs on local religious doctrines and practices. In this early documentation on Ceylon, they judged ordinary Sinhala Buddhist "folk" practices to be diabolical (Scott 1994).

While evangelists put a derogatory spin on Buddhist theology with the notion that the "idol" leaves an "empty space" for deities-cum-"false gods" and "demons," a neutral iteration of Buddhist theology has it that the human figure of the Buddha coexists in a moral hierarchy with a spectrum of intercessional deities, demigods, karmically incapacitated hungry ghosts, and fiercely powerful lower spirits. When stated in neutral terms, this idea is actually consistent with the spiritual division of labor found within Sinhala Buddhism. As delineated earlier, within ordinary practice one venerates the Buddha to accrue merit toward achievement of *nibbāna*, a supramundane (*lōkōttara*) pursuit, whereas one approaches deities for boons to fulfill samsaric this-worldly (*laukika*) needs (Obeyesekere 1963; Holt 1991). Traditionally, Sinhala Buddhists do not regard the practice of enlisting the gods to perform boons in one's favor as contravening nirvanic aims. Sinhala Buddhists engage deities through transactions of gifts, beseeching and venerating them, and vowing to return for further worship once the deity makes good on the deal. For fulfilling the prayer request, the supplicant returns to the shrine to worship and, most important, to share merit with the deity.

Other lower spiritual beings, such as *yakśa*, inflict themselves upon human victims, sometimes with malice. *Prēta* ("hungry ghosts") comprise a class of spirits, usually deceased loved ones, who have insufficient stores of good karma to move on to the next lifetime and thus remain stuck in an ontological and spiritual limbo. Having been unsated in the previous lifetime, they cling to their pasts. They are karmically incapacitated by their worldly attachments, and thus the actions of *prēta* chronically misfire in ways that unwittingly afflict the living. *Prēta* are thus biomorally base figures who substantively reflect negative karmic values. Yet *prēta*, and *yakśa* too, are worthy of compassion. The threat of spiritual hauntings by *prēta* impels various practices of ritual care for the dead and prophylaxis in the form of funerary and commemorative practices. Specifically, the rituals involve benefic transfers of the merit to the deceased so that they can fruitfully pass on to the next lifetime. For the living to witness the suffering embodied by the *prēta* as a reflection of negative karma also provides them with an opportunity to reflect upon their own moral conduct and remind them to live out Buddhist values, and thus ensure their own karmic upliftment.

Yakśa and *prēta* cause affliction by setting their sights (*dishtī*) on a socially vulnerable person (Scott 1994, 50; Kapferer 1997). Women are considered to be particularly predisposed to these vulnerabilities. A socially vulnerable person is considered an especially "porous self" because they have insufficient stores of merit and are thereby most prone to being captured in the sights of and become possessed by *yakśa* or *prēta*.[6] In addition to this visual capture, the soundscape is relevant in these interreligious contests too. Ritual drumming offers "sonic protection" against malignant spiritual forces during an array of Sinhala Buddhist rites (Sykes 2019). Jim Sykes demonstrates how Christian missionaries of the colonial era disparaged Sinhala rituals for involving boisterous drumming. The missionaries figured that sonorous rituals did not conform to Buddhist mores of quietude, and considered such noise to produce an aesthetic that was unbecoming of "religion" in general. Sykes demonstrates how the Christian missionary and "protestant secular" proclivity to deride traditional Sinhala Buddhist *tovil* ritual aesthetics, and to instead treat only the tranquil, reflective interiorized form as authentic Buddhist practice, inflects modernist imperatives of Buddhist reform and revival as well.

Quite differently from the modernist imperatives of interiorized reflection and quietude of prayer however, Pentecostalism entails an effusively exteriorized experience that generates a vivacious soundscape. The difference is a matter of dispute even today, as evident in the ways that Sri Lankan Catholic leaders disparage charismatic Pentecostalism for producing an unsavory "cacophonous exuberance" during worship. As I argue in the next chapter, that mainline Sinhala Catholic leadership disparages and dissuades Catholics from partaking in pentecostalist exuberance is part and parcel of a pointedly political project of social differentiation, distinction, and forging a nationalistic alliance with Sinhala Buddhists.

For Pentecostals, the Holy Spirit is the medium that easily and effusively bridges the divide between the person and their god. Conversion entails a perspectival change, wherein the believer retells the narrative of their life with a hermeneutic of wonderment and optimism that animates everyday experiences of miracles. An orientation toward a "miraculous life" hinges upon "disciplined seeing" (Goldstone and Hauerwas 2010). Such forms of seeing are inherent to the charismatic Christian notion of "witness." At the same time, the movements of the spirit are characterized in Pentecostal thought as pneumatic. In pneumatic theology, the idea is that the Holy Spirit traverses the air and is mediated through the breath to access the person's spirit or soul. Blanton describes this "materialization of the spirit" in the context of Pentecostal media transmission in the American South, whereby the pneumatic gesture involves "entwining of bodily movement, song, and breath," and how doing so "grants access to mnemonic surfaces of linguistic-formulaic capacities inaccessible to the everyday faculties of awareness and embodiment" (Blanton 2015, 148). Such experiences entail states of "absorption" that are unequivocally felt, as Bialecki (2017) describes in his ethnography on the Vineyard Pentecostal churches in California. Neo-Pentecostals emphasize that miracles transduced through the Holy Ghost are proof positive of their living God's powerful presence in the world.

Miracles are conceived of as reigning "sovereign over the Pentecostal self" (Marshall 2009). As Marshall demonstrates, in the Nigerian context born-again miracles engender authoritative and authoritarian religious and political convictions, and such a conception of sovereign exceptionalism has a profound impact on the form of governance imagined for the postcolonial nation.[7] Rather differently in the case of South Asia, various forms of Christianity persist as minority religions. Even still, ministerial discourses urge born-again believers to see miracles as sovereign over the self and thus as undeniable to the self. They thus shore up a confessional form of Christianity wherein belief in the miraculous character of God and his gifts is paramount.

In contrast to the ease with which Pentecostals believe they can access God, the "problem of presence" is rather more significant within Theravāda Buddhism, as I have intimated. In Theravādin doctrine, the vastness of the ontological and temporal gap between samsaric persons and the perfectly Enlightened sharer of the *Dhamma* underlies the difficulty of ordinary Buddhists to access and fully embody the *Dhamma*. The vernacular circulations of doctrinal Buddhism, recited in funerary rites and merit-transfer ceremonies, point to how the Buddha as exemplar, and the Buddha's *Dhamma* manifest in his enlightened teachings, are immediately available to humanity only in rare ages when a singular, fully awakened one is living in the world. As the doctrine goes, a Buddha is an awakened human who not only achieves *nibbāna* (enlightenment) but who also preaches the *Dhamma* (Harvey 2013). The presence of dharmic knowledge inevitably becomes weakened when a living Buddha is not present on earth to share the true *Dhamma* with the world (Gombrich 1971; Obeyesekere et al. 1972). With the Buddha's passing, the capacity for dharmic insight wanes and becomes difficult to access until the next Bodhisattva (Buddha-to-come) is to be born on earth. In the Theravādin scriptures, it has been written that there are to be only twenty-eight Buddhas in the history of the world, each of whom is a guarantor of dharmic immediacy for their own time. The current dispensation of the Gotama Buddha is the twenty-seventh, and the Buddha Maitreya, yet to come in the far, far future—after the millennial dissolution of the world and then a cyclical resurgence—is to be the twenty-eighth and final Buddha.

Being in the unmediated presence of a living Buddha and receiving the pure and lucid speech of the *Dhamma* directly from his lips automatically enlightens a hearer. Being able to absorb the *Dhamma* under such conditions, the hearer becomes an *arahāt*—an awakened being who attains *nibbāna* but does not attain Buddhahood because they cannot publicize the means to access the path toward *nibbāna*.[8] Upon death, those who have achieved *nibbāna* (either a Buddha or an *arahāt*) attain *Parinibbāna* (final *nibbāna*), escaping suffering once and for all; they are no longer reborn into *saṃsāra*, the cycles of life, death, and rebirth. Upon attaining *Parinibbāna*, the historical Buddha is reverently referred to as *Tathāgatha*, rendered in English as "the Thus-Gone One." At that point, a Buddha's obligations to the world are complete. In short, an idealist sensibility stems from the doctrines, including the *Cakkavatti-Sīhanāda Sutta*, which convey that it is only a living Buddha who is endowed with superhuman qualities that allows them to capably extoll the pure, lucid *Dhamma* (Collins 1998). His pure iteration of the *Dhamma* instantaneously releases all beings from suffering. Thus, for ordinary Buddhists, while one can strive to learn the *Dhamma* and follow it, to receive the *Dhamma* from the unmediated presence of a *living* Buddha is the only guarantee for perfect understanding and immediate release from *saṃsāra*.

Although a Buddha is capable of performing miracles while living, as a *Tathāgata*, he is "Thus-Gone" or "without karmic remainder," and as such he is generally conceived of as being beyond performing supernatural intercessions in worldly matters. Only within the relics of the Buddha are the remnants of power manifest. It is upon this principle that the king's custodianship of the relics legitimates his sovereign authority over ancient Buddhist kingdoms (Tambiah 1976; Malalgoda 1976; Trainor 1997; Seneviratne 1999). Given this, it is up to humanity to remember the teachings of the *Dhamma*; but as per the cyclical conception of the *yugas* (ages or eons) detailed in Buddhist doctrines, the capacities of living beings to remember the *Dhamma* perfectly and precisely and embody it gradually fade. The presence of dharmic insight and dharmic righteousness thereby goes into decline too.

The imperative to "save Buddhism" from the cosmologically ordained decline that is embedded in Theravādin doctrine coalesces with the imperative to protect Buddhism from the sense of threat posed by colonialism (Turner 2014; see also Obeyesekere et al. 1972). From quite early on in the era of European colonialism, Ceylonese Buddhist reformers and revivalists conceived of Christian missionaries as detractors and "heretics" who dissuaded Sinhala people from carrying out the obligations to remember the Buddha, to practice the *Dhamma*, and to be dedicated patrons of the Sangha (Roberts 1989; Young and Somaratna 1996). Yet, a political cosmology underpins the Buddhist revival—one that has a much longer genealogy than what the postcolonial and presentist debates over "postsecularist" religious freedom might imply.

THE ENCHANTMENTS AND DISENCHANTMENTS
OF BUDDHIST MODERNITY

While modernist and doctrinaire approaches have oriented the Buddhist revival toward an idealist religious formation that centers philosophy, ethics, and careful cultivation of interior states, in lived practice much of the cosmological, ritual, and material complexity of Buddhism is retained (Gombrich and Obeyesekere 1988; Obeyesekere 1963, 1981; de Silva 2006). A host of gods, demigods, and "demonic" spirits (*yakśa*) are prevalent within Sinhala Buddhism, both within rural lifeworlds and to a large extent also in urban and middle-class contexts. Paradoxically, despite the modernist approaches to Buddhism, near the top of the hierarchy of Sinhala Buddhist sovereignty stand four guardian deities. A sacred geography is associated with the guardian deities as well as the lesser deities and demigods of Sri Lanka. In the precolonial capital of Kandy, the relics housed at the palace authenticated the sovereign power of the king. In modern Sri Lanka, too, with its electoral democracy, the legitimacy of the postcolonial state is symbolically renewed through annual rituals involving the relic and its four guardian deities. In the annual *Perahera* ritual procession at Kandy, the Buddha's Tooth Relic is feted and venerated as it is led from the Dalada Maligawa (Palace/Temple of the Tooth) in a tour of the city. The circumambulatory pattern consecrates the entire kingdom. The movement of the Relic encloses and protects the city through a sanctifying process that "reinforces the centrality of the capital through its centripetal dynamic" (de Silva Wijeyeratne 2007, 171).

Satellite rituals are carried out in other areas of the country, each centering on one of the four guardian deities. (In theory, the deities guard the four cardinal directions to encompass the entirety of the country, but in reality the abodes of the deities are located in the central, western, southern, and southeastern parts of the country.) The dispersal of the ritual substances associated with the annual rites of the Tooth Relic "diffuse(s) the sacral power from the center to the provinces" (de Silva Wijeyeratne 2007, 171). In so doing, the statist rituals link to and reinforce the geomantic domains governed by each of the enshrined guardians. Under the spiritual authority vested in the Kandyan relic, the guardian deities reign over lesser tutelary deities and demigods, who govern "discrete, bounded territories" that "correspond to ... administrative villages, districts, and provinces," in what Deborah Winslow describes as "inter-nested sovereignty" (1984, 274–78). In theory, the veneration of each deity consecrates the land, so that taken together, worship of Buddhist deities allows the people to ritually and politically participate within a unified polity.

Considering the spatial and micropolitical involvements of the deities in structuring Sinhala Buddhist sovereignty, rituals to localized deities and demigods serve to integrate people in distant provinces into state administrative structures (Winslow 1984, 274). Winslow shows that in rural areas Sinhala people conceive of the deity as a feudal landlord (279). They contend that the local deity has "the right" (*ayiti*) to their patrimonial offerings of harvest shares. The deity "receives vows (*bara*, the same word as "rent") and other accoutrements of land ownership" from devotees (279). The various tiers of political authority coincide with distinctions between the demigods (*devatāva*) who are imbedded within a discrete region, minor deities, and the four guardian deities (*deviyō*) who are closely linked with the Buddha's Tooth Relic and who serve as protectorates over larger territories. Specific myths authenticate the deities' authoritative presence in any given locale (279). In the southern and southeasterly coastal villages where I carried out much of my fieldwork, my Sinhala interlocutors invariably named Viṣṇu-Kataragama as the duo of guardian deities to whom they were most dedicated (see chapter 6). The implications of theistic regionalism with respect to evangelical Christian efforts to establish new churches will become evident.

In short, for Sinhala Buddhists in rural contexts it is the deities who are the primary point of intercessional access to theopolitical flourishing. Yet, as with the tsunami miracles with which I introduced this chapter, many propounded the view that the Lord Buddha's substantive presence was awakened and became directed and unmediated in those most exceptional of circumstances. Miracles are validated in such exceptional moments and in states of emergency—for instance, miracles were also storied among Kandyan Sri Lankans, as when the Buddha's Tooth Relic was said to have "miraculously launched itself in the air" when a LTTE cadre bombed the Dalada Maligawa in 1998. In some instances too, Sinhala Buddhists also attest to the miraculous and magical capacities of a rare monk who emerges as an adept in mastering dharmic insights.

In the main, Sinhala Buddhists consider miracles to be extraordinary rarities to be cherished. In turn, they skeptically disparage the miracles that Pentecostals are purported to harness in abundance. From the point of view of dedicated Sinhala Buddhists, the profusion of miracles that born-again Christian "fundamentalists" espouse are without credibility, in part because of their sheer excess. Rhetorically cohering with the disparagements of unethical conversions, Buddhist activists and reformers assert that Christian "fundamentalists" chronically make false promises of miracles to "emotionally manipulate" people who are vulnerable to social suffering. In defending their own faith against the derogations of charismatic Christians, Sinhala Buddhist discourses suggest that although the Buddha is technically Thus-Gone, when the extraordinary intercessory powers of the *Dhamma* do appear, they are vitalistic and highly potent.

HAPTICS OF PENTECOSTAL SOVEREIGNTY

The southwesterly dry zone of Sri Lanka is known among Sinhala Buddhists for its resplendent stupas, ancient reservoirs constructed by Sinhala kings, and the Kataragama temple complex, which is home to the Sinhala deity of the same name (known among Tamil Hindus as Murugan or Skandakumara), who is claimed to reign sovereign over the region. That area has also seen a small pocket of new Pentecostal Christian growth, as richly addressed in Oshan Fernando's (2011) ethnography of an Assemblies of God congregation and the Christian NGO World Vision in the town of Tissamaharama. Fernando accounts for how in an era of globalizing Christian forms the evangelical entities he studied complicate the hegemony of majoritarian nationalist state ideologies through their "state-*like* effects." He does so by addressing the rhetorics of Christian nationalism in which they partake (2011, 6). He documents the sermonic discourses of one Sinhala deaconess, who proclaimed to a village congregation of some three hundred people that those who submit to the supreme deity will gain divine sanction: "God has given us the authority [*ādhipatya balaya*] to transform the village, town, and our *dēśaya* (country)" (Fernando 2011, 1). His ethnography underscores the spatial and temporal organization of these evangelists' endeavors (see also Woods 2013). Yet Fernando is clear that their rhetoric is aspirational and hardly totalizing; he reminds readers that according to census statistics, evangelical and Pentecostal Christians constitute just a tiny fraction of Sri Lanka's population.

In a similar vein, I am emphatic that the supersessionist rhetoric must be distinguished from the lived realities of conversion. But rather than simply play out in the realm of ideology, there are substantive, material features of religious difference at stake in these disputed, aspirational claims over religious sovereignty.

These practices of materializing the spirit that are common in Third-Wave Pentecostalism lead to the politicization of the encounter. The politicization is due, *in part*, to the inclination of Pentecostal Christian discourses to render other religions and their spiritual agents as diabolical. In the case of Sri Lanka, the political dimension is all the more pronounced because modern Sinhala Buddhist rituals of the state strive to consolidate the national encompassment of territory and people. It does so not only through the discursive reach of political administration and nationalistic ideology. The inclusion of Sinhala Buddhists into the fold of the nation is also reinforced through ritual enactments, veneration, and traditionalist patrimonial exchange with Buddhist demigods and deities—including those who theopolitically govern the most provincial of territories. Thus, the antagonistic cast of Christian ritual acts that "deliver" the social body from "demonic" agents, "into the arms of Christ," is tied to a theology of dominion—an orientation that is theocratic and nationalistic in its aspirations (Comaroff 2016; Bialecki 2017; Haynes 2021). In the Third-Wave deliverance ministries that engage such ritual acts, the pastoral team invites God's grace by pronouncing a battle against the spiritual agents that have taken up residence in the Sri Lankan landscape. The transduction of the Holy Spirit into the material world, down to the soil, is consonant with an ideology that territory can be spiritually and materially transfigured. Pastors rebuke any attempt to impede this sanctifying process as the machinations of the Devil's spirit (*Yakśa Ātmaya*).

One of the figures who most influenced and endorsed Third-Wave Pentecostal practices and inspired the dominionist theology that underpins it is the late theologian C. Peter Wagner (1930–2016). Since the 1990s, transnational charismatic Christian discourses have drawn from Wagner's writings on the "New Apostolic Reformation" to promote spiritual mapping and prayer walking, in a concerted effort to stamp out "demonic strongholds" (Coleman 1999; DeBernardi 2008). In his writings, Wagner identified these strongholds as encompassing regions that fall within "10/40 window"—that is, the latitudinal lines that include Africa, Asia, and Latin America (DeBernardi 2008; Freston 2008). He contended that it is within this equatorial span that people express the deepest resistance to Christianity because it is party to the densest concentration of demonic activity. Anthropologists and sociologists have documented how in Southeast Asia, certain charismatic Christian groups have actively engaged in territorial mapping techniques to guide their "prayer walks" to carry out "spiritual warfare" in regions dominated by non-Christian traditions (DeBernardi 2008; Goh 2009).

At Good News Calvary Church, Pastor Milton conducts a communion ritual known in Sinhala as *Awāsāna Rathrī Bōjhanāya* ("the Last Supper," lit. "last night meal"). Following bouts of sermonizing, testimonials, theatrical deliverance, and song and prayer that crossfade into glossolalia, Pastor Milton's pentecostalist self-service rendition of the Eucharistic Mass ritually marks a high point in the congregation's communion with god. The Christian devotees, garbed in white, form a line and approach spaces situated at one of several round tables. Women pull white shawls from their purses to cover their heads. Others clasp and pull the tail end of their saris to drape them over their heads before approaching the communion tables. Pastor Milton and his *sevakayo* (ministerial assistants or deacons, lit. "servants" [of God]) direct members of the congregation, one by one, to open spaces at one of five tables. Kneeling, each supplicant reverently partakes of the blood and body of Christ. With their own hands, they lift chalices of wine and flat *roti* (bread) to their mouths. The ministerial team stands back from the communion tables, allowing the devotees to partake in the ritual without any direct mediation by the pastor or the *sevakayo* assistants. The ministerial team merely facilitates the pentecostalist Mass by refilling the chalices and conducting congregational traffic. After partaking in the *Awāsāna Rathrī Bōjhanāya*, the congregation members file away from the communion tables and return to the open devotional space, shifting their postures to kneel in silent prayer until all who are present have sipped the blood and eaten the flesh of the transubstantiated victuals. It is after this Eucharistic segment of the ministerial service, when song and collective prayer recommence, that the most effusive expressions of possession and Holy Spirit baptism materialize. Men and women fall, flail, dance, scream, cry, and sometimes vomit out what afflicts them.

The *sevakayo*, the congregation members, and especially the pastor serve as conductors, channeling the Holy Spirit into the space of the prayer hall. The infusion of the Spirit penetrates individuals and exposes the demons that hide themselves away within the bodies and minds of the congregants. The demonic spirit (*Yakśa Ātmaya*) manifests as affliction, whereby bad mores and dangerous habits, illnesses, and financial impediments are all attributed to these possessing spirits—in essence, to Satan himself. The physical flailing aroused by exposing the possessing agent homed within a body can be injurious to the afflicted person or to others around them. The hands of the *sevakayo* physically restrain the flailing limbs. Working in pairs, the *sevakayo* "shepherd" those who become visibly possessed, firmly grasping wrists and ankles to haul the writhing figures toward a cordoned-off area within the reach of the pastor. Pastor Milton prays over the possessed bodies, laying on hands on the heads of individuals. Into the microphone, the pastor invokes Jesus, while loudly uttering maledictions against the *Yakśa Ātmaya*. "*Jesunuge nameya*, "*PAYA! PAYA! PAYAAA!*" ("In Jesus's name, GET OUT!"). *Paya* is an abbreviated form of the verb *paleyang*, a curse used to excoriate lesser beings. Ordinarily ethnic Sinhalas abusively hurl "*paleyang*" to repel stray dogs or demons who lurk at crossroads, burial sites, or other polluted, haunted locales. Pastor Milton forcefully shouts "*PAYA*" as he presses the forehead of the writhing, possessed person, laying on a strong healing hand to expel the demon. With the ministry as a conduit, the *Śuddha Ātmaya* (Holy Spirit) does battle with the *Yakśa Ātmaya* (Devil's Spirit). According to ministerial discourses, regular exposure to the Holy Spirit during weekly services holds the promise that the *Yakśa Ātmaya* will be cast out from the lifeways of churchgoers once and for all.

Toward the close of the Sunday praise and worship sessions in this suburban deliverance ministry, Pastor Milton directs devotees to ready an array of personal items to be sanctified by the Spirit. Devotees raise bottles of thick yellow cooking oil high above their heads, so that when Pastor Milton uses prayer to channel the Holy Spirit it will infuse and materialize within it. The congregation then proceeds to do the same with photos of loved ones, passports, visa applications, and then finally "prayer clothes" embroidered with the name of Pastor Milton's ministry. In doing so, blessings are transferred directly to the persons for whom these objects stand as metonyms. The intercessory act sends grace to sacralize the anointing oil, to bless children, to fulfill the desires of successful emigration, and to render travel safe.

As the Sunday service begins to wind down, Pastor Milton calls upon the congregation to direct their attention to the small kiosk in the back of the prayer hall where musical scores produced by his deliverance ministry are available for sale. His sales pitch is evocative: "If you have demons lurking in your home, hiding in the corner, behind your furniture, you can easily get them out. Just buy our ministry's songs on CD and play them in your home. All of the demons residing in your house will run right out! If you play the music loudly enough, they'll run out of your neighbor's house also!"

The Holy Ghost travels pneumatically, riding along with sacred sounds of charismatic song. Charismata (gifts of God's grace) are channeled, partly in the form of sound energy, and imbued into material culture (Blanton 2015). Anderson Blanton's ethnographic account illustrates how the pioneering American televangelist Oral Roberts performatively engaged the sensorial field through a critical "point of contact" so as to haptically reach audience members individually in the comfort of their own homes. Roberts would invite his remote audience to place one hand on their radios or analog television screens to take in the charismatic sensorium, using their own bodies as a conductor and conduit. The sound vibrations from the radio, and the static from analog television sets, vitally enhanced this sensorial experience. The haptics of Pentecostal televangelism are portable and are easily transduced into expressions of Pentecostal aesthetics worldwide. Even as transnational televangelical media outlets do not broadcast on Sinhala channels, there is certainly a continuity between the haptic ritual processes that had been promoted by Roberts in his radio and television broadcasts in the United States in the 1950s and 1960s and those that are localized in Sri Lankan deliverance ritual practices in the Third-Wave Pentecostal ministries that are prevalent today. Local pastors also transduce the Holy Spirit via YouTube, Whatsapp videos, and various other new media platforms to Sinhala and Tamil audiences in Sri Lanka and to the diasporas around the world.

Concern with efficacious modalities of transduction—that is, the conversion of something, such as energy or a message, into another form—has animated an array of studies under the rubric of religion, media, and mediation (deVries and Weber 2001; Stowlow 2005; Hirschkind 2006; Keane 2013). Pentecostalism involves transduction that is extended pneumatically through the air, breath, sound, and spirit and infused into the corporeal subject and into the surrounding material culture. These infusions generate conviction affectively, experientially, substantively, and spiritually. Armed with exclusivist rites and discourses, many evangelists feel emboldened to make rhetorical claims of sovereignty over space. Such rhetoric, paired with evidence of an apparent increase of Sinhalas who confessionally identify themselves as born-again Christians, has led vigilant Buddhists to denigrate the establishment of new churches in turn.

One of Pastor Milton's biggest rivals, Pastor Vinod, engages a similarly effusive practice through his ministry located in a neighboring town. The theatrical Pastor Vinod arrives at his open-air prayer hall in a different new luxury vehicle each Sunday. As his car rolls across the parched earth toward its parking space within the gates of the ministry, a handful of women draped in modest skirts and saris tattered with wear hurriedly follow. The tires of Pastor Vinod's car press patterns of soil into relief. The women bend over these tracks, reaching down to collect fistfuls of sand. With their hands, they proceed to funnel the sandy soil into small plastic bottles to take home with them. Mixing the soil from the pastor's car tracks into the earth near the threshold of their homes will bring a modicum of grace to their own lives, it is said.

As addressed earlier, the American evangelist C. Peter Wagner reinforced Pentecostalism's "Third Wave" through his endorsement of Dominion theology. Wagner's thought and practical methods had international reach among charismatic and evangelical Christian circles. Promoting what he called "strategic-level intercession" through his writing and preaching, he encouraged evangelists to work to root out the malevolent spirits in areas that are "untouched" by Christ. Wagner urged evangelists to familiarize themselves with vernacular religious knowledge in order to lay the ground for the planting of new churches. In a 2011 book, Wagner provided a secondhand account of a Sri Lankan Christian minister who had been facing difficulty in establishing a congregation in a Sinhala village. Eventually one of the villagers informed the pastor's wife of the name of the specific tutelary deity who held sway over their rural village territory. The Sinhala pastor shared with Wagner that it was only when he learned the name and the distinguishing features of that *particular* territorial deity that he became well equipped to carry out his church planting efforts. Reportedly, only after praying to God to unseat that *specific* deity did the pastor's congregation effectively begin to grow.

In this way, charismatic discourses imply that territorial mapping, planting, and growing a church requires as a first step something akin to weeding a garden. I did not observe any such mapping practices in Sri Lanka during the course of my fieldwork. Nevertheless, ministers and congregants invariably identify the southern coastal regions of Sri Lanka as having the most entrenched demonic afflictions. Within the course of charismatic deliverance practices in periurban ministries of the Western Province (outside of Colombo), it was often a point of comment that the churchgoers who had traveled from the southern districts had the most severe afflictions to overcome. The pastor would paint with his words a caricature of the southern coast as a demonically afflicted "hot zone" of Sri Lanka. Pastor Milton explicitly invoked the name of the southern village Ambalangoda, which is famed for mask-making and *yaktovil* "exorcism" rituals. He contended that because of the sway of these practices, the south bears the most entrenched demonic affliction in all Sri Lanka. According to these sermonic discourses, *yaktovil* rituals are indicative of how southern Sinhala culture is doggedly attached to "demonism," because people hailing from those regions perpetually "entertain the devil" with sumptuous ritual feasts.

3.1 In this annual *Yaktovil* performed in a southern Sri Lankan fishing village (2010), singers recite the story of the *akusala karmaya* (meritless karma) that the Gara Yakka committed during his past lives, which brought him to his current ontological state as a *yaksa*.

3.2 As the Gara Yakka dances, the singers narrativize his biography. Their drums punctuate his moves as he climbs a tree and shakes its branches.

Christians accustomed to Third-Wave Pentecostal discourses of spiritual warfare characterize these "devil dances" as celebrating and serving ultimately evil minions of Satan. However, others characterize *tovil* ritual play more sympathetically. For instance, a Sri Lankan ecumenical Jesuit Christian theologian, Father Aloysius Pieris (2009), renowned among theologians throughout Asia for his

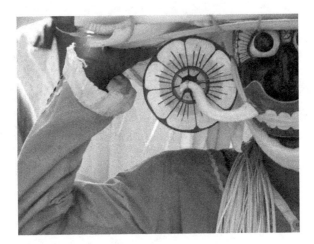

3.3 The *yakśa* is an embodiment of negative karmic values, and the narrativization of his life, in the course of his theatrical play, aims to discourage villagers from incurring the same bad fate. At the same time, the ritual performance draws *yakśas* lurking in the village to feast upon the tray of "base" foods.

3.4 Following the dance, the Gara Yakka hoists the tray upon his head, and the whole village follows behind him in a procession through the village, down to the docks. The villagers board fishing boats and travel far out to sea.

scholarship on interreligious dialogue, Christian pluralism, and for championing locally existing ways of knowing and being, offers a sensitive interpretation of these rites. Through his pluralistic and ethnographic attunement to local life, Pieris describes the Sinhala *tovil* rituals and suggests that they involve "taking the devil seriously, and laughing him out of existence" (Pieris 2009). Anthropologists,

3.5 Once at sea, the dancer impersonating the Gara Yakka tosses the tray of food into the sea, and all of the greedy *yakśas* are said to go down with it. The ritual is treated as a *pin kamma*, an act of merit that brings blessings to the village by alleviating it of *yakśas'* malevolence for another year.

too, have emphasized the importance of the curative ritual aesthetic of laughter in Sinhala Buddhist *yaktovil* rituals (Kapferer 1983). As detailed in the captions to the photographs of one such ritual, Sinhala villagers are not only entertained by the *yakśa* but also mock and laugh at them before luring them away from the village with tantalizing treats. The ritual play ends with a village-wide procession to the harbor, where the villagers board fishing boats, traveling together to cast the trays of food far out to sea. The idea is that the *yakśa* and other karmically incapacitated spirits, in their greed and gullibility, will be lured into following the feast of food to the bottom of the sea, leaving the villagers alone to ensure a plentiful annual harvest. Without the same good sense of humor, however, Pentecostal Christian are less sanguine about these rituals, characterizing them in mocking tones as "ineffective cures" at best, and at worst, as true manifestations of evil because they encourage people to willingly feed and "entertain" the devil.

SOVEREIGNTY, SOIL, AND SEEDING: TERRITORIAL COMPETITIONS OF RELIGIOUS DIFFERENCE

"Private *reason* is not the same as private *space*; it is the entitlement to difference, the immunity from the force of public reason," writes Talal Asad (1993, 8). To interrogate the competing Buddhist and Christian paradigms of religious sovereignty and freedom of conscience in Sri Lanka, it is worth dwelling for a moment on the contention leveled by Buddhists that new Christian churches are "springing up like mushrooms" in predominantly Buddhist areas.[9] The remark is a loaded one, implying that the churches are potentially dangerous outgrowths that interrupt an ideally imagined Buddhist landscape. The critique implies that these spore-like churches are without genealogical roots in Sri Lanka, and it thus condemns Christian churches for being disconnected from the land and as having parachuted in from a place without a legitimate history in the country.

To unpack how a mushroom-like entity might relate to the question of sovereign legitimacy, Thomas Hobbes's discussion of *De Cive* (*Of the Citizen*) is an instructive point of contrast. Hobbes urges examination of the "state of nature"—the condition of human existence that precedes the formation of a sovereign state—in order to understand what compels humanity's submission to sovereign authority. He suggests that in a state of nature, it is as if men (and their immediate families) are "sprung out of the earth, and suddainly (like Mushromes) come to full maturity" without any engagement or obligation to one another other (*De Cive*, 43). For Hobbes, this anarchic form of existence is undesirable—it is "solitary, poor, nasty, brutish, and short" (*Leviathan*, 73). The mushroom-like human families are atomized, and he implies that their lack of civilization stems from their paganism or lack of cultivation as moral Christians. For Hobbes it is crucial for human survival that they sacrifice their individual freedoms, renounce their atomized disengagement, and instead create mutual obligations and in turn an ordered form of sociality. Such a tightly knit body politic can be established only with the security offered by a sovereign.[10] It is the sovereign who is capable of realizing the optimally ordered commonwealth. In the European Enlightenment thinker's reasoning, the well-ordered earthly commonwealth is a providential reflection of the "future Christian kingdom" (Schwartz 1985, 7).[11] As above, so below—earthly providence under the sovereign is bound to reflect the kingdom of God in heaven.

As a metaphor, the "mushrooming" of churches that has Sri Lankan Buddhists so alarmed obviously has quite different connotations than Hobbes's discussion of a mushroom-like humanity in a state of nature. From the nationalistic view of Buddhists who are intent upon protecting their heritage, it is Christians who are the mushroom-like interlopers who dangerously interrupt the landscape of Buddhist sovereignty. The comparison reveals the ways in which competing

Buddhist and Christian political cosmologies project emplacement into the soil, each while seeking to deny the emplacement of the other. The praxis of evangelical and charismatic Christian emplacement is material as well as spiritual, as may be seen in the act of the Sinhala women who attempt to capture the grace laden in their pastor's tire tracks, which they then carry with them to mix with the soil of their home gardens. However, for my Sinhala Buddhist interlocutors, the mushrooming signifies the emergence of allochthonous (non-native) human institutions that are not embedded within, nor allegiant to, their established nation. Their discourses condemning the emergence of new churches imply that Christianity produces adherents to a credo that fails to shape subjects who will carry out their obligations to society and to the state. According to the allegations of Sinhala Buddhists who stand against "unethical" conversions, new Christian churches, in their autonomy and disengagement, are discontinuous with the existing cultural heritage of the Sri Lanka nation.

Further theorization of how miracles relate to sovereignty and territorial dominion can be found within the thought of Carl Schmitt ([1922] 1985), whose studies of illiberal democracy are as illuminating as he is controversial. As a jurist and legal theorist practicing under fascism, Schmitt made astute observations concerning illiberal polities. In *Political Theology* he discerned how political ideas carry a trace of antecedent theologies, drawing an analogy between the exception determined by a supreme deity and the exception determined by a king.[12] Addressing these two kinds of sovereigns, one religious and one political, Schmitt declared that "the sovereign is he who decides upon the exception." He ascertains how a miracle is an exception made by an omnipotent deity who decides to save a sinner from damning judgment, and analogously, a political pardon is an exception made by a sovereign who spares a convict from death row. Schmitt's thinking is derived from a particularly Catholic milieu in which miracles occur specifically within the rite of transubstantiation and in Final Judgment carried out in the Last Days. In contrast, Pentecostalist intercession via the Holy Spirit is an abundant and persistent phenomenon. Nevertheless, the Schmittian analogy is instructive for conceptualizing the authoritative, Manichean, and dominionist theopolitical directives that evangelical miracles serve to validate.

Furthering a discussion of sovereignty, exception, and charismatic territoriality, Maria José de Abreu elucidates the inherent "bounding" and the territorial entailments of Schmitt's concept of sovereignty as he developed it with respect to the Westphalian state (2020; 2021). De Abreu characterizes Schmittian states of exception as "reassert[ions of] sovereignty *in extremis*"—that is, as spaces of exception that are pushed to extend the bounds of the territorial nation-state (2023, 95). She engages the point ethnographically to analyze how charismatic Catholic preachers in Brazil claim territory through their theatrical performances. Relatedly, McAlister and Napolitano (2021) urge anthropological attunement to the theopolitical imbrications of Christianity, empire, conquest, and land appropriation. These critical retheorizations of Schmitt's territorial conception of political theology are relevant beyond the frame of Roman Catholicism too, considering how Pentecostal-charismatics and other evangelical Christians are ever made to feel compelled to the sacrificial endeavor to globally extend the zones of Christendom.

MEDIA INTERRUPTUS

Sri Lankan Buddhist anti-conversion activists engage Sinhala language news media to thwart the transmission of the "Good News" (*Subha Aranchiya*) and to ensure that Christianity does not further take root. As scholars have shown in the context of South Asia, popular media is often leveraged hegemonically to consolidate a unitary imagined community, which hinges upon steep hierarchies of social exclusion (Rajagopal 2001; Mankekar 2002). In India, teledramatic religious programing as well as television news have fueled anti-minority sentiment (Ghassem-Fachandi 2012; Ibrahim 2013). In that context publicity serves to affectively deepen nativist religious commitments while producing paranoiac calls to arms to defend the nation against the ostensible "dangers" posed by Dalits and Muslims. Since 2011, mediatized Islamophobia has similarly intensified in Sri Lanka, too.

Against the backdrop of cable televangelical transmissions of international and inter-Asian Christian imaginaries (see the introduction), as well as the circulation of localized charismatic Christian media productions of Sinhala language CDs and DVDs and social media, vernacular popular media had apparently consolidated Sinhala Buddhists' resistance to the advance of born-again Christianity. Episodically during the time of my fieldwork (2009–2011), Sinhala-language news media channels undercut evangelical Christians' expansionary efforts. Sinhala Buddhist activists used these platforms to shed negative light on Pentecostals' claims of miracles by asserting their falseness and by portraying Christian miracle workers as posing a danger to naïfs who are susceptible to being "duped" by their false promises.

In the midst of our dinner preparations, Thushari, who in her spare time ably worked to assist me with portions of my research, drew my attention to the evening newscast of the Swarnavahini Sinhala-language television station. From her south-coast village home we tuned into a segment showing a contingent of people who orchestrated a sting operation to expose the "false claims" made by a born-again Christian pastor. It captured a thirty-something Sinhala man making a phone call to a preacher in a nearby village. The Swarnavahini news cameras showed footage of the call and his collaboration with several Sinhala men who coached the caller on what to say to the pastor. Over the phone, the young man baited the pastor into asserting that he was able to heal his physical ailments owing to his God-given capacities to channel the power of Jesus Christ. The next day, on camera, the man, along with several other Sinhala Buddhist men and a couple of Buddhist monks, harangued the pastor, accusing him of making false promises of healing in order to unethically convert born-Buddhists to Christianity. The news spot caught the Christian pastor taken aback, anxiously stumbling over his words as he denied his healing capabilities on national television.

The same news bite documented a separate incident in another village wherein several vigilant citizen-interrogators, accompanied by a Buddhist monk, accused a Christian villager of having cut branches and burning the base of a Bo tree—the sacred symbol of Buddha's achievement of *nibbāna*. In his defense, the accused man declared that in cutting and burning parts of the tree he intended to reduce the presence of dengue-carrying mosquitoes to curb the epidemic in the area. Captured on camera, a figure in the assembled crowd angrily retorted, "if you were trying to prevent dengue, you could have cut the branches—but you needn't have burned the roots!"[13] With these nationally broadcast sting operations and other such news items showcasing harassment and violence against Sri Lanka's "new" Christians, anti-conversion advocates publicly articulated a sense of alarm that Christians have designs to supplant Buddhism by destroying the roots of the nation's heritage. With the vigilant and accusing discourses of the social actors centered on screen largely unmediated by critical newscaster commentary, this mainstream coverage appeared set upon conveying to a Sinhala Buddhist public that it was incumbent upon them to do something about the territorial encroachment. During the height of Sinhala Buddhist advocacy favoring the passing of the anti-conversion bill, numerous other such incidents were highlighted in a similar fashion in vernacular television news and mainstream print media.

In 2009, Sinhala- and English-language media exposed a fatal misstep that allegedly transpired in the course of one faith-healing minister's public "gospel rally," which he held regularly on Saturdays at Viharamahadevi Park (formerly Victoria Park), a prominent public space in Colombo. On one occasion at the open-air gospel rally, two women died, allegedly due to heat exhaustion. In the media coverage that followed, vigilant citizen groups consisting of Buddhist laity and monks were emphatic that the two women who died were Buddhists. They alleged that the women were prevented from promptly seeking medical help because the ministerial team insisted that the pastor's own healing abilities surpassed that of any allopathic medical care. The pastor denied accusations that his ministry had intentionally obstructed the women's access to medical care (Mahadev 2014). In lending their voice to shape the narration, the contingent of outraged Sinhala Buddhists insinuated that this public expression of Christianity led to the death of the women. They maligned the pastor, his ministry, and charismatic faith healing practices in general.

Several days after the tragic incident, a faction of Buddhist monks and laymen gathered outside of suburban prayer hall where the pastor regularly ministered to stage a protest against his "unethical" and "dangerous" activities. The protesters turned to vigilante violence, lodging an attack upon the premises. The monks and laypeople smashed and leveled the prayer hall to the ground within the view of video cameras, and they further threatened the pastor and the ministerial team associated with the church. Reportedly, the primary assailants belonged to the Jathika Hela Urumaya (Sinhala Heritage Party), the party of monks that had been elected to Parliament to push forth the legislation against Christian proselytism a few years earlier (see chapter 1). Although news teams captured and broadcast live footage of the demolition of the prayer hall, the monks denied any involvement. Ecumenical and evangelical Christian organizations and progressive Buddhist monks alike sharply condemned the vigilante violence. A lay Buddhist organization that avowed utmost support for the bill to criminalize unethical conversions condemned the violence as well. A lay spokesperson for the organization conveyed to the press that the monks' involvement in the destruction of the church was a deplorable "black mark on the sacred robe."[14] Nevertheless, the spokesperson used the example of the two "Buddhist" women who died in the course of the public Christian faith-healing deliverance service as an example of how "gullible people" are all too easily manipulated by "charlatans." Like the broader pattern of Sinhala anti-conversion discourse, she too cast the incident as symptomatic of the wider harm that can

3.6 Jagath Weerasinghe created "Decorated Kitchen Knives"—depicting loudspeakers that emit daggers and venomous snakes—in response to "The Noise of Silence" by Ameena Hussein. Hussein's writing is a meditation upon the "noise celebration" associated with Vesak holiday, which commemorates the Buddha's birth, Enlightenment, death, and attainment of *Parinibbāna*. Both pieces offer a critique of the exclusionary nature of public religion in Sri Lanka. From the exhibition *Mediated*, held at Saskia Fernando Gallery, in 2012.
Courtesy of Jagath Weerasinghe

befall people who are "illegally" lured into conversions propagated by proselytizers who peddle false miracles.

———◆———

Miracles are found within the doctrines and lifeworlds of Buddhists and Christians alike. Amid these entanglements, Buddhists and Christians regularly engage in comparison: Buddhists find Pentecostal-charismatic claims of miracles to be too commonplace—and also too effusive, and too incendiary—and they thereby consider them to lack credibility. At the same time, the born-again Christians who believe life is to be experienced through eyes that are disciplined to see the miraculous also find that Buddhism is framed as deficient—as lacking divine vitality, and rife with "empty" spaces through which the "devil" can seep in. Charismatic Christian theology, as espoused through Pentecostal sermons, emphasizes the profuse and democratically accessible possibilities of miracles via the exemplary Pauline modality of conversion. In a different tenor, for Sinhala Buddhists the Buddha's relics are understood to contain unmediated manifestations of the Buddha's power; likewise, in states of exception and emergency, the Buddha's sacred image is a repository that channels the pure and unmediated power of the cosmos, providing fateful good turns of fortune. For Buddhists, miracles spotlight the extraordinary power of the Dharmic cosmos—manifestations of power which are considered remarkable precisely because they are so rare. This rarity bespeaks the vastness of dharmic timescales, which are greatly stretched out in comparison to Christian millennialism. To see self-actualizing nibbanic progress, one must stay the course over a *longue durée*. Deep patience is necessary.

What is more, miracles present an enhanced opportunity for religious publicity. Abounding claims of miracles in themselves create substantial discord between neighbors. Indeed, miracle work, including healing and sensations of emotional catharsis, is essential to Pentecostals' experiences and imperatives to spread "the Good News" and create new converts. But in the Sri Lankan milieu wherein Buddhists seek to thwart the advance of Christianity, Buddhists harness local news media to undermine and defame these Christian ministerial forms. Through highly mediatized efforts to *remediate* the miraculous claims of born-again Christians, Sinhala Buddhists strive to act as custodians of the

Buddha *sāsana*—that is, the historical Buddha's dispensation—in moral, spiritual, ontological, territorial, and mediatic terms.

Differences concerning the character of religious agents, the locality and temporality that circumscribes their immanent power, the modalities and mediums through which these miraculous agents can be haptically accessed, and the theopolitical prognostications and geomantic prescriptions for ritually mapping out and securing the spiritual domain together undergird these rivalries. Collectives of Theravāda Buddhists and of Pentecostal Christians tap into and transduce these distinctive forms of sovereign religious power through state ceremonies and through ordinary ritual work of inhabiting and sacralizing territorial domains. Buddhist and Christian discursive practices seek to configure, reinforce, or reconfigure the theopolitical character of the land and the people that grow up upon its soil. Far from existing in siloed domains, adherents of these traditions put forth competing assertions of miracles and commonly stir up controversies over conversion in their wake.

CHAPTER 4

A Cacophonous Exuberance

Modulating Miracles, Defending Sovereignty

As the head of a world conquering movement, we expect that the Pope is both inclined and obliged to play the conqueror all the time. Besides, and for the same reason, we do not even for a moment require of him the same dignified academic detachment in the study and assessment of other religions that we would expect from elsewhere, from persons with less involvement and much less investment. Obviously, to err is human, even for a Pope. And to forgive, having pointed out to the offender his offence, is divine. But it must be remembered with an acceptable degree of sanity, that there are areas in the lives of a people where even angels fear to tread. At the same time, let not one lose sight of the fact that the entire world today, in spite of all international strategic indoctrination, is educated and alert enough to decry religious totalitarianism.

—Dhammavihari Thero (1994)

From an Asian perspective we cannot accept the conclusions of the traditional Christian orthodox theology that regarded the Church as the only path to salvation. Nor is it possible to accept that baptism in the "name of the Father, Son and the Holy Spirit" is the constituent element for belonging to the "community of saints" as mentioned by Pope Benedict XVI in his inaugural sermon on the 24th of April 2005. For Asians any thinking that holds that our ancestors for hundreds of generations were not cared for by God and were even sentenced to damnation cannot be reconciled with a concept of a Supreme Being or the understanding of God in Jesus Christ. We cannot think of a "communion of saints" that excludes not only the millions of ordinary persons who were killed, but even the sages and seers who are the pathfinders and gurus of our ancient religions and civilisations. The same reasoning can

*be used for the ancestors of the Christian West prior to the era of Jesus Christ
though few there reflect on it consciously.*

—Tissa Balasuriya (2006)

I n the epigraphs to this chapter, two Sri Lankan religious leaders—the
late Dhammavihari Thero, a Sri Lankan Buddhist monk, and the late
Father Tissa Balasuriya, a Catholic theologian—sharply criticized two
bishops of Rome for their commentaries upon and interventions into the religiosity of Sri Lankans.[1] Written twelve years apart, their critiques of two different
popes indicate how Vatican authority had proven contentious among different
religious demographics within postcolonial Sri Lanka over the last few decades.
The statements are striking because both men were prominent religious figures
in Sri Lanka during their lifetimes. Despite holding quite different conceptualizations of the nation—one from a Buddhist protectionist angle, the other oriented toward building a pluralistic form of civic belonging—both Dhammavihari
Thero and Father Balasuriya were forthright in their efforts to defend locally
relevant forms of religious commitment.[2] Although most Sri Lankan Catholics
constitute a body of believers who are normatively attached to the Church, these
two religious figures capture the fraught experiences that Sri Lankans have had
with the "official Church" in the postcolonial era. Their cutting correctives of
papal authority as it was received in Sri Lanka illuminate the spectrum of disputation, piety, and politicization of Roman Catholic practices and politics within
the country. Their critiques underscore some of the overarching resentments
against the reach of conservative Catholicism into public discourses on religion
in Sri Lanka.

Despite such vocal opposition to "the long arm of the Vatican," today the
country is home to a cardinal appointed by the conservative Pope Benedict XVI.
For a country to be home to a Catholic official at that high level of authority is
an indication that the Catholic Church enjoys stature and amicable relations
within that country. Yet, as I have shown in earlier chapters, Buddhists' political
invectives against Sri Lanka's Christians rose to a fever pitch from the mid-1990s
to the early 2000s, and Sri Lanka's Catholics had not been exempted from these
anti-conversion polemics. Indeed, Sinhala Buddhists' initial charges of "unethical conversions" tended to implicate Christians of all stripes. Given Sri Lanka's

majoritarian nationalist self-conception as a Buddhist country, it is thus remarkable that the state developed a fraternal relationship to the Catholic Church in such a time of heightened interreligious hostility. Considering too that interreligious tensions in Sri Lanka were exacerbated in the late stages of civil war, how did Buddhists and Catholics manage to forge an amicable relationship in an apparently hostile milieu?

Majoritarian nationalists of Sri Lanka have tended to hegemonically draw the lines of belonging to, and exclusion from, the nation. Amid a war of identity-based perceptions about what it means to belong within the context of postcolonial Sri Lanka, established Christian institutions have struggled to balance their national grounding and their ostensibly "suspect" international character. As detailed in previous chapters, Sinhala Buddhist discourses propelled generalized suspicions that Christian converts and their involvements in Sri Lanka serve to threaten national sovereignty. In the staunchest of these populist discourses, Sinhala Buddhists saw conversions to Christianity as estranging Sri Lankans from their nation. They condemned Christian proselytizers for their potential to create "anti-national" enemies who live in their midst. In chapter 3 we have seen how exclusivist Christian forms of deliverance ministering advances "warfare" against spiritual agents that are embedded within the existing religious landscape. Indeed, as detailed in chapter 1, it was a Sinhala convert to a charismatic demon-vanquishing strand of Catholic folk religiosity who became the object and emblem of majoritarian enmity. In turn, the inflammatory discourses critiquing Christianity as an expansionary religion that supposedly generates seditious sentiments and "anti-national" subjects have tended to be broad-based. So broad are the allegations that they implicated non-proselytizing groups of Christians too. This tense relationship has clearly perpetuated nationalistic anxieties and adds devastating fuel to populist politics.

At the same time, during the war, both ethnic and religious divides were exacerbated by territorial separation between warring factions. In regions of the country embroiled in war, Tamil Catholic priests commonly played an essential role in brokering peace efforts and negotiating with LTTE insurgents for the life and limb of Tamil civilian detainees (Johnson 2012; Brown 2015). From the point of view of Sinhala Buddhists, this willingness by Tamil Catholics and other Christian leaders to "negotiate with terrorists" connoted "non-neutrality" of local and international human rights initiatives during the war in Sri Lanka. Despite great factionalism and internal difference along lines of region, caste, class, religion, and political affinity among Sri Lankan Tamils themselves, the ideologues of Sinhala majoritarian revivalism and counterinsurgency logics tended to brand Tamils in general, and Tamil Christians and Tamil Catholic priests in particular, as loyalists and sympathizers of the LTTE. These circumstances of Sri Lanka's wartime and postwar politics in turn translated into substantive ethnic divisions that divisively cut across many of the country's Christian entities (Spencer, *Sinhala Village*). After the war, this ethnic divide was particularly ripe within the Catholic Church.

In the postwar context, despite conservativism that lends itself to seemingly interminable divisions, high-level leaders of the Catholic Church and the Sri Lankan state worked to secure a mutually beneficial relationship. The pages that follow delineate the causes and consequences behind Sri Lankan Catholic leaders' efforts to compromise with Sinhala Buddhist majoritarian leadership. They did so in a way that reoriented majoritarian nationalist politics of perception. The upshot of this maneuvering is that politicized Sinhala Buddhists came around to consider Catholics and the Catholic Church as an exceptional ally to the Sri Lankan national cause. Through careful engagement in theopolitical diplomacy and conservative measures in politics, theology, and even liturgy, Sinhala Buddhists and Sinhala Catholics mutually advanced their claims to entrenchment in and belonging to the sovereign nation. Sri Lankan Catholic Church leaders managed to do so by introducing a new, more conservative policy on religious liturgy, with explicit reference to imperatives to distinguish Sri Lanka's Catholics from proselytizing Christian "sects." By holding existing intra-Christian rivalries in view, the Sri Lankan state and the Vatican authority choreographed the emplacement of Catholic authority locally, enabling Catholic entities to better navigate their minority status in Sri Lanka.

After Sri Lanka's civil war, Sinhala Buddhist leaders and the Sinhala leadership of the Catholic Church, demonstratively pursued shows of interreligious friendship at the local and international levels. Two symbolic sovereigns—Pope Benedict XVI and Sri Lankan President Mahinda Rajapaksa—established a relationship through the mediations of the Sinhala Catholic Cardinal, Malcolm Ranjith. Pope Benedict XVI and Cardinal Malcolm Ranjith are staunchly conservative Catholic authorities. Both figures famously opposed Vatican II adaptations within the Catholic Church. In the view of Sinhala Buddhist revivalists, Rajapaksa had empowered the Buddhist legitimacy of the state through military victory in Sri Lanka. Paradoxically, these conservative figures consolidated their power within postwar Sri Lanka by extolling the value of interreligious friendship.

Together, these symbolic sovereigns and their intermediary engaged in political, theological, and liturgical maneuvering that served to distance the Catholic Church from proselytizing charismatics and in turn transformed nationalistic Buddhists' views of Catholics. Doing so enabled them to build a political alliance as a bulwark against international humanitarian criticisms of Sri Lanka. Nationalistic Buddhist and Catholic leaders carried out these theological and liturgical injunctions with the stated intention of ensuring interreligious harmony. But their efforts were firmly rooted in the preservationist instincts of Sri Lanka's religious and political institutions, that had profound micro- and macro-level theopolitical implications.

A BUDDHIST MONK'S CRITIQUE OF JOHN PAUL II'S COMPARATIVE THEOLOGY

The scholar of Buddhism and ordained monk, Dhammavihari Thero, known in his lay life as Professor Jotiya Dhirasekara, wrote in support of anti-conversion legislation throughout the early 2000s. Dhammavihari argued that Christian proselytism was creating a unique crisis for Sri Lanka, and that these exceptional circumstances demanded Buddhist clergy's political interventions (Hertzberg 2016). In the early phases of this Buddhist protectionist advocacy, Dhammavihari Thero publicly condemned Pope John Paul II for his "insensitive" and "ill-informed" remarks on Buddhism. The first epigraph to this chapter is an extract from a longer opinion piece published in *The Island*, an English-language newspaper with wide circulation in Sri Lanka. The Ecumenical Center for Study and Dialogue (Colombo) reprinted it in the journal *Dialogue* in a special issue on "The Pope and Buddhism." Dhammavihari Thero's 1994 statement on the "Papal Blunder on Buddhism" highlights a wider scenario in which the Vatican authority had grievously offended Buddhists of Sri Lanka.

Pope John Paul II was slated to visit Sri Lanka in early 1995 in a papal tour of Asia, with the purpose of beatifying Reverend Joseph Vaz, a seventeenth-century Portuguese Catholic missionary who arrived in Ceylon from India during an era of Dutch colonial "persecution" of Catholics. Among Catholics today, Vaz, canonized by Pope Francis in 2015, is known as the "Apostle of Sri Lanka." With the official announcement of the papal visit, Sri Lankan Buddhists turned their attention to Pope John Paul II's comments on Buddhism in *Crossing the Threshold of Hope* (1994). Sri Lankan Buddhists interpreted his responses to questions on the rising popularity of Buddhism within the West to be particularly disparaging. The pope maintained that *"the Buddhist doctrine of salvation* constitutes the central point, or rather the sole point of this system. Nevertheless, both the Buddhist tradition and the methods deriving from it have an almost exclusively *negative soteriology"* (85, emphasis his).[3] He described Buddhism as an "atheistic" system and alleged that it generates "indifference" in practitioners. The pope's stance stirred indignation and anger among the Sinhala Buddhist public. Sri Lanka's Mahanayaka Theros (leaders of the Buddhist clerical orders) reacted to the Holy See's comparative theology as a deep insult to Buddhists and called for an apology. Malcolm Ranjith, then the bishop of Colombo serving under Archbishop Oswald Gomis (chapter 1), sought to placate Sri Lankan readers by explaining that Pope John Paul II's theological exegesis was not meant to insult but rather to comparatively appraise and "praise" Buddhist philosophy.[4] Sinhala Buddhists were unappeased. They rejected the Sri Lankan Bishop's attempts to exonerate the pope for his assertions of Catholic superiority. They condemned his statement and treated it as evidence that Catholicism is enduringly linked to colonialism and neocolonial principles, consonant with persistent missionary endeavors to disestablish Buddhism.

Even as the conservative Bishop Malcolm Ranjith remained an apologist for the pope's theological critique of Buddhism by attempting to soften its reception in Sri Lanka, ecumenically oriented members of the Catholic Bishop's Conference of Sri Lanka issued a public apology. Appreciative of local Sri Lankan Catholics' conciliatory efforts though he was, Dhammavihari Thero considered the Holy See as characteristically tending to the obligation to "play the conqueror all of the time" (2005, 5). Other Sri Lankan Buddhist critics characterized the pope's flawed discussion of Buddhist doctrine as relying upon outdated nineteenth-century missionary reconnaissance reports on what Buddhists' belief systems entailed (Bodhi 1995; Wimalarathana 1995). Learned Buddhist monks and ecumenical Christians alike critiqued the pope's inclination to sustain the Church's "vested interests" (Jayaweera 1995) and criticized the fact that Sri Lanka was spending millions of dollars to entertain his visit during economic hardship and wartime strife. More pluralistically attuned Christian critics were careful to ensure that their reflections did not devolve into "an exercise in pope-bashing"

(Crusz 1995). Several of the Buddhist monks who wrote for the volume discouraged readers from having a "quarrel" with the pope, even as they made patient exegetical effort to correct his misconceptions of Buddhist soteriology, in layman's terms (e.g., Punnaji 1995).

With the controversy in play, in January 1995 Pope John Paul II visited Sri Lanka amid protests by Buddhists who remained incensed by his commentary. Whereas six Hindu and six Muslim religious leaders met with Pope John Paul II, Buddhist monastic invitees boycotted his visit. The pope gave a public address, saying, "You are very strong in faith. And very strong in . . . how to say? In *attacking*, no?–the Pope? [chortles and awkward laughter audible.] In *addressing* the Pope."[5] Afterward, Pope John Paul II made a spontaneous stop at the Catholic shrine to Saint Anthony, known as Kochikade Church, a site considered sacred and miraculous not only for Sri Lankan Catholics but also for Buddhists and Hindus. Analysts reporting upon the incident have suggested that the stop signified a moment of religious compulsion. The idea that God moved Pope John Paul II to make an unscheduled visit to the church with a substantial multireligious and multiethnic base could have served to quell Buddhists' discontent around his visit to Sri Lanka (Palakidnar 2005; Bastin 2012).[6] But for those Sinhala Buddhists who had existing grievances against Christians and Catholics, such subtle symbolic gestures by the pope to acknowledge the assimilation of Catholicism in the country as righteous and providential could hardly have had a conciliatory effect.

"RADICAL" ASIAN THEOLOGY AND PAPAL AUTHORITY

The second epigraph comes from the writing of Tissa Balasuriya (1924–2013), a Sri Lankan Catholic priest and theologian and a revered figure of the global ecumenical movement whom the Church famously excommunicated in 1997. It was Bishop Malcolm Ranjith of the Colombo Archdiocese who had initiated Father Tissa's excommunication under a Vatican body tasked with "promoting and safeguarding" Roman Catholic doctrine. Cardinal Joseph Ratzinger, at the time prefect of the Vatican's Congregation for the Doctrine of the Faith, oversaw and officiated Father Tissa's excommunication. In that role, Cardinal Ratzinger gained a reputation for being a conservative upholder of Catholic doctrine. In fact, in 1993 a reporter for *Time* magazine referred to the Congregation for the

Doctrine of the Faith as "the Inquisition's latest incarnation" and spotlighted Cardinal Ratzinger's pivotal role within it.[7] Ratzinger was subsequently elected Pope Benedict XVI in 2005 and reigned until his surprise resignation in 2013. It was under Cardinal Ratzinger's direct tutelage that Malcolm Ranjith Bishop of Colombo was promoted to Archbishop in 2009 and was later elevated to the cardinalate in 2010.

Throughout his life Father Tissa Balasuriya was a champion of Asian liberation theology and an advocate for social justice and for ecumenical and interreligious dialogue. He worked with other Catholic clergy members who supported Sri Lankans without regard to religion and ethnicity, in consonance with the values put forth in Vatican II (Fernando 1997). Vatican II (1962–1965) entailed a modernization of the church that was "born from the ashes of the medieval, counter-Reformation anti-modernist outlooks" of the official Church (Napolitano and Norget 2009). The Second Vatican Council allowed the Catholic Church to coordinate with wider changes in the Christian religiosity of postcolonies such as Sri Lanka. A "Christian left" emerged within postcolonial Sri Lanka, consisting of scholars, activists, priests, and nuns engaged in pastoral care of the poor and oppressed (Amarasuriya 2022; Mahadev 2022). This Christian left thrived in the country particularly in the period of 1960s to the 1990s, and associated figures intervened in Sri Lanka's political violence as conscientious objectors through periods of ethnoreligious unrest (Pieris 1995). The Christian social justice advocacy network within Sri Lanka was constituted by Protestant (typically but not exclusively Anglican and Methodist) and Jesuit Catholic scholar-priests. Father Tissa himself belonged to the Oblates of Mary Immaculate, a Catholic order historically associated with vocations of scholarship, teaching, asceticism, and pastoral care of the poor. The Christian left are advocates for a pluralistic and civic nationalism; arguably, some of them can be characterized as "post-nationalist" in their political leanings (Mahadev 2022).

A small subset of Ceylonese Catholic leaders in the postindependence era suppressed their inclination toward social justice advocacy, opting to remain within the conservative fold; they did so largely due to fears of becoming casualties of the Vatican's Cold War era fight against "communism" in decolonizing states (Fernando 1997, 2–3; Mahadev 2022). However, with the sanction of Vatican II, Father Tissa and a small cohort of Catholic thinkers and activists found their calling. He was a founding member of the Ecumenical Association of Third World Theologians (EATWOT), an organization that drew together religious thinkers committed to the Theology of Liberation throughout Asia, Africa, and Latin America. He remained integral to the association throughout his life.

In 1990 Father Tissa published a religious and feminist treatise in the form of a book entitled *Mary and Human Liberation*. At the incitement of Bishop Malcolm Ranjith, the Vatican's Congregation for the Doctrine of the Faith under the prefecture of Cardinal Ratzinger, scrutinized this work. The theologian's writing challenged the traditionalist Catholic image of Mother Mary's submissive character and instead celebrated Mother Mary for her fierce femininity, feminism, and righteous motherhood. Given the liberality of his thesis and the Marxian inflections upon it, conservatives within the modernizing Catholic Church deemed him a negative exemplar. Under the papal body's scrutiny, Father Tissa Balasuriya was excommunicated in 1997 at the age of seventy-two. After some time and much consternation, Father Tissa was compelled to show contrition and signed an official profession of faith; he was reconciled, "encompassed" back into the Catholic Church under the authority of that same Vatican body.[8]

In 2009 I traveled from Colombo to a remote plot of forested land to meet Father Tissa at his home and retreat center. I was struck by his gentle demeanor and simple clothing, his warm face framed by his long white hair. During a tour of the premises he pointed out the large file cabinet that housed all of the documents from his excommunication and reconciliation with the Church. As we sat across from each other, I spied a striking painting of an African Mother Mary and Baby Jesus propped up on display in the corner behind him. Following the direction of my gaze with his eyes, he turned with a laugh and said, "Obama," gesturing to the then-U.S. President's early reputation as a dedicated Christian who worked as a community organizer in service of disadvantaged Black Americans in the south side of Chicago.

Father Tissa and I discussed his own longstanding engagement with the ecumenical justice practices among the priestly community that constituted EATWOT. When I asked Father Tissa whether he considered himself to be a liberation theologian, he seemed to me to be somewhat reluctant to be labeled decisively as such, even as he had written on Asian theologies of liberation throughout his career. He remained a consummate critic of Catholic Church conservatives for attenuating the advances made through the Second Vatican Council and suppressing culturally grounded, socially liberative interpretations of engaged Christian theology. Staying with the spirit of the Christian left, in his

4.1 Father Tissa Balasuriya at his home office and ecumenical retreat center in 2010.

2006 book he questioned how the conservativism of Pope Benedict XVI might disarticulate local priorities to accommodate Asian adaptations of Catholicism. He also raised questions whether the Church under Benedict XVI would foster relationships and show respect for existing religious traditions, in accord with the values that are foundational for the indigenized Christian left. In the view of Catholics and other Christians committed to human rights activism in Asia, Father Tissa's excommunication and the terms of his reconciliation with the Church served as a potent reminder of the conservative Church's capacities to launch an offensive against pluralism (Fernando 1997; van Voohris 1997; Mahadev 2022).[9]

ROOTS AND WINGS

These two quarrels with the popes, one interreligious and one intrareligious, indicate the nature of the relationship between localized religious establishments in Sri Lanka and the conservative frame of Vatican authority. Over the last few decades Vatican leaders and Catholics more generally agitated Sinhala Buddhists because of their imperious approach to engaging religious difference. For the Christian left, which is oriented to social justice in ways that exceed the preservationist and expansionary imperatives of their respective churches, conservative Vatican authorities and their local emissaries appeared to be unwilling to meet local needs for socioeconomic justice, political reform, and interreligious pluralism.

Vis-à-vis Sinhala Buddhists' opposition to "unethical conversions," Christian groups—even those long established in Sri Lanka—have been categorically entangled in a war of identity-based perceptions. The Catholic Church of Sri Lanka had been no less subject to anti-minority sentiment than other evangelical Protestant, Pentecostal, and independent Christian groups that are typically classified as expansionary in their ambitions. However, in the postwar context, the Catholic Church of Sri Lanka strived to demonstrate the value of its international character and clout, and simultaneously of its rootedness in the nation (Mahadev 2013; Hertzberg 2016). It did so through its institutional center. Through careful coordination with Vatican officials, ethnic Sinhala leaders of Sri Lanka's Catholic Church sought to disentangle the Church from broader allegations of Christian anti-nationalism after the war. They publicized their strivings toward Buddhist-Catholic amity. In essence, Sinhala Catholic leadership strived to set the Catholic Church apart from "fundamentalist" Christianity.

Sinhala Catholic and Buddhist leaders deployed diplomacy and theopolitical maneuvering to transform hegemonic majoritarian populist determinations about who belongs to the nation. Through public performances of interreligious friendship, they activated the conditions of possibility for postwar Catholic exceptionalism within Sri Lanka. The new policies to promote interreligious harmony within the Church impacted postwar idealizations of Sri Lankan sovereignty as it played out on a global stage. Forging this relationship amplified conservativism through Catholic leaders' efforts to rein in the attractive charismatic movement known as the Catholic Charismatic Renewal (CCR), which the Church had authorized under Vatican II. These mediations and remediations are at once theological, liturgical, aesthetic, and politically pragmatic.

A NEW INJUNCTION

In October 2009 the Catholic Diocese of Colombo circulated a new dictum among Catholic parishioners with reference to lay Catholic performances of "paraliturgical services." Through the memorandum the newly appointed Archbishop Malcolm Ranjith expressed his concern that these services were interfering with the sanctity of the Mass. Addressing clergy and laypeople through a liturgical circular "concerning various Movements and Services," the archbishop censured the incorporation of charismatic "praise and worship" practices among Catholics. The Archdiocese of Colombo disseminated the memorandum to parishes throughout the entire country, to call upon Catholics to observe "sobriety" in worship. The circular included the following injunction:

> The so-called "Praise and worship" elements are not allowed during the entire rite of Mass. Inordinate loud music, clapping, long interventions, gestures which disturb the sobriety of the celebration are not permitted. It is very important that we understand the religious cultural sensitivity of the Sri Lankan people. Majority around us are Buddhists whose worship is thoroughly sober; and Muslims and Hindus too do not create any commotion in their worship. In addition, we know that there is strong opposition to Fundamentalist Christian sects in this country, and we as Catholics, have been striving to explain that Catholics are different from these sects. However, some of these so-called praise and worship exercises seem to resemble more of the Fundamentalist religious exercises than those of the Roman Catholics. Let us respect our cultural diversity and sensitivity.[10]

The archbishop used the liturgical circular of 2009 to denounce the Pentecostal-charismatic form for producing a "cacophonous exuberance" in what ought to be a contemplative practice of Christianity.

The Sinhala Catholic archbishop's dictum evinced conservativism and a traditionalist orientation to ecclesiastical authority. He advanced the injunction against charismatic "praise and worship" on the premise of Buddhist-Catholic harmony, which he suggested hinges upon shared aesthetic values of quietude and sobriety that inhere within both of these religious traditions. Insisting that

Sri Lankan Catholics must abide by those values, further on in the circular Archbishop Ranjith espoused how the Eucharistic liturgy carried out during the Catholic Mass forms "the source and summit from which all divine graces flow into the Church." The Catholic orientation to the containment of grace under the authority of the priesthood is built upon a Petrine apostolic genealogy. Within Catholicism, the priest is incorporated in the body of Christ as a descendant of Saint Peter and holds the liturgical keys to the sacraments. Quite differently, this priestly gatekeeping function is partially circumvented with the charismatic Christian notion that the Holy Spirit is activated in an effusive free-flow that directly sanctifies the individual.[11] That flow might be channeled by way of a minister but does not necessarily require the mediation of an ordained cleric. Pentecostals experience charismata as an effusive spiritual presence. Within the Catholic Charismatic Renewal, which is sometimes referred to as "Catholic Pentecostalism," charismata flow in a similarly effusive way. The movement is active in numerous localities where the Catholic Church thrives. Within it, distinctions between the Petrine and Pauline apostolic genealogies are fused and blurred (Mahadev 2013; de Abreu 2016). As evident in the circular, however, traditionalist strands of Catholic ecclesiastical authority demanded that the laity disentangle these religious forms. This remediating work of disentangling the Petrine from the Pauline religious form to restore a degree of Catholic orthodoxy in Sri Lanka was pragmatically invaluable for the Church in this fraught moment in Sri Lankan theopolitics.

Within Sri Lanka's Catholic Church, the CCR is referred to as "Pubuduwa," which in Sinhala means "flourishing" or "revival." Catholic laity in the United States originally developed the charismatic revival within the Church in the early 1970s, and it quickly became a global movement. The CCR gained the sanction of the Catholic Church in 1975. Vatican II allowances for "enculturation" and accommodation enabled the Catholic Church to incorporate and affirm the charismatic submovement (Csordas 1994).[12] Where it flourishes, the charismatic renewal movement is credited for keeping Catholics who have been keen to explore Pentecostal Christianity within the Catholic fold (Csordas 1997). Yet the Sri Lankan Archbishop's statement suggests that it is incumbent upon orthodox Catholic authorities to scrutinize Catholic Pubuduwa practices because they too closely resemble the "flamboyant" practices of Pentecostals. The Sri Lankan Church hierarchy cautioned Catholics who are involved in the Pubuduwa movement to be careful of such boisterous expressions of religiosity, lest Buddhist opponents of "unethical conversions" take notice, and mistake Catholics for born-again "fundamentalists."

In the days immediately after the archbishop broadcast the liturgical circular among Catholics across the country, a leader of the CCR Pubuduwa movement paid a visit to a senior Jesuit Catholic theologian in Sri Lanka's movement for ecumenism and interreligious dialogue and pluralism. I learned of their commiseration from the ecumenical leader. He had told me that the Pubuduwa lay leader—I will call him Brother Sunil—arrived at his doorstep an anxious state. He lamented to the ecumenical theologian that the new archbishop's liturgical circular directly took aim at the CCR movement and would impinge upon Brother Sunil's efforts to revive and renew Catholic devotion via the Pubuduwa movement. The learned social justice–oriented theologian and the charismatic Catholic lay leader could not be farther apart on the spectrum of Catholic religious affinity. What the two held in common though was the fact that conservative Sri Lankan Church leadership, under Archbishop Ranjith, was working to curtail possibilities for Catholic thought and practice that had been authorized under Vatican II, thus affecting the religious work to which they each were dedicated.

By the time that the Sri Lankan Archbishop Malcolm Ranjith had issued the liturgical circular, he was well known in the Church for his conservatism. Pope Benedict had appointed him as the Vatican's Secretary of Congregation for Divine Worship and the Discipline of the Sacraments. In that capacity, at the Vatican in February 2009 Ranjith made an impassioned argument for withdrawing a number of Vatican II liturgical reforms and reverting to several of the old Vatican I dicta.[13] Within the Vatican, Archbishop Ranjith was a foremost proponent of restoring the Latin Mass. He thereby solidified his position as a favorite among conservative Vatican authorities, especially Pope Benedict.[14] Applying these rules and regulations in Sri Lanka through the liturgical circular of October 2009, Archbishop Ranjith installed the mandate that Sri Lankan Catholic laity receive the sacraments while kneeling and by mouth, rather than in hand, to ensure that the avenue for communion with the divine is free of obstruction. Despite their unyielding dedication to the Church, several Sri Lankan Catholic priests quietly balked at the archbishop's directive when it arrived. Some voiced fears that this style of distributing communion would pose a public health hazard and stated that they would not abide by the order.

ASSUAGING TENSIONS

The October 2009 regulations on liturgy were crafted not only with the express purpose of upholding the integrity of ecclesiastic rituals. More crucially for the Sri Lankan Catholic Church, through the dictum that insisted upon devotional "sobriety," the archbishop emphatically sought to distance his Church from audibly charismatic and evangelizing forms of Christianity. In doing so he endeavored to secure the Church's exceptional capacity to coexist with Sri Lanka's Buddhist majority. Catholics comprise the majority of all Christian groups in Sri Lanka.[15] Sri Lankan Catholic leaders thereby worked diligently to "dialogue with" Buddhist protectionists so as to assure them that Catholicism is well seated in Sri Lanka, and as such that Catholics had little reason to seek new converts. Sri Lankan Catholic leaders asserted that Catholic "evangelism" does not entail an agenda to expand the church but rather is simply intended to deepen the faith of those Sri Lankans who are born as Catholics. They conveyed to Buddhist nationalist activists that they in fact faced bothersome incursion by born-again Christian proselytizers who sought to convert born Catholics, as much as Buddhists did. The archbishop conveyed this message to Sri Lankan Buddhists—a message that stood in apparent contrast to the broader messaging of the conservative pope.[16]

Officials of the Catholic Bishop's Conference of Colombo affirmed Archbishop Ranjith's reasoning for instituting the liturgical reforms. As one Sri Lankan Catholic official put it to me, "The anti-conversion efforts came up because fundamentalists in the Gospel business go in for direct conversions." He explained that by 2008 the original drafters of the 2004 legislative bill had come to recognize the distinction between "independent" (nondenominational) churches that freely evangelized and the established Catholic and mainline Protestant churches: "It is only the fundamentalist churches that are a threat (to Buddhism) actually. We have been dialoguing with the JHU [Jathika Hela Urumaya, the political party responsible for putting forth the original 2004 "anti-conversion" bill] for some time now to make them aware of our distinction from other Christian groups. So the original impetus driving the Bill has died out. It is a dead issue. The government is not interested in raising issues that will cause communal troubles." The Bishops' Conference and the archbishop himself drew parallels between Sri Lankan Catholicism and Buddhist institutions to convey their fraternity and similitude on the basis of shared devotional aesthetics—marking their distinction from Pentecostal-charismatic Christianity.

RITES OF DELIVERANCE: "SHEEP-STEALING," RIVALRY, AND DISPLACEMENT

This requirement of Sri Lankan Catholics to differentiate their worship from Pentecostalism has had implications for liturgical rites, and for the comportment of Catholic practitioners in the Pubuduwa movement. As discussed in chapter 3, the imperative to take on a "new life" with Christ is often marked by provocative discourses that condemn features of the newcomer's "past" as diabolical. Manichean distinctions of the divinely graced, and the diabolically afflicted, are imputed through born-again epistemologies (Marshall 2009). Within certain Third-Wave Pentecostal deliverance ministries, incitements to spiritual warfare sometimes play out as negative appraisals of religious others.

Prior to the arrival of Pentecostalism, powerful styles of Catholic deliverance that had been prevalent in the Catholic belt in the Gampaha District and northern outskirts of Colombo in the early 1970s significantly waned by the early 1990s (Stirrat 1992). That popular form of Catholic religiosity thrived in sites where institutional Catholic Church influence had long existed. As we saw in chapter 1, Buddhists alleged that a prosperous and high-profile figure who had converted under the authority of one such Catholic priest had been culpable for the death of a Buddhist monk, leading to the vilification of Christians in general and this style of deliverance in particular. The Catholic deliverance rituals involving exorcisms en masse arguably existed long before the arrival of born-again Pentecostalism in that region.

Elsewhere within South Asia, mass Catholic deliverance cults spanned back to the early seventeenth century, arising during the early phases of Jesuit Catholic missionization in the southern Indian state of Tamilnadu (Mosse 2006, 2012; Zupanov 2008). The Jesuit missionaries of the region subsequently endeavored to rationalize and modernize local Catholic practices that had taken root in the region. By the late nineteenth century, the Jesuit priests sought to supplant the practice of exorcism en masse, by instead giving prominence to hearing lay Catholics' confessions of sin (Mosse 2006). Confession became a new modality through which Catholic parishioners could expunge figurative demons, gain "discipline," enable healing, and, most important, reconcile with God. The Catholic deliverance and healing prevalent in Sri Lanka's Western Province in the 1970s–early 1990s (Stirrat 1992), arguably stemmed from those older styles of Catholic deliverance practice. Supplicants flocked to seek out exceptionally gifted Catholic priest-healers at Sri Lankan shrines, transforming these sites into pilgrimage destinations that were centered around the adepts' execution of power. Thousands of pilgrims—predominantly Catholic, but also Buddhist, Hindu, and occasionally Muslim—visited these shrines to seek the healing grace channeled through the Fathers. Each of these rival priests engaged rituals that demonstrated for believers their exceptional piety, Christlike renunciation, and command over sacred relics. The Catholic adepts' miracle work enabled each of these figures to appear as the very personification of and unique conduit for grace, and to enable healing and capacities for deliverance from demons.

As with contemporary Pentecostalism, the Catholic exorcism and deliverance rites of the mid- to late twentieth century in Sri Lanka involved spirited diabolization of Buddhist and Hindu deities.[17] In recent decades, in the coastal regions of Sri Lanka where Catholicism still predominates, Pentecostalism has largely supplanted the folk Catholic deliverance rituals and shrines of the kind described by Stirrat. What is more, neo-Pentecostalism nowadays competes with the authoritative reformist demands of the Sri Lankan Catholic Church, as implied within Archbishop Malcolm Ranjith's liturgical circular of 2009.

In chapter 3 I depicted how within some deliverance ministries charismatic pastors adaptively emulate the Catholic ritual form of the Eucharistic Mass, typically doing so without offering priestly mediation. What is more, in these shared regions of Catholic and Pentecostal influence, Pentecostal pastors make frequent mocking reference to Catholicism in the course of their sermons. For one, Pastor Sirisena sings, dances, jokes, and bellows his praise of Jesus, amplified with high levels of reverb. Capitalizing on sound technology, the pastor intersperses Sinhala pop songs, dances, exalting gestures, and jokes that elicit laughter, smiles, smirks, and applause from his massive congregation. Pastor Sirisena makes passionate, full-throated assertions proclaiming the ultimacy of Jesus's authority followed by rounds of halleluiahs. In another moment he imitates the slow, monophonic grandeur of Gregorian-style chant ordinarily voiced during the consecration of the sacraments in the Catholic Church. The recognizable gesture to the Catholic Mass, juxtaposed with the pastor's fast-talking performance style, creates provocative commentary that is taken to suggest to the laughing congregation how the Catholic Mass is a passive and inefficacious form of engagement, in contrast to his charismatically inspired style—*deviyange anugrahaya lath* (Sinhala, "received by the grace of God"). Pastor Sirisena's song and dance pokes fun of the established Catholic pathways to commune with God. This disparaging humor critiques the ossification of charismatic author-ity—in Weber's terminology, the "routinization of charisma"—that Pentecostal deliverance ministers aver is endemic to Catholic mediations of the divine. The pastor's jokes induce raucous laughter among the born-again congregants—laughter that, some devout Sri Lankan Catholics might fear, could initiate new-comers into disparaging their inherited Catholic faith as they are inducted into born-again charismatic forms of sociality. Indeed, eventually, for some of these Pentecostal newcomers, this laughter could come to index knowledge of things "past"—as spiritual forms of life that born Catholics might learn to cast to the margins of their community.

In these zones that have long been predominantly Catholic areas where Third-Wave Pentecostalism now flourishes, Pentecostals typically treat devo-tions to the Catholic patron saints and Mother Mary as detrimental, and poten-tially diabolical distractions "created by Satan" to prevent exclusive commit-ment to monotheistic or even Trinitarian principles. On this basis, born-again Pentecostal Christians engage their variety of piety as one vastly superior to Catholicism. According to the sermonic discourses of Pentecostal ministers, Catholicism appears as little better than Hindu and Buddhist forms of "idola-try." Pentecostal discourses derisively suggest that this "idolatry" (Sinhala: *rupa namaskarēya*, literally image worship or veneration) can enable demonic afflic-tion. Pastor Milton, for instance, disavowed the statue of Mother Mary that is stationed near the entrance of the rented factory building that houses his minis-try. The building's Catholic owner had installed it long before Pastor Milton had adopted it as the site of his prayer hall. Rather than struggle to remove it though, the Pentecostal minister affirmed that his congregation is constituted of true believers who are not tempted to worship the statue. They simply bypass it. As per Pastor Milton's insistence, members of his ministry piously worship "only in the name of Jesus and the Cross."

One of the primary targets of Archbishop Ranjith's dictum about cultural sensitivity and sobriety of worship was the internationally recognized Catholic Charismatic Renewal. What local amalgamations of Catholic practices emerged as a result of these remediating, anticharismatic injunctions put forth by Sri Lanka's central Catholic authority?

THE CATHOLIC CHARISMATIC RENEWAL IN URBAN SRI LANKA

Pubuduwa is promoted by a Colombo based lay Catholic group named the Community of the Risen Lord (CRL). Leading the movement is a Catholic charismatic lay leader, Lalith Perera, known among his followers as Lalith Thatha (Lalith Father).[18] During Wednesday night CRL prayer meetings in Colombo, the crowd swells well beyond the capacity of the Catholic school auditorium where it is held, with nearly two thousand people in attendance. The Wednesday night meetings are conducted in English, with simulcast translations in Sinhala and Tamil transmitted to separate outdoor corners where, anticipating the crowd, the *Sevakayo* (ministerial assistants) have set out chairs to accommodate the overflow. These outdoor areas are equipped with screens and audio equipment that capture the goings-on on the charismatic stage, including the song, testimonials, prayerful expressions of thanksgiving, and beseechments asking God to show his grace, all punctuated by glossolalic interludes. The projected images fade in and out to show different angles of the stage, the audience, the faces of the prayer leaders, and lyrics to allow devotees to follow along in song.

Lalith Thatha established the Catholic Community of the Risen Lord in the early 1970s, shortly after the movement had been developed in the United States. When news of the 2009 liturgical regulations reached his ears, he surmised that the archbishop had intended to rein in the CRL. Through conversations between Lalith Perera and the archbishop, they agreed that certain modifications of CRL practices were to be put into effect. As I learned from the charismatic lay leader in an interview, Archbishop Ranjith had newly barred the handling of the Holy Eucharist during these Wednesday night prayer meetings, even by an ordained priest. Prior to the regulations, I had observed that at the end of the CRL service a single Catholic priest would process across the length of the auditorium to the outer perimeter of the building, giving all of the devotees visible access to the divine presence within the Eucharistic monstrance. With the priestly display there was a palpable intensification of glossolalia. Following the new dictum on extraliturgical services, however, the devotees waited expectantly for the monstrance containing the charism to appear. But by the terms of the concession to Archbishop Ranjith, officiants of the service were required to keep the sacred host stationed in the middle of the stage. As representatives within the Catholic Bishops' Conference explained to me in an interview in February 2010, the CRL "had to make certain adjustments so as to not mislead the people. People may get things from CRL that they don't get from Sunday liturgy. But the objective [of CRL] must be to lead them back to their local parishes."

It appeared that this modification did slightly diminish the intensity of charismatic expression in the Colombo CRL prayer meetings in those final moments of the service. Speaking in tongues persisted at the services, but with notably less verve. Still, the numbers of Catholics who regularly attended the services had not been significantly affected. The Catholic Pubuduwa services continued to thrive, with the gifts of tongues gracing the participants. Lalith Thatha offers rousing biblical exegesis not ordinarily heard within the Catholic Church. For example, he delivered a sermon on the Jew named Saul who ardently "persecuted Christians" in his day. Lalith Thatha sermonized upon how the voice of God told him to stop his persecution: "Saul had a complete change of heart—Praise the Lord! The Jew named Saul had become the Apostle named Paul! Hal-le-lu-jah! Hal-le-lu-jah! Hal-le-lu-jah!" Engaging with the incorporeal manifestation of God through the Holy Spirit as Saint Paul had, the CLR promotes an "apostolic" Pauline attachment of the charismatic Catholic self to the God who is present in the immediacy of "the here and now."

CHARISMATIC CATHOLIC RENEWAL IN
SMALL TOWN PERIPHERIES

The Community of the Risen Lord (CRL) exports Catholic Pubuduwa devotionalism to various "outstation" Catholic parishes. Through CRL outreach programs, these parishes became occasional satellites to the Sri Lankan center of the Catholic Charismatic Renewal. One southern Sri Lankan coastal town, a predominantly Buddhist region where I conducted a major segment of my study, housed a Catholic parish that considered itself to be blessed to receive monthly visits from the CRL. At the time of my research (2009–2011), roughly two hundred Catholic families belonged to that parish. Father Stuart, the parish priest, affirmed and welcomed Pubuduwa as a lay Catholic practice within his church.

He explained that he was not troubled by this form of Catholic expression among his parishioners. Father Stuart found that CRL's emphasis on meditating upon Jesus resonated with the goals of advancing piety among Catholic laity.

Although Pubuduwa services were a relatively new component of Church activities, on the Sunday mornings during which the monthly Pubuduwa service was to be held, Mass was particularly well attended. The church swelled not only with the regular congregants of the parish, but also with Catholics who ordinarily attended Mass in smaller churches that did not play host to Pubuduwa services. Some Catholics traveled from upward of twenty-five kilometers away to take part. In spite of Father Stuart's embrace of Pubuduwa for Catholic laypeople and nuns, subsequent to the circulation of the archbishop's dictum on liturgical conformity I observed that some new regulations were instituted in the parish. Following the Sunday Mass and homily offered by the priest, in the week after the memorandum on Catholic liturgy had been circulated, Catholic parishioners were given special instructions on how to engage in the CRL services. Brother Francis, a seminarian and assistant to Father Stuart, explained to the congregation that CRL leaders had traveled from Colombo to conduct Pubuduwa services. "*Lalith Pererage athula kandayam aawa*," "Lalith Perera's inner circle has come," Brother Francis told the congregation members, rousing their attention.

On that Sunday after the liturgical circular had been issued, Brother Francis explained to us that the Pubuduwa service was to be relocated. Rather than conduct the Pubuduwa within the cathedral, which faced the main road and from which passersby could glimpse the pious activities of communion, the Pubuduwa service would take place in another building, tucked behind the church where parish social events were held. This relocation would not only maintain the sanctity of the liturgical and the ecclesiastical space as prescribed by Church authorities, but it would also prevent the sounds of ecstatic worship from escaping the premises and alerting those passersby that the Catholic parish had adopted the charismatic form.

Abiding by the directives of the circular, Brother Francis gave several caveats before allowing participation in the Pubuduwa service. He stated that if members of the congregation elected to take part in the service that they ought not yell or shout during the service: "*kaeae gahanne epaa.*" He insisted that the participants do not simply utter disconnected "letters" or nonsensical sounds: "*akuru kiyawenne epaa.*" "You must pray beautifully. Prayer for us is meditation": "*nyaaj-nyaa keriima bhavana tamay.*" Brother Francis continued his directive:

Prayer through song is famous in Lalith Thatha's services—there you find many different types of songs than the hymns we sing during our services. However, without praying in the correct way some people come and scold the priest or the bishop, and call them crazy [*pissu*]. Without praying the correct way, some deny the Father, or Bishop, call him crazy, and leave the Church. Practice prayer in the right way. We want to heighten our religious experience [*usas wenna oone*]. This is the way that we should protect our religion. This is the way we should behave in our religion.

He implicitly warned those who were eager to participate in the Pubuduwa service against Catholic defection to Pentecostalism. Brother Francis closed his statement with the quip, "We're not here for a birthday party!"

Following this announcement, the Father Stuart and Brother Francis took their leave. Most of the Catholic laypeople who were present during Mass, along with nuns from the adjacent Convent, filed out of the church building and filled an adjacent building. I followed the crowd. After some technical difficulties the services began. Alternating projections of a single image of Jesus and lyrics to devotional songs flashed upon the screen at the front of the room. The sermon preached by one Colombo-based CRL leader, Brother Arjith was structured so that the devotees would repeat the utterances involved in the sermon. Backup singers, instrumentals, the congregation's praise talk, and the exuberant exaltations of the praise leaders produced a dissonantly layered sound, which overlaid the song's baseline. Devotees closed their eyes and swayed with arms outstretched, nodding their heads to the pulse of the ambient sound. Perhaps out of obedience to Brother Francis's ground rules, or perhaps as a result of being novice to the charismatic form, the devotees of the church themselves did not talk in tongues. Rather, they quietly whispered their legible but enchanted praise. The praise of Brother Arjith and the other CRL leaders, on the other hand, crescendoed toward a passionate song-chant-prayer interspersed with a "shari-a-la-la-la-la-la-la . . ." of tongues. More utterances of "shia-la-la-la-la-la" pierced the soundscape as the prayer leaders spoke in tongues while the congregation quietly uttered their prayers.

Catholic clergy did not monitor or police the charismatic forms of Pubuduwa outright. Participation in the Pubuduwa practices of the Community of the Risen Lord is indeed encouraged by ecclesiastical authorities even in such "outstation" places as this southern parish. Nevertheless, following the release of

Archbishop Ranjith's liturgical circular there was a strict tempering of the charismatic form found within the Sri Lankan Catholic Church's official Pubuduwa movement.

SINHALA CATHOLIC NORMATIVITY AND
AN ECCLESIASTICALLY APPROVED CATHOLIC REVIVALISM

Compared to those Catholics who have adopted CRL Pubuduwa practices in Colombo and in southern "outstation" areas, Catholics dwelling in Catholic strongholds of Sri Lanka evidently abide by normative forms of attachment to Catholic Church authority. Deferentially committed Catholics in Sri Lanka overtly resist the Pentecostal-charismatic form. In the company of other traditionalist Catholics, they also tend to disparage the Pubuduwa charismatic Catholic form. I observed this in practice in the Catholic belt between the cities of Colombo and Negombo. There, instead, one finds another thoroughly Catholic form of revivalism that is popularly enacted through a service known as Kurusa Dähäna (the Enchanting Cross). A Catholic priest, Father Terrence, conducts the weekly Kurusa Dähäna service. It generates a soundscape that is quite different from that which emerges from Pentecostal-charismatic "praise and worship" practices that so easily draw the attention of its Buddhist and Catholic critics.

Roughly twenty kilometers north of Colombo, in the vicinity of Ja-Ela, I encountered many families dedicated to Catholicism who hold strong opinions about Pentecostals. It appears that those dedicated Catholics mark their distinction from Pentecostals with a pejorative tone. Catholics refer to their peculiar Pentecostal neighbors as "*Bible katīya*," connoting a Bible "gang" or "sect." However, the Pentecostal bearers of the nickname given to them by Catholics like to in turn spin the terms sympathetically to mean "people of the Book." One of my Catholic interlocutors from the village, Dakota *malli* explained to me in Sinhala that they referred to Pentecostals as such because "they require a lot of time [*wädiya waellāwa*] for Bible reading." "Too much of time!" Dakota repeated in his broken English translation. The term "*Bible katīya*" thus connotes an important aspect of faith that separates Catholics from Protestants and Pentecostals. Indeed, that relationship relates to the differential between the mediating force of the Catholic priest as opposed to an ideology of supposedly unmediated access to the word of God that one strives for through interiorized practices of Bible reading, which is primary for Protestants and prevalent to an extent among Pentecostals too. Dakota Dias and his family had also grown accustomed to seeing Jehovah's Witnesses going door-to-door evangelizing. Jehovah's witnesses, like Pentecostals, worship "without images" (*rupa naetuwa*), Dakota and his family emphasized. Dakota further specified that *Bible katīya* Pentecostals deny Mother Mary and the Saints. "*Bible katīya* refuse to pray to statues, and only pray to Jesus through the image of the Cross because of their exclusive focus on the Bible." Suranmaya, Dakota's cousin, added that she had heard Pentecostals call their god "Yeweh," which she understood to be a different god than her own. In fact, in the 2009 liturgical circular, Archbishop Ranjith had addressed the Pentecostal usage of "YHWH," condemning its usage among Christians: "The Tetragram 'YHWH' is not to be pronounced in prayers or hymns because of its sacred nature.... This takes into account the sensitivity of the Jewish community in this regard, from whom we inherited much into our worship," Archbishop Malcolm Ranjith had stated in the document.[19]

The entire Dias family, and their extended kin and neighbors of the village, were all devoutly Catholic and were clear about this in articulating their perceptions of Pentecostals as others. They evidently took distance from neighbors who they knew to be Pubuduwa *pauwla* or "Catholic Charismatic revivalist families" associated with the CRL. Jackson Dias in one breath commented that the head of the CRL was his own kinsman and in another insinuated that CRL practices are un-Catholic. As he spoke, he gestured to the oddness of charismatic Catholic practice and the practitioners themselves with a circling of his finger at his temple, implying that he viewed all charismatics, including those who considered themselves to be Catholic, to be "a touch crazy" (*pissu*).

Since these traditionally committed Sinhala Catholics conceive of themselves as devotedly and normatively Catholic, holding themselves to be distinct from Pubuduwa Catholics, Pentecostals, and other varieties of Protestants, I was intrigued to learn that the Dias family and many Sinhala Catholics of the area regularly participate in another variety of what might be called "extraliturgical services." The Thursday night "God's service" (*Deva mēhēya*) takes place weekly outside of their usual Sunday Mass at St. Rogus Church in Ja-Ela town. Dakota *malli* and Mrs. Dias (his mother, "aunty"), excitedly told me of this meeting, which takes place at another parish several kilometers away. This particular *Deva mēhēya* was decidedly not a Pubuduwa service; rather, the service, known as the Kurusa Dāhāna, conducted by a priest named Father Terrence on the grounds of

St. Helena Catholic Church, had the sanction of local Catholic authorities. Much buzz about Father Terrence's revivalism and healing capacities circulated among Colombo-based Catholics too. Father Terrence began conducting the Catholic prayer service "to enkindle the faith of the people" beginning in 2009, at the behest of the former Archbishop Oswald Gomis.[20] The stated objective of the Kurusa Dähäna service was to fortify Catholic piety, and implicitly to defend against the expansion of Protestant and particularly Pentecostal Christian institutions that had sprung up in the vicinity.

At dusk one Thursday, the Dias family, several neighbors, and I—about twelve of us—piled into a van slated to go from their village to St. Helena Church. We drove for over half an hour along dark, dusty, and winding roads until we reached our destination. Along the way my Catholic interlocutors excitedly told me that St. Helena Parish was located upon sacred grounds (Saint Helena is revered for having discovered the relics of the crucifixion during the fourth century). The sacredness is enhanced by the Way of the Cross (*pada namasakarēya*), fourteen articles of faith that are stationed in the church yard, around which parishioners communally retell and reenact Christ's Passion.[21] Father Terrence initiated Kurusa Dähäna at St. Helena's to shore up Catholic devotion in his own parish, and among Catholics living throughout the district.

As some of the last devotees trickling onto the grounds of the amphitheater, we lit small yellow Catholic candles and planted them in an alcove near the stage. The flames flickered, casting their light in the direction of a huge wooden crucifix. We made our way toward an edge of the large outdoor stage and found a place to stand alongside of the congregated mass. As my eyes adjusted to the dark, I was amazed to see that some three to four thousand people had assembled on the grounds of this rural parish. Judging from the enormous crowd, the popularity of the Kurusa Dähäna service went well beyond the few parishes for which the services had been prescribed. The congregants stood in a U-shaped formation facing the stage. A raised platform was stocked with images from the Passion, flanked by wooden angels. Altar boys donning vermillion cassocks stood at the bottom of the platform, while recorded Sinhala devotional hymns with strong male choral vocals and a female backup singer enveloped us in sound. The music and talk from the crowd came to a hush as Father Terrence approached the lectern, and the faces around me became solemnly focused.

Father Terrence began a solo praise in a cadence that resembled the authoritative, gentle speech uttered in the edifying homilies performed in traditional

4.2 and 4.3 Preparations for the Kurusa Daehaena.

St. Helena Church, Yakkaduwa, Ja-Ela, https://www.facebook.com/StHelenaChurchYakkaduwaJaElaSri Lanka (posted August 2, 2012).

Sinhala Catholic churches. Then he moved to elongate each of his utterances. The grandeur of his enunciation confessed to God the sin of the people and the country, and asked forgiveness for all people devoted to him. Into the microphone, he proclaimed in Sinhala: "We want to give thanks to you Lord!" This supplication reached a point of pause, opening to a round of praise utterances in English and in Sinhala, amplified by the elaborate outdoor sound system. Each phrase was uttered first by the priest. Each phrase was then followed by succinct, matching utterances from a small handful of female lay devotees with the monophonic intonation of a Mass reading. "Amen." "Amen." "Amen." "Amen." "Praise the Lord." "Praise the Lord." "Praise the Lord." "Praise the Lord." "Halleluuiah." "Halleluiah." "Halleluuuuiah." "Halleluiah." "*Prasansa wewa*" (we praise you). "*Prasansa wewa*." "*Mahimaya wewa*" (we glorify you). "*Mahimaya wewa*." "Halleluuuiah." "Halleluiah." "Praise the Lord." "Praise the Lord."

Returning in Sinhala to the priestly cadence of prayer, Father Terrence began offering a general pronouncement of thanks on behalf of the healed as he announced a miraculous event, naming a recent date on which one member of the congregation was delivered from a significant handicap. More rounds of praise for Jesus ensued. Directly following upon Father Terrence's leading utterances, the assembly uttered "*Prasansa wewa*" succinctly, in unison with the microphoned voices of the Church women.

Father Terrence then soloed his praise, addressing God: "The families you've freed, through your healing Grace . . . We want to give our thanks, dear God." His voice grew to a crescendo as he turned to speak of the Covenant:

> Since the experience on the Mountain, every single one of our lives has changed [*häma kenekagēma jīwitte wenas una*]! Out of love for us, you appointed Moses during his mountain experience [Mount Sinai, where Moses received the Commandments], you appointed Abraham, you appointed Jacob, you appointed Isaac. Our venerated one, You appointed Jesus *wahansii* to lead us to another experience on the mountain [where Jesus delivered the Sermon on the Mount prior to his Ascension]. We shall give our love, and our thanks, through this song [*gīthika*], "*mang adarē Jesu.*"

Following the song of adoration for Jesus, and a further round of exaltations, the *Dēva mēhēya* service came to a close when an assistant priest carried the monstrance containing the sacred host, shielded under a yellow parasol. Such is typical in Eucharistic processions at the Vatican, wherein the sacred host is displayed shielded by a canopy. In a similar fashion, the holy Buddhist relics are carried under a yellow parasol during processions in Sri Lanka. Now, as the monstrance was revealed, all who had gathered lit more yellow Catholic candles. The light set the open-air nave aglow, each visage evincing solemnity as the congregation grasped to take in the momentary manifestation of the Holy Spirit, with arms outstretched to receive God's grace as the sacred host passed by the nave. Father Terrence, together with the priest who carried the monstrance forward in procession, moved toward a separate building on the St. Helena Church campus. Father Terrence stationed himself adjacent to it, and the crowd quickly surrounded him. Each supplicant received a hand-to-forehead blessing from the priest. When the crowded dwindled, a handful of people stayed on, moving indoors for a brief, small-group prayer and healing session with Father Terrence. According to Dias family, the rite of exorcism, when called for, takes place privately, by appointment.

Father Terrence's Catholic ministry adopts certain features found in charismatic Christian prayer meetings and yet ensures that the authoritative tenets of Catholicism are upheld. Kurusa Dähäna sermons do not condemn the worship of the saints and Mary. Yet, the services placed emphasis upon the genealogy of the covenant and Christ's sacrifice, encouraging the deepening of belief less through focus on the pious intermediaries who were exemplars of faith and bearers of grace than through direct and unmediated praise of the Savior himself. The cadence of speech paralleled Catholics' regard of the Holy Spirit as concentrated and contained within the Eucharist. Further, as distinct from pentecostalist movements including the Catholic Pubuduwa, in the Kurusa Dähäna service the congregation matched Father Terrence's utterances word for word, without a single flourish. The spiritual power contained by the Eucharist appeared to emanate out from it, and the believing congregants reached out to receive this grace. But the manifestation was expressed subtly, with an air of relative containment. Within this extraliturgical service the experience and emanation of the Holy Spirit was enclosed by the utterances and ritual gestures of Catholic priestly authority.

The precise repetition of Father Terrence's utterances, without any flourish of speech or gesture from the congregation, distinguishes this local ecclesiastical form of Sri Lankan Catholic revivalism from the Pentecostal "excesses" of speaking in tongues. In accord with Archbishop Ranjith's directive, Pastor Terrence's Kurusa Dähäna avoided "cacophonous exuberance"—an exuberance that for charismatics signifies the pure and unmediated presence of the Holy Spirit. As I have argued, the overt and intentional effort to mark the differences between traditional Catholic and Pentecostal structures of charismata and the modalities of transmitting the Holy Spirit are consonant with distinct apostolic genealogies. Pentecostalism is rooted in a dispensation of the charism stemming jointly from Saint Paul and from the Pentecost. It is signaled by glossolalia, whereby grace is dispersed democratically, spontaneously, and exogenously. It appears to move outward from its source, lending to Buddhists' anxieties that it "spreads like mushrooms."

In Catholicism, the apostolic dispensation through Saint Peter—symbolized by a rock—is stable, slow and steady. In contrast to Saint Paul's spontaneous transmission and "acephalous" epiphany, Saint Peter was one of the original Disciples of Christ who received the body and blood of Christ at the Last Supper and was present at the Sermon on the Mount prior to Christ's Ascension. Peter was one among the original twelve who were set forth on the Great Commission and received the charism at Pentecost. Catholics regard Saint Peter to have received a unique charism from God and thus is known as "the rock" upon which the Catholic Church was built. As First Bishop of Rome, Saint Peter is understood to have directly passed the charism on to subsequent popes in an unbroken chain to the current pope. Ordained Catholic clergymen unbridle the charism through ritual consecration, enabling the Holy Spirit to hallow the Eucharistic Host. The Catholic liturgy is thus sacrosanct and is hence carefully guarded by the papacy. As such, despite Vatican II's general validation of global movements such as the Catholic Charismatic Renewal, in Sri Lanka, Catholic Pubuduwa troubled the line between exogenous outreach and stable reiteration of authority.

POLITICAL THEOLOGY, DIPLOMACY, AND SOVEREIGN DEVOTION

The Sri Lankan Catholic Archdiocese's 2009 statement on liturgy drew links of affinity between Catholicism and Buddhism. Under the circumstances of Buddhist protectionism and anti-conversion activism in Sri Lanka, the conjoined forms of Catholic and Pentecostal religiosity, manifest in the Catholic Charismatic Renewal (CCR), which remained valid in the post-Vatican II era, presented a conundrum for the Sri Lankan Catholic Church as a regulative body. The Sinhala Catholic Archbishop's injunctions sought to enjoin Catholic laity to abate Buddhists' concerns about Catholics' involvements in charismatic and evangelistic expansion. At the same time, it was incumbent upon Church leadership to curtail parishioner defection. The charismatic revivalist forms, when confined to the Catholic Church, could prevent Catholics from becoming apostates. Archbishop Ranjith's effort to tame while simultaneously allowing the existence of the charismatic forms that operate under Vatican II Catholicism was animated by reasons that are at once ecclesiastical and political. Having considered the diplomatic remediations in terms of their liturgical and theological impact, a discussion of their political logic and implications for debates over national sovereignty in postwar Sri Lanka is in order.

Following Sri Lanka's defeat of the LTTE insurgents in 2009, the Sri Lankan public sphere was filled with state pageantry and civilian fanfare of President Rajapaksa and the armed forces for executing a relentless final solution. By illiberally "securing peace" through military means, the president gained renown among majoritarian nationalist Sinhala Buddhists, as well as among other subsets of a citizenry eager to see an end to the long war. In his public address on Sri Lanka's victory, President Rajapaksa invoked the grand sweep of Sinhala triumphs over "foreign" detractors, in a way that reified the singularity of Sinhala Buddhist sovereignty. Rajapaksa positioned himself within a righteous lineage of guardians:

> It is necessary on this historic occasion to inquire as to how it was possible that we have obtained a proud victory, achieved today by defeating the world's most ruthless terrorist organization. We are a country with a long history in which we saw the reign of 182 kings who ruled with pride and honour for a period that extended more than 2,500 years. This is a country where kings such as Dutugemunu, Valagamba, Dhatusena and Vijayabahu defeated enemy invasions and ensured our freedom. As much as Mother Lanka fought against invaders such as Datiya, Pitiya, Palayamara, Siva and Elara in the past, we have the experience of having fought the Portuguese, Dutch and British who established empires in the world. As much as the great kings such as Mayadunne, Rajasingha I and Vimaladharmasuriya, it is necessary to also recall the great heroes such as Keppettipola and Puran Appu who fought with such valour against imperialism.[22]

State media too lauded Rajapaksa as the "King" in league with the great Sinhala Buddhist kings who vanquished "foreign invaders" in the ancient past, evoking the mythohistoric legends of the *Mahāvaṃsa* chronicles. One central legend of the *Mahāvaṃsa* chronicle valorizes the Sinhala King Dutugamenu who defeated the southern Indian Nayakkar King Elara in the second century BCE. Sinhala Buddhists have long mobilized the legend for nationalistic purposes, construing ethnolinguistic conflict with Tamils as an ancient conflict and constructing civilizational grandeur as having stemmed from that sovereign victory (Kapferer [1988] 2012; Gunawardana 1990; Spencer 1990). Eulogies of Dutugamenu project his rebirth in the *Tusita* heaven, placing him in close proximity to the coming Buddha. As with the past and present forms of Buddhist messianism that I elaborate in the next chapter, those who are born as deities into the *Tusita* heaven are destined to be reincarnated as the Maitreya Buddha (or as his right-hand disciple) and to attain *nibbāna* in the far future. Majoritarian rhetoric cast Rajapaksa's triumph of nationalistic statecraft in line with the karmic hallowing of Dutugamenu. In the immediacy of postwar reckoning, many Sinhala Buddhists valorized President Rajapaksa as an adept, karmically destined sovereign upholder of the nation.

Billboards in Colombo celebrated the president and the armed forces in the fraught aftermath of the war. Other signage throughout Colombo also depicted the president as an avid supporter of interreligious peace. In the dawning of a new, postwar era, Rajapaksa was suddenly posited as an exemplar who encourages "Sri Lankans who love the nation" to embrace possibilities for harmonious relations with people of other religions and ethnicities. This broader program by the Rajapaksa government to sympathetically align with religious minorities came at a time when many Christian leaders feared that hardline majoritarian nationalists would turn the full force of their attentions against Christians who had been categorically alleged to be anti-nationals. But Sinhala leaders at the helm of Sri Lanka's Catholic Church cast President Rajapaksa as a moderate partner who had the potential to undercut populist trajectories of anti-Christian violence and to deflect the passage of anti-conversion legislation (Mahadev 2013; Hertzberg 2016).

Created for the eyes of the Sri Lankan majority who supported Rajapaksa's leadership in the war, President Rajapaksa sought to present himself as a peaceable champion of interreligious harmony in the postwar period.[23] The Catholic

4.4 This poster depicts President Mahinda Rajapaksa in his iconic uniform of white and red, lighting clay oil lamps commonly used in Buddhist and Hindu devotions. In Sinhala it reads "*ēk sith pāna!*" "Everyone [of distinct religious communities] put your hands together and light the lamp in unity of heart/mind." It portrays the symbolic sovereign as an exemplar of interreligious unity and tolerance between the four major religions of Sri Lanka. This signage was a common sight throughout Colombo shortly after the end of the civil war in 2009.

archbishop and the Sri Lankan president built a demonstrative alliance. In the public campaign Rajapaksa postured himself in a way that allowed him to help extricate the Sri Lankan Catholic Church from generalized majoritarian perceptions of Christians as malign anti-nationals. Despite broader anxieties that Catholics were in league with other evangelizing "fundamentalist" Christians, Rajapaksa worked to transfigure nationalist and populist sentiments concerning the Catholic Church. Rajapaksa's trust in the archbishop and peace efforts with Catholics more generally ultimately compelled his Buddhist supporters—including anti-pluralistic activists within the sangha—to put trust in the Sri Lankan Catholic Church as a thoroughly dedicated nationalist entity.

Amid a slew of critiques by Western states and international human rights organizations, Archbishop Ranjith created a politically pragmatic link between Pope Benedict XVI, the sovereign of the Holy See, and President Rajapaksa, the symbolic sovereign of Sri Lanka. The alliance resulted in several amiable meetings between Rajapaksa, his Sinhala Catholic wife, and the pope, at the Vatican.[24] The visits are remarkable because non-Catholic heads of state are rarely given the opportunity to visit the Vatican unless that state is a major player in world politics. This transregional and interreligious relationship paved the way for Vatican diplomacy within the European Union on behalf of Sri Lanka. As a sanctioning mechanism for the country's widely alleged misconduct in war, the European Union was at that time threatening to strip Sri Lanka of invaluable trade benefits.[25] Seeking to block the sanctions, the archbishop and the Sri Lankan president worked to win over the Vatican and to ask the foreign minister to make a plea to the EU to "show respect for Sri Lankan sovereignty," since the country had "valiantly defeated an international terrorist group."

In November 2009, Archbishop Ranjith gathered an interreligious committee representing the major religions of Sri Lanka to travel to Vatican City. A committee consisting of Archbishop Ranjith, a Catholic cleric and director of Caritas Sri Lanka, two Buddhist monks, a Muslim cleric, and a Hindu priest approached Vatican officials with their appeal. The Sri Lankan religious leaders met Pope Benedict XVI and presented him with a gift, and they also met the Vatican foreign minister to present a memorandum on the postwar condition of Sri Lanka. The archbishop and the interreligious committee brought their case to the Vatican foreign minister, seeking to impress upon him that Sri Lanka was now at peace, reunified, and that the government was providing adequate care and "rehabilitation" for its internally displaced civilian population. They argued that EU sanctions would only deal a hard blow to Sri Lanka's economy that would effectively debilitate the Sri Lankan government's good-faith efforts to help Tamil civilians recover from war, displacement, and twenty-five years of "oppression" and "terrorism" under the LTTE insurgents. The Vatican minister agreed to vote in favor of allowing Sri Lanka to continue to receive the trade provision. But in the end the Vatican's connections and the cause itself were too tenuous to successfully support the appeals. The EU stripped Sri Lanka of the preferential trade status as punishment for atrocities committed in war.[26]

State media and other networks allegiant to the presidential regime publicized the diplomatic tour of the Vatican, highlighting how the Sri Lankan Catholic Archbishop used his ties to the papal authority to benefit the Sri Lankan national cause in an otherwise unfavorable international arena. In spite of the failed effort, the relationship between the Catholic Church and the symbolic sovereign protector of the Sri Lankan state helped to consolidate confidence among the Sinhala Buddhist public, and especially the politicized segments of the Buddhist sangha. Malcolm Ranjith remained solidly opposed to the international humanitarian criticisms of Sri Lanka and continued to advocate for the Sri Lankan government while it remained under the presidential authority of Rajapaksa. In the heat of international scrutiny and demands for humanitarian reckoning and reconciliation, the president assembled the Lessons Learnt and Reconciliation Commission (LLRC) and appointed the Archbishop Ranjith to it in May 2010.

The LLRC was tasked with conducting an internal review of Sri Lanka's military conduct and to provide recommendations on postwar development. In the main, Sri Lankan and diasporic critics of the wartime regime have seen the archbishop and other nepotistic appointees to the LLRC to be inadequate advocates for transitional justice and reconciliation.[27] Archbishop Ranjith propounded soft critiques of wartime and postwar initiatives—a small push to ensure that President Rajapaksa lived up to the promises of reconciliation (see the following conversation between the archbishop and the U.S. ambassador, documented in Wikileaks). Progressive Sinhala and Tamil activists in Sri Lanka insisted that although the regime may have won the war, it remained incumbent upon the government to also "win the peace." Some Tamil Catholics expressed feelings of embitterment by what appeared as "Sinhala chauvinism" on the part of the head of their Church. On the other side, Sinhala Buddhist nationalists continued to repudiate claims that Tamils of Sri Lanka had ever faced any historical injustice at all. At the 2012 UNHCR meetings in Geneva on these matters, as cardinal, Ranjith adamantly argued that the international community ought to suspend its "undue meddling" in the internal affairs of Sri Lanka.[28]

Although the international diplomatic effort was not a total success, the postwar campaigns between Colombo and the Vatican spotlighted for the Sinhala Buddhist public that the Catholic Church was not a liability but an asset, a

4.5 Pope Benedict XVI with Sri Lankan President Rajapaksa and Mrs. Rajapaksa in the pope's private library. Rajapaksa's visit assisted in building a politically pragmatic link between the Vatican and the Sri Lankan state.
©Vatican Media

friend and potentially powerful ally of the nation. In a time when a strident majoritarian campaign against Christians had come to a head, these flows of theopolitical influence enabled Sri Lankan Catholics to be extricated from such entrenched stereotypes of Christians. Put in other terms, the alliance between the Sinhala Catholic archbishop of Colombo and the Sri Lankan Buddhist President Mahinda Rajapaksa enabled a pardoning of sorts. Their politicized performances of interreligious dialogue went a long way to intervene in matters when hegemonic criteria for loyalty and questions of national belonging were at stake. For the Catholic Church to be validated in Sri Lanka as a recognizably "nationalist" entity has been institutionally opportune for the Church, too. The Vatican authority promoted Archbishop Malcolm Ranjith as a voting member of the Cardinalate in October 2010, the basic condition for which is a genial relationship between the Church and the political establishment of the candidate's home country.

FROM *WIKILEAKS*, THE U.S. EMBASSY, COLOMBO EDITION
REPRINTED IN THE COLOMBO TELEGRAPH, "MAHINDA
RAJAPAKSA IS A 'CHRISTIAN,' SAYS ARCHBISHOP"
SEPTEMBER 21, 2011

http://www.colombotelegraph.com/index.php/wikileaks-files-mahinada
-rajapaksa-is-a-christian-says-archbishop/

In a September 30 introductory meeting with Ambassador and PolChief, Roman Catholic Archbishop Malcolm Ranjith recounted the recent political evolution of Sri Lanka, of which he has been both an astute observer and important participant, and described the role of the Church in society. He noted that while he himself was a Singhalese, he was very sympathetic to the plight of Tamils, who had suffered greatly from pogroms and discrimination by the majority and from the disastrous results of LTTE separatist ideology. He explained that the Church had played a key role in brokering talks between the GSL and the LTTE over the years, including the 2002 cease-fire agreement. After the war, the church was advocating publicly for the release of IDPs and other controversial positions. This had led to criticism from the Buddhist right and even death threats against the archbishop himself. This was the opposite of the leading role in reconciliation the archbishop believed Buddhists should have been playing years ago.

Despite this criticism, the archbishop said he believed President Rajapaksa personally was a good man and in the constellation of Sri Lankan politics was a relative moderate (he reminded us that Rajapaksa used to attend human rights meetings in Europe as an opposition MP). Rajapaksa and his brothers were under great pressure from the Singhalese Buddhist right, and any show of what would be perceived as weakness before the international community could result in their losing ground to much more extreme elements. Indeed, he argued that if something happened to the president there would be "chaos" in Sri Lanka.

... This led to the archbishop addressing directly the question of war crimes accountability. He said "my suggestion is, in order to strengthen democracy in Sri Lanka, don't push accountability now." He reasoned that weakening the Rajapaksas could backfire. Moreover, if Sri Lanka were denied GSP-plus or the U.S. were to enact strong economic sanctions, leading to a sharp downturn in the economy, Sri Lanka—where democracy was not strong now—could suffer revolution from the right or a coup by the military, which currently had a very strong position in society. The archbishop said this was why he had recently come out publicly in favor of extending GSP-plus to Sri Lanka, despite the GSL's many human rights problems. Ambassador countered that this was a very interesting perspective, but if the Rajapaksas were in fact moderates, they needed to show it in at least a few ways. The archbishop said this was the challenge that he had been working on—how to get the president not to worry only about the "forces lurking beneath him" and to act as a moderate. He told the president it was important to work with Tamil leaders on reconciliation and to invite the diaspora to help re-build the economy. "The Rajapaksas will come and go," the archbishop opined, "but the Tamils will always be here."

SUBSUMING OPPOSITION: POLITICAL THEOLOGIES AND THE MAKING OF STRANGE BEDFELLOWS

Recognizing the force of ethnoreligious populism and nationalism in their war-torn country, Sri Lankan leaders endeavored to preserve the standing of Catholicism in Sri Lanka. The central authority of the Sri Lankan Church did so by seeking to temper the charismatic revivalist Pubuduwa movement that thrived within the Church, fearing that Buddhists may react to the "unsober" yet attractive religious form, and that the movement could jeopardize the possibility for Catholics to build amicable relations with Buddhists. Church leaders warned that lay Catholics must use caution when adopting charismatic styles of devotion. The Sri Lankan Catholic Church sought to prevent Catholics from participating in openly charismatic Christian practices in a way that was consistent with the theological and liturgical conservativism associated with the Petrine foundations of the Church. Moreover, to quell Buddhists' concerns about the "anti-national" character ascribed to Sri Lankan Christians in general, which loomed over Catholics as well, necessitated that Catholics do not appear to proselytize among non-Christians. Disassociating Catholicism from the charismatic and pentecostalist forms of worship was thus politically pragmatic too.

The Catholic ecclesiastical structure demands that charismata are accessed only via those Petrine authorities who are ordained to activate and disseminate the gifts of grace to confirmed Catholics via the liturgy. Clergy of the Catholic Church carefully guard charismata. So sacrosanct they are that Catholics have classically treated them as sequestered and contained within the Eucharist, made present and shared through liturgy only through capably graced and ordained figures of priestly authority. Comparatively then, the Pentecostal form might be seen as an effusive free-flow of charismata whereby the Spirit is discharged in ways that Pentecostals understand as overwriting established grounds that Buddhists, as well as Catholics, seek to guard as their own exclusive domains. Even as many traditionalists of the Catholic Church do aspire to evangelical expansion, they tend to promote it in a style and ethos that involves both pomp and relative quietude. In view of these competing strands of religiosity, concerns of relationality and public perception are paramount among religious activists in Sri Lanka. In this case, upholding conservativism aligns with the political expediency of going about things quietly.

Yet it was a very public effort through which the authoritative and conservative leadership of the Catholic Church worked to carve out a space of exceptionality for Catholics, as against those defined as allegedly "anti-national" kinds of Christians. Symbolic sovereigns negotiated these exceptions through different kinds of maneuvers—theological, apostolic, liturgical, and aesthetic on the one side and political, pragmatic, nationally allegiant, and internationally conversant on the other. These maneuvers worked in tandem with one another, tweaking and modulating the hegemonic thrust of majoritarian political perceptions. At its institutional center, the Catholic Church of Sri Lanka became quite successful in its diplomatic efforts, appearing to Sinhala Buddhists as striking a balance between its national grounding and its international character in a way necessary to secure the political fortitude and fortunes of the country. Catholic Church officialdom was rendered subject to certain demands of Sri Lankan nationalism. The obligation ran the other way as well. The Church sought to ambitiously advance its own claims to universality, enabling it to install a cardinal in the country.

The liturgical and theological concerns that sit uncomfortably within Sri Lankan Catholicism, and the political stance and posturing toward exceptionalism that allowed the Sri Lankan Catholic Church to be considered an adequately nationalist entity despite the overarching intolerances are strikingly analogous. Despite momentary purifications, this relationship of incorporating that which does not typically belong within a given category—the Pauline within the

Petrine inheritance of the Roman Catholic Church in the first instance, and the Catholic inclusion within a Buddhist majoritarian nation in the second—entails a kind of "opportunistic tolerance" (Schmitt [1923] 1996). An astute political observer of political theology, practitioner of illiberal politics, and onetime apologist for the Catholic Church, Carl Schmitt remarked upon the Church's capacity to find common cause with what may seem to be socially, religiously, and politically antithetical to its own principles. He found evident within the Catholic Church the tendency to embrace a "complexity of opposites" (in Latin terms, *complexio oppositorum*)—a pliability that is at the heart of the institution's "political form." This "astounding elasticity," he argued, could be seen in the way that in Europe, Catholicism articulated with such opposite positions on the political spectrum as liberal and conservative, royalist and republican.

In *Roman Catholicism and Its Political Form* (1923), Schmitt remarked, too, how in a seemingly counterintuitive fashion socialism could thrive within Catholicism. Schmitt's point can be extended to the way in which the Catholic Church eventually saw at its decolonizing fringes the emergence of liberation theology. The reckoning within the Church that led to Vatican II provisions in the mid-1960s gave sanction to liberation theology as well as to ecumenism and interreligious dialogue, and later also the charismatic renewal within the Catholic Church (see de Abreu 2021). Yet the limits of the official Church's tolerance evidently fluctuate with time, political circumstance, and personae of its sovereign leaders. Thus, even as there are incorporative capacities of the Church, excorporative possibilities also loom on the horizon of possibility.[29] When adaptations within the Church appear antithetical to the Catholic orthodoxy and political interests, they are liable to become points of contention and authoritative action by traditionalists of the Church hierarchy. What is striking is how personal connections and sovereign dispositions serve to mediate political and religious interests. As one observer of the Vatican put it, in "a rarefied political atmosphere . . . personnel is policy" (Horowitz 2017). Indeed, religious personnel and personality politics have been pivotal in shaping the trajectories of the Church and the partner institutions that the Church touched, much as it had been the case with certain Buddhist icons in the course of exceptional shifts in postwar Sri Lanka.

The irony of using interreligious dialogue in a way that shores up majoritarian nationalism is consonant too with wider tendencies toward "illiberal consequences of liberal institutions" in postwar Sri Lanka (Spencer 2008; Goodhand et al. 2010). The endemic illiberalism is found not only within strident and exclusionary populist nationalism in Sri Lanka, however. It also appears endemic in the exclusivist drives to carry out spiritual warfare to forge a born-again commitment as against non-Christian lifeways. The Catholic Church, too, is similarly capable of an anti-pluralistic political style. Yet, as a minority religion in Sri Lanka, Catholicism appears to be circumscribed by ethnoreligious nationalism and populism. Its conservatism becomes intensified in that context, despite the intra-Catholic and Christian plurality that exists within that milieu. The Church's surface-level efforts to mitigate interreligious tensions and appease Buddhist nationalist exigencies have served to diminish its capacities to support pluralistic and civic forms of nationalism.

The resignation of Pope Benedict XVI and the election of Pope Francis in 2013 signaled a new era for the Roman Catholic Church. Many Catholics throughout the Global South regard Pope Francis as a spiritual embodiment of the values set forth by the Second Vatican Council. He has effectively sidelined and angered conservative Catholics and ecclesiastical traditionalists.[30] Catholic social and environmental justice activists, as part of a broader Christian left, as I have observed in Sri Lanka, have delighted in the papacy of Francis as an inspiration for their own grassroots work (Mahadev 2022). Yet conservatives of the Sri Lankan state and the Cardinalate in Colombo persist in their roles as bureaucrats, religious exemplars, and pragmatists. It remains to be seen what shape the politics of the Sri Lankan state and the Catholic Church will take in an era wherein resurgent and ever-complicated interreligious hatreds flare episodically.

CHAPTER 5

Samsaric Destinies, Religious Plurality, and the Maverick Dialogics of Buddhist Publicity

---

Orthodoxy, straight, or rather straightened, opinion, which aims without ever entirely succeeding, at restoring the primal state of innocence of doxa, exists only in the objective relationship which opposes it to heterodoxy, that is, by reference to the choice—hairesis, heresy—made possible by the existence of competing possibles.

—Pierre Bourdieu, *Outline of a Theory of Practice*

Stepping into a Sri Lankan Dutch-era church that in recent decades had been converted from a mainline Protestant church to a denominational Pentecostal prayer hall, I looked around for Pastor Nimal. Finding me wandering about, a *sevaka* ("servant" of God, or deacon) of the ministerial team guided me through the labyrinth toward his office. Pastor Nimal devotedly sought to introduce newcomers to his church to "the Good News" (Sinhala, *Subha Aranchiya*), and in that spirit he handed me his business card as he shook my hand. When I found a moment to inspect it, I was surprised to find a four-sided piece of cardstock that listed not only his own credentials but also the many credentials of Jesus Christ. Printed in English prominently below Jesus's attributes was the statement, "HE is the shortest way to overcome *samsara*." *Saṃsāra* connotes the innumerable cycles of death and rebirth in the Buddhist trajectory of achieving the "salvation" that is *nibbāna* (Pāli, awakened extinguishment of suffering). The pithy statement enunciates how Sri Lankan Christian evangelists might translate and propagate the salvational promise of Jesus Christ amid the doxic presuppositions of Theravāda Buddhist eschatology. The slogan crystallized the evangelist's endeavor to "witness."[1] Although it can be attributed to the pastor himself, I learned that the premise behind it found resonance with other Sinhala Christians. It is an expression of competitive theologizing, an assertion that is symptomatic of the contentious discursive interplay between Christian evangelism and Buddhist nationalism in millennial Sri Lanka.

When I asked Pastor Nimal about his effort to relate Christian salvation to *nibbāna*, he emphasized the conundrum that Buddhist people must face with regard to the sheer duration of duress: "Buddhism & Hinduism have a very long *saṃsāra*. It takes many births [to be saved from suffering]. If you are reborn as an animal or a spirit—how terrible! If you believe in Jesus, you can be with Him in heaven after only one life." In making their presence known in Sri Lanka, especially in the last three decades, Pentecostals have seized upon the theological advantage that Christianity seems to offer with respect to Theravāda Buddhism. Sinhala Christians conceive of the advantage through theological comparison. In Pentecostals' efforts to witness among Sinhala Buddhists, they competitively theologize—actively comparing incommensurable eschatologies to make claims of capably foreshortening the possibility of achieving an end to suffering. As detailed in the last chapter, embedded in Pentecostal-charismatic theology and practice is the idea, and the sensation, that the pneumatic power of the Holy Spirit can make Christ immediately available to believers. Charismatic Christianity is thus cast in contrast to Theravādin doctrine whereby the power imbued in the dharmic teachings of the *Tathāgata*, or the "Thus-Gone One," appear to be far distant. Sharers of the Good News like Pastor Nimal regard the path to *nibbāna* as a slow-going approach to an eternal end to suffering, and consider the labors required to achieve it to be far too onerous.

Responding in turn to the "crimes" against Buddhist heritage that evangelists are alleged to routinely commit, vigilant Sinhala Buddhist agitators attempt to strike down Christians' evangelizing efforts through interventions broadcast over television news media, as we saw in chapter 3. But in a different register, dedicated Sinhala Buddhists commonly offer a pointed retort to such Christian promises that Jesus offers a shortcut out of *saṃsāra* by claiming that one cannot absolve oneself from sins (*akusala karmaya*) accumulated over many lifetimes by deflecting them onto a savior. In this vein, Rohini, a Sinhala friend in her late sixties, asserted in English, "No one else can suffer for the sins that we have committed in our own lifetimes, no?" She made the assertion while speaking with me informally about the conversion disputes in 2009, in the space of her own home in the outskirts of Kandy. Rohini had offered the remark as if she were shadow boxing with the Catholic theology she had first been exposed to through her convent education. In the era of Ceylon's nationalization when Rohini had been in school, there was no requirement for Sinhala Buddhists to convert in order to be taken into the Catholic educational system—yet it was there where she learned the central tenets of Christianity.[2] As a result of her "secular" immersion in a Catholic educational milieu, Rohini, although a Buddhist, had built many amicable lifelong relationships with Christian and especially Catholic friends.

Although the era of sharpened anti-conversion politics might have oriented Rohini, as a Sinhala Buddhist, to hold deep contempt or retaliatory enmity toward Catholics and Christians, it was clear that this was hardly the case. But even so, Rohini occasionally did feel disturbed by the material manifestations of Christian power. On several occasions she had witnessed how the material accoutrements associated with Christianity could be used to undercut people's Buddhist commitments. This became clear and present to me when nearly a decade after our initial conversations on conversion, I saw how distraught Rohini became at a funeral of a mutual friend, Estelle. Estelle had converted from Protestantism to Buddhism in her early thirties. But even though Estelle had a long-standing commitment to Buddhism, in circumstances beyond Rohini's control, Estelle was about to be buried as a Christian. As I sat holding Rohini's hand in the funeral parlor, her eyes became glassy as she blinked back tears for her dear friend.

Rohini told me that she had given some money to a friend of Estelle's to pass on to yet another friend who had assumed responsibility for organizing Estelle's funeral. She had done so with the stated intention to invite Buddhist monks to perform the funerary rites and sermon, to accept alms (*dāna*), and in turn to perform the requisite transfers of merit to our late friend to ensure her safe passage to a better rebirth and ultimately *nibbāna*. But in the busy swell of funeral preparations, the organizers did not carry out Estelle's last wishes. Despite her instructions, no invitations had been extended to the monks of the neighboring village temple to whom Estelle regularly offered *dāna*. In broken-up whispers, Rohini conveyed to me, her daughter, and her son-in-law how upset Estelle would have been that the authorities of the Christian orphanage at which she had been christened insisted on holding a Christian burial for her. I thought back to the point that Rohini had made, years earlier, that one could not expiate the bad karma accumulated in one's present and past lifetimes by deflecting sin onto a savior. Her words, "No one else can suffer for the sins that we have committed in our own lifetimes, no?" echoed in my head. She had been emphatic that Christian shortcuts could not allay the consequences of one's own bad karma: one had to undertake the moral work of good karma (*puñña karmaya*), accumulate merit, and share it with others, over the course of many, many lifetimes.

As we sat in the funeral parlor that day, Rohini resigned herself to the fact that Christian priests would conduct Estelle's funeral as if Estelle were a Christian rather than as the Buddhist that she had become. Later that morning, as the funeral pyre burned, we all cried for the loss of our friend. Anglican fathers associated with the school Estelle had attended as a child said grace in Sinhala, offering blessings for the eternal salvation of Estelle's soul. Rohini squeezed my hand. She turned to me and to her family to confirm that they would gather together to carry out the Buddhist rituals for Estelle at their home. They would hold almsgivings for the monks on the requisite days in order to make merit, and in turn to transfer that merit to Estelle in the Buddhist way. In doing so, they reassured themselves, Estelle would be reborn with better conditions for her next lifetime. The stores of merit that she had made over her lifetimes and had received from other Buddhists who loved her would ultimately enable her to obtain *nibbāna*, too. In doing so, they averred, there was a way forward so that Estelle could continue on in her samsaric path as a Buddhist.

***

As is evident with these clashing salvific and samsaric conceptions of religious destiny, a complex field of religious influence is opened up with the lived interactions between Buddhism and Christianity in Sri Lanka. In previous chapters I have discussed how the circulations of antagonistic religious discourses and the majoritarian anxieties that a new religion could overwrite the existence of a firmly established one through conversion have served to intensify the mutual currents of religious exclusivism. Rather differently, in this chapter I examine the novel ways in which Buddhist revivalists have sought to contend with the persuasive forces and the powerful intercessory promises offered by a host of other rival religions. Considering how samsaric, nibbanic, millenarian, and salvific conceptions of destiny intermingle and are lived in the Sri Lankan public sphere, how do these competing soteriologies intersect one another and inspire religious innovation? In the face of new and old varieties of charismatic, intercessional, and media-savvy styles of propagation that rival religions set forth in the Sri Lankan public sphere, what new repertoires of persuasion have emerged within the scope of the Sinhala Buddhist revival?

One answer to these questions can be found within the revivalist practices of a maverick Buddhist monk named Pitiduwe Siridhamma Thero. The movement that began to consolidate around the monk and his style of dharmic teaching and practice first came across my radar when, shortly after I arrived in Sri Lanka for fieldwork in 2009, I began receiving automated text messages on my mobile phone network advertising paid subscriptions for his recorded sermons. Within the months that followed, Pitiduwe Siridhamma Thero's name came up quite often in Buddhist circles, particularly during my stints living in the cities of Colombo and Kandy. In Colombo, regular *Dhamma* study groups emerged, mainly constituted by youthful urban Buddhists led in learning by lay followers who, through careful training, became well versed in the monk's particular takes on dharmic discourse. I learned from Nimesh, who had traveled with me from Maharagama following the death anniversary commemoration of Gangodawila Soma Thera (see the introduction), that he too had become drawn to the teachings of Pitiduwe Siridhamma Thero. A woman in her early thirties, who I will call Anoja, followed a similar trajectory in that she too had been inspired by Soma Thera's teachings, but after his sudden and mysterious death she found herself discovering that her own commitment to Buddhism deepened further as she became a dedicated follower of Siridhamma Thero. Anoja was a regular devotee at Siridhamma Thero's temple and belonged to one of his *Dhamma* study groups. She soon became a friend and interlocutor, and she enthusiastically offered to introduce me to Siridhamma Thero's temple and teachings. Through Anoja and other Sinhala Buddhists in her circle, I found myself observing the rising tide of devotional commitment that the monk had begun to garner.

Many Sinhalese Buddhist laypeople felt moved by the thirty-something's *Dhamma* talks, which regularly aired on Sinhala-language television. While watching Pitiduwe Siridhamma Thero's arresting sermon on television with Rohini at her home in Dangolla, I asked her opinion. "He gives very good *bana* (sermons)—I will give him that," she conceded. "He knows the *Dhamma* very well." But Rohini also mentioned how the press gave airtime to his elaborate celebrity birthday festivities, almsgivings, and other high-profile events that his followers organized to fête the monk. Unlike some of my younger, Colombo-based interlocutors, Rohini was skeptical of the media-savvy monk. In a subsequent conversation, she hinted at his impropriety of holding such self-glorifying events and suggested that she found him to be "too showy." For Rohini and other Sinhala Buddhists of her generation, Siridhamma Thero's flashy ways were unbecoming of a monk. Meanwhile, in Colombo, many of my urban, middle- and upper-class Sinhala Buddhist interlocutors found Siridhamma Thero's expositions on the *Dhamma* to be especially compelling—a quality they attributed to his "science-mindedness" (*widayāwēdīya*). They cited the fact that he received a bachelor of science degree before his ordination as evidence of his scientific orientation. Siridhamma Thero quickly built a concentrated following in the city of Colombo and beyond, consisting mainly of young to middle-aged urban Sinhala Buddhists. Sinhala television networks regularly broadcast his temple activities and sermons, and in turn he gained some degree of popularity in smaller cities and towns all over the island. The maverick Buddhist monk galvanized his personal charisma in a way that for many enlivened Sinhala Buddhism.

VIRTUOSITY AND RELIGIOUS ATTRACTION

Siridhamma Thero's temple, Siri Sadaham Ashramaya, is located in a southern stretch of Colombo known as Bellanthara. The uniqueness and popularity of the devotional style engaged there was evident when I first attended *Poya* (full-moon) day services with Anoja in 2009. Well over a thousand Buddhist laypeople, clad entirely in white, crowded the grounds of the temple/monastery in that September morning's heat. Anoja had instructed to me wear white, too, according to the Buddhist norm, and Siridhamma Thero was especially strict about this convention. We sat on rattan mats with her aunt, mother, and cousin while we waited for the monk to make his appearance. Alongside of where we were seated, three *dāyakayo* painstakingly created floral mandalas with fragrant rose petals, to flank a lush red carpet (*pāvadē*) that they unfurled for the venerable to tread upon. Siridhamma Thero emerged, donning mahogany robes. A *dāyaka* accompanied him as he made his entrance, holding a golden yellow parasol above his shorn head. Siridhamma Thero moved ceremoniously past us to take an elevated seat upon an ornately carved wooden chair.

The assembled crowd attentively listened as the monk delivered a sermon that instructed expecting parents to conduct themselves virtuously so as to exercise good influence upon their children. He recounted how just before becoming the Buddha, the meritorious Bodhisattva Gotama sat in the *Tusita* heaven until the gods invited him to select the earthly couple who would be the most suitable parents for him.[3] He emphasized that likewise, every karmic seedling "chooses" the parents to whom they will become incarnate to, and that thus it behooves expecting parents to mindfully collect merit. In doing so, the karmic seedling will "be born and grow into a child who brings benefits rather than suffering to the family." Devotees absorbed the lesson on the practical effects of striving to emulate the perfections (*pāramitā*) of Gotama Buddha—the same set of character virtues that Maitrī, the Buddha yet-to-come, will ultimately embody. The devotees beamed with the contentment they felt in being in the presence of Siridhamma Thero and in hearing the *Dhamma* from his lips.

Following the sermon, the devotees presented themselves in front of Siridhamma Thero, and folded themselves in prostration at his feet. After doing so ourselves, Anoja and I toured the temple premises. Following a stream of devotees, we walked to the open-air rooftop where twenty-eight larger-than-life Buddha statues stood along the perimeter. The figures were newly erected, painted in bright and glossy colors, with each of the Buddha's names listed on a placard below. Processing along with the queue ahead of us, we gazed at each of the Buddhas, slowly taking in each of their names and attributes. We ventured back downstairs. Anoja had picked up her pace, but I stopped short when I encountered a bronze deity that I did not recognize. Calling her name just loudly enough to get her attention amid the solemn temple crowd, Anoja doubled back to respond. She stepped next to me to gaze at the figure. I was intrigued that any deity at all was featured in a newly reconstructed temple that attracted urban Buddhists like Anoja.

I had discerned that Anoja's sensibilities fit within reform-oriented Buddhist modernism, with its requisite tendencies to shun deity veneration—an ideal common among middle-class Sri Lankans since the early phases of the Buddhist revival that had been sparked during the late colonial era of nationalization (Obeyesekere 1970; Gombrich and Obeyesekere 1988). Modernist tendencies within Sinhala Buddhist religiosity redoubled since the late 1990s, as a result of the preaching of Gangodawila Soma Thera (1948–2003), whose life and conspiracy theories concerning his death I discussed in the introductory chapters of this book. Many Buddhists, including Anoja, had foremost credited Soma Thera for awakening them to "real" Buddhism (*äthamata Budhudahama*). Like other revivalists before and after him, Soma Thera had called upon Sinhala Buddhists to reject deity veneration. He overtly attributed the incorporation of the deities into Sinhala Buddhism to syncretic cultural accretions owing to proximate forms of Hindu and pre-Buddhist religiosity. He thereby encouraged Sinhala Buddhists to purify their intentions as Buddhists rather than to focus their energies on worshipping deities.

Anoja anticipated my confusion over the presence of a deity in the context of an urban, stylized modern Buddhist temple. She identified the bronze deity I had set my gaze upon as Maitrī Bōsat. Preempting my question, she stated in her clear, colloquial English, "You see, our Buddhist people are always chasing after Hindu gods. Instead of worshipping Hindu gods, Siridhamma Thero says it is better to worship a *Buddhist* god. So he has encouraged us to worship Maitrī Bōsat—the Bodhisattva who will become the next Buddha." Within Theravāda Buddhist doctrine, Maitreya is positioned as the next and final Buddha of twenty-eight Buddhas in the entire existence of the world. Sinhala Buddhists conceive of the coming Buddha as a supremely meritorious figure, but in his present state he is neither accessible nor yet incarnate. Given the non-intercessory nature of the Buddha-to-come, it is striking indeed that Siridhamma Thero actively guided Buddhist devotees to venerate and ritually propitiate Maitrī as a deity and to treat him as a "Buddhist god."

Shortly after my initial visit to Siri Sadaham Ashramaya, Pitaduwe Siridhamma Thero publicized a new ritual movement centered on the Bodhisattva. Under the auspices of the temple-monastery, in late 2009 the television station Swarnavahini aired a ritual and grand procession, *pūja* and *perahera*, dedicated to Maitrī Bōsat. A voiceover narration by Siridhamma Thero in Sinhala conveyed to viewers that the practice of venerating and ritually propitiating the "god" Maitrī Bōsat was not new to Sri Lanka but rather had ancient roots. The evening program panned between live footage of Siridhamma Thero's *perahera*, Maitrī Bōsat icons and statues featured within his temple, and scenes of the tenth-century rock carvings of the coming Buddha located at Buduruvagala, in the Monaragala District.

Siridhamma Thero drew attention to one especially exquisite feature of the imagery, a seated Buddha emplaced within the center of the Bodhisattva's crown. The iconography of the "Buddha in the crown" bespeaks Maitreya Bodhisattva's future destiny as the Buddha-to-come (Holt 1991). Yet, from the accounts of several Sri Lankan Buddhists with whom I spoke, they, like me, were witnessing the

5.1–5.2 Tenth-century rock carvings of the Bodhisattva Avaloketeśvara, the coming Buddha, at Buduruvagala, Sri Lanka, June 2018. Archaeologists and scholars interpret the images as indicative that elements of Mahāyāna Buddhist cosmological principles had some influence upon the Theravāda Buddhist sangha during that era.

Maitrī Bōsat *pūja* for the first time ever through that evening's telecast. Siridhamma Thero claimed to be reviving the practice of venerating the Buddha-to-come, and his ethereal voiceover elucidated the logic of doing so. He summoned Sinhala Buddhists to share their merit (*pīn*) with Maitrī Bōsat as they would with any deity to whom they have committed themselves to by a vow (*bāra*). Siridhamma Thero emphatically told his televisual audience that this new ritual orientation to Maitrī Bōsat, paired with Buddhists' efforts to act in accordance with Gotama Buddha's teachings, would help those who aspire to overcome *saṃsāra* and to see *nibbāna* relatively quickly.

For followers of this movement, Siridhamma Thero's innovation held the promise that with devoted effort, the end of *saṃsāra* and the attainment of *nibbāna* can potentially be within reach. In classic Theravādin cosmology the Bodhisattva Maitreya, the final Buddha, is scheduled to arrive only in the far, far future.[4] But the monk's unique reinvention involved summoning the Bodhisattva as one who, through ritual and moral cultivation, can be made accessible in the relatively near future. The otherwise inaccessible Buddha-to-come was now being called upon to respond to demands for heightened Buddhist commitment. With the publicity first given to the ritual movement through the Sinhala language evening telecast in 2009, the monk, his temple, and the movement began to gain wider appeal.

The maverick monk, in coordination with monastic and lay Buddhist adherents to his stylized teachings, produced a highly mediatized response to the sense of anxiety that robust commitments to the ultimate goals of Buddhism are too often deterred because Theravādin trajectories through *saṃsāra* demand arduous spiritual evolutions that require many, many lifetimes to achieve. Buddhist modernism (or "Protestant Buddhism") has tended to encourage devotees to dispense with enchanted and deistic features of Buddhism, and instead steers people toward focus upon the *summum bonum* task of attaining *nibbāna*. Even as Sinhala Buddhist cultural forms, including deity veneration and colorful *perahera* (relic and deity procession) festivities, remain popular in Sri Lanka, Sinhala Buddhist reformers and revivalists enculturate lay devotees into modernist ritual austerities and to consistently extend patronage support through *dāna* (alms-giving) practices, thus ensuring the continuity of the Buddha, *Dhamma*, and Sangha. Siridhamma Thero's innovation rather differently addresses the commonly held anxiety that the promises of *nibbāna* do not easily generate the appeal of soteriological immediacy that rival traditions like Pentecostalism and even popular Hinduism can more easily galvanize. Through live temple activities, scintillating sermons, and televisual and online publicity, Siridhamma Thero created and curated attractive new elements within the scope of Buddhist thought and practice. Most remarkably, he did so through the new Buddhist ritual directed toward the veneration of Maitrī Bōsat.

As Anoja and I ambled around the Siri Sadaham Ashramaya premises on another occasion, she spoke of her intensifying commitment to the path that Siridhamma Thero had shown her. She confessed, "Though I am a married person, I want to attain *nibbāna*." This is striking since, as an immediate pursuit, attaining *nibbāna* is a vocation, a calling of the "heart and mind" (*sita*) that in Theravāda Buddhism is archetypically reserved for spiritually advanced and karmically well-seated mendicant monks.[5] The modernist transformation and "laicization" of Sinhala Buddhism in the early twentieth century created new imperatives for Buddhist laity to attempt to more closely approximate high-level monastic pursuits (Obeyesekere 1970; Gombrich and Obeyesekere 1988). In spite of being tied by marriage to mundane matters of family, Anoja was keen to maintain those ties while declaring her commitment to the word of a monk who teaches his lay devotees that, with dedicated striving, *nibbāna* can be near at hand. Siridhamma Thero's innovation to introduce worship of Maitrī Bōsat was a deft response to the worry that strong lay Buddhist commitments might be thwarted because overcoming *saṃsāra* would require innumerable lifetimes of karmic fortitude.

Through a maverick innovation, the monk kept Sinhala Buddhism in step with other rival forms of religiosity. He developed a ritual form that can dissuade Sinhala Buddhists from their inclination to worship "Hindu" gods. The new ritual movement also mitigates the allure of the "shortcuts" offered by millenarian premises of Christian salvation. In the agonistic and anxious encounter with evangelistic expansionism, this particular strand of Buddhist practice has apparently absorbed the affective charge of the millennial urgency and promise proffered by Pentecostal-charismatic discourses that circulate in Sri Lanka. This sense of urgency and anxiety at once stems from millenarian soteriology and from the competitive threat posed by evangelical Christianity. Indeed, one finds "Jesus Christ is Coming Very Soon"—the polyvalent threat and promise—splayed in large block letters across the parapet wall of a Galle Road church a few kilometers away from Siri Sadaham Ashramaya, where the maverick monk launched this new strand of Maitreya veneration. The act of ritually approaching the deity is, in part, animated by manifold rivalries prevalent within this patently multi-religious milieu. This innovative effort to venerate Maitrī Bōsat and to hasten his arrival on Earth illustrates how Sinhala Buddhism is dialogically responsive to the provocations of other religious traditions.

THE RIVALROUS FRONTIER

Pivoting upon the imagination of a far-future apocalyptic end to the world order, in Siridhamma Thero's maverick revivalism the Buddha-in-the-making is drawn into the present to call forth millenarian promises. The anticipated "savior" is conceived of being capable of redeeming the future for the devout. Within modern Theravādin contexts, evocations of the coming Buddha (*Bodhisattva*) have typically emerged only under circumstances of acute sociopolitical turmoil, a point I will elaborate on. In the case at hand however, it is under circumstances of simmering interreligious rivalry that Theravādin Buddhists began to invoke the messianic figure. In orthodox Theravādin soteriology the Bodhisattva Maitreya, as a not-yet present redeemer of the Dharmic future, is presently considered to be absent from everyday life, preoccupied with his own asceticism and nibbanic ascent. Yet with Siridhamma Thero's ritual innovation, subsets of Sinhala Buddhists newly treated the messianic figure as a deity. This new ritual movement and the practices of moral cultivation promoted by the maverick monk offer devoted Sri Lankan Buddhists a means to hasten their journeys through *saṃsāra*.

In effort to fortify, revive, and expand their respective religious constituencies, Buddhists and Christians occasionally borrow practical-theological elements of the rival tradition. But in considering the interreligious mingling that has produced the veneration of Maitrī Bōsat, "syncretism" as a concept falls short by implying that the new religious form merely builds upon elements borrowed from the rival form of religiosity.[6] Rather than an amalgamation of Christian millenarian eschatology and Buddhist deity veneration, I suggest that the new rise of Maitrī veneration offers a competitive and dialogical response to expansionary forms of Christianity by building upon *Buddhist* conceptions of the future. The movement seizes upon millenarian and messianic soteriologies that are native yet ordinarily latent within contemporary Theravāda Buddhism. Located within a heterogeneous religious milieu, the maverick monk's efforts to shore up commitment to Buddhism in the face of the expansionary ambitions of rival groups animates this new movement. The founder and followers of the movement contend that what distinguishes their practices from the nationalistic and exclusionary drives typically associated with prevailing strands of Buddhist revivalism in Sri Lanka is the movement's "skillful" attunement with contemporary realities. It is precisely this attunement, his followers aver, that makes Siridhamma Thero's orientation to teaching the *Dhamma* profoundly magnetic and most apt for the present and the future.

Far from imitating Pentecostalism to entertain the competitive calls for a shorter and faster means to attain the salvational promise offered by the Buddha's teaching, however, the monk's innovation draws upon certain cosmological and ritual elements that are ingrained within Sinhala Buddhism. This maverick emphasizes messianic promises essential to the Buddhist canon to drive his

5.3 Maitrī Bōsat/Bodhisattva Maitreya at the Ashramaya's rooftop terrace.

innovation. The initiative encourages the deepening of faith by drawing on ritual forms traditionally reserved for the deities who have been absorbed into the pantheon of Sinhala Buddhism. To be sure, the monk does not simply resort to rationalizing mechanisms that distill Buddhism down to its philosophical and ethical premises, or that create strict interiority to bolster Sinhala Buddhist religious commitment. Rather, by drawing a latent, messianic figure who is central to Theravāda Buddhist futurity into the present, the new rites help curb the competitive threat of evangelical Christian promises. Put simply, rituals for Maitreya respond to evangelical challenges by celebrating, and hastening a Buddha's doctrinally prophesied arrival.

ICONOGRAPHY AND THEOGRAPHY OF MAITREYA

The figure of Maitrī Bōsat that one finds at Siri Sadaham Ashramaya is royally clad. At the center of his crown is an image of a Buddha seated atop a lotus flower. The "Buddha in the crown" is the iconographic feature that Maitrī Bōsat of Siri Sadaham Ashramaya shares with two other deities who have established links to Sri Lanka: Avalokiteśvara and Nātha (Holt 1991). Today both deities are

identified with the coming Bodhisattva Maitreya. Avalokiteśvara was introduced by itinerant Mahāyāna Buddhist monks to Theravādin shores and to
monastic communities of Anuradapura (north-central Sri Lanka) by the eighth
century CE. Nātha stands as one of the four guardian deities in the contemporary pantheon of Sinhala Buddhism, and thus is conceived of as a protector of
the nation's sovereignty. Tracing the iconography shared between the two figures, John Holt argues that the identity of the foreign Mahāyāna Avalokiteśvara
figure evolved and eventually transformed into the Sinhala deity Nātha, such
that the identity of the latter subsumed the former.

Avalokiteśvara was initially a deity valorized for both "this-worldly" (*laukika*)
and "otherworldly" (*lōkōttara*) capabilities. Nātha's identity was developed circu-
itously according to Holt's historicization: the figure was considered a demon-
vanquishing warrior deity in the eighth century. But centuries later, when the
myths told of his defeat in battle by a foreign deity, he was said to have "retreated"
into asceticism (Holt 1991, 130–37).[7] Although the Mahāyāna Avalokiteśvara has
largely been forgotten in Sri Lanka, the icon's transcendent status was restored
with the common identification of Nātha as the future Maitreya (127). The
identities of Avalokiteśvara, and eventually also Nātha, evolved into future bodhisattvas in the Theravādin sense. In this historical transformation, each figure
ultimately underwent a further apotheosis that transformed their identities
from ascetically disengaged deities to singular Buddhas in the making. Even
though both of the deities were considered to be preoccupied with asceticism
and nibbanic aspiration, within the context of the exchange of Theravāda and
Mahāyāna Buddhist influences both figures came to be revered in the land that
is now known as Sri Lanka. This is so even as Sinhala Buddhists insist upon
upholding a pure practice in accord with Theravādin doctrine.

Doctrinally, Maitreya Bodhisattva and his deified antecedents Avalokiteśvara
and Nātha are considered to be disengaged from worldly matters. However, it
was clear that the Maitrī Bōsat of Siri Sadaham Ashramaya was not considered
an otiose figure. The new ritual movement oriented toward the "Buddhist God"
at Siri Sadaham Ashramaya is remarkable because according to the followers of
Siridhamma Thero, in spite of the shared iconography and their proximity to
Buddhahood, the identity of Maitrī Bōsat is utterly distinct from that of Nātha
Deviyō, who contemporaneously stands as a guardian deity within the pantheon
of Sinhala Buddhism. Strikingly, whereas many Sinhala Buddhists see Nātha as

destined to be reborn as Maitreya, devotees at Siri Sadaham Ashramaya with whom I conferred considered Nātha to be just one possible contender with the karmic potential to become the next Buddha.

In spite of a modicum of ancient cross-pollination between Theravādin practices and Mahāyāna influences that is apparent with the presence of Avalokiteśvara statues in Sri Lanka, the two Buddhist schools maintain distinctly different conceptions of a bodhisattva. A bodhisattva in Mahāyāna traditions is any extraordinarily virtuous being who suspends attainment of *nibbāna* to help others along the path until all beings achieve it. Thus, Mahāyāna soteriologies give credence to the idea that there are many, many Buddhas who exist "through all space and time."[8] In contrast, a Theravādin bodhisattva is one who ultimately becomes a Buddha, a "peerless" man of virtuosity, who attains all of the insights of *nibbāna* through his own volition (Harvey 2013). A Buddha (*Sammā-Sambuddha*) in the Theravādin sense is an *arahāt* (awakened one) who "rediscovers the Path after it has been lost to society" (29). Within the Theravādin tradition Buddhists consider achievement of Buddhahood to be rare; in the whole history of the cosmos the doctrine typically acknowledges the existence of only twenty-eight Buddhas (including Gotama and Maitreya). As many statues depicting the various Buddhas stand in a rectangular formation on the rooftop terrace of the Ashramaya. Following these "perfect Buddhas," a second class of *arahāt* is one who attains *nibbāna* through discipleship under a Buddha and goes on to preach, known as *Sāvaka-Buddha*.[9] However, doctrinally, the present *kalpa* (eon) is a time when the purest iterations of the *Dhamma* are lost to the world. Thus, in this day and age, although very rare, it is possible for one to achieve *nibbāna*, but only forest dwellers known as *Pacceka-Buddha* can achieve it through ascetic disengagement from the world. Archetypically, *Pacceka-Buddha* are to be mute and utterly modest about their status, according to *Vinaya* (monastic codes); they do not share the *Dhamma* by preaching or reveal their enlightened status (Harvey 2013, 99).

In short, according to the Theravādin school of thought, in our present times, the existence of an *arahāt* remains obscure to unenlightened eyes. As a result of these sectarian distinctions in doctrine, the Theravāda Sinhala Buddhist orthodoxy tends to consider Mahāyāna Buddhists to hold to overly liberal notions of a bodhisattva ideal that foreshortens the moral ascent required to achieve *nibbāna*. The implication is that from an orthodox Theravādin vantage, the Mahāyāna bodhisattva concept dilutes and depreciates the virtuosity exemplified by one who singularly deserves the title "Buddha" (Enlightened Proclaimer of the *Dhamma*). The import of the continuing preoccupation with upholding the boundaries between the Mahāyāna and Theravāda schools on this matter will become apparent further on.

SITUATING MAITRĪ BŌSAT IN SRI LANKA

Within Theravādin logics, the ultimate aim of following the Buddha's *Dhamma* is to rise above the murky waters of *saṃsāra*. Yet traditionally for Sinhala Buddhists, anyone who lives outside of the lifetime of a Buddha faces a long course ahead, because the pathways to *nibbāna* typically involve arduous and nonlinear spiritual evolutions. Although a Buddha is exemplary in his compassion, the Bodhisattva figure in his present state as a deity tends to be seen as spiritually superior and ascetically disinterested in the mundane concerns of human supplicants. Thus, among Sinhala Buddhists, as in other Pāli Buddhist contexts, worship of Maitreya is considered to yield very little fruit, and thus Maitreya is generally not approached in a posture of supplication. Traditionally, Sinhala Buddhists referentially *evoke* Maitreya only in the course of merit-making ceremonies (*pinkama*).[10] Laypeople acquire merit (*pin gatta*) by giving alms (*dāna*) to Buddhist clergy, and in return, the monks deliver sermons (*bana*) for edification of lay donors.

The gestural evocation of Maitrī remains prevalent in the ritual discourses of most almsgivings today as well. Following the death of a loved one, the bereaved gather together to make a ritual transaction with the monks, and all who partake earn merit. To transfer merit to a loved one (*pin anumodhang karannawa*), the family of the deceased crouches down around a small pitcher of water, each holding it, or gesturally doing so by placing a hand upon the arm of the water bearer. Led by the closest and most senior kin member, together the family, facing the monks, pours the water into a bowl with another container beneath for catchment. They allow it to overflow. Channeling the water into the bowl stands as a metonym for the flow and proliferation of merit.

As the family performs this ritual gesture, they chant the words to convey merit to the dearly departed, and extend the merit further with their words and intentions, sharing it "with all beings who are suffering." Within the practice of Buddhist almsgiving and ritual transfer, karmic merit undergoes a spiritualized

5.4 A Sinhala Buddhist family transferring their merit on the death anniversary of a loved one.

proliferation—"somehow, the more you give, the more you have, as with love or cell division" (Doniger 1980, xix). As the ritual comes to a close, the monk-officiant expresses the prayerful wish (*prārthanava*) that the merit ought to allow all participants to achieve their nibbanic ambitions by enabling them to be reborn in the far future when Maitrī Bōsat is born on Earth.[11] For to hear the future Buddha's *Dhamma*—supernaturally lucid in its articulation by the perfected being—consolidates perfect understanding of the *Dhamma*, thereby guaranteeing that the hearers instantaneously attain *nibbāna*. Here again is a core doctrinal expression of a Buddhist ideology of immediacy, mediation, and persuasion relating to the matter of presence and absence, discussed also in previous chapters.

These traditionalist practices of Sinhala Buddhism hinge upon a bifurcated religiosity: monastics prototypically abide by the Buddha and *Dhamma* (the Buddha's teachings, and the cosmic order itself) to attend to *lōkōttara* (supermundane) aspirations, while lay Buddhists simply strive to obtain a better rebirth and attend to *laukika* (mundane) concerns. As underscored in chapter 3, Buddhist laypeople typically attend to such everyday concerns with the aid of deities. They enter into a ritual pact with a specific deity or deities, making vows (*bāra*) and thus securing a patronage bond to morally, materially, and affectively navigate the suffering inherent in *saṃsāra*. In a hierarchical logic that takes nibbanic ascent as the *summum bonum* spiritual goal, deities, humans, "demons" (*yakśayo*), and lesser spirits (*prētayo*) are subsumed under the cosmic authority of the ordinarily inaccessible, "Thus-Gone" (*Tathāgata*) Lord Buddha.

Although the reorientation of Buddhist laity toward *nibbāna* is a kind of modernization that has been a feature of the nationalist revival for more than a century, it appears that Siridhamma Thero's innovation to direct devotees to worship (*wandinawa*) the Bodhisattva Maitreya as a deity to hasten the possibility of collectively achieving *nibbāna* is unprecedented in modern Sri Lanka. The new ritual actively serves *to invoke*, whereas prior ritual traditions merely served *to evoke* the Buddha to come. In this case, interreligious mingling generated a new strand of religiosity. The millenarian urgency inherent within Pentecostalism spurs interreligious competition and in turn generates an equal measure of urgency within Sinhala Buddhism. The upshot is that Sinhala Buddhist revivalism exhibits an imperative to address the call of immediacy and the issue of presence. However, even as the Maitrī Bōsat *pūja* is highly innovative, it does not simply imitate contemporary Christian messianism. It is clear that veneration of Maitrī Bōsat cannot be deemed "syncretism" insofar as that would imply that the new religious form simply borrows elements from the rival form of religiosity. Rather than an amalgamation between Christian millenarian eschatology and Buddhist deity veneration, the new rise of Maitrī veneration is evidently a competitive and dialogical response to expansionary forms of Christianity that builds upon *Buddhist* conceptions of the future.

TIME IN DECLINE: MESSIANIC THEOLOGIES OF MAITRĪ BŌSAT

Indian religious traditions, with their cyclical cosmological trajectories, commonly denote the present as an age of epistemological, ontological and moral disintegration. The messianic Buddha Maitreya figures as a palliative for dark times. Inscribed in the *Cakkavatti-Sīhanāda Sutta*, an integral text within the canon of Pāli Buddhism, is the future projection of a cataclysmic decline of society (Collins 1998).[12] The scripture conveys that when Gotama Buddha lived he uttered the pure *Dhamma*. The truth of his teachings infused all of human conduct, enabling the rule of law and morality to prevail. Unmediated access to dharmic insights underpins civilizational advance. But after Gotama Buddha's *Parinibbāna* and departure from the world, the passing of time is destined to ravage the memory of his words and teachings, resulting in slippages of judgment and morality. The erosion of dharmic memory lends specifically to the failure of the sovereign to keep the "two wheels of the *Dhamma*"—the wheel of worldly power (*ānācakka*) and the wheel of righteousness (*dhammacakka*)—continually turning and in balance (Obeyesekere, Reynolds, and Smith 1972). Throughout the canon is the idea that following from foundational sovereign violence, the "world conqueror" will renounce his violence and turn instead to rule righteously in line with the *Dhamma*, as the historical exemplar King Aśoka had (Tambiah 1976). But as the truth of the living Buddha's *Dhamma* fades from memory, the sovereign inevitably blunders and fails to fairly distribute land, triggering poverty and thievery, which corrupts the polity and the moral order. As the pure, unmediated iteration of the Buddha's *Dhamma* further recedes from memory, the moral impoverishment of humanity deepens and violence proliferates. Over time, the degeneration becomes so heavy that humanity is plunged into cataclysmic violence. The few who manage to hold onto the last vestiges of merit (*pīn*) accumulated in past lives retain enough sense to hide themselves from the utterly degenerate segments of humanity. After the dust settles, the survivors garner their shreds of merit and reason to work collectively to reorient themselves toward goodness and its karmic consequences.

The scripture promises that over the course of many, many generations humanity gradually works to restore moral action. By the time collective societal righteousness and human intelligence is sufficiently restored, a virtuous king will again come to rule. By then the Bodhisattva Maitreya will have amassed a superhuman quantity of merit, and the gods will invite the Bodhisattva to cede his place in *Tusita* heaven and descend to earth to be born as a human. The Bodhisattva will attain *nibbāna*, and the "Awakened One" (Buddha) will reiterate the *Dhamma*. With this pure iteration in the far, far, far future, all virtuous beings who hear the lucid teaching will gain perfect understanding and will instantaneously become enlightened.

This soteriology (salvational trajectory) of decline and resurgence was especially pronounced in Siridhamma Thero's discourses. Posters sold in the Ashramaya bookshop depicted a colorful Maitrī Bōsat, and Siridhamma Thero's renditions of the *Sutta* in Sinhala, which I quote at length:

The prosperous and heavenly kingdom of Ketumathi, ruled by a universal monarch, is the home state for the aspiring Buddha.... Having consumed only what is suitable for life as an ascetic for one week ... Maitrī ordains as a monk, and accompanied by *Devas, Brahmas* and a retinue of million men, sets out to the Bodhi tree. Ascending ... the Bodhisattva attains *Samma Sambuddhahood* after scaring away Vasavaththi Mara.

Maitrī Buddha, one hundred and thirty-two feet in height, will live for eighty thousand years. Those fortunate to see Maitrī Buddha would have the minimal requirement of offering a handful of flowers, a lamp, or some rice in Buddha's name. Those who committed deadly sins [*ananthariya*], entertained false views, born in *prēta, asura* realms, are deformed in body, or use that belonging to the Triple Gem without permission or knowledge, shall not meet the Maitrī Buddha.

According to the classic and contemporary iteration of the prophecy, Maitrī will achieve *nibbāna* and extol the *Dhamma* as the Gotama Buddha did before him, thereby reestablishing the supremacy of Buddhist morality.[13] All who hear the Buddha's direct iteration of the *Dhamma* will automatically understand the teaching and be compelled to follow the path. With the lucidity and immediacy of his words, virtuous hearers will instantaneously achieve *nibbāna*.

Ordinarily, it is only in exceptional circumstances that Buddhists become animated by prophetic millenarian discourses that promise the near-future arrival of a redeemer of the dharmic order of things. In episodes throughout the history of Asian Buddhist contexts, the messianic Maitreya prophecy was activated in conjunction with popular uprisings in times of economic and political crisis. During periods of internal instability during decolonization, as well as in "Cold" War battles between European forces and Maoists, millennial Buddhist movements of various sorts emerged in such places as Sri Lanka (then Ceylon), Thailand, Myanmar (then Burma), and Khmer Cambodia. These millenarian tropes engendered visions of dharmic magic capable of igniting profound political-economic reversals. In their battle against powerful aggressors, oppressed but meritorious Buddhists were slated to be spontaneously endowed with powers of invincibility (Keyes 1977). In such states of millenarian exception, prophecies held that Buddhist *weikza* would unleash the powers of apotropaic amulets to guard the meritorious oppressed, while their magic would transform pigs and buffaloes into demons to avenge meritless oppressors (Keyes 1977; Malalgoda 1970; Patton 2018). Given that within the Pāli tradition the forest is archetypically the seat of monastic virtuosity while the city is the seat of

5.5 The poster depicts Bodhisattva Maitreya (center), embodied as a manifold deity conjoined in karmic continuity with several previous Bodhisattvas. The caption below exalts the Bodhisattva as the true embodiment of the *Dhamma* and the immanent way forward for the whole universe.

power and potential site for moral corruption, preexisting millenarian prophecies of dharmic avengers also implicitly fortified revolutionary violence, by feeding hopes that embattled virtuosos would redeem the debased world by strategically descending from the forest to undertake battle in the city (Tambiah 1977; Salter 2000). With the promise of a coming *dharmaraja* or *dharmadēva* (dharmic king or deity)—sovereign protectors who prepare the ground for the coming Buddha—episodic visions of redemption in that era took on theopolitical force.

During such key crises within Theravādin contexts, messianic and millenarian doctrines came to life. But despite the drive that this rich imagery provided in key moments of conflict, Buddhists' evocations of the Maitreya Bodhisattva in those circumstances had primarily been metonymic and gestural. To my knowledge, historically, the image of Maitreya as deity had not been consecrated and ritually summoned in ways akin to the practices that Siridhamma Thero inaugurated at his temple. The act of venerating, ritually propitiating, and invoking the Bodhisattva Maitreya as if he were a Buddhist god appears to be a unique phenomenon—one that is apparently Siridhamma Thero's invention. The fact that this maverick monk newly encouraged devotees of his temple to "worship" (*wandinawa*) and share merit (*pīn dennawa*) with Maitrī Bōsat—a figure who is ordinarily not beseeched and propitiated through ritual means, is a significant innovation in the revivalist mediations of Sinhala Buddhism.

MERIT AS RITUAL CURRENCY

To elucidate the compelling procedures that Siridhamma Thero used to deflect attention away from the gods who reformers consider exogenous to Buddhism and instead to direct it toward Maitrī Bōsat, it is necessary to first consider the mechanics involved in "worship" and supplication of Sinhala Buddhist deities. Lay Buddhists interact with the deities (*dēviyō*) through beseechment and exchange. First, a devotee propitiates a deity with offerings (*dēva dāna*) of fruits, flowers, incense, garlands, and lighted oil lamps to implore them for assistance. The supplicant then binds himself to the deity by a vow (*bāra dennawa*). When the requested boon has evidently been fulfilled, the supplicant returns to the deity to fulfill the vow by again making offerings and by sharing merit (*pīn dennawa*) of one's good *karma* with the deity (Obeyesekere 1977; Goonasekera 2012).

Sinhala Buddhists use their own karmic merit as a ritual currency in beseeching the gods. The transactional basis for the relationship between a deity and lay Buddhist supplicant illuminates how the deities are positioned within the hierarchy of the cosmos. Under the rubric of Buddhism, unlike the actions of humans, the actions of deities do not produce merit (*pīn*) no matter how selfless a deity's actions may be (Southwold 1983; Bechert 1992). Only as a human being is one karmically capacitated to pursue *nibbāna* for oneself. But gods, like humans, nevertheless need merit for their spiritual journey toward *nibbāna*. Thus a deity's progress toward *nibbāna* is contingent upon merit offered to them by human devotees, a point my interlocutors emphasized in discussing the rituals for Maitrī Bōsat. Human efforts to share merit with a deity is a necessary condition for the deity's own karmic advancement along the path. The merit accumulated by a deity has an inverse relationship to their interest in powerfully intervening in worldly affairs of humans. Otherwise put, a deity with ascending levels of merit will at the same time gradually begin to wane in their capacity to intercede in the world and provide boons for human supplicants. One who collects supreme amounts of merit will become ever more disengaged from worldly matters as a deity, retreating until ultimately that being is reborn as a human in some far-off future lifetime.

Being reborn on earth as a human—as the Bodhisattva Gotama had been after spending a penultimate lifetime dwelling as a deity in the *Tusita* heaven—is the singular avenue through which a god may ascend toward attainment of *nibbāna*. Within Sinhala Buddhist ritual life, the interactional processes of veneration and exchange with gods of relatively lesser merit is axiomatic and is as taken for granted as Maitreya Bodhisattva's high and non-intercessory position within the Theravādin conceptualization of the cosmos. Thus, when Siridhamma Thero first introduced the Maitrī Bōsat *pūja*, even those Sinhala people who were not familiar with his new invention immediately recognized the implications of the ritual practice. For instance, Crystal, a Pentecostal woman who is knowledgeable about and avows respect for Buddhism because she sees it as a constitutive part of her culture (see the next chapter), was excited when she learned from me that Siridhamma Thero was encouraging his devotees to worship Maitrī Bōsat. Until then, Crystal had not heard about the Maitrī Bōsat *pūja*, but she became animated in hearing my report on the televised event: "It must be because Maitrī needs merit! . . . Maitrī can only be born on Earth and become a Buddha if he has enough merit. Siridhamma Thero must be urging people to worship Maitrī because he must need more merit to come to Earth!" Giving merit to Maitrī in fact had a dual purpose in Siridhamma Thero's devotional scheme. First, directing Buddhist laity's attention to Maitrī averts their inclination to focus on purportedly syncretic adaptations of "Hindu" gods who have been absorbed within the Sinhala Buddhist pantheon. Second, gathering the Buddhist laity to direct their attention and merit to a non-intercessory deity could only serve to make

Maitreya's arrival more proximal and render attainment of *nibbāna* feasible in a relatively near future. These mutually reinforcing components of the practice served to heighten lay Buddhists' commitment. By venerating Maitrī Bōsat and using the currency of merit to ensure Maitrī's further spiritual assent, Sinhala Buddhists could envision a more accessible pathway to overcome *saṃsāra*.

THE MAVERICK GOES ROGUE

In November 2011, some months after I had left Sri Lanka and nearly two years after the first Maitrī Bōsat *pūja* and *perahera* had been telecast, Pitiduwe Siridhamma Thero donned new golden yellow robes. Facing a crowd of devotees who gathered at his Ashramaya, and several video cameras atop tripods too, the monk made a special announcement. Siridhamma Thero conveyed how during his recent journey abroad he had experienced overwhelming sensations indicating a significant leap in spiritual advancement. Stemming from his intensive reflections upon the *Budhudahama* during this retreat abroad, he claimed to have had sensations that signaled his attainment of a level of *jhāna*, a stage of heightened Buddhic consciousness. In his mind's eye, he had had a rebirth of sorts. With this message to his devotees, Siridhamma Thero implied that he had become extraordinarily adept at absorbing the light of the *Dhamma*. He maintained that he had "entered the stream" (Pāli *sotāpanna*, Sinhala *sōwan*)—arriving at one of the final stepping stones to *nibbāna*. Sinhala Buddhists understand *sōwan* as a stage that will lead to *nibbāna* after just seven further rebirths. Pitiduwe Siridhamma Thero announced that with this experience of entering the stream his name too had changed, and that he thenceforth would be known as Siri Samānthābādhrā Thero. The monk dropped his village name "Pitiduwe," evoking the sense that he had transcended his local origins. He explained to his followers that the name Samānthābādhrā had been among the names of monks who Gotama Buddha proclaimed would one day become *arahāts*, and that no one in the last fifty thousand years, the present *kalpa*, had borne the name before him. Anoja and several other dedicated followers of the maverick monk expressed feeling more intensely dedicated to him and a sense of heightened enthrallment with his discourses on the *Dhamma*. To them, his spiritual advancement was palpable.

Upon learning of this announcement from outside of the Ashramaya, skeptics vocally condemned the monk. Specifically, the Bodu Bala Sena (BBS, Army of Buddhist Power), a contingent of monks that had been policing heterodox Buddhist activity in Sri Lanka, fixed their crosshairs upon the monk who deigned to call himself Samānthābādhrā Thero and claimed to be a *sōwan*. For some of the maverick monk's followers, the challenges cast significant doubt upon his claims. With that challenge in play, the newly self-minted stream-enterer entreated members of the broader monastic community to find an *arahāt* who could verify his spiritual advancement for the skeptics among them. However, according to Buddhist doctrines, the contemporary age is a time of insufficient dharmic insight, and thus an *arahāt* could only be a solitary ascetic whose status is obscure to the ordinary eye (Gethin 1998, 32-34). Hence, Samānthābādhrā Thero opened the invitation to any learned monk to test his knowledge of the *Dhamma*, to challenge his ascendant status in an open forum on the temple premises. Upon hearing this news, this contingent of the sangha became incensed. By the rules of monastic conduct (*Vinaya*) any *sōwan* must be modest about his status. Taking issue with his pretension, a monk who was well known for his political activity within the National Bhikkhu Front bombastically declared that Pitiduwe Siridhamma had gone mad and should be institutionalized and heavily medicated. Several BBS monks attempted to storm the temple to confront the monk and to talk him down from his conceits. Afraid for his life, his devotees deterred the vigilante monks from entering the temple—some pelting stones at the robed *bhikkhus* while police officers lined the streets to prevent a direct altercation. Following this encounter, the BBS vigilantes and other orthodox members of the sangha publicly denounced Siridhamma Thero, accusing him of going rogue. They alleged that he defiantly misled the Sinhala people by inducting them into Mahāyāna Buddhist beliefs and practices.

What led to this transformation in the perception of the monk's persona from that of a maverick revivalist to a rogue? The monk challenged his devotees to drop their attention to "Hindu" gods—ironically, some of which are guardian deities, considered to be central to the protection of Sinhala Buddhist sovereignty. But again, this is not a new trend in the modernist Buddhist revival. What is new is that in their stead he introduced the messianic Maitreya, who is latently present within Theravāda Buddhist discourses but is to become incarnate only within Theravādin visions of the far future. He enlisted Sinhala Buddhist devotees to set their sights on *nibbāna* and to share their merit with the Bodhisattva, for in giving their merit to Maitreya they could hasten his arrival on Earth. Until that point Pitiduwe Siridhamma Thero's innovation was entirely within the pale of Buddhist modernist revivalism. For the monk to position himself as an agent who helps deepen lay Buddhist commitment with the promise of hastening Maitreya's arrival is distinct from his secondary innovation that so riled up politicized monks who insisted upon upholding Theravādin orthodoxy. Whereas Sri Lankan Buddhist monastic authorities received the introduction of Maitrī Bōsat as a focus of veneration as an innocuous if maverick innovation, the secondary move raised hackles among the sangha. The conservative clerical body considered Siridhamma Thero to be roguishly scheming to introduce Mahāyāna Buddhist concepts to a place and a people they insist must righteously remain Theravādin. In essence, what these religious authorities found to be scandalous was that by characterizing himself as *sōwan* or stream-enterer, the monk was posturing as a candidate who had the karmic potential to approximate the virtuosity of, *or to even become*, the Bodhisattva himself, thus prompting Theravādin objections to the liberality of the Mahāyāna bodhisattva concept.

Disapproving of the maverick's pretenses, the activist monks petitioned the National Media Ministry to prohibit networks from broadcasting sermons delivered by the monk formerly known as Pitaduwe Siridhamma Thero. Responding to their authority, television and radio networks ceased all programming that showcased his preaching or other proceedings from the grounds of his temple. For a time, only one Sinhala news outlet continued to support the monk. They aired a radio and online interview of Siri Samānthābādhrā Thero, allowing him the opportunity to explain his revised spiritual status. In the Sinhala-language broadcast, he expounded how his mission had become all the more urgent:

> This *Dhamma* that I understand is not only . . . for Lanka, but for the whole world. I must publicize the *Dhamma*. There are scientists, intellectuals, millionaires, and it is time to tell them this message. Why, even Arthur C. Clarke has said that 2050 is the time that the Buddha *Dhamma* will become the world's greatest religion! This cultural custom and religious philosophy which we behold in our country, I am designed to promote and preserve it. Now the biggest challenge is this: How can we make it *their* religion? How do we show it to the world?[14]

The maverick monk exalted the *Dhamma* as universally relevant, much as evangelicals avow Christianity's universality. In the context of growing rivalries between Pentecostal-charismatic evangelists and Sinhala Buddhist nationalists in Sri Lanka, this is not surprising.

Although Siridhamma Thero's methods were unconventional, his efforts to attract Buddhist laity to higher nibbanic pursuits were at first in concord with nationalistic efforts to reform and revive Buddhism in the face of renewed Christian inclinations toward expansion. However, because Siridhamma Thero pronounced that he had "entered the stream" toward *nibbāna*, insinuating that he himself had become a candidate capable of *becoming* Maitreya in a near future lifetime, he asserted his own dharmic virtuosity. In turn, Sri Lankan Buddhist monastic authorities denounced him. Amid these clerical objections to his ostentation, he lost several lay followers, including Nimesh *malli*, and also the bulk of the *podi hamaduruwo* (novice monks) who had newly ordained within this uncommon style of Sinhala Buddhism. But Samānthābādhrā Thero called upon those of his devotees who remained convinced by his teachings to join him in a common mission. Anoja was one among several consistent devotees and patrons of the monk. She had witnessed a deep and genuine change in his person. To her, his discourses on the *Dhamma* had become more lucid than ever. Anoja and other devotees at the temple continued to insist that he was worthy of his stream-enterer status, or even beyond. Tech-savvy devotees found ample ways of circumventing the media blackout and enabled live-streaming of Samānthābādhrā Thero's religious programs through the temple's website, Facebook, and You-Tube channel. This publicity reached people in Sri Lanka as well as Sinhala Buddhists living abroad.

Sometime after the initial controversy, some Sinhala language media networks resumed broadcasting Siri Samānthābādhrā's *Dhamma* programs to meet popular demand. Shortly thereafter, in July 2013, I made a return visit to Sri Lanka and Siri Sadaham Ashramaya, allowing me to reconnect with some remaining devotees and to meet several newcomers. They described how Siridhamma Thero's entire retinue of monks had left the temple, bowing to pressures from the Mahasangha. But several new monks joined the temple, as did new lay devotees. These new adherents described the intense attraction of the heart and mind (*sith adaganīma*) that they felt toward Samānthābādhrā Thero's preaching. The mother of one newly ordained monk who was still studying for his O-level exams explained to me that Samānthābādhrā Thero typically does not allow ordination until one has finished schooling, but the boy's apparent dedication compelled the monk to make an exception. Referring to the boy's early attraction to the monk's teachings, his mother said to me, "it must be his *saṃsāra*"—implying that her son was karmically destined to take up robes under the virtuoso.

Anoja similarly used the idiom of samsaric destiny to explain the intense attraction she felt in listening to Siri Samānthābādhrā Thero's iterations of the *Dhamma*: "it must be my *saṃsāra*." Her persistent dedication to Buddhism and work toward perfecting her practice under the monk's tutelage had been karmically written. While explaining to a casual attendee who recently joined the temple that Samānthābādhrā Thero had uniquely "become a *sōwan*—or even beyond," Anoja stressed to her that "to *me* he is *like* a Buddha." I reminded Anoja how four years before when I first met her, she told me that the writings of Gangodawila Soma Thero (chapter 1) had initially persuaded her to follow "the religion of her birth." She affirmed that both venerable monks had encouraged lay Buddhists to strive for *nibbāna*. But what was unique about Samānthābādhrā Thero was that "he is showing us the *method* to attain *nibbāna*." Followers of Samānthābādhrā Thero emphasized the monk's inspired qualities (*anu hās*)—what I might be inclined to translate as "charisma" if not for the Christian origins of the term. Recalling how members of the sangha had objected to the monk's declarations of his ascendant status, Anoja underscored that the sangha relied on "traditional" interpretations of the *Dhamma*.[15] She implied that Samānthābādhrā Thero's relationship to the *Dhamma* was that of a virtuoso—one that innovated beyond the capacities of other monks who held to established pathways of thought and practice. For Anoja, Samānthābādhrā Thero defied the gravity of the declining collective memory of Gotama Buddha's *Dhamma*.

In my fieldwork during the immediate postwar years (2009–2011), I observed how nationalistic Sinhala Buddhists had edged away from propagating anti-Tamil sentiment, and instead focused their attention on anti-Christian activism. By 2011, the ground had shifted again. During my 2013 follow-up visit, Anoja and I discussed the crisis in which the Bodu Bala Sena had grown into an extreme but influential contingent within the sangha, which had begun to unleash violence and vitriol against Sri Lankan Muslims. It was the BBS that had sought to shut down Samānthābādhrā Thero's pretensions in 2011 by barring his broadcasts too. By 2012 the BBS urged attacks on mosques and Muslim-owned shops. It also campaigned for a ban on *halal* labeling, to which many Sri Lankan Buddhist monks, especially in Colombo, had begun to assent. These intolerant and paranoiac acts upset Anoja as much as they upset me. As she pulled the car away from the temple's parking lot, she pressed on with her point about the BBS. She stressed that if Buddhist monks were so concerned about Sinhala people converting to other religions, then they should lead by example rather than use violence. "In our temple, young men have ordained as Buddhist monks from other religions because they are persuaded by Thero's teaching. In addition to Sinhalese, two Muslims, one (Sinhala) Christian, two Tamil Catholic boys, and one Hindu boy have all joined!" In the view of Anoja and other dedicated followers, the monk known as Siri Samānthābādhrā Thero was adept at making Buddhism attractive.

In a subsequent incident in 2017, the maverick monk yet again courted controversy among members of the sangha. In a series of Sinhala-language YouTube videos launched by Siri Sadaham Ashramaya, the monk formerly known as Pitaduwe Siridhamma Thero asserted that he had attained some *margapala*, "supermundane fruitions" or capacities to perform certain kinds of Buddhist miracles. In a move most offensive to established clerical authorities, the self-styled *arahat* this time stated explicitly on his YouTube channel that the *Dhamma* he taught was more profound and more important to Buddhists of the day than what the historical Gotama Buddha himself had taught. Sinhala Buddhist authorities and the lay Buddhist public once again chastised Siridhamma Thero for his insubordination. The chief prelate of the Malwatte chapter of the Siam Nikaya, the monastic sect in which Siridhamma had been ordained, called upon him to issue a public apology.[16] This branch of the sangha is linked with the authority of the Sri Lankan state in connection to its historical seat within the precolonial capital of Kandy. They required Siridhamma Thero to meet them in person and to submit a written statement retracting his pretentious assertion that he had surpassed the capacities of the Lord Buddha to offer a *Dhamma* relevant for Buddhists today. Various Buddhist commentators penned editorials condemning Siridhamma Thero. In an editorial published in an online Sri Lankan news source, one commentator contended that Siridhamma Thero ("self-styled" as Siri Samānthābādhrā Thero) was likely not a monk at all but rather a "subversive anti-Buddhist" agent who sought to "create internecine conflicts within the Buddhist establishment."[17] Despite all of this clamor, Anoja and several other followers remain committed to Siri Samānthābādhrā Thero to this day.

In the canon and within the historical episodes of Buddhist millenarian movements described earlier, the appearance of Maitreya is a metonym for Theravādin theopolitical ascendance. Strikingly, however, Siri Samānthābādhrā

Thero's discourses on Maitrī Bōsat were devoid of any overt political manifesto, even as an expansionary manifesto is evident. In several incidents the maverick monk offended the wider Buddhist sangha with his pretensions that he was close to achieving buddhahood. Amid his propensity toward scandals of self-aggrandizement, and against a backdrop of polarizing identitarian politics that escalated over the last couple of decades in South Asia, the monk presented a surprising new configuration born out of media trends and channels for maverick self-styling. As to the question of whether these dynamics of interreligious interaction give rise to religious pluralism, the case of a maverick who initiates the veneration of Maitrī Bōsat does indeed pluralize Buddhist religiosity, insofar as it adds to the diversity of existing religious forms. Yet it is also evident that without explicitly engaging in the politicized discursive repertoires of Buddhist revivalism, the maverick monk introduced this ritual form with the intention to consolidate exclusivist commitments against rival practices that are constitutive of the wider religious field. As much as the Theravāda Buddhist clergy who reacted strongly against the monk formerly known as Pitiduwe Siridhamma Thero are attentive to ambitions of evangelists who urgently seek to expand the ambit of Christianity, the sangha recognizes much older rivalries and imperatives to mark the Sinhala Theravādin tradition as distinct from Hinduism, as well as from the Mahāyāna school of Buddhism. Evidently, dominant statist discourses do not provide the only scripts for the protection of a nation's boundaries and inheritances. Attending to such conjunctures and contingencies reveals the dialogical nature of religious disputation and adaptation, bringing into relief a layered account of religious heterogeneity.

THE DIALOGICS OF RELIGIOUS RIVALRY

The maverick's effort to consolidate commitments among urban Buddhists by ushering forth the arrival of the Bodhisattva Maitreya served in part as an implicit rejoinder to evangelical Christian efforts at expansion. In conceiving of the phenomenon as emerging from the tension with rival forms of religiosity, it is instructive to move beyond the dialectics of interreligious conflict and to think instead with dialogical approaches. Even as revivalist Buddhism and evangelical Christianity tend to demand exclusivist commitments of their religious subjects, the orthodoxies set forth by religious authorities are not totalizing forces. The unifying and authorial discourses of Buddhist nationalism and Christian evangelism each provide competing sets of "centripetal" forces that may be set in dialogical relation to one another (Bakhtin 1981). Yet the maverick monk's unconventional approach to the revival of Buddhism exhibits a centrifugal, decentralizing aspect, which is not a straight vector of either resistance against or compliance with any of these authorial regimes of Buddhist or Christian power.[18] Dispensing with conceptual binaries of religious revival and resistance, conversion and anti-conversion—or for that matter, singularly nationalistic orientations to karma, or evangelistic orientations to grace—allows for contingencies to bear out through these forces. Abandoning the idea that any force is singular or produces a predetermined trajectory of dialecticism makes it possible to see that complex configurations may invigorate possible vectors of newness.

In the opening of this chapter, a Pentecostal minister incorporatively treated the Buddhist principle of *saṃsāra* as a means to translate Christian eschatology to persuade Sinhala Buddhists that Christian salvation is superior to the Buddha's slow path out of suffering. In doing so, the evangelist contends that Buddhist points of access to *nibbāna* are far too distant. At the same time, in a coinciding development in Sri Lanka's capital city, Siridhamma Thero's innovation involved articulation of concern that Sinhala Buddhists were "chasing after" (*pasu pasa yannawa*) and worshipping "Hindu" gods, reflecting a well-established modernist criticism of traditional Sinhala Buddhist practices. Responding to the provocations leveled from the vantage points of other rival religiosities, the maverick monk reclassified the messianic Buddha as a "god" superior to the "Hindu" deities, yet as accessible through a Buddhist economy of merit transactions. For devoted Sinhala Buddhists this does not represent a simple compensatory mechanism: although there are chronic concerns among revivalists over the quality and durability of Buddhist commitment, it does not entail any shortcoming on the part of their Lord Buddha, as evangelical Christians would have it. What is clear, though, is that the maverick monk's innovations to enhance Sinhala Buddhist lay religiosity are born out of a dense and dynamic multireligious milieu. This maverick religiosity is dialogically responsive to anxieties stoked by competing religious traditions. At the same time, the vicissitudes of his innovations are complex and rendered tenuous, threatening to be treated as heresies that challenge the orthodoxy insisted upon by the sangha—the clerical body whose institutional memory spans back to much older rivalries with schismatic Mahayanists. Indeed, the second innovation threatens a heresy of a type that for monastics may conceivably seem as dangerous as the renewed trend of lay Buddhist conversions to Christianity. The processes of legitimizing these innovations in Sinhala Buddhist ritual life are evidently being shaped by the contours of religious rivalries—rivalries that are quite new, and others that are very old—and that are inevitably mediated through varied channels for publicity.

In a time of heightened interreligious disputation, religious leaders and practitioners may seek to consolidate commitments in an exclusivist fashion. Yet, despite the overarching milieu whereby Sinhala Buddhists might experience adversarial affronts at the hands of powerful rivals, they offer a range of novel rejoinders. For example, the bereaved Rohini acted with patient reserve when Christian funerary rites were performed for Estelle, a Buddhist. Despite what might have felt like a hegemonic Christian assertion, the unsettling implications of that turn of events for a conscientious Buddhist's reflections upon the samsaric trajectory of her loved one, Rohini and her family found the quiet resolve to carry out the appropriate rituals for Estelle at home. In quite a different vein, the Buddhist revivalist movement spurred by the innovations of the maverick monk, ensured that his devotees did not succumb to vitriolic methods of shoring up religious commitment. Despite the overarching forces of exclusivism and against the "allure" of the shortcuts offered by other religions, these Buddhists find creative pathways to remain dedicated and even magnetically attracted to the religion of their birth and to living out their *saṃsāra* as it has been written.

CHAPTER 6

A Spectrum from Sincerity to Skepticism

Ordinary Biographies of Converts, Apostates, and Dual Belongers

In Sri Lanka and elsewhere in Asia, a dialectic of sincerity and skepticism thrives in the evangelical discourses on religious conversion and the antagonistic politicization against it. One side of this dialectic is enlivened through the concept of grace, which born-again Christians understand to impel conviction spontaneously, producing radical ruptures in the lives of converts. Holding an expansionary mission, born-again ministers espouse supersessionist aspirations for the church that hinge upon Manichean framings of the divine and diabolical. On the other side, Buddhists promulgate the established inheritances of the nation, implicitly through nativist framings of karma. Karmic logics enable the exaltation of religious continuity in the face of nativist apprehensions concerning the encroachment of proselytizers who envision altogether other religious futures. The interplay of karma and grace discourses produce divisive imperatives to steady, or to unseat, established religious sovereignties. These countervailing tendencies toward continuity and discontinuity correspond with the formation of religious stereotypes that, as demonstrated in chapter 1, articulate with disparate economic ideologies and party politics. These marked epistemological differences, coupled with distinctive "sensational forms," create the perception of ontological differences that exacerbate communal tensions and contribute to episodic violence. Yet, at the level of quotidian experience, Buddhists and Christians of Sri Lanka find various ways to negotiate these overarching antipathies. Taking the context of charismatic Pentecostal exclusivism and corresponding inclinations toward anti-pluralistic Buddhist discourse in the public sphere, in this chapter I document some of the lived complexities of interreligious relations between Buddhists and Christians in Sri Lanka.

There is often a gap between discourses of religious exclusivity and singularity that religious practitioners put forth, and the ways in which religious commitments are actually lived. For instance, during my fieldwork in Sri Lanka, people would typically ask me about the nature of my own religious affiliation and commitment. In turn, I would give a loose and abbreviated explanation in Sinhala concerning a complex of personal choices and family dynamics, concluding with, "so: I like all of the religions." If speaking with Anglophone urbanites, I would sometimes also add, "I'm a pluralist." My ambivalent disclosures were typically met with consternation and raised eyebrows. In a southern village that I call Weligoda, where I conducted a major segment of my research, my Buddhist and Christian interlocutors tended to insist upon having singular dedication and suggested that I ought to declaratively choose "only one religion." This discursive insistence on religious singularity, however, belies a more complex set of everyday realities. Among many Sri Lankans, religious experimentation and multiple-belonging are more common than what confessionally declared faith commitments tend to reveal. Rather than living their faiths in a strictly exclusivist frame, Sri Lankan Buddhists and Christians ordinarily strive and struggle to live relationally. An ethnographic view of these religious entanglements complicates the sense that conversion produces a binary set of religious commitments that plays out hostilely. Despite overarching interreligious antagonism, Sinhalas often took pains to make gestures to ensure "mutuality of being,"[1] resorting to do so with varying degrees of appeasement, sincerity, ambivalence, and agonism.

SINCERITY, SKEPTICISM, AND RELIGIOUS LENIENCY

In my earliest ethnographic inquiries concerning conversion and allegations of "unethical conversions" in Sri Lanka in 2005, I found that Sinhala Buddhists and Tamil Hindus commonly mocked proselytizers and converts who had dabbling dalliances with multiple religious forms. Despite the anxieties that Christian conversion cuts to the ontological core of persons, Sinhala Buddhists who were politicized by the matter alleged that only weak threads attached the vulnerable poor to their adopted Christian faith. Reformist Sri Lankan Hindus made similar allegations with regard to Christian converts. Riding along one day in 2005 in the tea plantation district outside of the upcountry town of Hatton with a

Tamil tea estate manager, Mr. Aravind, my companion slowed his vehicle along a dirt road as we passed a church nestled between a school and endless rows of tea bushes. Sunday services had just let out, and Mr. Aravind allowed his pickup truck to crawl past. Tamil men and women were filing out of church, chatting with one another congenially. They were dressed in Western-style clothing. The gleam of Sunday taffeta dresses caught my eye too. Some of the men were placing their hats back on their heads as they exited the church building.

Glaring into the sun at the Sunday families in their finery, Mr. Aravind said to me in Tamil: "Look at them. Look at how they are dressed! Do you think that this is who they really are? They forget their heritage, their roots." He motioned to their style of dress, and their adopted religion. I asked him in turn, "Couldn't it be that they have been born as Christians?" Switching to English, he scoffed and said, "Our people, they're poor, you know, they get attracted only to the charity. Many of them, they take what they can get. Once the gifts and charitable funds dry up, they can't get anything more from the church, they simply come right back [to their prior habits and religious practices]!" Mr. Aravind, a dedicated Hindu, conveyed the point to me at a time when the initial phases of anti-conversion advocacy in Sri Lanka and also in India had begun to inflect Hindu reformist discourses common among upwardly mobile Sri Lankan Tamils too.[2] I discovered later that Sinhala Buddhists expressed scorn of nonexclusivist religious commitment in a similar way—characterizing Christian converts as people who hold false, fleeting, and pragmatic faith commitments. At the same time, born-again Christians likewise find "backsliding" among new Christian converts to be a bedeviling problem. Within evangelists' discourses, the fragility of faith commitments was a problem that required correction: returning Christian backsliders to the Christian fold would ensure a totalizing sanctification of a community "living in Christ." Being enfolded in this way was critical both for proselytes' and converts' capabilities of reaping the rewards associated with God's grace.

Anthropologists specializing in the study of Christianity have amply demonstrated that Christianity, and Protestantism in particular, demands and almost inevitably evokes "sincere" expressions of belief (Keane 2007).[3] From the emic and doctrinal point of view, Christians are quintessentially "believers" in the profundities of the sacrifice, miracle of resurrection, and the salvation that Christ offers (Ruel 1982; Bynum 2004). Doctrines of the Protestant Reformation further reified monotheism and the jealous demands of sincere and exclusivist devotion. With the emphatic declaration that it was faith alone, *sola fide*, and not material "works" that guarantees salvation, Martin Luther placed primary importance upon an individual's state of grace as an experience of believing, which for the individual is marked by interiorized affects and sensations (Weber [1905] 2001; Keane 2007; Mahadev "Karma").[4] The reification of the sincerity of belief was part and parcel of the vernacularization of the Word of God, which empowered Christian laity to access the divine directly, circumventing the mediations of clergy. Thus, it was particularly within Protestantism that the demand for Christians to achieve sincerely embodied belief crystallized, and this recurs as a religious imperative in the array of locales that Protestant missions have reached (Keane 2007).[5] The pentecostalist revival of Protestantism also takes the charge of sincerity forward, but through altogether different aesthetic forms and modalities of religious transmission. While the Protestant Christian Reformation story may appear to be the paradigmatic case of a religious reform that places demands upon laity to maintain sincere commitments, cognate processes of laicization are evident in other non-Christian religious revivals too. As detailed in earlier chapters, transformations that concertedly extended aspects of monastic practice as essential to lay practice (laicization) have been prevalent in Buddhism, too. Buddhist revivalists' modernist injunctions toward purification of *Dhamma*-following conspire to impel relatively elite Buddhists to express scorn toward cultic practices, as well as toward nonexclusivist commitments—much as Christian evangelists tend to revile and to discipline ambivalent attachments to Christianity.

Countering the preponderance of scholarly attention to "earnest" subjectivities of morally ambitious religious devotees within the anthropology of religion over the last couple of decades, a subset of anthropological scholarship on religion complicates this fixed orientation to sincere and exclusivist ontologies and pious religious commitments (Khan 2012; Mayblin 2017). A few anthropologists have drawn attention to the ambiguities and unscripted features of religious life that persist alongside trenchant sectarian and interreligious disputes (Das 2010; Chua 2012; Bush 2020). In the context of Brazil for instance, Maya Mayblin (2017) considers the religious experience of the "lapsed" and "lenient" lay adherent to Catholicism. Whereas the Protestant Reformation generated vernacular accessibility to the word of God, Catholicism retained a strong divide between monastic and lay forms of religiosity. Thus "leniency," Mayblin argues, is available to lay Catholics precisely because the Church retains a strong division of spiritual labor. In a time of the conversion controversies in Sri Lanka, I address the ways that Sri Lankan Christians and Buddhists embody a spectrum of commitments that complicate binary categories of sincerity and skepticism. In doing so, this chapter reveals some of the textures of social complexity that are conducive to religious plurality.

Given that skeptics and anti-conversion activists characterized conversions as "instrumentalist" or "pragmatic" at best, or "unethical" at worst, it is not surprising that skeptics seek to invalidate the claims put forth by those who might devote themselves to another religion. Yet, inconstancy and experimentation in religious practice became especially discernible through the "multicameral" ethnographic approach that I employed, since it placed me at the interstices between multiple kinds of religious influences, and sometimes at the relative margins of religious communities rather than consistently at the center. A multicameral approach may of course conceal certain aspects of religious life that stand out in other modes of ethnographic study. But by traveling in between, and not taking too seriously the overarching institutional and theopolitical imperatives that underpin demands for singularity and sincerity of commitment, in this chapter I provide another angle on inter-religion. Examining the rhetoric and the reality of deep conviction, as well as experimental and lightly held commitments, I interrogate what the interchanges between Buddhists and Christians mean in the scope of religious affinity, plurality, and social belonging.

The ethnography that follows captures kinds of commitment among wholly Christian families; in interreligious marriages where both Buddhism and Christianity thrive in single households; in places where religious difference creates tangible divides; and in cases where individuals return or "backslide" into former ways of being. Sometimes apostates bend to pressure of Buddhist kinspeople, or sometimes an evangelist's promises simply turned up short and failed to create indelible conviction. The final conversion story of a Sinhala migrant worker to Singapore presents the added complexity of inter-Asian religious transmission and itinerancy, as well as a broader discussion of the negotiations of competing desires of kin, ministers, mediums, spirits, and the people whom spirits possess.

Variegations in social environments shape the conditions of possibility for religious attraction and conversion. In the urban centers of Colombo and Maharagama, anti-conversion sentiments tend to be most politically charged. It is in Colombo where Christians and Buddhists tend to find the most consolidated networks for support of exclusivist religious aspirations. In contrast, within rural, predominantly Buddhist domains, Sinhalas who are attracted to Christianity must navigate threats of ostracization. In some respects, on the rural southern coast of Sri Lanka from which I make my case ethnographically, lay practitioners appear to be less habituated to the exclusivist claims that are characteristic of urban and periurban religious revivalism. In other respects, urban anonymity allows for greater degrees of religious experimentation. To consider these structural features, ideologies, and contingencies of religious attraction, I start with born-again conversion narratives at some of the centers of the Pentecostal movement in Colombo before moving "outward" to consider the "peripheral" habitations of evangelical Christianity as well as the peripheral habitations of politicized Sinhala Buddhist nationalism. Doing so illuminates the wide spectrum of being and belonging together—which ranges from the possible, to the impossibly constrained—for Buddhists and Christians in these milieus.

COSMOPOLITAN CHRISTIANITY: PROTOTYPES OF TRANSNATIONAL TRANSCENDENCE

Born-again Christian testimonies pivot upon the drama of sincere conviction. During interludes within Pentecostal praise and worship, a church's ministerial team performatively draws out Christian witnesses, giving established believers and newcomers a platform to offer testimonies of how God has graced their lives, radically transforming their person, spirit, and conditions of life. When invited or otherwise feeling safe to do so, individual believers testify in casual introductions too, and in more targeted acts of witnessing. In paradigmatic narratives of born-again believers, a convert may testify by enunciating the precise date, context, and sometimes the time of day during which they recognized themselves as having "gotten saved." When I met the head pastor of Grace United over tea in his Colombo office, he conveyed his own born-again experience to me. The pastor professed how, although he could easily have inherited his Christian identity as the son of Grace United Church's founder, he had once completely "lost his way" during his late teens. He narrated how God lovingly called him to see the error of his ways and how his grace had brought him fully back into the fold of his church, so that he came of age as a born-again man.

Grace United is a preeminent Assemblies of God church in Colombo—one of a handful of denominational churches in Sri Lanka that can be characterized as a "megachurch" in terms of its size, membership, and resources. The ministry was established during mid-1960s, and its storied "revival" marked reinvigorated charismatic growth in congregant numbers in the mid-1970s, true to Pentecostal form. Just before the turn of the millennium, the ministry established itself in a freshly built permanent building structure. Several of the Colombo church's established members are notables within Sri Lankan society. The congregation is partly made up of cosmopolitans, and yet the church also bears the stated mission to "reach the unreached"—implying, in part, a mission of subaltern care. Relatedly, like other Pentecostal churches in the Assemblies of God denominational franchise in Sri Lanka, Grace United is host to services in Sinhala, Tamil, and English. People of Sinhala, Tamil, mixed ethnic Eurasian ("Burgher"), and occasionally Euro-American backgrounds attend the church. To accommodate the linguistic diversity of the congregational body, the services are demarcated into distinct linguistic "fellowships." The English language fellowship at Grace United is the most populous of the sessions and is held during prime time on Sunday mornings, followed by the Sinhala and then the Tamil services.

Urban and rural dynamics of cosmopolitan desire, and habituated drives to achieve social distinction, and "development," correlate with discourses of diabolization (Brow 1996; Meyer 1998). As detailed in chapter 3, dominionist practices of Christian spiritual warfare render untoward habits and troublesome ways of being as the work of the devil. The diabolization involved in Christian spiritual warfare is intended to processually rouse the religious subject's receptivity to conversion. With this subjectification, a center-to-periphery ideology of transmission structures born-again Christian ideals of indelible conversion. Relatedly, for urbane Sri Lankan Christian evangelists, a cultivated and distinguished comportment and steady aesthetics of worship are tightly connected to cosmopolitan (and Anglicized) social habitus, which is taken to be a mark of grace. This became clear when I asked two core members of the Grace United ministerial team, why the intense charismatic energy associated with (Third-Wave) Pentecostal deliverance ministries is not palpable in their cosmopolitan denominational Assemblies of God church. Over lunch in the Samaweera's palatial home, the deacon gave me a ready answer: "Most of us who belong to Grace United Church are long-established and committed devotees—some of us have been Christians for more than one generation. But for many of the people who go to those deliverance churches, they have other, very strongly negative influences that affect their lives. So they are in very desperate need of that healing."

The deacon and his wife suggested that the members of their urban church constitute an established community of devotees who are firmly ensconced within the Christian fold, and who are thus fully and indelibly sanctified and graced by the Holy Spirit. The deacon also implied that the wholeness of grace and thus the prestige of their megachurch accrues with the embodied cosmopolitanism of its devotees, and with relatively "sober" charismatic devotional expressions. In contrast, he suggests, in nondenominational deliverance ministries such as those situated outside of Colombo city (see chapter 3), believers live in proximate relation to non-Christians, and that those people, although churchgoers, are routinely subject to negative influences which are dangerously inclined to inspirit and ensorcell them, creating tangible life impediments. According to Mr. Samaweera's logic, such demonic afflictions are more deeply entrenched in these devotional peripheries.

For dedicated Pentecostals there is a strong ideology of center-periphery intensity of charismatic church "planting," wherein those at the center of the movement see themselves as firmly embodying cosmopolitan mores. Urban elite Christians like the Samaweera family, and others at the core of Grace United Church, sense that a high concentration of grace surrounds them because they constitute a tightly knit community that forms a bulwark that blocks non-Christian forms of influence from entering their lives. Believers who are relatively peripheral to this intense cosmopolitan charismatic core may find themselves struggling to access the fullness of grace. In accord with millenarian logics, born-again Christians who engage this struggle commonly feel that they must wait for grace to come to fruition in their lives. This phenomenon of waiting for the fructification of grace appears to be a pattern in anthropological studies of charismatic Christianity, particularly among those who remain economically disadvantaged and at the relative social and geopolitical margins.

Otherwise put, Christian cosmopolitanism is an embodied genre, which pentecostalist and born-again discourses treat as vital to the development of a civil society that holds global relevance. Christian cosmopolitanism is an embodied social form, a habitus, which easily translates across international borders and is treated by believers as a material and aesthetic aptitude toward the achievement of "health and wealth" that can only be enabled by grace.[6] To be set upon a path toward upward mobility, ministerial discourses implore subaltern converts to

Pentecostalism to "make a complete break from the past," a discourse that dove-tails with aspirations of rural to urban migration (Meyer 1998).

A pentecostalist ideology of a total conversion that breaks the believer wholly from the past coincides with the idea of a sanctified, born-again self—one who ought to be enveloped in a normatively cosmopolitan frame. The ideal sits uncomfortably with the fact of religious mixing, since non-Christian influences are seen as engendering affliction and sin, and ultimately are to be vanquished. It stands to reason that from the point of view of a believer, as in Deacon Samaweera's discussion of the popularity of Third-Wave deliverance ministries outside of Colombo, that the non-Christian influences that are injected into one's life through religious mixing pose the risk of shattering the sanctified state of born-again personhood.[7] Nevertheless, for the vast majority of my Christian and Buddhist interlocutors, interreligious intimacy and even multiple religious belonging was an essential feature of their daily lives.

CRYSTAL'S AND ANOJA'S STORIES

Crystal is an aspiring figure in the Colombo fashion industry, and although she hails from modest means, she has had considerable success and what seemed to be an ever-growing clientele. We struck up a friendship when I met her at her small Colombo boutique in 2009. Our friendship, and our mutual curiosity, deepened as I began telling her about my research and she began telling me her stories and her ever-healthy opinions on everything from love, religion, politics, the war and ethnic reconciliation, and life. Crystal and her family are Christians, but I struggled to categorically place them within a specific denomination since they did not consistently belong to a single church. But they are dedicated Christians indeed. For a few years, Crystal, her sister and their mother, belonged to Grace United Church, but they eventually defected from the congregation. Crystal insinuated that overbearing demands of tithing, paired with the minis-terial team's inadequate attention to personal relationships with her and her family, were the primary reasons that drove her to relinquish her relationship to the outsized church. Since leaving Grace United, her mother and sister typically attend Mass at a Catholic Church near their home. But for her own part, she preferred to have more intimate pastoral guidance. Instead of attending church with a wider congregation, Crystal gave Pastor Erick a standing appointment to come to her place of business, to pray with her, for the boutique, and to bless her family and all of their endeavors, to supplement the prayers she conducted on her own. The namesake of Crystal's boutique, a variation on the Hebrew term for "grace," marked her commitment to God in a way that was indiscernible to most other Sri Lankans. Often their curiosity led them to ask Crystal to decipher the name of her boutique, which, in the right circumstances, allowed her to offer witness and share testimonies of her faith.

In our long discussions, Crystal commonly prefaced her discussions of her Christian commitments by stating that although she had become a Christian, that she "really respects Buddhism" and the Buddhist monks. She was emphatic that as a Sinhala person, Buddhism is an integral part of her culture. I witnessed her respect for the Buddhist clergy who participated in her father-in-law's funeral. A set of monks officiated the death rituals, delivered the *bana* (sermon), and afterward had their fill of a pre-noon alms meal doled out by Crystal, her in-laws, and her own immediate family. The whole family then carried out a ritual transfer of merit to the deceased. At her boutique the following week, Crystal remarked to me about her respect for Buddhism while acknowledging that other Christians may not see things her way. She then recounted her family history, wherein her own grandfather died of a "spiritual attack," which led the family's Catholic neighbors to fault a Buddhist monk for the tragedy. My eyes grew wide as Crystal began telling me how, long before she was born, during a period of economic recession in the country, her grandfather had died. Some jealous distant relatives of her grandfather's had leveraged sorcery "charms" (*sunnīyan*)—some next level, extra-dark black magic—against him, cursing him out of jealousy relating to his material success. Noting his symptoms, his immediate family took him to seek treatment from a Catholic priest, an exorcist. The priest did the necessary incantations as thoroughly and as quickly as possible but urged them to leave their family home with haste to avoid any untoward outcome from the afflicted residence. Since those were days when there were precious few roadside amenities, the family wanted to cook and take food with them before departing. The priest conceded to their need to prepare for departure but cautioned them against wasting time, for the grandfather's condition could worsen. The family returned home to cook and pack as quickly as possible. Just then, a Buddhist monk who was close to the family had heard of her grandfather's illness had come to chant *pirit* to bless him. In between the cooking, listening to the chanting, and paying respects to the monk, her grandfather's youngest son, Crystal's uncle, darted off to play cricket and was nowhere to be found, creating a delay in their departure from the site of spiritual infestation. Crystal's grandfather died—long before she had the chance to meet him—because of prolonged exposure to the malefic spirit. She explained to me that although in those olden days her family had mainly been Buddhist, the surrounding village was Catholic. Hearing the news of their neighbor's death, the Catholic villagers blamed the Buddhist monk for allowing her grandfather's untimely demise. "Though they blamed that Buddhist priest, I would have never blamed him. He was innocent," Crystal averred as she recounted this family history.

Despite her own dedication to Christianity, and broader born-again inclinations to admonish those who might appear to be backsliding, Crystal's occasional nonexclusivist religious dalliances were remarkable. On one occasion when Crystal and her family wanted to divine the whereabouts of some missing valuables that they believed had been stolen, they invited me to a small village shrine to the god Kataragama to seek help from a deity medium (*kapurala*). Crystal, her sister, and her mother picked me up at six in the morning one Sunday to travel out of the city to meet the *kapurala* who came highly recommended by one of her Buddhist employees. They carried out all the necessary rituals. The divination offered a ritual prescription; yet its success was indeterminate. The experience at the shrine was at once pacifying to Crystal, yet it appeared to leave a subtle trace of guilt upon her.

In spite of her own occasional experimentation, with regard to her friend, Anoja (who we met in chapter 5), a dedicated Buddhist married a born-again Christian man, Crystal expressed concern. Crystal was eager for me to get to know Anoja and understand her nontraditional approach to becoming a dedicated Buddhist. Even as Crystal was fond of Anoja and generally respectful of her choices, she seemed incredulous and somewhat disconcerted by her friend's headstrong dedication to the *Dhamma* when her affines would prefer her to lead a Christian lifestyle. But when Anoja first met me through Crystal's introduction, she stressed the capacities for romantic and marital love across religious bounds. "Though I am a Buddhist, my in-laws really love me," she said to me, as she expounded upon her confessional commitment to Buddhism. Anoja would sometimes go with her husband and in-laws to their church, even as she always went to the temple on Sundays and poya days. As detailed in the last chapter, Anoja made it her priority to strive for *nibbāna* in this lifetime rather than to take for granted that *saṃsāra* was insurmountable. In all, I was persistently struck by how deeply Crystal was dedicated to her Pentecostal born-again faith, even as she held an ambiguous and unconventional set of attitudes toward religious difference and religious experimentation. She persistently kept me guessing.

PERIURBAN DELIVERANCE: CHRISTIAN WOMEN BEARING THE BURDEN OF MALIGN HUSBANDS

At a deliverance ministry in the suburbs of Colombo I became acquainted with two women, Dhanushka and Thilini. They both strived to be wholly encompassed within the sanctified charismatic field through their associations with Pastor Milton's ministry (chapter 3), and through their friendships with one another. Although they lived in suburbs located at opposite ends of Colombo city, Dhanushka and Thilini solidified their friendship through their involvements in church. Each woman renarrativized her lifeway prior to becoming incorporated into her Christian community, describing a chronic sense of affliction which she attributed to her non-Christian intimates. Each told me of harrowing life experiences that resulted from difficult associations with her marriage partner. In both accounts, the deliverance and healing practices offered through their adopted Christian faith trajectories allowed each of the women to endure and "overcome" the corrupt lifestyles led by their husbands.

During a long worship session at Pastor Milton's deliverance service one Sunday, in one of the quieter, prayerful moments of sermon and Bible study, Pastor Milton had us all take a seat on the floor. A jumble of limbs, we organized ourselves and made space for neighbors. I took out my notebook, jotting down Bible verses and pieces of his sermon. Since I was without a Sinhala Bible of my own to reference, a puzzled look must have appeared on my face as I wrote, prompting the woman next to me to smile at me and lean in to share her Bible. After the ebb and flow of calm and charismatic exuberance of the three-hour church service had ceased, I introduced myself to her and learned that her name was Dhanushka. I showed her my notebook, and she sweetly laughed at and then corrected my Sinhala. Dhanushka and her forthright fourteen-year-old son Shyam invited me to their home for lunch. A bus filled with a multitude of Virgin Mary images and flashing lights—common in this largely Catholic area—carried us for a few short stops. We landed in a large roadside town and walked along a street filled with posters with the iconic kelly green elephant advertising the United National Party (center-right) platform for the upcoming presidential elections. Once we settled into their home with a preliminary cup of plain tea, Dhanushka began preparing lunch for us. I explained to them that I had adopted a semi-vegetarian, pescatarian diet—a choice that for Sri Lankans tends to connote adherence to reformist Buddhism. Dhanushka opted to make me an omelet to go with my rice and *dhal* curry. As she did, Shyam expressed concern about my dietary choices. Answering Shyam's queries as to why I didn't eat meat, I explained that I had originally adopted a vegetarian diet while at university because, as I understood it, vegetarianism had a lower impact on the earth and that the earth would be better equipped to "feed more people" if more of us adopted a vegetarian diet. He listened carefully but readily answered with a proselytizing tonality: "If people are hungry, all you need to do is pray to God. You don't have to become a vegetarian, Sister. Just believe, and God will provide everything!" I tried not to argue with the young witness as Dhanushka slid the omelet onto my plate alongside of the mound of rice and curry she had heaped upon it. They then turned the conversation toward how they, along with Shyam's elder sister, had come to identify as born-again (*näwatha ipadhīma*).

The mother and son told me the harrowing story of how they had survived the criminality of Dhanushka's late husband, who ultimately took his own life. Shyam was not shy about discussing how his father had gotten taken up with all matter of demonic influences, and how he had become possessed by Yakśa Ātmaya (the devil's spirit). His father courted danger, stockpiled guns, and had been convicted for his criminal business activities. In the midst of the trouble he courted, Dhanushka and her children began attending a nearby Pentecostal church and gained the spiritual counsel of Pastor Milton. Through their prayers, they were able to steel themselves "with the grace of God" against the deviant behaviors of the head of their household. Although they prayed and prayed for him, he was too embroiled in "the work of the Yakśa Ātmaya." He ultimately committed suicide due to his difficulties with the law and the failure of his business. When the sordid details of his death surfaced, a business partner falsely accused Dhanushka of killing her husband. Shyam explained that the threat of his mother being arrested and their house being seized loomed large, but that "because of Jesus" such ill fate did not befall them.

It was striking how forthright Dhanushka and especially Shyam were in expressing the story to me, a newcomer and visitor to their church and their home. Face-saving discourses are commonplace in Sri Lanka, particularly under conditions as extreme as those they recounted to me. Anthropologists have documented this inclination toward face-saving silences in terms of culturalist arguments; Sinhala families archetypically insist upon restraint, modesty, and shyness, and young ones are socialized in such a way that they are scolded, or at least teased, if they display insufficient "*lajja-bayya*," glossed in English as "shame-fear."[8] Yet, in Dhanushka and Shyam's telling of the story of hardship created by the negative influences of their late kinsman, they demonstrated no sense of embarrassment or concern with keeping up appearances. With their spiritual and moral separation from the husband and father, Dhanushka and her children were able to supplant their relationship to him with a close spiritual relationship to their church and to Pastor Milton. The absence of shame, fear, or remorse in the telling of their story, was a crucial feature in their born-again testimony of overcoming.

Dhanushka urged me to also speak to her friend Thilini Ratnasara, who she introduced me to on another occasion at the church. Over tea at her home, Thilini told me the story of how she led a life wherein her devotion to Jesus allowed her and her family to endure the dangers of her husband's political life. Mr. Ratnasara went from being a simple civil servant to campaigning and being elected to office as a minister of parliament in one of the major political parties. While campaigning, his opponents set fire to his office and shot at his vehicle. On another occasion there was an arson attempt on his family's home, and on a third occasion he was beaten and sustained severe injuries involving more than a hundred stitches and a broken limb. "Miraculously," he survived other violent incidents too, all meted out at the hands of his thuggish political opponents. Thilini's husband was a Buddhist and worshipped a number of Buddhist deities. When Pastor Milton learned that Thilini's husband had sustained such violence, the minister called her from South Africa, where he was visiting on a mission trip, to send blessings for her husband's speedy recovery.

"I stay up and pray all night, Sister." She spoke to me in Sinhala, but per the evangelical convention, she called me "Sister" in English. "When he is out with his work, I cannot sleep at night, because I'm worried about my husband and our family. Even when he is at home, I stay awake at night to pray." By then, Thilini had been a member of Pastor Milton's church for over two years. Her husband not only had a number of thuggish political associations and enemies, but he was also a devotee of some "rough" Sinhala deities and demigods. There are strong parallels between the operations of modern political patronage and religious patronage in Sri Lanka, as evidenced by anthropological studies of the cognate political and moral practices of politicians and Sinhala deities (Obeyesekere 1966; Winslow 1984; Stirrat 1992).[9] Thilini intimated too that her husband's devotions sometimes require him to engage in *bilipuja*, or animal sacrifice. Blood sacrifice to deities like Bhadrakali, shores up potency in the political domain, even as it constitutes a "demerit" (*akusala karmaya*) within the scope of Dharmic aspirations (Bastin 2002; Mahadev, "Post-war Blood"). Sinhala politicians engage *bilipuja* when they need to make sweeping political advances, though they typically feel compelled to do so furtively, so to appear as if they are maintaining their moral composure. In telling me her story, Thilini referred me back to Dhanushka's story of conversion, as a way of acknowledging their sisterhood. They each struggled to endure the corrupt pursuits of their husbands. Each of them believed that withstanding their troublesome spouses was possible "only through Jesus Christ" and the blessings he conferred through the Holy Spirit.

LOVE IS A BATTLEFIELD—CONVERSION AND APOSTASY IN THE SOUTHERN LITTORAL

For stints between 2009 and 2011 I spent long days in Weligoda (a pseudonym) and a cluster of neighboring villages in the southern littoral of Sri Lanka. I did so with Thushari *akka*, a woman a few months my senior, who hails from another village not far from there. In her time off from her primary employment as the principal of a school located some twenty kilometers away, Thushari worked with me as a field assistant and an occasional translator in Weligoda. We became fast friends. I learned that Thushari and I held many opinions in common, as she introduced me to her coworkers, husband, daughter, parents, siblings, extended kin network, friends, and acquaintances. Besides being located nearby to her home village, Thushari was familiar with Weligoda in her capacity as a short-term staff member with the Red Cross's humanitarian action there in the aftermath of the tsunami.

In that lush littoral zone, where the air is scented by salt and dried Maldive fish, I encountered families that had been affected horribly by the tsunami a few years earlier, and others who had not, with the aid of Thushari's introductions. Some lived in reconstructed homes. Many people of the area were relocated to

"tsunami villages," built one kilometer inland per new governmental requirements to install a buffer zone to stave off future disasters by sea. In Weligoda
village, I became well acquainted with a set of kin belonging to a moderately
well-off Salāgama family, the Kulatungas, who fortunately did not lose their
homes thanks to the natural buffer of mangroves and a strip of swampy inter-
tidal land. The Kulatunga clan lived within three separate adjacent houses that
directly faced the main road. Beyond the road and a gnarly patch of mangrove
trees, the sea gurgled and churned. The men of the family were involved in a
relatively lucrative sale of timber, and the female head of one of the households,
Geethika, a woman in her mid-sixties who I addressed as "Aunty," was well
known in the village for being a gossip and a bearer of strong opinions. In the
post-tsunami period, Geethika Aunty was employed to distribute aid through a
local Christian organization.

   True to broader patterns of gendered religious affinity in Sri Lankan evangelicalism, Geethika Aunty and her sisters were Christian; the three sisters, all
of whom had chosen not to marry, initially followed the religion of their late
mother who had been a devout Catholic. Subsequently, the Kulatunga sisters
joined a Pentecostal church, and experimented with other varieties of Christianity thereafter. The three Kulatunga brothers followed the religion of their father,
as Buddhists, and their wives were all Buddhist too. The religious difference
between the siblings seemed to pose little to no problem within this extended
family. The sisters' pastor, Pastor George visited the sisters' home, and I joined
them for a prayer meeting there one day. Those prayers were directed to their
brother, Herath, who had fallen grievously ill. A few nights later at their home
the sisters hosted an all-night *prēta pidinēya*, a Sinhala ritual appeasement to get the
pretēyo (malignant apparitions) out of his afflicted body. The Kulatunga sisters
invited an *ädura* ritual specialist to their home. Upon his arrival the *ädura* set to
work to construct ornate structures made of palm fronds. The family also
arranged a *thatuwa* (platter), also made from pale green palm leaves, and upon it
placed fried oil cakes, betel nut, cigarettes, arrack, and other symbolically "base"
and "impure" food items to lure the *prēta* outward from Herath's body.

   After the arrangements were set in place, Geethika and her sisters stayed at
the periphery of the room, wandering in and out of the kitchen, only half paying
attention to the *ädura*'s chanting and the liturgies of the elaborate healing ritual.
For a soothing effect during the ritual, their other brother, Susila, laid down on
a rattan matt next to his sick brother, the patient. Susila's adolescent son tensed

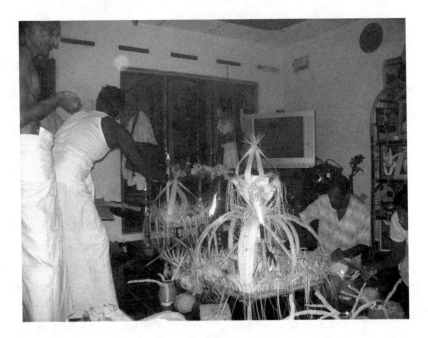

6.1 With ritual architecture constructed from palm fronds, *ädura* work their magic in a *bali tovil*—a ritual to pacify malignant planetary influences. After making astrological prognostications, an *ädura* may prescribe a *bali tovil* to cure an afflicted person. Such rituals are most commonly held in southern villages of Sri Lanka.

6.2 *Ädura* performing an expiatory *bali tovil*.

and fearfully urged his father to get up and move away from his sick uncle Herath, lest the malign spirit become dislodged from his uncle's body and capriciously leap into the body of his father, as spirits are wont to do. After a moment, Susila bent to the pleading and panicked look on his son's face. As he slowly rose from the floor, he steadied himself with a hand from one of his sisters. Susila looked dazed, perhaps partly entranced or perhaps just lightheaded. I turned to Geethika Aunty to query whether she was afraid, as her nephew apparently was. She scowled, making an incredulous and disdainful face, squeezing her eyes shut while vigorously shaking her head and her hand at me. In a later conversation Geethika explained her emphatic no, stating that it is Jesus who makes her unafraid of such things as *prēta* and *yakśa*.

Geethika Aunty and her sisters had a remarkable habit of switching between churches and even denominations. Their late mother had been a devout Catholic and had belonged to the seaside parish in Matara town, and they had attended alongside her. However, after their mother passed away, Pastor Jayanth arrived to Weligoda village by bicycle for the first time. It was the early 1990s, and the Pentecostal pastor had initiated prayerful home visits, to spread "the Good News" (*Subha Aranchīya*) in remote areas away from his slow growing ministry in the town. Geethika and her sisters took to attending his charismatic praise and worship services, traveling by bus into the town some sixteen kilometers away. By the time I spoke to her in 2009, however, Geethika had nothing kind to say about Pastor Jayanth, and the depth of her cantankerousness (for which she was well known in the village) came out as she disparaged the pastor and his "selfish" wife. She gave various justifications for defecting from the Pentecostal church, but she and her sisters ultimately had a viable opportunity to take leave of the church when, with the tsunami, a new man of God in the area, Pastor George, came to the village offering aid from funds gathered by a small church based in the southern United States. Geethika made it sound like common sense that because they had accepted provisions from Pastor George, they were obliged to attend his church.

Perhaps the most surprising thing about the choice made by Geethika, her sisters, and Saman and his wife to attend this new church, simply called Church of Christ, was its unique doctrine (see also chapter 2). The head of mission of the Church of Christ in Sri Lanka, a friendly man with graying dreadlocks who asked me to simply call him Joshua, insisted that his church community are not to be characterized as "Protestants" but simply as "Christians." The parent Church of

Christ in the United States was one of three churches that arose from the American Restoration Movement, also known as the Stone-Campbell Movement, which pointedly resisted the emotive pentecostalist revival of the Second Great Awakening (Garrett 1994). The Church of Christ denomination places emphasis on the New Testament and unification of all Christian forms by striving to subdue divisive doctrinal interpretations and undermining denominationalism itself. As their doctrine has it, Christ intended the existence of a single, unified church.

According to Joshua and Pastor George, the ethos of Church of Christ required that they work to dispel the misconception that miracles exist as evidence of the intercessional workings of Christ in the world. At the small Church of Christ ministry in the area, with a handful of families in attendance, Pastor George preached in a demure fashion. The *Awāsāna Rathrī Bōjhanāya* (the Last Supper) Eucharistic ritual was foregrounded within the service, with each congregation member receiving a small single serving of grape juice and a morsel of *roti*. Very differently from Pastor Jayanth's Assemblies of God ministry in the nearest town, and the other Pentecostal-charismatic churches that tended to be so attractive to newcomers (chapter 3), Pastor George's church establishment actively preached cessationism—the doctrine that we exist in a postapostolic, postbiblical dispensation wherein God no longer intervenes in the world, and thus the flow of divine miracles has ceased. This cessationist church imperative is comparable to Jack Miles's (1995) thesis that God has a biography that dispensationally shapes the deity's living engagement and disengagement in the world. This implication is captured in the Church of Christ's credo that, "Where the Scriptures speak, we speak; where the Scriptures are silent, we are silent" (Garrett 1994, 138) According to both Pastor George, and Joshua, to produce worldly miracles through "special effects" would be to dangerously mislead people. The critique of "special effects" took a tone of rebuke of the performativity of miracles associated with the advance of new audiovisual technologies, as widely seen with modernization in the Global North. It was striking indeed that Geethika and her sisters shifted from adherence to a form of Pentecostal religiosity that is very appealing precisely because of the cathartic, miracle-working movements of the charism, to a form of Christianity that actively disavows the theatrics of charismatic practice. The three sisters did select from among a small sampling of churches in the area. They settled upon Pastor George's church largely in accordance with a sense of obligation to donors of material enrichment.[10]

Other local demands of religious patronage put the Christian sisters in a strained relationship with the Buddhist clerics of Weligoda village, and particularly with the abbot of the local temple. Before the temple's annual festival, lay Buddhist devotees and patrons of the temple (*dāyakayo*) routinely made rounds to request monetary assistance from fellow villagers. I happened to be present, chatting with Geethika Aunty on her veranda while trying to catch a breeze with her in the sweltering afternoon air, when a young man approached to invite her to be a sponsor of the *katina* festival. The Buddhist festival, which followed a traditional period of monastic retreat during the rainy season (*Vassa*), was a prime time for laypeople to give monks the eight essential offerings (*ata pirīkara*). Without standing up, and without looking the man in the face, Geethika begrudgingly reached into her purse and pushed a share of money into the young *dāyaka*'s hand. Before he even took our leave, she thrust her arthritically angled elbow into my side while loudly muttering to me about the obligations of being a "big woman" (*lokku nona*) of the predominantly Buddhist village.

Some distance down a jungly trail from Geethika's home lived Dhanika, a Christian woman who remained a dedicated member of Pastor Jayanth's New Covenant Church (see chapter 3). Some weeks after we had first met Dhanika at the church, I was in Weligoda with Thushari. Through a neighbor passing by, Thushari sent word to Dhanika that we would pay her a visit later that afternoon. As we approached her home we found Dhanika perched upon a large landscaping boulder in her yard. She sat atop of that rock, intently studying her Bible. Or, as it seemed to me, she may have been anticipating our arrival, and for our benefit she sat in a demonstrative state of prayerful reflection upon the gospels. After we settled passed the small talk of tea in Dhanika's sitting room, I was quick to clarify that Thushari and I had no affiliation with the church or any other Christian entity, so as to ensure that she didn't hold any impression that our intent was to gauge or to report upon her dedication.

Dhanika proceeded to tell us about her longstanding born-again Christian attachments. She joined Pastor Jayanth's church in 1991. Dhanika's husband was a dedicated Buddhist, yet he remained highly tolerant of her dedication to her practice of churchgoing and prayer. However, as we had learned in prior conversations from some of Dhanika's neighbors living further afield from Weligoda, some of them deeply resented her proselytizing. Even so, they peaceably ignored her efforts to share with them the "Good News" because they recalled a time when, twenty years prior, the abbot of the village temple had led an attack on a prayer meeting which had taken place at Saman's home. Stones were thrown, windows were shattered, and insults were hurled. All of this occurred at the hands of Buddhist assailants from their village. It was a frightening incident indeed, in the recall of Dhanika, her niece, Saman, and a handful of others who had been present. With time, however, Dhanika ultimately managed to make peace with the chief monk and the other Buddhists of the village who had become agitated by her turn to Christianity. Although she generally did not go to the temple, she continued to cook for the monks on behalf of her husband and her sons who remained dedicated to Buddhism. Dhanika ensured that her household retained its position in the village-wide rota of *dāna* (alms) provisions to the temple.

Dhanika recalled how in 1997, her church, located several miles away in the nearest town, had also come under assault. Pastor Jayanth and other members of the Pentecostal congregation separately corroborated the incident. In their accounts, a Buddhist temple near to the church had installed loudspeakers to broadcast the temple's proceedings. The chief monk authorized the installation immediately in front of the Church building. With that, *pirit* chanting and *bana* (sermons)—both live and recorded—began to blare and disrupt the church's soundscape. Pastor Jayanth in turn filed a formal noise complaint, requesting that the loudspeaker be removed. He did so on the grounds that without a permit such an installation was illegal. Placed so near to another site of worship, an elevated loudspeaker was more than just a public nuisance but was also an incursion upon the church's territory. In accord with the local authority's mitigating determination the loudspeaker was ultimately removed. But in the interim, several monks and a contingent of lay and monastic Buddhists from the temple staged a protest (a "hartal"), in a move to intimidate the pastor and his congregation. Buddhist supporters of the temple's initiative carried signs in procession through the neighborhood, passing directly in front of the church. They allegedly pelted churchgoers with rocks as they attempted to enter the ministry grounds.

Dhanika's twenty-four-year-old niece, Somaya, vividly remembered the two attacks. "Apo!" she exclaimed when Thushari and I asked her about those tense and distressing days. Prior to our arrival Dhanika had told Somaya that we would come to speak to her on matters of faith. When we knocked on her front door, Somaya led us outside, a few meters beyond the entry of her family home. She offered us seats on red plastic stools astride a pile of kindling under a corrugated tin roof. That second outdoor kitchen space preserved Somaya's ability to speak to us candidly, comfortably out of earshot of her in-laws. We learned that she had first begun attending New Covenant Church at Dhanika's behest in the early 2000s ("before the tsunami"), while she was still in school. Somaya described having felt completely drawn in. She attached herself to the church community as a believer and attended for many years. Since getting married though, Somaya began working as a teacher at the *Daham pasal*, a Buddhist Dhamma School ("Sunday School") for young children. Her return to Buddhism was the upshot of a complex set of life decisions. Somaya had gotten engaged at age nineteen after a "love affair" with her now husband, Tharindu. In order to be wed, his family asked Somaya to relinquish her Christian faith. Tharindu is a military man, and they reasoned that because he is an army officer, it would be inappropriate for him to marry a Christian.

Reflecting comparatively, Somaya maintained that "Buddhism is a free religion—you can worship when you want. Christianity is not a free religion, you *must* worship; you must participate in seeding [*sam adhama*, collections], and also in tithing [*dasa gunaking kotesa*]." Exhaling, she said that her husband's family had insisted that she must give up Christianity, because, as they had it, "conversion away from the religion of one's birth [*upathima*] brings *pau*" ("demerit," typically rendered in English as "sin"). "Is it because conversion away from the religion of one's birth [*upathima*], goes against one's *saṃsāra* (karmic path or destiny) in their view?" I asked for clarification as the implications of her assessment began to dawn in my awareness. "Yes, that's right," Somaya nodded. But Christianity had helped her to "relinquish greed" (*thusnāva*) and has many other positive moral qualities, she explained. "It also helps us to cultivate good habits in our heart. We learn to give to others through Christianity," Somaya averred. Her reflection ran in obvious contradistinction to Buddhists' generalized critiques of the Christian prosperity gospel. Despite her earnest expressions of attraction to Christianity, Somaya peaceably complied with the demands made by her husband's family. Alongside of them she worships and lights a lamp for Lord Buddha each evening, and she works with her mother-in-law to cook and coordinate *dāna* offerings to the temple on a monthly basis, in addition to teaching Buddhism to children on Sundays at the *Daham pasal*.

JAYASENA AND DALMINI

Another part of Weligoda village is composed primarily of people of a caste grouping that is traditionally associated with the Beravā occupation of drumming and drum making. Broadly speaking, inheritors of the traditional Beravā occupation are classified as masters of Sinhala Buddhist systems of apotropaic (protective) rituals, astrology, geomancy (*vāstu*), the making of amulets, and the expunging of lower spirits through ritual appeasement. The social status of Beravā drummers and their kin is complex. The basis for caste distinctions in Sri Lanka is quite different than in India.[11] As briefly delineated in chapter 2, in Sri Lanka caste is primarily a designation of traditional hereditary occupation, and it only secondarily involves hierarchical arrangement of biomoral ontologies of purity and pollution (Simpson 1997). As such, caste among ethnic Sinhalas is relatively mild and mutable in comparison to Hindus in India.

Insofar as *Beravā* is used nominally for drummers and ritualists as a caste, families contained by the social classification do bear some degree of social stigma as a result of their association with the Beravā drum, substantively base forms of leatherwork used in the craft of drum-making, and dangerous ritual work with malignant lower spirits. Thus, the term *Beravā* itself, *if* used in reference to people outside of the context of naming their occupation as drummers, can act as a pejorative classification by unfairly confining people of the community to bald associations with the "impurity" of the drum, which sets them at the margins of the Sinhala Buddhist hierarchy (Ambos 2012). In the main, people in the southern regions of Sri Lanka politely tend avoid discussion of caste, and especially "*adu kuliya*" (people consigned to lower caste statuses). Since the caste term *Beravā* is often considered demeaning, nowadays, most Sinhalas avoid the caste appellation, even as it remains the revered name for the drum. Instead, the revisionist term *Näkäthi*, associated with "auspiciousness," has become elevated as a modernized caste and occupational name that replaces several prior terms, including *Beravā* and *Nawandanna*. Näkäthi" stems from the association with the Nawandanna caste, the traditional term for metalsmiths and artisans who crafted amulets and talismans (*näkath* and *yāntra*) to protect against ensorcellment and malefic astrological alignments (*graha apala*). This relatively recent innovation in caste naming positively identifies people with their capacities for divining, discerning, and dealing in auspicious material culture (apotropaic metals and biomoral substances), including the work of geomancy (*vāstū*), arranging marriages, and the prediction of fortuitous times to initiate life-cycle events.

Some members of these Näkäthi communities do persist in their traditional hereditary occupational niches, but these occupational arrangements are far from immutable. During the 1990s, young people in the south irrespective of caste have had expanding opportunities for social mobility (Kapferer 1997; Simpson 1997). Thus, many Beravā drummers rejected their hereditary occupations, not least of all because they have tended to be treated with "social odium" (Simpson 1997). By the time of my research in the late 2000s and early 2010s, people associated with this community were involved in nonritual-oriented income generating activities, including fishing, coir production, and crop cultivation as well as blue-collar work and teaching. South coast dwellers of various social backgrounds also engage in more lucrative service industries like driving, hospitality, and tourism. Due to this moderate degree of mobility in these southern villages during that time, there is a fair amount of social mixing among caste groups—certainly so in comparison to most contexts in India. What is more, nowadays marriages far less frequently result from arranged partnerships. Thus, even though one's economic mobility can generally limit marriage prospects, in contrast to India, proximal-caste marriages are relatively common, as was evident in rural Sinhala milieus such as the southern rural stretches of Sri Lanka where I carried out segments of my fieldwork.

Despite the relatively "mild" forms of casteism that are prevalent among Sinhalas in Sri Lanka, it would be misleading however to suggest that the caste boundaries are utterly immutable among Sinhala communities in the southern littoral. Middle- and upper-caste provincial types do occasionally enunciate derogations against Näkäthi people, as against their own sense of being of "high birth."[12] In one instance in Weligoda, I heard a Salāgama woman cruelly tease a younger woman of her own caste who had fallen in love and married a man of the Näkäthi caste with the mocking statement that "your husband must have used sorcery (*sunnīyan*) to gain your love." The confident young woman easily shrugged off the condescending implication that her husband was inferior to her and therefore that he would have had to use love magic (*washi bandana*) to impel her attraction to him. Letting it roll off her back was easy enough, she suggested, because that village elder was known to spew derogatory social judgments. The young woman later told me that she herself had little awareness of caste divisions in the course of her life in the village, and that, aside from ethnic differences in the country that were so intensely discussed during the war years, Sinhala people lived "without divisions" (*bädha näthuwa*) of caste. She expressed no derision toward the ritual involvements of her Näkäthi affines. In fact, she celebrated them.

Apart from the reformist Buddhist moderns who disparage Näkäthi ritual work as "superstitious," Sinhala Buddhists typically covet the expertise and ritual energy that these specialists wield. Näkäthi ritualists, including *ädura* who expunge malign spirits, are locally referred to with the honorific *gurunānsē* (teacher of the craft). In the varied types of work that they carry out, they are guarded in transmitting their knowledge (Simpson 1997). Their esoteric guardedness, paired with the fact that Sinhalas tend to attribute to this traditional occupational niche a relatively low biomoral status, has meant that the social reproduction of *gurunānsē* ritualists has been limited. In turn, Näkäthi ritual practitioners are fewer and farther between. But since their ritual work is socially valuable across a variety of social domains, established Beravā drummers and Näkäthi ritualists travel with a good deal of social capital and celebrity status and are able to "perform respectability," even though in some circles they encounter stigma attached to their work (Simpson 1997; Reed 2002; Ambos 2012). As hereditary practitioners, the talent of these ritual adepts is ideologically sustained in terms of their karmic inheritances. Practitioners from within the caste are affirmed for their special "aptitude" or "pre-disposition" (*pera purudukāma*) which is said to make them virtuosos in the ritual arts (Simpson 1997, 47). In Weligoda I met Mr. Somapala, known as Somapala Gurunānsē, along with some other members of his cohort of ritual specialists. As I found to be the case with Somapala, various high-status people from Colombo (ministers, businesspeople, army generals, presidents, and other urban celebrities) commonly consulted him. As such, despite his status-ambivalent ritual work, Somapala maintains high levels of local social capital. He is a respected elder in his village community and has also become something of a celebrity within Colombo.

Amid the grouping of Näkäthi families living in Weligoda, just next door to Somapala Gurunānsē lives a Karāva Sinhala family in barely built house.[13] The homeowner, Jayasena, his wife, Dalamini, and the eight-year-old daughter of Jayasena (from his first marriage), Somali, lived in some of the poorest conditions that I encountered in any Sinhala village. Just prior to our first meeting, they had newly joined a house-church affiliated with the international Pentecostal denomination, Four Square Church. They essentially lived on the bare foundations of a two-room home under a corrugated tin roof, with an attached open space where the family did their cooking. The rains of the southern monsoon and the scorching sun made life in their unfinished living quarters difficult.

6.3 A *jothiyṣa* (astrologer, a.k.a. *śāstrakāraya*) producing an etched *yāntra* astrological chart for a client. The talismanic scroll is housed in an ornamental metal cylinder worn around one's neck or waist.

Jayasena and Dalamini informally consulted their neighbor, Somapala Gurunānsē, concerning their housing problems.

Somapala Gurunānsē was well versed in astrology and *vāstu* geomancy, and he freely offered his time for consultations with Jayasena and Dalamini. He advised them to properly exhume and relocate the grave of Jayasena's mother, which was squeezed between the outer wall of their house and the edge of their property. With his geomantically attuned sense faculties, Somapala diagnosed that the grave was too close to their house and discerned that its location was the cause of their ill fortune. Since they could not afford to exhume the grave, Somapala promised to do a ritual appeasement to settle and pacify the lurking apparition of his mother that was plaguing them—clinging on yet karmically maladroit, as *prēta* are wont to be. Somapala charitably carried out the ritual on behalf of his neighbors, but the couple's financial position was simply too weak to pay him for the fullest elaborations necessary to lend full relief from their poverty. Jayasena worked as a nighttime chef for a mobile food cart, which he himself did not own, and he struggled to make ends meet. Before marrying him, Dalmini had worked on the staff of a hospital in a city some forty kilometers away. She moved with him to his home upon marriage. Although he was a good man, Jayasena was rumored to be an alcoholic. As a result of his alcoholism, their poor financial situation, and the dilapidated conditions in which the family lived, their neighbors often expressed concern for the well-being of his daughter, Somali.

One day, Dalmini walked out on Jayasena. Distraught, he went in search of her and traveled to her hometown in attempt to track her down. He managed to reach her on the phone. He pleaded with her to come back to him, but she met his pleas with persistent refusal. Overhearing his conversation, a police officer approached Jayasena after he hung up with Dalmini and offered him unsolicited advice. "Come and meet my Pastor." The police officer placed a call to Pastor Vipun, and the minister beckoned them to come meet him at his house church, located in a town not far from Weligoda. The friendly evangelizing police officer escorted Jayasena to meet Pastor Vipun, where the pastor and his wife prayed for Dalmini's speedy return home to Jayasena. Jayasena followed their lead and earnestly tried to pray with them—his first time attempting to pray in such a fashion, to the Christian God. Pastor Vipun promised him that, with the grace of God, Dalmini would return home within three days, and that when she did, they should come together to the church and dedicate their lives to Jesus Christ.

By a "miracle," Dalmini returned home three days later. Dalmini later told me that she had no intention to come back to Jayasena and that she did not know why she did, but she felt compelled, as if a force outside of her had directed her back to their home. Thereafter, Jayasena and Dalmini attended Pastor Vipun's Four Square house church, together with Somali. The family became involved in church activities, and Jayasena was invited to cook the meals for church events and was given basic provisions with which to do so. During Sunday services we'd sit in the open air congregation space in front of the threshold of Pastor Vipun's new, partly constructed, two-story home, atop thick plastic chairs that would heat up almost unbearably under the morning sun. As the service intensified, charismatic tongues, interspersed with hallelujahs, went on at a moderate din. During praise and worship, the police officer who had invited Jayasena to the church was the most exuberant in his absorptive state of them all, shaking his head vigorously as his body swayed, and speaking in a fast clip. Once I observed Dalmini set her gaze upon him while he was in such a state. She then turned toward me, met my observant eyes, and shyly smiled with raised eyebrows, almost smirking, signaling to me a feeling of bewilderment at the charismatic force by which the officer and many others around us had been absorbed.

The pastor, his wife, and some members of the ministerial team paid a visit to Jayasena and Dalmini at their home. They gathered to pray that by the grace of God the construction of their home would be completed without further delay. Jayasena and Dalmini initially expressed great pride in their attachment of Pastor Vipun's church. For this impoverished family, it was a point of pride indeed that Jayasena and his employer were hired to provide food for church functions, and that Dalmini could assist him in this regard too. With the increase in income, Jayasena was able to purchase a scooter that made his work commute manageable. Grateful for Pastor Vipun's help, the couple told me enthusiastically that the pastor had told them that he had connections to the Red Cross and other NGOs through which he might be able to assist the couple in financing the construction of their home. Within a few weeks of joining the church, the couple was baptized in the sea, on the shores of a nearby beach. One of the lay ministers at the church, a young woman named Tamara, lived very near to Weligoda. She was assigned to spiritually mentor the family. Tamara regularly went to their home and led the family in prayer.

Dalmini recalled to Thushari and me that during her first time at church, she felt scared. "I had never prayed that way before. I was used to praying with my hands together. At the church, they pray with their hands open," she demonstrated for us the gesture of open-handed prayer that signifies readiness to receive the Holy Spirit, under the open-aired portion of her barely built home. She went on, describing the charismatic prayer meetings: "there are songs, with violin, and organ. They pray out loud. But when we're at home, we can pray in our hearts." Expressing her reservations though, Dalmini conveyed to us that, "We have been baptized, but we haven't received a Bible yet. Tamara Sister explained to us that, "when we give you a Bible and you read it at home, all at once, you won't like it, you may miss the deeper meaning, and you'll drop it. You'll get bored reading it on your own. After one year of being in the church, we will give you a Bible.'"

The practice of delayed presentation of a Bible to newcomers was intended to assure that the text would be treated with sufficient reverence. The delay also allows anticipation to build, such that one can remain excited about the trajectory of coming into the fullness of one's faith.[14] But being deprived of access to a Bible of their own, Dalmini took as a sign that the pastor considered their faith to be insufficient. She felt the foment of mutual distrust between them. Dalmini then gestured to her persistent feelings of fear over the hauntings of the *prēta* that lingered around the grave that stood too close to their home, which she perceived as serving to leach away their wealth. With all of that, Dalmini wondered out loud if her fears would be appeased by continuing to attend church. She did say that she was enjoying her involvement in the church community. Her optimism read to me as if she was still trying to convince herself.

In the weeks that followed, Dalmini and Jayasena appeared more conflicted and bothered by the demands put upon them by the church community. One Sunday, during a time of year that is high season for the nearby Devinuwara ("Dondra") temple, Dalmini and Jayasena mentioned to church members that they had packed a lunch and intended to spend the afternoon with their daughter at the Perahera festivities. The Perahera is a ritual procession, which in this case celebrates the deity Upul Devīyo, the brilliant blue-colored "Buddhist Viṣnu," one of the four guardian deities of Sri Lankan Buddhism.[15] South-coast Sinhalas, when discussing the deities which they most devote themselves to, often name Viṣnu along with the deity Kataragama (revered as Skanda Kumara or Murugan among Tamils). The temple complexes dedicated to the two deities jointly protect the place and the people of the southern regions in a form of worship akin to patron-clientelism (see chapter 3). Upon hearing of Dalmini and Jayasena's plan for their day ahead, members of the church staged an intervention. Pastor Vipun and his wife involved themselves too, approaching the family to reiterate to them that believers should not attend the Perahera under any circumstances. "To attend the Perahera is to honor Lord Buddha, and doing so would be to go against Jesus." The family of three was crestfallen.

When Thushari and I spoke to Dalmini at her home, she expressed sadness over having to miss the Perahera. "I had thought that since we were born as Buddhists, we must die as Buddhists. So after that lady [the Pastor's wife] said those things, I felt sad. Since childhood I've gone to the temple and have trusted Buddha's religion. Even now, I prefer *gātha* and *pirit* (venerative Buddhist songs and chanting), more than the Christian songs; our Buddhist way of worshipping is really a treasure. So I feel I must see the Perahera."

Dalmini told us that they would organize a trip to the Perahera, later in the week. Dalmini then recounted to us how, at their church each week, one or two new couples were newly confirmed as converts at the church and Baptized in the sea. "If someone cannot attend for one or two weeks, the ministerial team will visit the family at their home, to ensure that they come back. Last week, we didn't attend church, so we received a phone call to ask us why."

While weighing the possibility of renouncing her Baptism, Dalmini reminded Thushari of a common acquaintance of theirs who had gone abroad to work as a maid in Kuwait. She had converted to Christianity while working for a Christian family there. "But when she returned to our village she never went to any church again. She came back to Buddhism." Dalmini then confessed to us that her heart doesn't feel attracted to Christianity (*Cristian āgamanta sith adaganna naeae*). I turned to asked her, "do you feel attracted to Buddhism?" Even with her shy, understated nod of affirmation, Dalmini's pride shone through. She then said, "I have even gotten used to the grave that is on our property. I don't worry myself about *prēta* or *bhūtha* (malevolent ghosts) anymore."

By way of her conversation with us, in her own terms, Dalmini was reasoning through and finding affirmation for a difficult decision that she and her husband were about to undertake. Over a span of a few months, disappointments with the unfulfilled promises made by Pastor Vipun and other dedicated members of the ministry piled up in the minds of Dalmini and Jayasena. Offering further justification for their impending move away from the church, Jayasena recalled to us an incident in which he noticed that there were extra construction materials laying around near the pastor's house church. He inquired after them, and Pastor Vipun promised to give him the leftovers once the construction of his house church was finished. When Jayasena followed up to ask again, though, the pastor's wife refused to allow the building materials to be handed over to him. Jayasena fumed as he spoke to me, reflecting upon his disillusionment by the promises that had been made and broken. The church kept a careful account book of the tithe and seed offerings received from each household, but Jayasena and Dalmini complained that their work of cooking and contributing in nonmonetary ways had never been registered in that ledger. A couple of weeks later, during one of my visits to their home, Jayasena ranted with anger and hurt, stating that they had left the church. Unprompted, he said to me, "No one can say that they are unethically converting people [*egolla waerädhi harawenna kiyala kauruwoth kiyanne baeae*]—I could never accuse them of that. That is not the problem. The problem is, Pastor Vipun and his church have made endless promises to us. But they have not fulfilled any of them! I'm so angry."

Jayasena's caveat, that no one had undertaken to facilitate their conversion unethically, was striking to me since, to my knowledge, no one had tried to dissuade them from joining the church. Despite not being deeply beholden to the overt demands of Buddhist anti-conversion activists, and despite not having a television in their home, they were well aware of rhetoric concerning conversion that permeated the air in the Sri Lankan milieu.

With their decision to leave Pastor Vipun's church, their Christian friends and acquaintances urged the couple to join another church. They said that if Pastor Vipun's ministering did not suit them, they ought to find another pastor. They noted that there was a popular church ministry in another small inland town just a few kilometers away from their village. Tamara too came around, inquiring why they had left the church—"what about your baptism?" she asked, alarmed that they were forsaking the promises associated with having taken that ritual bath in the Laccadive Sea, Dalmini recounted. "The church gets a 'commission' for converting people. That's why they have to find out why we have stopped coming to church, and try to persuade us to return," she told us cynically.

The exclusivist demands of their new church and their "new life" ultimately drove the family away. The pleadings of Tamara and their Christian friends did nothing to affect a "steadying" of their hearts and minds (*hita*). Jayasena, Dalmini, and Somali, did not return to church. Shortly thereafter, the family moved away from the village. Some months later, Thushari learned that Jayasena and Dalmini separated, and Somali was sent to live with a relative. Their former neighbors gossiped and speculated that Jayasena had taken to drinking again. Yet, again, Jayasena and Dalmini resumed their relationship, and eventually Somali was happily wed. When I returned after a few years away from Sri Lanka, Thushari and I went to meet Mr. Somapala, the *gurunānsē* ritual specialist neighbor who Jayasena and Dalmini had consulted about the grave located on their property, situated a little too near to their house. Somapala Gurunānsē had purchased the property and their skeletal home, with an eye toward completing the construction. He did so and had painted the house in a brilliant *upul* blue hue. Having ceded his original home to his son and daughter-in-law, Somapala and his wife are now living there on Jayasena and Dalmini's former property, using the house as their new home and as a workshop for his specialized production of amulets, *yāntra*, and astrological charts. On the day of my return to Weligoda, Thushari and I popped by for a visit. We found Somapala there, lighting an oil lamp in front of a shrine to Lord Buddha, which he had established atop of the very site where the gravestone that had so troubled Jayasena and Dalmini had once stood.

TRANSNATIONAL AMBIVALENCE

In another inland village in the vicinity of Weligoda, a Sinhala deity medium, diviner, and soothsayer (*śastra kāraya*) known as Dakshini Mäniyo operates a popular deity shrine complex (*dēvāla*).[16] The priestess channels the blessings of the Goddess Lakshmi and seventeen other deities (see also Mahadev, "Post-war Blood"). According to the adept and her followers, Goddess Lakshmi confers her divine authority (*varam*) upon Dakshini Mäniyo. Lakshmi spiritually enters and possesses her, and in this state of possession Dakshini is believed to directly channel the Goddess's divine presence. The deities carry out their divine and dharmic wills through mediumistic adepts like Dakshini Mäniyo, blessing and transacting boons to aid supplicating Sinhala devotees.[17] Sinhala Buddhist revivalists and reformers typically dismiss such deistic forms of practice as "Hindu" and thus improperly Buddhist, but these rustic rituals fall squarely within the scope of moral and ontological hierarchies of Sinhala Buddhism (Obeyesekere 1966, 1981, 1984; Kapferer 1997; de Silva 2006).[18] Indeed, practitioners consider these rituals to garner efficacy precisely because of their emplacement under the authority of the Buddha's *Dhamma*. Decked in a tangle of gold amulets and bangles, Dakshini enters into her Lakshmi-possessed state each morning, processing past the early crowd of supplicants, who queue up, in wait to meet with her. With verve, she swings open the doors of her shrine, first performing a *pūja* of veneration and obeisance to Lord Buddha. Worshipping Lord Buddha capacitates Dakshini as a deity medium, enhancing her *varam* (sanction) from the Goddess Lakshmi, and steels her against incursion by malevolent spirits and *yakśas*.

I first encountered Dakshini Mäniyo at her shrine in 2016, when Thushari and I sought her out to participate in and observe goings-on at the site of her *dēvāla* where the eighteen deities are enshrined. The priestess's assistants granted us admission to the inner chamber where Dakshini Mäniyo diagnosed what ailed her clients, issuing sacred prescriptions to them to propitiate specific

6.4 Dakshini *Mäniyo* (pictured to the left of the shrine), a Sinhala priestess, guides devotees to pour milk over the goddess Lakshmi, the god Shiva, and the goddess Pattini in veneration. Before doing so, she and the worshippers pay obeisance to the Buddha to ensure that merit flows easily from their ritual actions.

deities. During our visits Dakshini Mäniyo took time to show off, wowing us with her magical energetics, and boasting about her adeptness at alleviating her clients' woes. Most impressively, Dakshini Mäniyo's channeling provided boons to assist fishermen on their long sea voyages, to help families overcome marital and reproductive health problems, to effect positive outcomes for people embroiled in legal issues, and to aid in securing jobs for underemployed men and women.

After a series of conversations with Dakshini Mäniyo that we carried out over the course of several weeks, I moved the conversation forward with a slight provocation. I compared the rituals she performs as a deity medium and diviner (*śastra kāraya*) to the deliverance rituals performed by Christian ministers, stating in Sinhala, "As I have heard, many people believe that Christian pastors are especially adept at curing possessions by malevolent spirits." I then asked her opinion of that view. To my surprise, she did not assert the superiority nor exclusivity of her own healing abilities. Instead, Dakshini Mäniyo told me a story of how she once collaborated with a Christian minister to facilitate a cure for a woman named Puja, a longtime client and devotee of hers.

Dakshini Mäniyo prefaced the story by telling us that she has a good relationship with Puja, who often sends her gifts from Singapore, where she is employed by an elderly Singaporean woman as a domestic worker. During her time in Singapore, Puja developed some "diseases" (*laeda*) in her body. According to Dakshini's diagnosis, these diseases were symptoms of a spiritual attack. The physical manifestation of the spirit possession coincided with the breakup of Puja's long-distance relationship with her husband. Emotional disturbances leave laypeople, especially women, open to spiritual attack, and a spirit (*prēta*) was believed to have set its sights (*dishtī*) upon Puja. Consumed as she was by her work in Singapore, and distraught over the failure of her marriage, Puja wanted to travel home to Sri Lanka to be treated by Dakshini Mäniyo. Her employer was demanding, causing delays in her return. Unable to bear her symptoms any longer, Puja insisted upon taking leave. Upon arrival in Sri Lanka, Puja's sister took her to see Dakshini Mäniyo in her southern abode.

Dakshini Mäniyo had asked Puja to ritually cook and bring a meal with her to the shrine and instructed her to eat it there on the premises. Malign spirits have voracious appetites and are attracted to relatively "base" foods, and thus, she prescribed a greasy carnivorous meal to lure the spirit outward, inducing an obvious expression of the spirit in Puja's body. In exposing it, Dakshini Mäniyo could communicate with the spirit. As she ate, Puja's *dishtī* (state of possession) became evident, and she started talking aggressively and angrily in a man's voice, in a language that Dakshini Mäniyo didn't recognize. It was a Singaporean spirit, speaking a Singaporean language. Puja's sister offered translation. The spirit was clearly afraid of Dakshini Mäniyo. But the spirit was also stubbornly transfixed to the person of Puja.

A thundering spirit voice was propelled forth from Puja's throat, hurling abuses at Dakshini Mäniyo: "Stay away from me. I don't want you near me. I want to go to the church. I want to go abroad, back to Singapore. I can't be cured by you, because I don't believe in you!" (*oyāta viśwāsa karanna naeae*).

My eyes widened, and I searched for clarification of Dakshini Mäniyo's account: "the spirit said that it wanted to go to *church*?"

"Yeah, yeah. The spirit is a Christian one, no? The spirit said, 'I am not trusting these deity shrines,'" Dakshini Mäniyo recounted the translation that Puja's sister provided.

Eventually the spirit fearfully conceded that Dakshini Mäniyo could do whatever she wanted, but that it did not want further maledictions to be inflicted upon him on the premises of the shrine. The priestess asked the spirit what it did want, and the spirit said, "I want to go to another place." Negotiating with the spirit, Dakshini Māniyo said, "I can take you to Kataragama" (a deity shrine where Buddhists and Hindus worship).

The spirit said, "no, no, I don't believe in the God Kataragama. . . . I want to take a bath. I want to take a bath in the sea. And I want to go beyond the sea! Because I do not belong here. I am from another place, another country." A Chinese Singaporean Christian spirit had been entrapped in Puja's body—a spiritual remnant of the man for whom she had served as a caretaker. The *prēta* spirit evidently wanted to be released to return to his home, just as much as Puja wanted the spirit to leave her the hell alone. The spirit resisted Dakshini Māniyo's ritual work. Having conferred with the spirit, Dakshini Māniyo encouraged the family to do as the spirit requested. They in turn asked a pastor to come to the beachfront, as prescribed. The pastor led them all in song. After bathing in the sea, Puja was finally rid of the spirit.

Strikingly, Dakshini Māniyo did not recognize Puja's ritual bath in the waters at the local beach as the baptismal rite of Christian conversion. The ritual took place at precisely the location where Jayasena and Dalmini had experienced their baptismal baths in the Laccadive Sea, and where other new converts were baptized under the auspices of Pentecostal ministries in the area. Yet, as Dakshini Māniyo averred, after returning to Singapore, Puja remained in close contact with her. She explained that if Puja doesn't maintain contact with her, she complains of becoming ill again.

One might surmise that Dakshini Māniyo had been duped. However, this is not necessarily the case. Even as the baptismal rite archetypically signals adoption of born-again Christianity, it seems that Puja had not undertaken a wholesale and exclusivist conversion to Christianity. It's possible that Puja's family may have placed a multivalent set of demands upon her, taking her to Dakshini Māniyo's shrine, while simultaneously calling for her baptism. Given that Puja had been a devotee at Dakshini Māniyo's shrine in the past, Puja may not have renounced her ties to the priestess of Goddess Lakshmi, out appreciation and love for the boons that she had bestowed, or fearing a spirited retribution if she broke from her association with the priestess Dakshini and the goddess. The account suggests that Puja and her family sought a way to experiment with Sinhala Buddhist and Pentecostal-charismatic Christian deliverance forms, at one and the same time, to doubly assure her cure.

This fragmentary moment of the migrant experience of religion, recalled by Dakshini Mäniyo, reveals transboundary crossings that are not only territorial and oceanic but also ontological and epistemological. This transregional religious traffic includes traffic in portable, recalcitrant and even homesick spirits. The account points to why, in Sinhala Buddhist milieus, just as in Chinese Singaporean ones, people see the need to carefully attend to filial piety, and to satiate the needs of spirits of the dead. Quite differently from Pentecostal deliverance, wherein all spirits are deemed to be ultimately evil agents to be vanquished once and for all, in the Sinhala Buddhist conceptualization, it is simply that karmic residues may have the spirit caught up in clinging to relational threads of past lives. "Lovelorn" and terrifying, these apparitions are left to express themselves through misguided exertions of karma, sometimes revealing themselves to immediate kinspeople while clinging in place to their ancestral village or place of death (McDaniel 2011).[19] Accordingly, *mäniyo* and *gurunänsē* (priestesses and *ädura* priests) cajole the spirits with ritually offered victuals to pacify hunger, to ritually expunge possessing spirits from the bodies of the living, relocating them and leaving them to haunt crossroads, marginal spaces, and out-of-bounds places. These adepts also use the power of their incantations to set these spirits on a homeward path to attend to the unfinished business that will alleviate their longing and allow them to move on to the next lifetime.

ALL IS FAIR IN LOVE AND SPIRITUAL WAR

Modernist variations upon Christianity commonly shape condemnations of spirit cults and ritual magic as "superstitions" (Pina-Cabral 2015), and as involving "fetishizations"—critiques that signify the presumed dangers of forsaking the monotheistic God through inappropriate attributions of divine power (Pietz 1985). Modernist reformers in Buddhist contexts treat "lesser" spiritual agents and associated ritual practices as mere figments of uncultivated minds. However, particularly in its charismatic-Pentecostal form, Christianity is "revived" in taking spiritual incursion altogether more seriously. Between spaces of Pentecostal deliverance and the extensions of Sinhala news media, religionists treat the public sphere as a battleground for claims of religious supremacy (see chapter 3). Charismatic Christian imperatives to spread "the Good News" cohere with ideological emplacements of cosmopolitan social distinction, and peripheries requiring reform and remedial social and spiritual action.

Although born-again Christian ministerial paradigms emphatically call for breaking with past religious inheritances and are thus fundamentally opposed to Buddhists' nativist efforts to restore past glories, in this chapter, I have shown that far from creating a totalizing set of irreconcilable differences, Buddhists and Christians receive experiences with difference in myriad complex ways. Among Sri Lankans in the city, in periurban areas, and in rural contexts, one finds varying intensities of conversion, hostility, and ambivalence concerning difference. Sometimes religious conversions "stick," and in other instances they do not. Sometimes transitory, unstable conversions result from family pressures, or from falling short on promises. Accusations of "unethical" conversion, or of being an impressionable convert, can result in harm to the life and limb of minorities and present grave danger to social harmony. Yet families seek out a range of ways to manage the bedeviling influences of "wayward" religiosities in their intimate lives. People demonstrate capacities to pacify interreligious antipathies through love, friendship, and often too, by bending to social pressure.

Tolerance, as many have argued, seems to imply little more than "putting up with" a social fact of plurality (van der Veer 1994; Walton 2017; Walton and Mahadev 2019). Yet sometimes, that is precisely what people resort to in order to guarantee social peace. In other instances, navigating a maze of networks and kin relationships goes beyond mere "tolerance." Engaging religiosity leniently or experimentally, as in several instances I have delineated above, flies under the radar of much theopolitical analysis. An "ordinary ethics" concerning difference is tacit, quotidian, and transpires among laity outside of the ambit of religious authority. How it is that people live together in social proximity, sometimes with a good measure of "agonism," can be captured ethnographically (Das 2010; Lambek 2010; Singh 2010; Bush 2020).[20] Such a view complicates any sense of a prefigured and unilinear experience of conversion, or a dogged commitment to the singularity of declared identitarian inheritances.

These complex religious possibilities exist not only through cosmopolitanism or through intellectualist capacities for ecumenism and interreligious dialogue. They often transpire through structural constraints of living adversaries and aggrieved rivals. Agonistic forms of inter-religion might require, for instance, maintaining alms donations in a continued gesture of hospitality and care for established patterns of religious inheritance. These ordinary emergences of social complexity might be seen as a lived analogue to nondialectical thinking, which positively reconfigures what might otherwise lend to a clash of belief and skepticism. Even in the absence of effective, programmatic work of religious exemplars who persistently model interreligious tolerance and a pluralistic religious ethos (as happens to be the case in most rural reaches of the country), Sinhala Buddhists and Christian converts find a number of small ways to mitigate conflict and simply persist in the experiment of living together.

Epilogue

"Jesus Christ is coming very soon." This polyvalent statement extolling the proximate return of the messiah is sprawled in English in red block letters on a white parapet wall facing a major thoroughfare near the coast of Colombo. The sign has been there for so long that for many Sri Lankans the assertion simply fades into the plurality of urban life. Yet it may also call believers (adhahiliwāntayo) to attend to the urgency of the second coming. For born-again Christians it articulates both a promise of salvation, as well as the threat that non-believers will be left behind. At the same time, for dedicated Sinhala Buddhists it can add to the foment of nativist anxiety, portending that established religious inheritances could be overwritten by newcomers' promises that a more proximate end of suffering is nigh. For Sinhala Buddhists oriented toward nationalistic commitments, the message may be taken as a call to fortify their religious inheritances against the threats posed by these relative newcomers.

Religious end goals—and the gaps to be mediated in their pursuit—vary greatly across majoritarian-nationalist forms of Buddhism and various kinds of born-again Christianity. Depicted in the preceding chapters, Buddhists and Christians undertake material and political mediations, and remediations, that relate to eschatological distances, both temporal and spatial. They also address questions of ontological depth versus epiphenomenal and ostensibly "insincere" surfaces of religious personhood. Despite incommensurable soteriological differences between Buddhism and Christianity, authorial voices often endorse religious supremacy through rhetorical acts of comparison and commensuration. These tensions are amplified through conjunctures between doctrine and histories of material difference. On their own, the tensions might well have been either extended or settled through the continual meeting of Sri Lanka's plural religious inheritances. But as we have seen, these tensions are reinvigorated in the entanglement with new "pneumatic" and muscular influences that appear to be parachuting in from "the outside" and that seek establishment through conversion. Between Buddhists' skepticism and contempt toward believers' conviction, and evangelists' persistent—and *at once, very real, and really elastic*—claims of religious persecution there is a thick tangle of perspectivism with regard to these questions of religious depth and surface, and of being and belonging.

<hr />

When I arrived in Sri Lanka to carry out an ethnographic study of the politics and practices of conversion and anti-conversion in 2009, some of my Sri Lankan interlocutors, particularly Sri Lankan Catholics, were convinced that Sinhala Buddhists' anti-conversion drives were by then already a "dead issue." Some wondered why I would bother to study the ephemeral social phenomenon at all. But the significance of the resurgence of anti-Christian and broader anti-minority sentiment in the millennial and postwar period of Sri Lanka's history is difficult to overstate.

Indeed, a conglomerated set of challenges to the existence of religious pluralism have become evident in the postwar and millennial context. This crystalized in one spectacular, fringe act of majoritarian nationalist protest in 2013. A single Buddhist monk, Reverend Bowatte Indarathana, set himself ablaze in front of the Temple of the Tooth Relic in Kandy. Just ahead of the media spectacle, he publicized his protest against the various offenses that religious minorities are alleged to routinely commit against Buddhism and Buddhist values. Reverend Indarathana stood in protest against *halal* slaughter, animal sacrifice at Hindu temples, and against the proliferation of "unethical" conversions of Buddhists to both Christianity and Islam (see also Mahadev, "Post-war Blood"). In public discourse, Sri Lankan Buddhists condemned the act of self-immolation as "extremist," and "un-Buddhist," and the state denied the monk a state funeral. Yet many conservative Sinhala Buddhists, animated by an ethos of religious protectionism, concurred with the monk's underlying objections to the activities of these minority groups. The anti-pluralistic agenda that animated Reverend Indarathana's attempt at martyrdom spectacularly reveals a constellation of resentments against religious minorities, and especially against Christian and Muslim minorities, whose proportions are perceived to be swelling through the injection of muscular foreign influences.

In several instances, some of which are documented in chapter 3, politicized Buddhists engaged in a series of televised sting operations to unveil the "truth" of charismatic Christians' promises of miraculous healing. They did so with an eye toward dissuading those Sinhalas deemed most vulnerable to being "duped" into converting. Sinhala news media widely publicized these incidents, giving politicized monks a platform to publicly scrutinize these charismatic Christian forms and censure them for having all of the trappings of Christian "fundamentalism." As recently as 2020, Sri Lanka's former president, Mahinda Rajapaksa, promised his most devoted nationalist supporters that he would endorse their efforts to lobby for legislation that would criminalize proselytizers' efforts to secure conversions "unethically." In the Sri Lankan public sphere, Sinhala Buddhists' multifarious interventions served to remediate the influx of international and localized efforts by born-again Christian believers to publicize and share the promise of "the Good News" (*Subha Aranchiya*). Despite hegemonic control of mainstream vernacular media, ever new conduits for religious transmission are emerging in this era of neoliberal transformation. Inevitably, these technologies and new media platforms present various means for Christians to circumnavigate these controls and for Buddhists to amplify and sacralize their revival.

It is worth noting that while majoritarian nationalists actively seek to invalidate Christian "miracles" of conversion, doing so may not necessarily have the intended effect. This is because for those who are interpellated into born-again Christianity, nonbelievers' efforts to denigrate these miracle claims may only serve to fill the narrative "gaps" which allow witnessing Christians to situate their own life stories within the ongoing story of "postbiblical" miracles. As Susan Harding so deftly argued with respect to the rhetorical practices of Jerry Falwell and other conservative Protestant preachers who entered the public eye in the United States beginning in the 1970s, "necessarily, there is something incredible—in the simple sense of unbelievable—about a miracle, if only because disbelief is a precondition of miraculous action" (Harding 2000, 86). Indeed, that there is "disbelief" allows believers to punctuate their rhetoric of ascendance with rhetoric of miracles—of surviving and even flourishing against the odds of violence, persecution, and bad publicity.[1] Situating the acrimony over conversion and miracles that stands between Sri Lanka's Buddhists and born-again Christians in this way illuminates the trenchant potential for impasse.

Amid a war of identity-based perceptions about the requirements of national belonging within the context of postcolonial and postwar Sri Lanka, established

Christian institutions and relative newcomers alike have struggled to balance their national grounding, with their "suspect" global character and claims of universalist charm. New contingencies create ever-new possibilities of drawing and redrawing the boundaries of belonging and exclusion. For instance, Sinhala Buddhist nationalists tended to become inflamed with anti-Christian sentiment as a result of how the ethos of Christian charity appeared to coalesce with both secular Western humanitarian interventions and opportunistic conversion drives in the aftermath of the tsunami and the civil war. Secular aid and Christian charity, along with the liberal sensibilities concerning humanitarianism, resulted in broad charges of "neocolonialism."

Yet the lines of conflict and belonging are ever rearticulating over a shifting set of issues in this plural milieu—one that is necessarily a meeting place for global influences of various kinds. Majoritarian nationalists drew the lines of belonging in the late-war and postwar era with hegemonic force. These particular antipathies and identitarian stereotypes gain, and episodically wane, in their immediate political import. In the intervening years since I carried out the main fieldwork for this book, religious tensions have ebbed and flowed. But these lines were rearticulated once again in 2011 with intensified Islamophobia and anti-Muslim violence within the Sri Lankan milieu. Subsequently, this problem was exacerbated with the horrific bombings of Easter Sunday 2019. The bombings, claimed to be the work of ISIL (Daesh), targeted Catholic and Pentecostal worship sites and several secular commercial zones that attracted tourists to Sri Lanka. Initially, suspicions, political blockages, and violence rebounded, targeting Sri Lanka's diverse Muslim population. As Sharika Thiranagama (2020) put it, after the closure of a long ethnic war, new "figurations of menace" are ever emerging in Sri Lanka, whereby "fear is always in search of an object," producing a chronic condition that breaks into episodes of anti-minority violence. Throughout this book I have sought to track some of these rearticulations of conflict and belonging by examining how soteriological differences—the very logics of karma and grace, and ideologies of continuity and discontinuity—have tended to track variously with elite and subaltern subjectivity, senses of righteous or villainous personhood, ideas of intercessional efficacy and presence, and the proper aesthetics of religious conveyance. Perpetually, religious authorities define themselves and their constituents against others—to validate their public self-assertions, to forge new, persuasive configurations, and to extricate themselves from perceived associations with unseemly, dangerous, "anti-national" or "demonic" beings.

During the pandemic in Sri Lanka, discourses on the spread of COVID-19 virulently traced transmission to "suspect" (*sakakārēyo*) others (Silva 2020; Gajaweera and Mahadev 2023). In majoritarian nationalist milieus of India, as well as in Sri Lanka, Muslims were commonly demonized as "super spreaders," actively engaged in "Corona jihad" (Roy 2020; Silva 2020). Yet there is counter-vailing evidence that Sinhala Buddhists also make careful discernments amid the rising trend of Islamophobic paranoias that intensified after the bombings. As Thushari, my research assistant, observed, Sinhala Buddhists described those Muslims who are familiar to them through regular interactions in the village market as "*ahinsakay*"—a term in Sinhala that is commonly translated as "inno-cent" or "harmless"—a ordinary word linked to the Sanskrit term *ahimsā*, denot-ing that these "known neighbors" are inclined to be nonviolent (see Gajaweera and Mahadev 2023). In this way, a group is definitionally captured, once again, by categories—but perhaps in this case the categories are indeterminate enough to stave off identarian enmity and potentially sustain friendship. What is more, in some of the southern areas where I carried out my research, Catholic, Protes-tant, Buddhist, Muslim, and Hindu leaders engage in dialogue sessions, particu-larly amid the ubiquitous scapegoating that transpired in aftermath of the 2019 bombings. Even as these intercommunity tensions proliferate and "go viral" through rumor and channels of mass mediation, interreligious organizations are actively working to offset those conflicts, programmatically engaging as repre-sentatives and peacemakers to mediate and mitigate interreligious hostilities.[2]

In 2022, the concerns of the Sri Lankan public have veered in a radically dif-ferent direction, when profound financial mismanagement and corruption by the reelected Rajapaksa regime (under President Gotabaya Rajapaksa, the hawk-ish former minister of defense) converged with pandemic-era GDP borrowing deficits and resulted in crisis-level sovereign debt. Facing long power cuts and devastating fuel, food, and medical supply shortages, nearly all sectors of Sri Lankan civil society became embroiled in mass social protest and calls for "Gota Go Home"—to eject the prime minister and his corrupt band of brothers from political office. Whereas in 2009 Sinhala Buddhists had celebrated the Raj-apaksa government's triumph in the civil war and tended to dismiss humanitar-ian violations as "recolonizing" political spin, in 2022 some of these very people had become animated in their fury against these symbolic sovereigns. The parti-san divide detailed in chapter 1 appears to have come undone over the last decade, with political authorities increasingly drawn into neoliberal development undertakings. As usual with structural adjustment, ordinary citizens are being held responsible for sustaining themselves through imposed austerities. Drawn together in this crisis, urban activists from various social backgrounds, including middle-class Sinhala Buddhists, took to protesting alongside of minoritized Tamils, Muslims, and Christians who have had long-standing grievances against the regime. Alongside concurrent calls by Catholics and other Christians of Sri Lanka to investigate the 2019 Easter Sunday bombings in the course of the *Aragalaya* ("struggle") protests of 2022, Sri Lankan Buddhists, Hindus, and Christians set up sanctuary spaces for Muslims to pray within the site of the protests at Galle Face Green.[3] As this book goes to press, the political leadership has returned and barely shifted from their extractive and draconian course. Protestors have been threatened and forced to roll back on their political gatherings.[4] The dire effects that are being felt among ordinary Sri Lankans will likely deepen, as this crisis remains unresolved.

———◆———

As I have argued in this book, the millennial intensification of conflicts between Buddhists and Christians over religious conversion is at once imbedded in disparate ideologies of abiding by religious heritage, as against the new, discontinuous arrival or "incursion" of grace. At the same time, it is material realities that serve to channel religious influence. The antipathies of belief and skepticism appear as conceptually bounded identitarian conflicts, thus making religious difference a site of discursive sparring, and trenchant conflicts. Interreligious contentions play out in ways that sometimes forcefully constrain and shape religious choice. However, rather than offer an account that solely captures dialectically opposed religiosities, I have detailed how even in conflict, a complex religious field is conducive also to dialogically responsive emergences, innovations, multifaceted devotional repertoires, quotidian leniencies, and concerted mitigating efforts. Certainly new adaptations will come in such a milieu. Under the weight of social contention and economic disparities, various kinds of religious rivalries are sparked. Unfortunate negative judgments against difference are symptomatic of these tense configurations. They are also extended through innovative forms of mass mediation, some of them involving technologies and platforms that are now only in their infancy or are yet to be born. At the same time, various authorities of the established religions push back against these reformulations concerning which pathways lead to the achievement of salvific and nibbanic end goals. In the standoff between the millennial Christian urgencies and rebounding Buddhist nationalist anxieties, religious authorities occasionally propose to settle the issue, in ways that reassert interreligious friendships while also creating deflections that amp up conflict in other arenas.

In rivalry, certain Christian and Buddhist leaders transform their traditions. They innovate, performing a variety of ritual, theological, and mediatic maneuvers to attract devotees and to shield their practices from the affronts of rivals of other religions, denominations, and sects. Attentive to the overarching political context of Sri Lanka, they invariably do so while underscoring their love of the nation. Religious laity too often must work to navigate religious tensions that hit close to home. At the intersection between these Buddhist and Christian forms of religious life, emerges an antagonistic mirroring between nationalistic and evangelical discourses—a dialogical set of "oppositional symmetries."[5] Through this work of reckoning, mirroring, and commensurating between incommensurate soteriological goals, innovations may also arise. Rather than have a homogenizing effect, religious difference thrives in spite of trenchant antagonisms. Taking care not to assume that these are necessarily enduring expressions of religious pluralism, however, it is imperative to recognize that it takes concerted, programmatic efforts to extend interreligious friendship and to enhance ordinary intimacies. In places that have seen the starkening of categorically wrought identitarian enmities, such boundary-crossing intimacies are too often unrecorded and unremarked upon. These kinds of daily peacekeeping in plural and even agonistic conditions are worthy of attention, and cultivation too.

Notes

INTRODUCTION

1. The temple is associated with the Amarapura Nikaya, a monastic sect established in Ceylon in the early 1800s, its ordination lineage stemming from Burma.

2. Throughout this book I have used pseudonyms for all of my interlocutors except for public figures whose stories are widely circulated within Sri Lanka. In most instances I have used pseudonyms for place names and changed other identifying features.

3. For elaborated discussion of the lineage, and temple founder Venerable Reverend Madihe Pannasihe Thero (1913–2003), see Kemper 1991. Pannasiha Thero was revered teacher of Soma Thera and many other monks trained and ordained at the monastery. His larger-than-life image was displayed in the Maharagama temple hall alongside Soma Thera's image during my 2010 visit.

4. Scholars argue that modernist transformations and ethicization of Buddhism in fact began long before the encounter with European modernity (Obeyesekere 1963; Hallisey 2007). Obeyesekere (2002) makes the point with regard to Buddhist eschatology of karma by drawing upon Jasper's (1953) thesis on the Axial Age (8th–3rd c. BCE), allowing him to cross-culturally examine metaphysical emergences of transmigration and their implications for ethics in several religions of the world.

5. Csordas argues that under conditions of postmodernity the self is susceptible to "commodification and fragmentation," manifesting as the "uncanny" (demonic) within the self (1997, 152). Thus, incoherent ritual processes are instrumental in reintegrating a "sacred self" capable of withstanding those societal forces (62).

6. The televised *Ramayana* epic that serially aired across India in the late 1980s provided fodder for the Ram Janmabhumi movement, which sought retribution against Muslims for erecting the Babri Masjid (16th c. CE) supposedly upon the hallowed grounds of their Lord Ram's birth. The movement culminated in the atrocious demolition of the mosque in Ayodhya in 1992 (Rajagopal 2001; Mankekar 2002).

7. Chathuri Dissanayake, "Buddhist Leaders Say God TV on Dialog No Threat," *Sunday Times*, August 5, 2007, https://www.sundaytimes.lk/070805/News/nws3.html.

8.   Rohan Mathes, "Development Should Incorporate Economic and Spiritual Values—President," *Daily News*, July 2, 2007, http://archives.dailynews.lk/2007/07/02/news20.asp.

9.   Dissanayake, "Buddhist Leaders." According to a press release, viewer access to the channel is enabled for subscribers only by special request to cable providers rather than as a default, thus ensuring that televangelical programming can reach Christian audiences in a measured way.

10. The fact that South Korea also has a vast tradition of shamanism, Buddhism, and ancestor worship goes unacknowledged in such narratives and does not matter for the Sri Lankans who seize upon the comparison.

11. As widely documented by scholars of Sri Lanka, mythohistorical accounts of the *Dipavamsa* and *Mahavamsa* propels the idea that Gotama Buddha had once set foot in Sri Lanka to preordain the island as *Dhammadipa*. As the accounts have it, in the moment of Buddha's death and attainment of *Parinibbana* (ultimate release from cycles of life, death, and rebirth [*saṃsāra*]) the seafaring Prince Vijaya touched ground in Sri Lanka, establishing the Sinhala "race," which laid the groundwork for the uptake and gradual establishment of Buddhism on the island.

12. As early as the mid-1700s, Portuguese Catholic missionization bred nascent hostility, which appears encoded in myth (Roberts 1989; Young and Somaratna 1998).

13. Comparing census statistics from 1981 and 2012: http://www.statistics.gov.lk/PopHouSat/PDF/Population/p9p9%20Religion.pdf and http://www.statistics.gov.lk/PopHouSat/CPH2011/index.php?fileName=pop43&gp=Activities&tpl=3.

14. "International Religious Freedom Report, Sri Lanka," U.S. State Department. In 2018, there were eighty-eight attacks on Christian Churches according to the NCEASL. https://www.state.gov/wp-content/uploads/2020/05/SRI-LANKA-2019-INTERNATIONAL-RELIGIOUS-FREEDOM-REPORT.pdf.

15. A robustly researched report published in 2022 by the NCEASL and Verité covers violence committed against Christians, and secondarily against other minorities. It notes the negative bias by the Sri Lankan authorities in policing these matters and documents the uptick of religious violence during election periods.

16. Portuguese rule from 1505 to 1658 introduced Roman Catholicism, particularly in coastal regions of Ceylon. The Dutch (1658–1796) brought Calvinism. The Dutch confiscated Portuguese properties in Ceylon, persecuted Portuguese Catholics, and ultimately sent them into exile (Perniola 1989, xiv). With the British takeover of the Kandyan Kingdom in 1815, the Anglican Church and other Protestant forms were established. The Catholic Church, too, was allowed protection under British rule.

17. Without attempting to neutralize or deny atrocities committed under the banner of empire and missionization, in these newer takes on the colonial era scholars have been emphatic that supremacist and supercessionist practices were not totalizing features of these encounters (Biedermann 2010). Historians of the Ceylonese colonial era have demonstrated that there were substantive moments of political agency on the part of local people, as well intercultural and interreligious diplomacy, cosmopolitan extraversion and mutual respect, political pragmatism, and syncretism, that occurred within the encounter (Strathern 2007; Biedermann 2010; Harris 2006). Scholars of the

Luso–Sri Lankan encounter (1505–1658) demonstrate that conversions occasionally went in both directions (Strathern 2007) and argue that Sri Lanka was a "crossroads of history" (Biedermann and Strathern 2017). Likewise, Zupanov (1996) describes how "Jesuit orientalism" constructively shaped a respectful form of encounter with Hindus in India.

18. K. M. de Silva shows that the Colonial Office incorrectly assumed that Buddhism had a centralized authority structure. In the handover of the relic to the new authority, the British inadvertently provided Ceylonese Buddhism a more centralized authority structure (1965, 92).

19. De Silva (1965) examines the vicissitudes of such missionary projects to seek the "disestablishment" of Buddhism during British colonialism. Protestant missionaries were by no means unified on the matter.

20. Schonthal details how the first iteration of the Constitution of Ceylon passed in 1948, had been crafted to obviate interference of religious groups in secular political processes (2016, 23–37). However, the Pali scholar G. P. Malalasekera subsequently asserted how Buddhism had been the "state religion" of the precolonial polity (Schonthal 2016, 51). In a report produced by the All-Ceylon Buddhist Congress (1956), Malalasekera argued that the 1948 Constitution of Ceylon had "enthroned" Christianity over the newly independent state and deemed it necessary to reestablish Buddhism through constitutional reforms that would restore Buddhism to its "rightful place" (Schonthal 2016, 51).

21. Somaratna (1996) historicizes how the Second Wave of Pentecostalism established robust connections between Ceylonese and Indian denominations and ministries.

22. *Evolution and Conversion* (2008) extends the thesis of *Violence and the Sacred* (1977), whereby René Girard develops his theory of sacrifice in Christianity. He takes Saint Paul as the quintessence of the Christian injunction to sublimate blood sacrifice, and to instead evangelize (and achieve martyrdom) as the correct avenue for sacrifice.

23. To quote the title of an important retrospective on Asad's work by Hirschkind and Scott (2006).

24. Historians and anthropologists of Buddhism in Southeast Asia elucidate the relationship between monastic and lay activism, anticolonialism, millenarian movements, and "communist" insurgencies (Keyes 1977; Tambiah 1984; Salter 2000; Ford 2017; Ladwig 2014, 2017; Hansen 2019). Even as both Christianity and Buddhism were conceived of as a potentially pacifying force throughout the region, during the colonial era episodic emergences of millenarian Buddhism gained the watchful eye of colonial administrators who feared their anticolonial and insurrectionary potential (Keyes 1977; Tambiah 1984). Generally in Sri Lanka, authorities regarded millenarian tendencies as relatively innocuous, even quaint, if heterodox, new Buddhist movements, rather than providing animus for revolution (Malalgoda 1970).

25. Herzog (2011) and other historians have shown how Christian ministries represented a "spiritual-industrial complex" in the battle against communism that was consonant with U.S. geopolitical imperatives since the start of the Cold War.

26. Schonthal (2016) makes the observation through close reading of archivally inscribed debates over constitutional policy-making processes and contemporary litigation in

Sri Lanka. He finds that Sinhala Buddhist protectionists argued that Buddhism and other religions are incommensurable. They used a broad-based concept of *sāsana* (Buddha's dispensation and legacy) rather than *āgama* ("religion"), he observes. Accordingly, Schonthal argues that Buddhist litigants sought protections for Buddhism that went beyond the confines of an individual's freedom of thought and conscience. By endeavoring to conceive of the Buddha's dispensation as all-encompassing, Sinhala Buddhists injected conceptualizations of religious freedom in order to make legal claims to retain established Buddhist territories and properties (171–72).

27. See Mahadev 2016 and 2018. In a different context, Islamic disputation in Pakistan is commonplace in part because learned Muslims consider it a form of moral striving to grasp at divine truths (Khan 2012, 10). Khan argues that Islamic disputation gained further visibility in the region as Muslims began to tackle "the onslaught of Christian proselytizing while continuing to spar with authorities over other Indian religions" (10).

28. Only rare adepts in astrology and other divination practices might offer visions of past lives and future trajectories.

29. Their critiques primarily addressed the Marxian analysis of Jean and John Comaroff's *Of Revelation and Revolution* (1991) and other works.

30. Adding to Robbins's point, Cannell (2006) emphasizes that this is a carryover from anthropological imperatives to engage in "salvage ethnography" in an era when cultural forms were (presumed to be) facing extinction due to colonial incursion and assimilation to imperial hegemony.

31. Matthew Engelke finds evidence for this in the way that the Friday Masowe relate the "live and direct" experience of their God to the original Apostles of Christ, and in the congregational use of the "old-fashioned" formal language of "deep Shona," which he argues serves a metadiscursive function by linking their sacred, indigenous speech to a vision of a precolonial African past (2010, 187).

32. Walton and Mahadev (2019) distinguish between the empirical fact of "religious plurality" (theological, ritual, and communal difference) and prescriptions for "interreligious pluralism" that enhance and celebrate existing plurality. Sudipta Kaviraj (2021) has made a more elaborated argument for analytically distinguishing between the fact of alterity and the political embrace of pluralism. In a similar assessment as Klassen and Bender (2010) on pluralism, Mahmood (2011) has argued that feminism scholarship is complicated precisely because of the dual orientation to prescriptive and the analytical stakes of her writing.

33. Here I find resonance and inspiration in Das's (2010) and Lambek's (2010) work on "ordinary ethics."

34. The dividing lines of enmity and amity, conflict and belonging, are at the center of the "concept of the political," as the illiberal theorist of the political Carl Schmitt [1932 (2007)] has argued. The contemporary political theorist Chantal Mouffe (2005) somewhat more optimistically argues that the middling effects of "agonism" abound in political life, despite the antagonisms concerning majoritarianism and minority rights that paradoxically lie at the core of liberal democracies.

35. Thanks to Jeremy Walton for pointing me to this work. See also GhanneaBassiri and Robertson 2019; Walton and Mahadev 2019.

1. TANGLES OF RELIGIOUS PERSPECTIVISM

1. Although Theravādin monks in Sri Lanka are often seen flanking politicians to lend "gravitas" to political causes, historically it has been uncommon for monks to formally enter electoral politics because it is seen as inconsistent with their vows of asceticism and mendicancy (Spencer 2007, 33). Illustrating this principle, one of Benjamin Schonthal's Sinhala Buddhist interlocutors stated, "Religion has to be different from politics . . . monks can be king makers, but should never become kings" (2016, 236). See also Abeysekera (2002) on the disputed political role of Buddhist monks. After the Jathika Hela Urumaya (JHU) was elected to Sri Lankan Parliament on the anti-conversion platform in 2004, popular support for them waned when Sinhala Buddhist voters came to see them as "extremists" who engaged in vitriolic speech and highly publicized acts of destruction of Christian properties. However, the election of the JHU opened the floodgates for the election of other Islamophobic and anti-Christian Buddhist monks.

2. S. Aluthwatte, "The Government Plan to Conflagrate the Entire Country on the Day Soma Thera Was Cremated," *Lanka*, January 4, 2004.

3. By the 1940s–1950s, English language education was expanded to rural populations with the promise of upward mobility. Soon there was an overabundance of educated youth who aspired to take up roles in clerical jobs (Venugopal 2018). With the glut of unemployment in the 1950s, the promises of Western-style Anglophone education did not pan out for many Ceylonese, lending to populist discontent.

4. Sri Lanka introduced a quota system in the 1970s to enable majority Sinhalese to gain proportionate admission into national universities, thus depriveleging Tamils (many of whom were Protestant or Catholic), of whom there were high concentrations in professional ranks owing to their high levels of proficiency in English (Silva 1978).

5. Bandaranaike became reluctant to abide by the demands of extreme coalition partners. Ultimately, hardline majoritarian nationalists perceived Bandaranaike to be equivocating, and he was assassinated by a Buddhist monk.

6. During 1970s and 1980s UNP politicians were directly culpable for fueling political violence against minorities, but by the 1990s the UNP reformed its image under Ranil Wickremesinghe who strived to ensure that his party was making a "break from the past" through progressive work toward a civic form of nationalism (Venugopal 2018).

7. The SLFP splintered and practically dissolved when the Rajapaksas created the Sri Lanka Podujana Peramuna (SLPP) party in the lead-up to the 2019 election, which has perceptibly moved their political ethos to the right. Under the SLPP banner, the Rajapaksas returned to power a decade after the war. What is more, during the fallout from the sovereign debt crisis of 2022, the Rajapaksas aligned with UNP leadership. Arguably, the formation of the SLPP has inaugurated a new era in Sri Lankan politics that one might characterize as Buddhist neoliberalism.

8. Perera (2001).

9. Perera (2001, 14).

10. Perera (2001).

11. It appears that Jayamanne's clerical practices entailed a homegrown syncretic form of Catholicism, which fuses local Buddhist and Hindu ideas of spirit possession with

diabolizing Catholic practices of exorcism. It is unlikely to have been directly influenced by the international Catholic Charismatic Renewal (CCR) movement ("Catholic Pentecostalism"). However, in my estimation of Stirrat's account, it appears that this variety of Catholic religiosity evolved locally in response to or even in anticipation of competing forms of Third-Wave Pentecostalism that arrived on the scene in urban milieus around the same time. I discuss the CCR movement in chapter 4.

12.   Savithri Rodrigo, "Interview of Kotelawala," *Lanka Monthly Digest*, December 2006, http://lmd.lk/archives/2006/December/public.htm

13.   Frances Harrison, "Sri Lanka Peace Movement Launched," BBC News Online, August 27, 2001, http://news.bbc.co.uk/2/hi/south_asia/1511600.stm.

14.   Rajesh Venugopal (2018) a political scientist, also examines Kotelawala's involvement in the broader "business for peace" initiatives during this period of the Sri Lanka civil war with Eelamist insurgents. He similarly shows that there is an overlap in the constituencies of cosmopolitan capitalists, religious minorities, and UNP partisan support (2018, 147). Complementing Venugopal's argument, my analysis articulates the implicit and overt theological and political tenor of Kotelawala's initiatives and iconicity, which contributed to the convergence of religious identity and ontological conceptions of karma and grace, economic ideology, and partisan affinities, and which consolidated the divides between Buddhists and Christians over the issue of conversion.

15.   In 1999, the People's Alliance ruling party (partially constituted by the SLFP) and the UNP opposition were at loggerheads over the president's initiative to engage in peace talks with the LTTE. The UNP opposed the proposal. Though Kotelawala consistently voted UNP, he was disappointed by partisan obstinance toward Kumaratunga's (SLFP) efforts at peace. http://news.bbc.co.uk/2/hi/south_asia/420519.stm.

16.   "Gulf News," Weekend Review, November 9, 2006, http://gulfnews.com/about-gulf-news/al-nisr-portfolio/weekend-review/articles/business-with-philanthropy-1.39768.

17.   Ministry of Defense "SL Army Is Fully Committed to Protect Human Rights Laws—Army Chief/ Lalith K, Pride (Shame) of the Nation," November 27, 2006, http://www.defence.lk/new.asp?fname=20061127_03.

18.   B. Sirimanna, "Central Bank Rescues Three Crisis-hit Finance Companies," *Sunday Times*, March 27, 2011, http://www.sundaytimes.lk/110327/BusinessTimes/bt35.html.

19.   Shirajiv Sirimane, "CB Bails out Seylan," *Daily News*, December 30, 2008, http://www.dailynews.lk/2008/12/30/news01.asp.

20.   The question remains as to whether in another context the captains of finance might not have publicized this scenario so widely to prevent inevitable investor panic that resulted in the bank run and liquidity crisis.

21.   Dharmitha Kotte, "Ceylinco Crisis: Golden Key Credit Card Scam and the Aftermath," LankaWeb, January 1, 2009, http://www.lankaweb.com/news/items09/050109-3.html.

22.   Shirajiv Sirimane, "Three Years After Ceylinco Scandal," Daily News Online, December 19, 2011, http://archives.dailynews.lk/2011/12/19/bus19.asp.

23.   I take inspiration from Peter van der Veer's (2016) essay on "the Future of Utopia" and Jean and John Comaroff's (2001) work on "millennial capitalism" to think through the meaning of "futures" dually in the economic and cosmological sense.

24.   For historicization of this shift, see Jayawardena 2000.

25. Morris specifically discusses South Africa since apartheid, building her argument largely upon the historical anthropology authored by Jean Comaroff (1990).

26. As anthropologists have long argued, outside or alongside of the capitalist economy, social cohesion thrives through a moral economy of the gift (Mauss [1925] 2016).

27. It appears that an appetite for purchasing insurance policies increased in South Asia in the 1970s and was potentially amplified by civil strife between the JVP (Marxist-Leninist) and the Sri Lankan government. By 2020, market analysts suggest, only 14 percent of Sri Lankans owned insurance policies. Hence, insurance companies are ever trying to expand the market even into the rural and lower-income sectors. https://www.3blmedia.com/News/Bringing-Affordable-Life-and-Health-Insurance-Low-Income-Earners-Sri-Lanka.

28. Two 2020 advertising campaigns for Sri Lankan insurance were Ceylinco's, https://www.worldfinance.com/wealth-management/ceylinco-life-is-breathing-life-into-sri-lankas-insurance-space, and KPMG's, https://assets.kpmg/content/dam/kpmg/lk/pdf/kpmg-sri-lanka-insurance-report-april-2020.pdf.

2. CHARITY AND DĀNA

1. Incorporated in 1955. For the significance of the All-Ceylon Buddhist Congress, see also Schonthal (2016).

2. Idigbe (2020).

3. Sykes (2019) suggests that this European paradigm did not wholly penetrate the Sinhala Buddhist lifeworld. Sykes's usage of "zoopolitics" is derived from Derrida's concept of the same, used to distinguish the modern Western ontology of the human from the ontological stature of the animal.

4. I have also shown how the "reckoning of accounts" relates to moral accountancy, as Buddhists and Christians in the Sri Lankan milieu engage in a dialogical process of judging religious others' moral worth ("Karma").

5. Noted in sections 239 and 573 of the ACBC Report. These organizations are known in other world regions for faith-based initiatives that engage in evangelism through charitable and humanitarian work.

6. Simpson (1997) attributes this to the fact that the Sinhala caste system of Sri Lanka is rooted in quite different premises from in India. The caste system among Sinhalas is based upon a feudal form of service tenures to the king (*rajakariya*), rather than strictly on the basis of hierarchical scales of purity and pollution as one finds in Brahmanical Hinduism (45). He demonstrates that in the Sinhala case, members of a given caste are traditionally associated with service niches first and foremost, and notions of purity and pollution are only secondary.

7. Simpson shows that by the 1990s, members of the "lowest" Beruvā ("Näkethī") caste of drummers and ritualists had a fair number of opportunities for upward mobility, even in the face of castigation by upper-caste groups. Yet he shows that in their own self-conception, those who perform these Buddhist ritual activities on a hereditary caste basis consider themselves to be uniquely adept at this ritual work on the basis of their karma.

8. "Charity and commerce entail quantification, calculation, and careful accounting, suggesting that the economy of the market and the economy of piety can easily come together to sustain modalities of accumulation in which material wealth and spiritual merits might appear simultaneously as incommensurable and sustaining each other," writes anthropologist and scholar of South Asian charity, Filippo Osella (2018). Since the early colonial encounter, reckoning—in the forms of economic and moral accountancy—was pivotal in shaping the judgments that Christians and Buddhists made of one another's traditions of religious thought and practice (Mahadev, "Karma").

9. It has been well documented that the plantation industry extracted wealth from the upcountry lands. Sinhala villagers were ousted from some of these lands but refused to work the hard terrain. The British imported Tamil laborers, called "coolies," from southern India through a *kangany* system (comparable to debt peonage), creating chronic debts among Tamil workers today (Jegathesan 2019). The displacement contributed to interethnic resentment (Moore 1989; Venugopal 2018).

10. T. W. Rhys Davids (1843–1922), a British founder of the Pāli Text Society, came to extoll the virtues of Buddhism as an ethical system (Harris 2006). The American Theosophist Colonel Henry Steel Olcott (1832–1907), author of *The Buddhist Catechism* (1881), remains a celebrated figure of the Buddhist revival (Gombrich and Obeyesekere 1988; Prothero 1996).

11. Anagarika Dharmapala, a Sinhala layman, spearheaded the Buddhist revival in Sri Lanka and internationally (Gombrich and Obeyesekere 1988; Jayawardena 2002). Dharmapala designed the international Buddhist flag.

12. Mahinda Deegalle (2012) points out that Sinhala speakers make a distinction between *āgamaṭa harīma* and *āgamaṭa haravīma*. The former implies religious conversion is undertaken by one's own volition, and the latter, he argues, is "forcible" conversion because it relates to conversion carried out at the hands of another (3). The implication is lodged in a subtle grammatical difference: the former is the intransitive form. In contrast, the latter is the transitive form, which implies that the conversion is carried out under the influence of someone else (e.g., a proselytizer: for example, *they converted her*). Deegalle argues that Sinhala Buddhists consider conversion mediated by the influence of someone else, as opposed to a choice which is made through conviction that first arises in one's own mind, as "forcible" or "unethical."

13. David Rohde, "Mix of Quake Aid and Preaching Stirs Concern," January 24, 2005, http://www.nytimes.com/2005/01/23/world/asia/23iht-preach.html.

14. I am grateful to Farzana Haniffa for encouraging me to think about what kind of sovereignty Sinhala Buddhists assert in these postwar claims. She usefully suggested that the "Api wenawen api" campaign might be related to notions of *Swaraj*, the Gandhian insistence upon Indian home rule.

15. Public intellectuals and government officials in Sri Lanka maintained that if casualty counts were high it was because the LTTE used civilians as human shields and that Tamil civilians were conscripted in plain clothes, so that civilian bodies were indistinguishable from those of combatants.

16. Stated in her appearance before the House Committee on Foreign Affairs. http://indiatoday.intoday.in/story/World+disappointed+with+Sri+Lanka:+Clinton/1/38272.html.

17. Nalin De Silva, "Get Ready for a Humanitarian Attack," May 10, 2011,. http://www .island.lk/index.php?page_cat=article-details&page=article-details&code_title =25022.

18. De Silva, "Get Ready for a Humanitarian Attack." Such anxieties that the Western humanitarian NGO community was "propping up" the LTTE's agenda had fomented since the turn of the millennium, when a Norwegian envoy came to Sri Lanka to facilitate peace talks and was widely viewed as showing favoritism to the LTTE.

19. Goonatilake (2006).

20. Calhoun (2010) distinguishes between humanitarian organizations and human rights organizations, detailing that the former express political neutrality, whereas human rights organizations are more deeply committed to secularism and aim to critique political and military actions of states and parastate groups (37). "Charitable humanitarians pursued the mitigation of suffering rather than the transformation of institutions." However, humanitarian organizations would not necessarily be able to draw such lines in the course of violent action. Sri Lankan critics of the "NGO mafia" tended not to make this distinction.

21. See Korf et al. (2010).

22. Korf et al. (2010) detail how recipients of aid from Smyrna Fellowship, a U.S.-based evangelical church that relies on private funding from a Swedish family, complained that their own churches (Catholic and Methodist) had not helped them much. As the recipients of this charity saw it, Smyrna Fellowship deserved their loyalty (570). Matthews (2007) also discusses how evangelical groups were often conflated with secular NGOs in the post-tsunami humanitarian context of Sri Lanka.

23. The Church of Christ is a Protestant "nondenominational" church that came out of the American "Restoration Movement." The church follows "cessationist" New Testament principles in reaction against the trends of the Great Awakening which generated Pentecostal charismatic Christianity. See: Allen, Crawford Leonard (1988).

24. For a comparable discussion of "biomoral" entailments of associated with caste in Hinduism see Parry 1986.

25. In Sri Lanka there has traditionally been a caste basis for admission to the sangha's *nikayas*.

26. Bowie's ethnography (1998) details how during periods of drought, Thai Buddhists pliably and "alchemically" transformed their conception of meritorious giving to include laity. Hallisey (2007) demonstrates how there is premodern textual precedent for the Buddhist ethic of giving to the indigent poor.

27. In "A Tribute to G. D. Wijayawardhana," *The Island Newspaper*, March 15, 2007, http:// www.island.lk/2007/03/15/features4.html, Hallisey movingly commemorated his late teacher, a professor of Sinhala at the University of Colombo.

28. Leve (2017) makes a similar observation in her ethnography of the Theravādin turn in Nepal.

29. Responding to my characterization of this phenomenon in a paper on "ordinary ethics," Lawrence Cohen aptly commented that it might be called "karmic neoliberalism" (UC Berkeley South Asian Studies graduate student conference, 2006).

30. On Madihe Pannasiha Thero and the monastic turn toward social service, see especially Seneviratne 1999; Abeysekara 2002; Holt 1998.

31.   Abeysekera (2002) highlights how Sinhala Buddhists tended to look to Japan and other East Asian sources of capital and patronage to sustain the growth of Buddhist infrastructures.

32.   Narayan Swamy (2004, xiii).

33.   A common assumption held among Sinhala Buddhists is that the rebel leader converted from Hinduism to Christianity. The view is based upon the fact that he had given his child a Christian name after one of his closest friends and associates within the secessionist movement.

34.   Scholars have long put forth such a "post-ethnicity" argument, whereby rather than arguing that the Sri Lankan civil war was caused foremost via ideologies of ethnolinguistic difference shored up by mythohistories of ethnic supremacy, it was material inequities that were the main drivers of conflict (Winslow and Woost 2004; Spencer, *Sinhala Village*; Spencer 2007; Moore 1997).

3. MEDIATING MIRACLES

1.   Daswani (2013) demonstrates that in the context of Ghana, Pentecostalism does not give rise to singularity, as the idea of sovereignty implies. Considering the array of disputes among believers as to how one might best engage being born again, there is evidently great variation in how Pentecostals attempt to go about enacting and embodying Pentecostalist ethics and lifeways in Ghana.

2.   Justin McDaniel (2011) has described how certain Thai monks gain a following of "fans," in many cases because of their magical abilities.

3.   Anthropologists have demonstrated how Sinhala *yaktovil* practices "celebrate" demons while ritually expelling their malignancy (Kapferer 1983; Scott 1994). Highlighting the complex ritual mechanics, Kapferer argues that *yaktovil* rituals serve to "re-encompass" ontologically fragmented and socially deviant people, and as such, the exorcism rites ultimately reincorporate "patients" into the social body and the dharmically righteous cosmos (Kapferer 1983). Scott (1994) problematizes the colonial translation of *tovil* as "exorcism," since it is loaded with the missionaries' interpretations of these cosmological agents. Sinhalese *tovil* rituals are not reducible to exorcism since the "demons" do not represent ultimate evil as they do in Christianity.

4.   I do not wish to overstate the distinction between the traditionalist and modernist forms of Sinhala Buddhist religiosity. Likewise, as Gombrich and Obeyesekere (1988) argue, "Protestant Buddhism" (or Buddhist modernism) is an "ideal-type" heuristic approach in the Weberian sense.

5.   Gooneratne, an elite English-educated Sinhala, was known as the "Macaulay of Ceylon" because of his advocacy of installing English in the colony and for his long correspondence with Lord Macaulay himself (Gunaratna 2008). He discusses three categories of "demonism:" "Demonism," or engaging and expunging malignant spirits; "Capuism" or mediumistic deity engagements; and "Grahaism" or astrology ([1865] 1998, 5–6). Gooneratne was baptized and entered the ranks of the colonial administration in the mid-nineteenth century. K. L. Guneratna (2008) suggests that despite being an anglophile, Gooneratne the Mudliyar later championed the efforts of Buddhist petitioners on

various matters, especially as their grievances against the evangelical expansion in Ceylon became more prominent.

6. I invoke Charles Taylor's famous distinction between the (premodern) "porous self" and the secular modern "buffered self" (2008), detailed in brief at https://tif.ssrc.org/2008/09/02/buffered-and-porous-selves/.

7. Pentecostal political theology shores up exclusivist convictions and "authoritarian forms of pastoral power" that are as dangerous for Nigerian politics as they are for the endurance of pluralism (Marshall 2009, 214). A somewhat different orientation to Christian nationalism and the gospel of prosperity can be found in the context of Zambia, as well documented by Haynes (2014).

8. All Buddhas are considered arahats; but not all arahats become Buddhas. The difference is that Buddhas not only become Enlightened, but they also share the *Dhamma* through teaching. Arahats rarely emerge from the forest, and because of their commitment to asceticism their enlightenment remains hidden from the world.

9. As stated in English. In Sinhala, the analogy is *"panduru palliya,"* which translates as "bush churches," similarly connoting the tendency of churches to spring up wildly.

10. Section on "The Rights of Lords Over Their Servants" (VIII).

11. As the political theorist Joel Schwartz explains, Hobbes's theory distinguishes the Jewish kingdom of God, which he believed to be sullied by "instability and confusion resulting from incorrect notions of sovereignty, liberty, and human nature—and its subjects," from the "well-ordered commonwealth in Leviathan," which avoids those missteps by modeling itself on "the future Christian kingdom" (Schwartz 1985, 7). The parallel here between Hobbes's anti-Semitic supersessionist picture of sovereignty and that of Schmitt's is evident—and according to context, it can evince an illiberal and dominionist orientation of religious commitment (Fischer 2010).

12. See also Catherine Colliot-Thélène's (1999) essay on the mutual influences between Weber and Schmitt.

13. LIVE@8 television news broadcast, Swarnavahini Television, Colombo, October 21, 2010.

14. N. Kannangara, "JHU Vows Legal Action Against Prayer Services," *Sunday Leader*, November 14, 2009, http://www.thesundayleader.lk/?p=1689.

4. A CACOPHONOUS EXUBERANCE

1. Dhammavihari (1921–2010), a Sri Lankan Buddhist scholar-monk, published his remarks in response to Pope John Paul II's comments on Buddhism in *Crossing the Threshold of Hope* (1994). "Papal Blunder on Buddhism" was first published in *The Island*, an English-language newspaper, and reproduced with permission in *Dialogue* in a special issue on "The Pope and Buddhism" (1995). Father Tissa Balasuriya (1924–2013) published his book in Sri Lanka in 2006.

2. Neil Devotta productively drew attention to "civic nationalism" in the context of South Asia in his presentation "Whither Civic Nationalism?" at the Rajaratnam School of International Studies at Nanyang Technological University, Singapore, August 11, 2020.

3.   Pope John Paul II argued that the world-renouncing orientation that is an end point for Buddhist *nirvana* was a life-affirming starting point for Christian mystics (1994, 85–86). He specifically referred to Tibetan Buddhism, which had been growing in popularity in the West due to the public work of the Dalai Lama.

4.   Donald Mitchell, "Remarks of Pope on Buddhism Cause Reactions," Monastic Interreligious Dialogue, Bulletin 52, January 1995, http://monasticdialog.com/a.php?id=478.

5.   Associated Press Archive, "Sri Lanka: Pope John Paul II Visit," YouTube, July 22, 2015: https://youtu.be/2ZoadNdH940.

6.   The iconic church was demolished in the Easter Sunday bombings of 2019. It was home to a shrine to the Virgin Mary. Her statue was considered miraculous for having eyes that "turned from blue to brown," which, Bastin deftly argues, signifies how Catholicism became disinherited from a blue-eyed European colonial elite and inherited by the brown-eyed people of Sri Lanka (2012, 106). Sri Lankans perceived the pope's spontaneous worship of the miraculous Mary as papal validation of Sri Lanka as home to genuine Catholic sacraments. Bastin argues this may have softened the controversies over the pope's visit. A different take in *The Sunday Observer* (Palakidnar 1995) secularizes the incident, attributing the stop to the pope's requirement to "answer the call of nature," which coincidentally gave bystanders an opportunity to receive the papal blessing. http://www.sundayobserver.lk/2005/04/10/fea31.html.

7.   Richard Ostling, "Keeper of the Straight and Narrow: Cardinal Joseph Ratzinger," Time.com, December 6, 1993, http://content.time.com/time/magazine/article/0,9171,979775,00.html.

8.   http://ncronline.org/news/people/fr-tissa-balasuriya-loving-and-gentle-rebel.

9.   Sri Lankan rights activist Basil Fernando wrote that Balasuriya and a cohort of left Catholic activists were subject to "intense dislike" and "endless harassment" by the official Church. These circumstances, he averred, only confirmed the "authenticity of the spirituality they represented" (Fernando 1997, 25–26).

10.   Archbishop of Colombo Diocese, Most Rev. Malcolm Ranjith, "Liturgy Circular—No. LT CR / 01: Circular Concerning Various Religious Movements and Services," October 7, 2009, http://www.archdioceseofcolombo.com/LiturgyCircular_07.10.2009.php.

11.   Bloch (1994) draws a similar contrast between the gatekeeping function of Catholic priests and the spontaneous Marian possessions that liberated enslaved peoples of the slums of Antananarivo, Madagascar.

12.   "Message from the Holy Father Pope John Paul II to the Catholic Charismatic Renewal," April 24, 2000, http://www.vatican.va/holy_father/john_paul_ii/speeches/2000/apr-jun/documents/hf_jp-ii_spe_20000424_catholic-charismatic-renewal_en.html.

13.   "Vatican Liturgical Official Makes New Plea for 'Reform of the Reform,'" Catholic World News, February 23, 2009, http://www.catholicculture.org/news/features/index.cfm?recnum=60291. Following Ranjith's polemics against Vatican II, Pope Benedict XVI delivered a homily "on the solemnity of the Pentecost" in May 2009, in which he explained that the gifts of the Spirit allowed the Apostles to overcome fear and undertake Christ's mission. It sought to discipline Catholics, cautioning that they are not to be swept away by neo-Pentecostal exuberance and emphasizing that Pentecostals

do not have the monopoly over the biblical event (http://www.zenit.org/en/articles/benedict-xvi-s-homily-for-solemnity-of-pentecost).

14. In 1985 Cardinal Joseph Ratzinger asserted that "the true time of Vatican II has not yet come." http://www.catholicculture.org/news/features/index.cfm?recnum=60291.

15. Catholics constitute 6.1 percent of the population, while "other Christians" make up 1.4 percent of the population, according to the latest Sri Lanka census (2012).

16. After his resignation from the papacy, Benedict XVI asserted that interreligious dialogue is not a substitute for spreading the gospel and that relativistic truth would be "lethal to faith." Francis X. Rocca, "Retired Pope Benedict: Inter-religious Dialogue Is No Substitute for Mission," Catholic News Service, 2004, https://www.ncronline.org/news/vatican/retired-pope-benedict-xvi-interreligious-dialogue-no-substitute-mission.

17. In Stirrat's ethnographic account, in the course of an exorcism rite, the demon possessing a person announced itself bellicosely as Kataragama, the Sinhala Buddhist deity, who is known as Lord Murugan among Tamils (1992, 81–85). Within the practices of Catholic exorcist healer priests, Buddhist and Hindu deities are unambiguously cast as demons, easily vanquished with grace. Stirrat shows that Sri Lankan Catholic Church authorities attempted to keep this popular devotional form at the margins of the official Church until it eventually faded out of practice. What becomes clear is how these folk forms of religiosity compete with the authority of the institutional Church in ways that can be as political as they are religious.

18. The usage of *Thatha* (the kin term of address for one's own father) is more casual than the term used for ordained priests, who are ordinarily addressed formally as *Piyathumi*, or in English as "Father."

19. See Liturgical Circular, http://catholocity.net/documents/LiturgyCircular.pdf. Ranjith cites the Holy Decree "NAME OF GOD," Prot. N213/08/L.

20. The services were pioneered at St. Helena's Church in Yakkaduwa by Father Terrence's predecessor. It seems there had been a ten-year hiatus of the *Kurusa Dāhana*, then known as *Kurusa Yagaya* and *Suva mēhēya* (Cross Oblation Ritual and Healing service), before Fr. Terrence revived the practice. http://kurusadahana.com/ky/index.php. These services became especially popular after Fr. Terrence's arrival at the parish in 2009. http://kurusadahana.com/guidance/locate.php?id=43.

21. In Sri Lanka this pre-Vatican II institution is widely encouraged as a "dramatic reliving of Christ's Passion" and remembrance of the savior. Although elsewhere Catholics individually engage the Way of the Cross as an interiorized meditation, in Sri Lanka it typically takes place in a communal ceremony performed in front of a series of icons or statues to mark each station (Stirrat 1992, 68).

22. Victory speech at Parliament, Sri Jayawardenapura, Kotte, May 19, 2009, http://www.defence.lk/new.asp?fname=20090519_04.

23. In doing so, he performatively enacted what Stanley Tambiah (1976) has productively called the Asokan paradigm, whereby following a stint as a violent conqueror King Asoka felt deep remorse, which led him to renounce violence and become a Buddhist: an epitome of nonviolence and a dedicated patron of the sangha (see also Obeyesekere 1989).

24. Rajapaksa's wife is Catholic. As a rule, Pope Benedict XVI was not known to condone interreligious marriage, in consonance with his general conservativism concerning marriage and the family.

25. http://www.asiantribune.com/news/2009/11/06/italy-spearhead-damage-control-act -urge-eu-review-gsp-suspension.

26. The Generalized Scheme of Preferences (GSP+) is a set of trade concessions that had been critical for the growth of Sri Lanka's manufacturing industries. http://ec.europa .eu/trade/policy/countries-and-regions/development/generalised-scheme-of-preferen ces/index_en.htm.

27. Tisaranee Gunasekera, "Cardinal Malcolm Ranjith Speaks Truth to Power on Justice, Reconcilation and Peace," Transcurrents, November 7, 2010, http://transcurrents.com /tc/2010/11/cardinal_malcolm_ranjith_speak.html.

28. With the persistent humanitarian criticisms from Western nations, Sri Lanka took a hiatus from relying upon Western aid and took advantage of China's ambitions to expand westward through its Belt and Road Initiative.

29. Ironically, the Church excommunicated Schmitt a few years after the publication of the book for remarrying without annulment of his first marriage.

30. Pope Francis ousted several conservatives from the Congregation for the Doctrine of the Faith. Jason Horowitz, "Pope Francis Ousts Powerful Conservative Cardinal," New York Times, July 1, 2017, https://www.nytimes.com/2017/07/01/world/europe/vatican -pope-doctrine-mueller.html.

5. SAMSARIC DESTINIES, RELIGIOUS PLURALITY, AND THE MAVERICK DIALOGICS OF BUDDHIST PUBLICITY

1. Harding (2000) explains that "witness invites or exhorts the listener to receive Christ as his or her personal savior."

2. Stirrat (1992) delineates how decolonization and nationalization policies compelled the Church to accommodate difference within its schools.

3. This is a common teaching in Dhamma textbooks in Buddhist "Sunday schools" (Daham pasal) throughout Sri Lanka (Gombrich 1971, 101).

4. Pāli, Metteyya Bodhisatta; Sinhala, Maitrī Bōsat. Although the Pāli is more accurate for this context, I use the more familiar Sanskritic spelling or the colloquial Sinhala as appropriate.

5. Scholarship on Hinduism and Buddhism emphasizes the traditional distinction between householders (laypeople), and ascetics (sannyasi and sadhu). Processes of "laicization" serve to partially blur these distinctions. Jeffrey Samuels (2010) writes of the "aesthetics of emotions" in the monastic culture of Sri Lanka necessarily involves the attraction of the heart (sita).

6. There is no consensus over whether syncretism creates the conditions of possibility for pluralism. Some anthropologists contend that syncretism and religious intermingling serve as an unrationalized pluralizing force that mitigates interreligious hostilities (e.g., Pfaffenberger 1979; Whitaker 1999). Other studies challenge such optimistic outcomes

(Obeyesekere 1977; van der Veer 1994; Viswanathan 1998; Asad 2001). Possibilities ranging from inclusivity to exclusivity may transpire from religious heterogeneity.

7. Nātha was once considered a "responsive deity who maintains order in the face of *dukkha* (suffering)-causing agents" (Holt 1991, 130). The attributes of Nātha were transfigured when a another deity mythically vanquished Nātha, and he "retreated" to "higher ground" and became preoccupied with "attainment of buddhahood, rather than fighting battles on behalf of the . . . Sinhalese" (127).

8. In some varieties of Mahāyāna Buddhism, Buddha-nature is immanent in the world and, through practice, accessible to all.

9. Gethin (1998, 32–34); Harvey (2013, 29).

10. Occasions for gestural evocation of Maitreya include festivals marking the beginning of the rainy season (*katina pīnkama*) (Gombrich 1971, 93).

11. Through observations carried out among Sinhala Buddhists in the 1960s and 1970s, Gombrich suggests "It is only a few fundamentalists who eschew this formula and condemn this postponement, urging the necessity of striving for *nirvana* here and now" (1971, 256).

12. From the *Dighana Nikaya* (Long Discourses), a text that comprises a portion of the *Tipiṭaka*, canonical to Theravāda Buddhism.

13. The cyclical ascendancy, decline, and return of a redemptive force are rooted in Indic conceptions of the *Mahayuga*.

14. Broadcast by Randiwa, Golden Island Radio, YouTube post, October 13, 2011, http://m .youtube.com/#/watch?v=Y3q9w4jU6Qk&desktop_uri=%2Fwatch%3Fv%3DY3q9w4 jU6Qk.

15. Abeysekera (2002) discusses how one Buddhist monk pioneered "casteless ordination" in Dambulla, in defiance of the *Mahasangha*'s (Asgiriya chapter) construction of legitimate and "traditional" Theravādin monastic authority (174). Differently, in this episode of Siridhamma Thero's heterodoxy, we see that even as monastic authorities contest the movement, popular support attributed to the monk's inspired qualities served to diminish the force of "traditional" authority.

16. The monk later publicly claimed to have attained *nibbāna*. http://www.dailymirror.lk /opinion/172-opinion/40308-i-have-attained-nibbana-able-to-stand-aloof-on-any-attack .html.

17. Rohana R. Wasala, "Closure of Modern Day Arahant case," Lankaweb, October 17, 2017, http://www.lankaweb.com/news/items/2017/10/17/closure-of-the-modern-day-arahant -case/.

18. Anthropologists engage Bakhtin's idea beyond its linguistic framing to capture social complexity. For instance, in their critique of the dialectics involved in Benedict Anderson's (1983) construction of nationalism, John Kelly and Martha Kaplan detail how a dialogical process can allow thinkers to conceive of history as an "open series":

> In a dialogical account even global history is a series of planned and lived responses to specific circumstances that were also irreducibly constituted by human subjects, creating not a single vast chain of "the subject" changed by "the object" and vice versa, but a dense, complex network of individual and collective subjects continually responsive to one another. These constitutive, irreducibly

subjective dialogics add enormous contingency and complexity to what dialectic there is between material realities and human realities. (2001, 7)

6. A SPECTRUM FROM SINCERITY TO SKEPTICISM

1. I invoke the turn of phrase that Marshall Sahlins (2011) used to describe the workings of kinship.

2. This point of convergence created temporary solidarities among Sri Lankan Tamils and Sinhalas outside of the war zones. Tamils later argued that this threatened to create a rift among them in their demands for equal rights.

3. Anthropologists have critiqued earlier trends wherein the concept of belief that is essential to Christianity was presumed to be commensurately found in other religious forms. They argued that this transposal of belief, based upon Christian terms, leads to inaccurate scholarly renderings of non-Christian religions (Needham 1972; Ruel 1982; Asad 1993; Masuzawa 2005).

4. In Luther's Reformation, "no compensation through action ('works') could suffice to expiate sin and enable Salvation. Otherwise put, no human activity, nor material mediation, could enable reconciliation with God" (Mahadev 2019). Drawing upon Weber, I emphasize there that "in the ideal-typical Protestant Christian form, grace is seen as being given miraculously and exceptionally, irrespective of the qualities of one's conduct."

5. Webb Keane (2007) argues that the upshot for the demand for sincere belief in Protestantism is that it gives rise to a "semiotic ideology" that structures imperatives and modalities to demonstrate sincerity, to be evinced via material and linguistic signs.

6. Anthropologists of charismatic Christian forms describe this as an orientation to "transnational transcendence" (Csordas 2010; Robbins 2010).

7. Marilyn Strathern's (1988) argument about dividuality has been fruitfully deployed by a number of anthropologists to emphasize the partitive and porous nature of persons, especially with respect to pentecostalist ontologies.

8. As detailed by Obeyesekere (1984, 504); Spencer (1990, 606).

9. In this phenomenon we see a manifestation of Sinhala Buddhist political cosmology. Stirrat (1992) suggests that the power of parliamentarians is contingent upon associations with the political center, but that the most charismatic MPs switch parties. He argues that this party switching prevents these figures from becoming beholden to a central authority (170–175). By dissociating themselves from central authority, ambitious MPs, resemble holy men and popular deities, by establishing personal fiefdoms (173). Accruing power in this way, deities begin to develop an "amoral" character (Obeyesekere 1966; Winslow 1984; Stirrat 1992).

10. Korf et al. (2010) elaborate such inclinations toward a "patrimonial rationale," as discussed in chapter 2.

11. Bob Simpson contrasts caste in Sinhala society to that in Indian Brahmanical Hinduism; whereas the latter is fixed to notions of substantive biomoral conceptions of purity and pollution, among Sinhala people, caste is tied to feudal service tenures to the king

(rajakāriya) (1997, 45). He argues that in Sinhala society, notions of purity and impurity are only secondary.

12. Salāgama (or Halāgama) were the first among the low-country Sinhalese to be recruited to plantation work in the coconut, cinnamon, and tea industries. Goyagama are the landowning farming castes, the highest caste within the Sinhala caste system.

13. Karāva are traditionally of the fishing caste.

14. The practice resonates the millennial structure of anticipation evident in Courtney Handman's (2014) ethnography. She shows that in the circumstances of Papua New Guinea's babel-like linguistic diversity, local converts inferred from the Summer Institute of Linguistics' Protestant language ideology that only upon receipt of a Bible translated into one's own vernacular heart language would an ethnolinguistic community be saved. Yet her Guhu-Samane interlocutors commonly worried that they might not be saved because they had not yet received the gains promised by economic development.

15. See Holt (2004).

16. Devotees address female mediums with the honorific *Māniyo* (mother).

17. Receiving the goddess is a burden and also a blessing to socially marginal priestesses, who struggle with ailments and financial difficulties. Mediumship is invaluable in preventing the social neglect of these disadvantaged women in a hierarchical society (Obeyesekere 1981).

18. Anthropologists have argued that amoral activities and even activities that constitute demerit, are powerful modalities to wield power. Their holistic examinations of Sinhala Buddhist society are not constrained by modernist definitions of what Buddhism is or is not.

19. McDaniel (2011) beautifully chronicles the stories of the infamous "lovelorn ghost," Mae Nak, and the magical monk Somdet To, who famously tamed her in the context of Phrakhanong District, Thailand. In Sri Lanka, monks rarely partake of this ritual work.

20. In the context of India, where nationalistic Hindu rhetoric warns young women of "love *jihad*," alleging that Muslim men seek conversion through the bonds of marriage, Veena Das's (2010) ethnography gives an account of a love marriage between a Hindu man and Muslim woman. She shows how despite early parental opposition to marriage, the partners each partially adopt each other's modes of devotion without renouncing their own. In conditions of "agonistic intimacy" (Singh 2011), affinal love introduces Islam into a Hindu home. She nuances her point, stating, "there isn't one single conversion as a turning away from a previous mode of life but rather a slow flowering . . . [wherein] each member of the family is given the opportunity to learn to inhabit this newness" (Das 2010, 396).

EPILOGUE

1. I thank Zé de Abreu for encouraging me to address this point.

2. OMNIA Interfaith Peacemaking Teams, as well as other unaffiliated religious leaders, are working on these efforts in Sri Lanka.

3. I thank Vajra Chandrasekara, Geethika Dhammasinghe, Praveen Tilakaratne, and Nalika Gajaweera, for their firsthand and secondhand accounts.

4.   Local activists point out that arrests have been unjustly made with the misuse of the Prevention of Terrorism Act of 1979, which had originally decreed a state of emergency during the start of guerrilla warfare with the LTTE. https://www.hrw.org/news/2022/08/31/sri-lanka-end-use-terrorism-law-against-protesters.

5.   I borrow the turn of phrase "oppositional symmetry" from literary character development, which borrows from dance. To quote the writer Thomas Filbin at length:

> Most theories of the novel stress the notion of conflict as a necessary component of plot; a protagonist must be frustrated in seeking his goal by events, another character, or even physical obstacles, otherwise he is just in stasis. "And they all lived happily ever after" is bad enough as an ending but intolerable as a beginning. Someone has to want or need something to set in motion a series of events we call a drama. Often, however, the conflict is the main character being at war with himself as he tries to sort matters out. The term "oppositional symmetry" in dance conveys the concept. Two dancers, paired, opposite or beside, make the same movement in mirror image, reversing themselves, as if two halves of the same whole. Looking at fictional beings in some recent books suggested to me that the primordial struggle is really about the forces inside of them, even when occasioned or prompted by other characters or events. (Filbin 2013, 600)

Bibliography

Abeysekera, Ananda. *Colors of the Robe: Religion, Identity, and Difference.* Columbia: University of South Carolina Press, 2002.

Adorno, Theodor W. *Negative Dialectics.* 1966. New York: Continuum Publishing, 2004.

All Ceylon Buddhist Congress. *Sri Lanka Buddhist Commission Report on Conversion by Fraudulent Strategies.* (In Sinhala.) Colombo: ACBC, 2009.

Allen, C. Leonard. *Discovering Our Roots: The Ancestry of Churches of Christ.* Abilene, TX: Abilene Christian University Press, 1988.

Amarasuriya, Harini. "Beards, Cloth Bags and Sandals: Reflections on the Christian Left in Sri Lanka." In *Multi-Religiosity in Contemporary Sri Lanka,* ed. Mark Whitaker, Darini Rajasingham-Senanayake, and Sunmugeswaran Pathmanesan, 220-32. New York: Routledge, 2022.

Ambos, Eva. "The Changing Image of Sinhalese Healing Rituals: Performing Identity in the Context of Transculturality." In *Transcultural Turbulences: Towards a Multi-sited Reading of Image Flows,* ed. Christiane Brosius and Roland Wenzlhuemer, 249-69. Berlin: Springer, 2012.

Anderson, Benedict. *Imagined Communities: Reflections on the Origin and the Spread of Nationalism.* London: Verso, 1983.

Anidjar, Gil. *Blood: A Critique of Christianity.* New York: Columbia University Press, 2014.

—. "Christians and Money (The Economic Enemy)." *Ethical Perspectives: Journal of the European Ethics Network* 12 (2005): 497-519.

Appadurai, Arjun. *Fear of Small Numbers: An Essay on the Geography of Anger.* Durham, NC: Duke University Press, 2006.

Asad, Talal. *Formations of the Secular: Christianity, Islam, Modernity.* Stanford, CA: Stanford University Press, 2003.

—. "Reading a Modern Classic: WC Smith's 'The Meaning and End of Religion.'" *History of Religions* 40, no. 3 (2001): 205-22.

Ashton, S. R. "Ceylon." In *The Oxford History of the British Empire,* ed. Judith Brown and Wm. Roger Louis, 4:447-64. Oxford: Oxford University Press, 1999.

Bakhtin, Mikhail. *The Dialogical Imagination.* Austin: University of Texas Press, 1981.

Balasuriya, Tissa. *Jesus Christ and Human Liberation.* Colombo: Center for Society and Religion, 1976.

—. *Mary and Human Liberation*. Colombo: Center for Society and Religion, 1990.

—. *Which Way Pope Benedict XVI?* Colombo: Logos (Center for Society and Religion), 2006.

Bastian, Sunil. *The Politics of Foreign Aid in Sri Lanka: Promoting Markets and Supporting Peace*. Colombo: International Centre for Ethnic Studies, 2007.

—. "The Politics of Social Exclusion, State Reform and Security in Sri Lanka." *IDS Bulletin* 40, no. 2 (2009): 88–95.

Bastin, Rohan. *The Domain of Constant Excess: Plural Worship at the Munneswaram Temple of Sri Lanka*. New York: Berghahn, 2002.

—. "Saints, Sites and Religious Accommodation in Sri Lanka." In *Sharing the Sacra: The Politics and Pragmatics of Intercommunal Relations around Holy Places*, ed. Glenn Bowman, 97–117. New York: Berghahn, 2012.

Bechert, Heinz. "Buddha-Field and Transfer of Merit in a Theravāda Source." *Indo-Iranian Journal* 35, nos. 2–3 (1992): 95–108.

—, ed. *Buddhism in Ceylon and Studies on Religious Syncretism in Buddhist Countries*. Göttingen: Vandenhoeck & Ruprecht, 1978.

Bellah, Robert. "Civil Religion in America." *Daedalus: Journal of the American Academy of Arts and Sciences* 96, no. 1 (Winter 1967): 1–21.

Bergunder, Michael. *The South Indian Pentecostal Movement in the Twentieth Century*. Grand Rapids, MI: Eerdmans, 2008.

Berkwitz, Stephen. "A Buddhist Media Pioneer: Ven. Kiribathgoda Gnānānanda Thera." In *Figures of Buddhist Modernity in Asia*, ed. Jeffrey Samuels, Justin Thomas McDaniel, and Mark Michael Rowe, 30–32. Honolulu: University of Hawai'i Press, 2016.

—. "Resisting the Global in Buddhist Nationalism: Venerable Soma's Discourse of Decline and Reform." *Journal of Asian Studies* 67 (2008): 73–106.

Bialecki, Jon. "Angels and Grass: Church, Revival, and the Neo-Pauline Turn." *South Atlantic Quarterly* 109, no. 4 (2010): 695–717.

—. *A Diagram for Fire: Miracles and Variation in an American Charismatic Movement*. Berkeley: University of California Press, 2017.

—. "The Third Wave and the Third World: C. Peter Wagner, John Wimber, and the Pedagogy of Global Renewal in the Late Twentieth Century." *Pneuma* 37, no. 2 (2015): 177–200.

Biedermann, Zoltán. "An Island under the Influence: Soqotra at the Crossroads of Egypt, Persia and India from Antiquity to the Early Modern Age. In *Aspects of the Maritime Silk Road: From the Persian Gulf to the East China Sea*, ed. Ralph Kauz, 9–24. Wiesbaden: Harrassowitz, 2010.

Biedermann, Zoltán, and Alan Strathern, eds. *Sri Lanka at the Crossroads of History*. London: University College London Press, 2017.

Blackburn, Anne M. "Ceylonese Buddhism in Colonial Singapore: New Ritual Spaces and Specialists, 1895–1935." Asia Research Institute, Working Paper series, no. 184, National University of Singapore, Singapore, May 2012.

—. *Locations of Buddhism: Colonialism and Modernity in Sri Lanka*. Chicago: University of Chicago Press, 2010.

Blanton, Anderson. *Hittin' the Prayer Bones: Materiality of the Spirit in the American South*. Chapel Hill: University of North Carolina Press, 2015.

Bloch, Maurice. "The Slaves, the King, and Mary in the Slums of Antananarivo." In *Shamanism, History, and the State*, ed. Nicholas Thomas and Caroline Humphrey, 133-45. Ann Arbor: University of Michigan Press, 1994.

Bloch, Maurice, and Jonathan Parry. *Money and the Morality of Exchange*. Cambridge: Cambridge University Press, 1989.

Blunt, Robert W. *For Money and Elders: Ritual, Sovereignty, and the Sacred in Kenya*. Chicago: University of Chicago Press, 2019.

Bodhi, Bhikkhu. "Replies to Questions from 'Source.'" *Dialogue* 22 (1995): 20-28.

Bond, George D. *Buddhism at Work: Community Development, Social Empowerment, and the Sarvodaya Movement*. West Hartford, CT: Kumarian Press, 2004.

Bourdieu, Pierre. *The Logic of Practice*. Stanford, CA: Stanford University Press, 1980.

—. *An Outline of a Theory of Practice*. Cambridge: Cambridge University Press, 1977.

Bowie, Katherine A. "The Alchemy of Charity: Of Class and Buddhism in Northern Thailand." *American Anthropologist* 100, no. 2 (1998): 469-81.

Brac de la Perrière, Bénédicte. "Religious Donations, Ritual Offerings, and Humanitarian Aid: Fields of Practice According to Forms of Giving in Burma." *Religion Compass* 9, no. 11 (2015): 386-403.

Brac de la Perrière, Bénédicte, Guillaume Rozenberg, and Alicia Turner, eds. *Champions of the Buddha: Weikza Cults in Contemporary Burma*. Singapore: NUS Press, 2014.

Brow, James. *Demons and Development: The Struggle for Community in a Sri Lanka Village*. Tucson: University of Arizona Press, 1996.

Brown, Bernardo. "Jesuit Missionaries in Post-Colonial Conflict Zones: The Disappearance of 'Father Basketball' in Batticaloa, Sri Lanka." *South Asia: Journal of South Asian Studies* 38, no. 4 (2015): 589-607.

Bush, J. Andrew. *Between Muslims: Religious Difference in Iraqi Kurdistan*. Stanford: Stanford University Press, 2020.

Bynum, Caroline Walker. "The Power in the Blood: Sacrifice, Satisfaction, and Substitution in Late Medieval Soteriology." In *The Redemption: An Interdisciplinary Symposium on Christ as Redeemer*, ed. Stephen T. Davis, Daniel Kendall, SJ, and Gerald O'Collins, 177-204. Oxford: Oxford University Press, 2004.

Calhoun, Craig. "The Idea of Emergency: Humanitarian Action and Global (Dis)order." In *Contemporary States of Emergency: The Politics of Military and Humanitarian Interventions*, ed. Didier Fassin and Mariella Pandolfi, 29-58. New York: Zone Books, 2010.

Cannell, Fenella, ed. *The Anthropology of Christianity*. Durham, NC: Duke University Press, 2006.

Carrithers, Michael B. "Hell Fire and Urinal Stones: An Essay on Buddhist Purity and Authority." In *Contributions to South Asian Studies*, ed. Gopal Krishna, vol. 2. Delhi: Oxford University Press, 1982.

Castelli, Elizabeth. "Persecution Complexes: Identity Politics and the 'War on Christians.'" *Differences* 18, no. 3 (2007): 152-80.

—. "Praying for the Persecuted Church: US Christian Activism in the Global Arena." *Journal of Human Rights* 4, no. 3 (2005): 321-51.

Chandrasekera, Vajra. 2021. "අබෞද්ධකම/UNBUDDHISM," *Vajra Chandrasekera* (fiction author blog), October 27, 2021. https://vajra.me/අබෞද්ධකම/-unbuddhism.

Choi, Vivian Y. "Anticipatory States: Tsunami, War, and Insecurity in Sri Lanka." *Cultural Anthropology* 30, no. 2 (2015): 286–309.

Chua, Liana. *The Christianity of Culture: Conversion, Ethnic Citizenship, and the Matter of Religion in Malaysian Borneo.* New York: Palgrave Macmillan, 2012.

——. "Conversion, Continuity, and Moral Dilemmas among Christian Bidayuhs in Malaysian Borneo." *American Ethnologist* 39, no. 3 (2012): 511–26.

Coate, Stephen, and Martin Ravallion. "Reciprocity without Commitment: Characterization and Performance of Informal Insurance Arrangements." *Journal of Development Economics* 40, no. 1 (1993): 1–24.

Coleman, Simon. "The Charismatic Gift." *Journal of the Royal Anthropological Institute* 10, no. 2 (2004): 421–42.

——. *The Globalisation of Charismatic Christianity.* Cambridge: Cambridge University Press, 2000.

Collins, Steven. *Nirvana and Other Buddhist Felicities: Utopias of the Pali Imaginaire.* Cambridge: Cambridge University Press, 1998.

Colliot-Thélène, Catherine. "Carl Schmitt versus Max Weber: Juridical Rationality and Economic Rationality." In *The Challenge of Carl Schmitt,* ed. Chantal Mouffe, 138–54. New York: Verso Books, 1999.

Comaroff, Jean. *Body of Power, Spirit of Resistance: the Culture and History of a South African People.* Chicago: University of Chicago Press, 1985.

Comaroff, Jean, and John Comaroff, eds. *Millennial Capitalism and the Culture of Neoliberalism.* Durham, NC: Duke University Press, 2001.

Cone, Margaret, and Richard Gombrich. *The Perfect Generosity of Prince Vessantara.* Oxford: Oxford University Press, 1977.

Connolly, William E. *The Ethos of Pluralization.* Minneapolis: University of Minnesota Press, 1995.

——. *Pluralism.* Durham, NC: Duke University Press, 2005.

Cotterill, Sarah, James Sidanius, Arjun Bhardwaj, and Vivek Kumar. "Ideological Support for the Indian Caste System: Social Dominance Orientation, Right-Wing Authoritarianism and Karma." *Journal for the Social and Political Psychology* 2, no. 1 (2014): 98–116.

Crusz, Robert. "Guest Editorial." *Dialogue* 22 (1995): i–ii.

Csordas, Thomas. *Language, Charisma, and Creativity: The Ritual Life of a Religious Movement.* Berkeley: University of California Press, 1997.

——. *The Sacred Self: A Cultural Phenomenology of Charismatic Healing.* Berkeley: University of California Press, 1994.

——, ed. *Transnational Transcendence: Essays on Religion and Globalization.* Berkeley: University of California Press. 2009.

Das, Veena. "Engaging the Life of the Other." In *Ordinary Ethics: Anthropology, Language, and Action,* ed. Michael Lambek, 376–99. New York: Fordham University Press, 2010.

Daswani, Girish. "On Christianity and Ethics: Rupture as Ethical Practice in Ghanian Pentecostalism." *American Ethnologist* 40, no. 3 (2013): 467–79.

de Abreu, Maria José. "Acts Is Acts: Tautology and Theopolitical Form." *Social Analysis* 64, no. 4 (2020): 42–59.

——. "Afterword: Thoughts on Governance, Punctuation, and Authoritarian Populism." *Cambridge Journal of Anthropology* 41, no. 1 (2023): 87–97.

—. *The Charismatic Gymnasium: Breath, Media, and Religious Revivalism in Contemporary Brazil.* Durham, NC: Duke University Press, 2021.

—. "Economies of San Paolo: Image, Space, Circulation." Lecture delivered at the Max Planck Institute, Göttingen. May 24, 2016.

de Alwis, Malathi. "A Double Wounding? Aid and Activism in Post-Tsunami Sri Lanka." In *Tsunami in a Time of War: Aid Activism and Reconstruction in Sri Lanka and Aceh,* ed. Malathi de Alwis and Eva-Lotta Hedman, 121–38. Colombo: International Centre for Ethnic Studies, 2009.

de Silva, C. R. "The Politics of University Admissions: Aspects of Sri Lankan University Admissions Policies 1970–78." *Sri Lankan Journal of Social Sciences* 1, no. 2 (1978): 85–23.

de Silva, K. M. *A History of Sri Lanka.* Berkeley: University of California Press, 1982.

—. *Social Policy and Missionary Organizations in Ceylon 1850–1855.* London: Longmans, 1965.

de Silva, Premakumara. "The Anthropology of Sinhala Buddhism." *Contemporary Buddhism* 7, no. 2 (2006): 165–70.

—. *Globalization and the Transformation of Planetary Rituals in Southern Sri Lanka.* Colombo: ICES, 2000.

de Silva Wijeyeratne, Roshan. "Buddhism, the Asokan Persona, and the Galactic Polity: Rethinking Sri Lanka's Constitutional Present." *Social Analysis* 51 (2007): 56–78.

de Vries, Hent, and Samuel Weber, eds. *Religion and Media.* Stanford, CA: Stanford University Press, 2001.

Deegalle, Mahinda. "Buddhist Protests over Non-Buddhist Evangelism: All Ceylon Buddhist Congress Commission Report on 'Unethical' Conversion." *International Journal of Buddhist Thought and Culture* 22 (2012): 65–86.

—. "Politics of the Jathika Hela Urumaya Monks." *Contemporary Buddhism* 5, no. 2 (2004): 83–103.

DeVotta, Neil. *Blowback: Linguistic Nationalism, Institutional Decay, and Ethnic Conflict in Sri Lanka.* Stanford, CA: Stanford University Press, 2004.

—. "Sri Lanka's Structural Adjustment Program and its Impact on Indo-Lanka Relations." *Asian Survey* 38, no. 5 (1998): 457–73.

—. "Whither Civic Nationalism in South Asia?" Unpublished lecture, S. Rajaratnam School of International Studies, Nanyang Technological University, Singapore, August 11, 2020.

Dhammananda, Galkande. "Religion for Reconciliation: Is It Feasible?" *Colombo Telegraph,* July 26, 2013. https://www.colombotelegraph.com/index.php/religion-for-reconciliation-is-it-feasible/.

Dhammavihari Thero (Jotiya Dhirasekara). "Papal Blunder on Buddhism." *Dialogue* 22 (1995): 4–7.

Doniger O'Flaherty, Wendy, ed. *Karma and Rebirth in Classical Indian Traditions.* Berkeley: University of California Press, 1980.

Douglas, Mary. "No Free Gifts." Foreword to Marcel Mauss, *The Gift,* ix–xxxiii. New York: Routledge, 1990.

Edwards, Michael. "Drowning in Context: Translating Salvation in Myanmar." *Comparative Studies of South Asia, Africa, and the Middle East* 41, no. 2 (2021): 175–84.

Egge, James. *Religious Giving and Invention of Karma in Theravada Buddhism.* New York: Routledge, 2002.

Eisenlohr, Patrick. "Media and Religious Diversity." *Annual Review of Anthropology* 41 (2012): 37-55.

Engelke, Matthew. *God's Agents: Biblical Purity in Contemporary England.* Berkeley: University of California Press, 2013.

—. "Past Pentecostalism: Notes on Rupture, Realignment, and Everyday Life in Pentecostal and African Independent Churches." *Africa: The Journal of the International African Institute* 80, no. 2 (2010): 177-99.

—. *The Problem of Presence: Beyond Scripture in an African Church.* Berkeley: University of California Press, 2007.

—. "Religion and the Media Turn: A Review Essay." *American Ethnologist* 37, no. 2 (2010): 371-79.

Fassin, Didier. *Humanitarian Reason: A Moral History of the Present.* Berkeley: University of California Press, 2012.

Fernando, Basil. *Power vs. Conscience: The Excommunication of Fr. Tissa Balasuriya.* Hong Kong: Asian Legal Resource Centre, 1997.

Fernando, Oshan W. N. "The Effects of Evangelical Christianity on State Formation in Sri Lanka." PhD dissertation, University of California Santa Barbara, 2011.

Filbin, Thomas. "Oppositional Symmetry." *Hudson Review* 66, no. 3 (2013): 600-607.

Findly, Ellison Banks. *Dana: Giving and Getting in Pali Buddhism.* Delhi: Motilal Banarsidass, 2003.

Fiordalis, David. "Miracles and Superhuman Powers in South and Southeast Asian Buddhist Traditions." *Journal of the International Association of Buddhist Studies* 33 (2010): 381-408.

Fischer, Karsten. "Hobbes, Schmitt, and the Paradox of Religious Liberality." *Critical Review of International Social and Political Philosophy* 13, nos. 2-3 (2010): 399-416.

Ford, Eugene. *Cold War Monks: Buddhism and America's Secret Strategy in Southeast Asia.* New Haven, CT: Yale University Press, 2017.

Freeman, Dena. "The Pentecostal Ethic and the Spirit of Development." In *Pentecostalism and Development: Non-Governmental Public Action*, ed. Dena Freeman, 1-38. London: Palgrave Macmillan, 2012.

Freston, Paul. "Globalization, Southern Christianity, and Proselytism." *Review of Faith & International Affairs* 7, no. 1 (2009): 3-9.

—. "Pentecostalism in Brazil: A Brief History." *Religion* 25, no. 2 (1995): 119-33.

Gajaweera, Nalika. "The Mothers of the Righteous Society: Lay Buddhist Women as Agents of the Sinhala Nationalist Imaginary." *Journal of Global Buddhism* 21 (November 2020): 187-204.

—. "Situated Humanitarianism: Doing Good in the Aftermath of Disaster in Sri Lanka." PhD dissertation, University of California Irvine, 2013.

Gajaweera, Nalika and Neena Mahadev. "Sonic Fields of Religious Protection in Sri Lanka's Covid-19 Pandemic." In *CoronAsur: Asian Religions in the Covidian Age*, ed. Emily Z. Hertzman, Natalie Lang, Erica M. Larson, and Carola Lorea. Honolulu: University of Hawai'i Press, 2023.

Garland, Robert. "Miracles in the Greek and Roman World." In *The Cambridge Companion to Miracles*, ed. Graham H. Twelftree, 75-94. Cambridge: Cambridge University Press, 2011.

Garrett, Leroy. *The Stone Campbell Movement: The Story of the American Restoration Movement.* Joplin, MO: College Press, 1994.

Geiger, Wilhelm. *The Mahavamsa: The Great Chronicle of Ceylon*. London: Pali Text Society, 1912.

Gethin, Rupert. *The Foundations of Buddhism*. Oxford: Oxford University Press, 1998.

——. "Tales of Miraculous Teachings: Miracles in Early India Buddhism." In *The Cambridge Companion to Miracles*, ed. Graham H. Twelftree, 216-34. Cambridge: Cambridge University Press, 2011.

GhaneaBassiri, Kambiz, and Paul Robertson, eds. *All Religion Is Inter-Religion: Engaging the Work of Steven M. Wasserstrom*. London: Bloomsbury Academic, 2019.

Ghassem-Fachandi, Parvis. *Pogrom in Gujarat: Hindu Nationalism and Anti-Muslim Violence in India*. Princeton, NJ: Princeton University Press, 2012.

Girard, René, Pierpaolo Antonello, and Joao Cezar de Castro Rocha. *Evolution and Conversion: Dialogues on the Origins of Culture*. London: Bloomsbury Academic, 2008.

Goldstone, Brian, and Stanley Hauerwas. "Disciplined Seeing: Forms of Christianity and Forms of Life." *South Atlantic Quarterly* 109, no. 4 (2006): 765-90.

Gombrich, Richard. *Precept and Practice: Traditional Buddhism in the Rural Highlands of Ceylon*. Oxford: Clarendon Press, 1971.

Gombrich, Richard, and Gananath Obeyesekere. *Buddhism Transformed*. Princeton, NJ: Princeton University Press, 1988.

Goodhand, Jonathan, Jonathan Spencer, and Benedict Korf. *Conflict and Peacebuilding: Caught in the Peacetrap?* London: Routledge, 2010.

Goonasekera, Sunil. "*Bara*: Buddhist Vows at Kataragama." In *Dealing with Deities: The Ritual Vow in South Asia*, ed. Selva J. Raj and William P. Harman, 107-28. Albany: State University of New York Press, 2012.

Goonatilake, Susantha. *Recolonisation: Foreign Funded NGOs in Sri Lanka*. New Delhi: Sage Publications, 2006.

Gooneratne, Dandris de Silva. *On Demonology and Witchcraft in Ceylon*. 1865. New Delhi: Asian Educational Services, 1998.

Government of Sri Lanka. "Gazette Notification: Prohibition of Forcible Conversion of Religion Act." *Daily News* (Colombo), May 28, 2004.

Gunaratna, K. Locana. "Dandris de Silva Guneratna: Recalling His Times and Some Landmarks in His Career." *Journal of the Royal Asiatic Society of Sri Lanka* 54 (2008): 225-42.

Gunawardana, R. A. L. H. "People of the Lion: The Sinhala Identity and Ideology in History and Historiography." In *History and the Roots of Conflict*, ed. Jonathan Spencer, 45-86. London: Routledge, 1990.

Guyer, Jane. "Prophecy and the Near Future: Thoughts on Macroeconomic, Evangelical, and Punctuated Time." *American Ethnologist* 34 (2007): 409-21.

Hallisey, Charles. "Challenges to the Study of Religion and Understanding Southeast Asia." SEASSI Summer Lecture Series, Madison, WI. 2007.

——. "A Tribute to G. D. Wijayawardhana." *The Island Newspaper*, March 15, 2007. http://www.island.lk/2007/03/15/features4.html.

Handman, Courtney. *Critical Christianity: Translation and Denominational Conflict in Papua New Guinea*. Berkeley: University of California Press, 2014.

Hansen, Ann. "The Prophetic Mood of 1957: Stories from the 2500th Anniversary Celebrations of Buddhism in Bangkok and Phnom Penh." Unpublished paper presented at AAS-Asia, Bangkok, 2019.

Harding, Susan F. *The Book of Jerry Falwell: Fundamentalist Language and Politics*. Princeton, NJ: Princeton University Press, 2001.

Hardy, Robert Spence. *The Legends and Theories of the Buddhists: Compared with History and Science, with Introductory Notices of the Life and System of Gotama Buddha*. Edinburgh: Williams and Norgate, 1866.

Harris, Elizabeth. *Theravāda Buddhism and the British Encounter: Religious, Missionary and Colonial Experience in Nineteenth-Century Sri Lanka*. London: Routledge, 2006.

Hart, Keith. "Religion and Economy." The Memory Bank, October 26, 2015. https://thememory bank.co.uk/2015/10/26/religion-and-economy/.

Harvey, Peter. *An Introduction to Buddhism: Teachings, History, Practices*. Cambridge: Cambridge University Press, 2013.

Haskell, Thomas L. "Capitalism and the Origins of the Humanitarian Sensibility, Part I." *American Historical Review* 90, no. 2 (1985): 339–61.

Haynes, Naomi. "Affordances and Audiences: Finding the Difference Christianity Makes." *Current Anthropology* 55, no. S10 (2014): S357–65.

——. *Moving by the Spirit: Pentecostal Social Life on the Zambian Copperbelt*. Berkeley: University of California Press, 2017.

——. "Taking Dominion in a Christian Nation." *Pneuma* 43, no. 2 (2021): 214–32.

Heim, Maria. *Theories of the Gift in South Asia: Hindu, Buddhist, and Jain Reflections on Dana*. New York: Routledge, 2004.

Heo, Angie. *The Political Lives of Saints: Christian-Muslim Mediation in Egypt*. Berkeley: University of California Press, 2018.

Hertzberg, Michael. "The Anti-Conversion Bill: Political Buddhism, 'Unethical Conversions' and Religious Freedom in Sri Lanka." PhD dissertation, University of Bergen, 2016.

Herzog, Jonathan. *The Spiritual-Industrial Complex: America's Religious Battle Against Communism in the Early Cold War*. Oxford: Oxford University Press, 2011.

Hirschkind, Charles. *The Ethical Soundscape: Cassette Sermons and Islamic Counterpublics*. New York: Columbia University Press, 2006.

Hirschkind, Charles, Maria José de Abreu, and Carlo Caduff. "New Media, New Publics? An Introduction." *Current Anthropology* 58, no. S15 (2017): S3–S12.

Hobbes, Thomas. *Leviathan: Or the Matter, Forme and Power of a Commonwealth, Ecclesiasticall and Civill*. 1651. Ed. A. R. Waller. Cambridge: Cambridge University Press, 1904.

——. *Man and Citizen (de Homine et de Cive)*. 1642. http://www.public-library.uk/ebooks/27/57.pdf.

Holt, John C. *Buddha in the Crown: Avalokiteśvara in the Buddhist Traditions of Sri Lanka*. Oxford: Oxford University Press, 1991.

——. *The Buddhist Visnu: Religious Transformation, Politics, and Culture*. New York: Columbia University Press, 2004.

——. "The Persistence of Political Buddhism." In *Buddhist Fundamentalism and Minority Identities in Sri Lanka*, ed. Tessa J. Bartholomeusz and Chandra R. DeSilva, 186–95. Albany: State University of New York Press, 1998.

Horowitz, Jason. "Pope Francis Ousts Power Conservative Cardinal." *New York Times*. July 1, 2017. https://www.nytimes.com/2017/07/01/world/europe/vatican-pope-doctrine-mueller.html/.

Hurd, Elizabeth Shakman. *Beyond Religious Freedom: The New Global Politics of Religion.* Princeton, NJ: Princeton University Press, 2017.

Ibrahim, Amrita. "'Who Is a Bigger Terrorist Than the Police?': Photography as a Politics of Encounter in Delhi's Batla House." *South Asian Popular Culture* 11, no. 2 (2013): 133-44.

Idigbe, Rosie K. "What Will Be the Fate of Religious Minorities in Sri Lanka?" Groundviews, Journalism for Citizens. August 28, 2020. https://groundviews.org/2020/08/28/what-will -be-the-fate-of-religious-minorities-in-sri-lanka/.

Ivan, Victor. *Revolt in the Temple: The Buddhist Revival up to Soma Thera.* Colombo: Ravaya Publishers, 2009.

Jaspers, Karl. "The Origin and Goal of History." Trans. Michael Bullock. New Haven, CT: Yale University Press, 1953.

Jeyaseelan, Gnanaseelan. "A Critical Discourse Analysis of a Newspaper Editorial Promoting Insurance." *Journal of Business Management* (Faculty of Business Studies, Vavuniya Campus, University of Jaffna) 3, no. 1 (2020): 48-67.

Jayawardena, Kumari. *Nobodies to Somebodies: The Rise of the Colonial Bourgeoisie in Sri Lanka.* Colombo: Social Scientists' Association and Sanjiva Books, 2000.

Jayaweera, Stanley. "The Pope, the Mahanayakes, and Buddhism." *Dialogue* 22 (1995): 8-12.

Jegathesan, Mythri. *Tea and Solidarity: Tamil Women and Work in Postwar Sri Lanka.* Seattle: University of Washington Press, 2019.

John Paul II. *Crossing the Threshold of Hope.* Ed. Vittorio Messori. New York: Knopf, 1994.

Johnson, Deborah. "Sri Lanka: A Divided Church in a Divided Polity—The Brokerage of a Struggling Institution." *Contemporary South Asia* 20, no. 1 (2012): 77-90.

Kapferer, Bruce. *A Celebration of Demons: Exorcism and the Aesthetics of Healing in Sri Lanka.* New York: Routledge, 1991.

——. *The Feast of the Sorcerer: Practices of Consciousness and Power.* Chicago: University of Chicago Press, 1997.

——. *Legends of People, Myths of State: Violence, Intolerance, and Political Culture of Sri Lanka and Australia.* 1988. New York: Berghahn Books, 2012.

Karunanayake, Nandana. "Communication Scenes: Sri Lanka." In *Asian Communication Handbook,* ed. Indrajit Banerjee and Stephen Logan, 446-59. Singapore: Asian Media Information and Communication Centre, 2008.

Kaviraj, Sudipta. "Plurality and Pluralism: Democracy, Religious Difference, and Political Imagination." In *Negotiating Democracy and Religious Pluralism: India, Pakistan, and Turkey,* ed. Karen Barkey, Sudipta Kaviraj and Vatsal Naresh, 221-48. New York: Oxford University Press, 2021.

Keane, Webb. *Christian Moderns: Freedom and Fetish in the Mission Encounter.* Berkeley: University of California Press, 2007.

——. "On Spirit Writing: Materialities of Language and the Religious Work of Transduction." *Journal of the Royal Anthropological Institute* 19, no. 1 (2013): 1-17.

——. "What Is Religious Freedom Supposed to Free?" In *Politics of Religious Freedom,* ed. Winnifred F. Sullivan, Elizabeth Shakman Hurd, Saba Mahmood and Peter G. Danchin, 57-65. Chicago: University of Chicago Press, 2015.

Kelly, John D., Beatrice Jauregui, Sean T. Mitchell, and Jeremy Walton. *Anthropology and Global Counterinsurgency.* Chicago: University of Chicago Press, 2010.

Kelly, John D., and Martha Kaplan. *Represented Communities: Fiji and World Decolonization*. Chicago: University of Chicago Press, 2001.

Kemper, Steven. *The Presence of the Past: Chronicles, Politics, and Culture in Sinhala Life*. Ithaca, NY: Cornell University Press, 1991.

——. *Rescued from the Nation: Anagarika Dharmapala and the Buddhist World*. Chicago: University of Chicago Press, 2015.

Keyes, Charles. "Millennialism, Theravāda Buddhism, and Thai Society." *Journal of Asian Studies* 36 (1977): 283–302.

Khan, Naveeda. *Muslim Becoming: Aspiration and Skepticism in Pakistan*. Durham, NC: Duke University Press, 2012.

Klassen, Pamela E., and Courtney Bender. "Introduction: Habits of Pluralism." In *After Pluralism: Reimagining Religious Engagement*, ed. Courtney Bender and Pamela E. Klassen, 1–30. New York: Columbia University Press, 2010.

Klem, Bart. "The Problem of Peace and the Meaning of 'Post-War.'" *Conflict, Security and Development* 18, no. 3 (2018): 233–55.

Klem, Bart, and Sidharthan Maunaguru. "Insurgent Rule as Sovereign Mimicry and Mutation." *Comparative Studies of History and Society* 59, no. 3 (2017): 629–56.

Korf, Benedict, Shahul Hasbullah, Pia Hollenbach, and Bart Klem. "The Gift of Disaster: the Commodification of Good Intentions in Post-Tsunami Sri Lanka." *Disasters* 34, no. 1 (2010): 60–77.

Kwon, Heonik. *Ghosts of War in Vietnam*. Cambridge: Cambridge University Press. 2008.

Ladwig, Patrice. "Millennialism, Charisma and Utopia: Revolutionary Potentialities in Premodern Lao and Thai Theravada Buddhism." *Politics, Religion and Ideology* 15, no. 1 (2014): 308–29.

——. " 'Special operation pagoda': Buddhism, Covert Operations and the Politics of Religious Subversion in Cold War Laos." In *Changing Lives in Laos: Society, Politics and Culture in a Post-Socialist State*, ed. Vanina Bouté and Vatthana Pholsena, 81–108. Singapore: National University of Singapore Press, 2017.

Lakshman, W. D. "The IMF-World Bank Intervention in Sri Lankan Economic Policy: Historical Trends and Patterns." *Social Scientist* 13, no. 2 (1985): 3–29.

Lambek, Michael, ed. *Ordinary Ethics: Anthropology, Language, and Action*. New York: Fordham University Press, 2010.

Leve, Lauren. *The Buddhist Art of Living in Nepal: Ethical Practice and Religious Reform*. New York: Routledge, 2017.

Mahadev, Neena. "Buddhist Nationalism and Christian Evangelism: Rearticulations of Enmity and Belonging in Postwar Sri Lanka." PhD dissertation, Johns Hopkins University, 2013.

——. "The Charism of the Christian Left: Dissidence as Habit in a Time of Bi-polar Theopolitics." *Cambridge Journal of Anthropology*, 40, no. 1 (2022): 84–103.

——. "Conversion and Anti-Conversion in Contemporary Sri Lanka." In *Proselytizing and the Limits of Religious Pluralism in Asia*, ed. Juliana Finucane and R. Michael Feener, 211–35. Singapore: ARI-Springer, 2014.

——. "Economies of Conversion and Ontologies of Religious Difference: Buddhism, Christianity, and Adversarial Political Perception in Sri Lanka." *Current Anthropology* 59, no. 6 (2018): 665–90.

——. "Karma and Grace: Rivalrous Reckonings of Fortune and Misfortune." *HAU Journal of Ethnographic Theory* 9, no. 2 (2019): 421–38.

——. "The Maverick Dialogics of Religious Rivalry." *Journal of the Royal Anthropological Institute* 22, no. 1 (2016): 127–47.

——. "Post-war Blood: Sacrifice, Anti-Sacrifice, and the Rearticulations of Conflict in Sri Lanka." *Religion and Society: Advances in Research* 10 (2019): 130–50.

——. "Secularism and Religious Modernity in Sri Lanka and Singapore: Transregional Revivalism Considered." In *Secularisms in South, East, and Southeast Asia*, ed. Peter van der Veer and Kenneth Dean, 287–311. Cham, Switzerland: Palgrave, 2019.

Mahmood, Saba. *The Politics of Piety: The Islamic Revival and the Feminist Subject*. Princeton, NJ: Princeton University Press, 2011.

——. *Religious Difference in a Secular Age: A Minority Report*. Princeton, NJ: Princeton University Press, 2015.

Malalgoda, Kitsiri. *Buddhism in Sinhalese Society 1750–1900: A Study of Religious Revival and Change*. Berkeley: University of California Press, 1976.

——. "The Buddhist-Christian Confrontation in Ceylon, 1800–1880." *Social Compass* 20, no. 2 (1973): 171–200.

——. "Millennialism in Relation to Buddhism." *Studies in Society and Culture* 12, no. 4 (1970): 424–41.

Mankekar, Purnima. "Epic Contests: Television and Religious Identity in India." In *Media Worlds: Anthropology on New Terrain*, ed. Faye Ginsburg, Lila Abu-Lughod, and Brian Larkin, 134–51. Berkeley: University of California Press, 2002.

——. *Screening Culture, Viewing Politics: An Ethnography of Television, Womanhood, and Nation in Postcolonial India*. Durham, NC: Duke University Press. 1999.

Manor, James. *The Expedient Utopian: Bandaranaike and Ceylon*. New York: Cambridge University Press, 1989.

Marshall, Ruth. "Christianity, Anthropology, Politics," *Current Anthropology* 55, no. S10 (2014): S344–56.

——. *Political Spiritualities: The Pentecostal Revolution in Nigeria*. Chicago: University of Chicago Press, 2009.

Matthews, Bruce. "Christian Evangelical Conversions and the Politics of Sri Lanka." *Pacific Affairs* 80, no. 3 (October 2007): 455–72.

Mauss, Marcel. *The Gift*. 1925. Trans. Jane Guyer. Chicago: Hau Books, 2016.

Mayblin, Maya. "The Lapsed and the Laity: Discipline and Lenience in the Study of Religion." *Journal of the Royal Anthropological Institute* 23, no. 3 (2017): 503–22.

Mazusawa, Tomoko. *The Invention of World Religions*. Chicago: University of Chicago Press, 2005.

McAllister, Carlota, and Valentina Napolitano. "Political Theology/Theopolitics: The Thresholds and Vulnerabilities of Sovereignty." *Annual Review of Anthropology* 50 (2021): 109–24.

McDaniel, Justin. *The Lovelorn Ghost and the Magical Monk: Practicing Buddhism in Modern Thailand*. New York: Columbia University Press, 2011.

McKinnon, Andrew. "Elective Affinities of the Protestant Ethnic: Weber and the Chemistry of Capitalism." *Sociological Theory* 28, no. 1 (2010): 108–26.

Meyer, Birgit. "Aesthetics of Persuasion: Global Christianity and Pentecostalism's Sensational Forms." *South Atlantic Quarterly* 109, no. 4 (2010): 741–63.

—. "Introduction: From Imagined Communities to Aesthetic Formations: Religious Media-tions, Sensational Forms, and Styles of Binding." In *Aesthetic Formations: Religion/Culture/Critique*, ed. Birgit Meyer, 1–28. New York: Palgrave Macmillan, 2009.

—. "Make a Complete Break from the Past: Memory and Post-colonial Modernity in Ghana-ian Pentecostalist Discourse." *Journal of Religion in Africa* 28, no. 3 (1998): 316–49.

—. *Mediation and the Genesis of Presence: Towards a Material Approach to Religion*. Utrecht: University of Utrecht Press, 2012.

Miles, Jack. *God: A Biography*. New York: Vintage, 1996.

Mohan, P. Sanal. *The Modernity of Slavery: Struggles Against Caste Inequality in Colonial Kerala*. New Delhi: Oxford University Press, 2015.

Moore, Mick. "The Identity of Capitalists and the Legitimacy of Capitalism: Sri Lanka since Independence." *Development and Change* 28, no. 2 (1997): 331–66.

—. "The Ideological History of the Sri Lankan 'Peasantry.'" *Modern Asian Studies* 23, no. 1 (1989): 179–207.

Morris, Rosalind. "Accidental Histories, Post-Historical Practice." *Anthropological Quarterly* 83, no. 3 (2010): 581–624.

Moss, Candida. *The Myth of Persecution: How Early Christians Invented a Story of Martyrdom*. New York: HarperCollins, 2013.

Mosse, David. "Possession and Confession: Affliction and Sacred Power in Colonial and Con-temporary Catholic South India." In *The Anthropology of Christianity*, ed. Fenella Cannell, 99–133. Durham, NC: Duke University Press, 2006.

—. *The Saint in the Banyan Tree: Christianity and Caste Society in India*. Berkeley: University of California Press, 2012.

Mouffe, Chantal, ed. *The Challenge of Carl Schmitt*. New York: Verso, 1999.

—. *The Democratic Paradox*. New York: Verso, 2005.

Needham, Rodney. *Belief, Language, and Experience*. Chicago: University of Chicago Press, 1972.

Napolitano, Valentina, and Kristen Norget. "Economies of Sanctity." *Postscripts: The Journal of Sacred Texts, Cultural Histories, and Contemporary Contexts* 5, no. 3 (2009): 251–64.

Narayan Swamy, M. N. *Inside An Elusive Mind: Prabhakaran, the First Profile of the World's Most Ruthless Guerrilla Leader*. Colombo: Vijitha Yapa Publications, 2004.

Obeyesekere, Gananath. "The Buddhist Pantheon and Its Extensions." In *Anthropological Stud-ies in Theravada Buddhism*, ed. Manning Nash, 1–26. New Haven, CT: Yale University Press, 1966.

—. "The Conscience of the Parricide: A Study in Buddhist History." *Man* 24, no. 2 (1989): 236–54.

—. *The Cult of the Goddess Pattini*. Chicago: University of Chicago Press, 1984.

—. "The Great Tradition and the Little in the Perspective of Sinhalese Buddhism." *Journal of Asian Studies* 22, no. 2 (1963): 139–53.

—. *Imagining Karma: Ethical Transformation in Amerindian, Buddhist, and Greek Rebirth*. Berkeley: University of California Press, 2002.

—. *Medusa's Hair: An Essay on Personal Symbols and Religious Experience*. Chicago: University of Chicago Press, 1981.

—. "Religious Symbolism and Political Change in Ceylon." *Modern Ceylon Studies* 1 (1970): 43–63.

——. "Social Change and the Deities: Rise of the Kataragama Cult in Modern Sri Lanka." *Man* 12, nos. 3-4 (1977): 377-96.

——. "Theodicy, Sin, and Salvation in a Sociology of Buddhism." In *Dialectic in Practical Religion*, ed. Edmund Leach, 7-40. Cambridge: Cambridge University Press, 1968.

Obeyesekere, Gananath, Frank Reynolds, and Bardwell Smith, eds. *The Two Wheels of Dhamma: Essays on the Theravada Tradition in India and Ceylon*. Chambersburg, PA: AAR Studies in Religion, 1972.

Osella, Filippo. "Charity and Philanthropy in South Asia: An Introduction." *Modern Asian Studies* 52, no. 1 (2018): 4-34.

Outreville, François. "Life Insurance in Developing Countries: A Cross-Country Analysis." United Nations Conference on Trade and Development (UNCTAD) Review Discussion Papers, 1994.

Palakidnar, Ananth. "When the Pope Visited Sri Lanka." *The Sunday Observer*. April 10, 2005. http://archives.sundayobserver.lk/2005/04/10/fea31.html.

Parry, Jonathan. "The Gift, the Indian Gift and the 'Indian Gift.'" *Man* 21, no. 3 (1986): 453-73.

Patton, Thomas N. *The Buddha's Wizards: Magic, Protection, and Healing in Burmese Buddhism*. New York: Columbia University Press, 2020.

Perera, Sasanka. *New Evangelical Movements and Conflict in South Asia: Sri Lanka and Nepal in Perspective*. Colombo: Regional Centre for Strategic Studies, 1998.

Perera, Sreema. *Deshamanya Lalith Kotelawala*. Ratmalana: Sarvodaya Vishva Lekha Printers, 2001.

Peristiany, J. G., and Julian Pitt-Rivers, eds. *Honor and Grace in Anthropology*. Cambridge: Cambridge University Press, 1992.

Perniola, V. *The Catholic Church in Sri Lanka, 1505–1565*. Vol. 1. Dehiwela, Sri Lanka: Tissara Prakasakayo Ltd., 1989.

Pfaffenberger, Bryan. "The Kataragama Pilgrimage: Hindu-Buddhist Interaction and Its Significance in Sri Lanka's Polyethnic Social System." *Journal of Asian Studies* 38, no. 2 (1979): 253-70.

Pieris, Aloysius. "Dialogue and Distrust between Buddhists and Christians: A Report on the Catholic Church's Experience in Sri Lanka." In *Buddhism and Christianity, Interactions between East and West*, ed. Ulrich Everding, 104-21. Colombo: Goethe Institut Colombo, 1995.

——. *Prophetic Humour in Buddhism and Christianity: Doing Inter-Religious Studies in the Reverential Mode*. Colombo: Ecumenical Institute for Study and Dialogue, 2009.

Pietz, William. "The Problem of the Fetish, I." *RES: Anthropology and Aesthetics* 9 (Spring 1985): 5-17.

Pina-Cabral, João. "On the Resilience of Superstition." In *Religion and Science as Forms of Life: Anthropological Insights into Reason and Unreason*, ed. Carles Salazar and Joan Bestard, 173-87. New York: Berghahn, 2015.

Povinelli, Elizabeth. *Economies of Abandonment: Social Belonging and Endurance in Late Liberalism*. Durham, NC: Duke University Press, 2011.

Premawardhana, Devaka. *Faith in Flux: Pentecostalism and Mobility in Rural Mozambique*. Philadelphia: University of Pennsylvania, 2018.

Premawardhana, Shanta. "The Politics of Conversion: The Anti-Conversion Bill in Sri Lanka." Ethics Daily Online, November 2, 2004. http://www.ethicsdaily.com/the-politics-of-conver sion-anti-conversion-bill-in-sri-lanka-cms-4925.

——. *Religious Conversion: Religion Scholars Thinking Together.* West Sussex: Wiley-Blackwell, 2015.

Prothero, Stephen. *The White Buddhist: The Asian Odyssey of Henry Steel Olcott.* Bloomington: Indiana University Press, 1996.

Punnaji, Madawela. "Why Buddhists Should Not Quarrel with the Pope." *Dialogue* 22 (1995): 13–19.

Rajagopal, Arvind. *Politics after Television: Hindu Nationalism and the Reshaping of the Public in India.* Cambridge: Cambridge University Press, 2001.

Rajasingham-Senanayake, Darini. "From National Security to Human Security: The Challenge of Winning the Peace in Sri Lanka." *Strategic Analysis* 33, no. 6 (2009): 820–27.

——. "The Sinhala *Kaduwa*: The Double-Edge Sword and Ethnic Conflict." *Pravada* 5, no. 2 (1997): 15–19.

Rambukwella, Harshana. *The Politics and Poetics of Authenticity: A Cultural Genealogy of Sinhala Nationalism.* London: UCL Press, 2018.

Rao, Anupama. *The Caste Question: Dalits and the Politics of Modern India.* Berkeley: University of California Press, 2009.

Reed, Susan A. "Performing Respectability: The Beravā, Middle-Class Nationalism, and the Classicization of Kandyan Dance in Sri Lanka." *Cultural Anthropology* 17, no. 2 (2002): 246–77.

Robbins, Joel. "Anthropology and Theology: An Awkward Relationship?" *Anthropological Quarterly* 79, no. 2 (2006): 285–94.

——. "Anthropology, Pentecostalism, and the New Paul: Conversion, Event, and Social Transformation." *South Atlantic Quarterly* 109, no. 4 (2010): 633–52.

——. "Continuity-Thinking and the Problem of Christian Culture." *Current Anthropology* 48, no. 1 (2007): 5–38.

——. "The Globalization of Pentecostal and Charismatic Christianity." *Annual Review of Anthropology* 33 (2004): 117–43.

Roberts, Michael. "A Tale of Resistance: The Story of the Arrival of the Portuguese in Sri Lanka." *Ethnos* 54, no. 1–2 (1989): 69–82.

Roberts, Nathaniel. *To Be Cared For: The Power of Conversion and the Foreignness of Belonging in an Indian Slum.* Berkeley: University of California Press, 2016.

Rogers, John D. "Historical Images in the British Period." In *Sri Lanka: History and the Roots of Conflict*, ed. Jonathan Spencer, 87–106. London: Routledge, 1990.

Roy, Arundhati. "The Pandemic Is a Portal." *Financial Times.* April 4, 2020. https://www.ft.com /content/10d8f5e8-74eb-11ea-95fe-fcd274e920ca.

Ruel, Malcolm. "Christians as Believers." In *Religious Organization and Religious Experience*, ed. John Davis, 9–31. London: Academic Press, 1982.

Sahlins, Marshall. "What Kinship Is (Part One)." *Journal of the Royal Anthropological Institute* 17, no. 1 (2011): 2–19.

Salter, Richard. "Time, Authority and Ethics in the Khmer Rouge: Elements of the Millennial Vision in Year Zero." In *Millennialism, Persecution and Violence*, ed. Catherine Wessinger, 281–98. Syracuse, NY: Syracuse University Press, 2000.

Samuels, Jeffrey. *Attracting the Heart: Social Relations and the Aesthetics of Emotion in Sri Lankan Monastic Culture.* Honolulu: University of Hawai'i Press, 2010.

Schlieter, Jens. "Checking the Heavenly 'Bank Account of Karma': Cognitive Metaphors for Karma in Western Perception and Early Theravāda Buddhism." *Religion* 43, no. 4 (2013): 463–86.

Schmitt, Carl. *The Concept of the Political.* 1932. Trans. George Schwab. Chicago: University of Chicago Press, 2007.

——. *Political Theology: Four Chapters on the Concept of Sovereignty.* 1922. Trans. George Schwab. Chicago: University of Chicago Press, 1985.

——. *Roman Catholicism and Its Political Form.* 1923. Trans. G. L. Ulman. Westport, CT: Greenwood Press, 1996.

Schonthal, Benjamin. *Buddhism, Politics and the Limits of Law: The Pyrrhic Constitutionalism of Sri Lanka.* Cambridge: Cambridge University Press, 2016.

Schonthal, Benjamin, and Matthew Walton. "The (New) Buddhist Nationalisms? Symmetries and Specificities in Sri Lanka and Myanmar." *Contemporary Buddhism* 17, no. 1 (2016): 81–115.

Schwartz, Joel. "Hobbes and the Two Kingdoms of God." *Polity* 18, no. 1 (1985): 7–24.

Scott, David. *Formations of Ritual: Colonial and Anthropological Discourses on the Sinhala Yaktovil.* Minneapolis: University of Minnesota Press, 1994.

Scott, David, and Charles Hirschkind, eds. *Powers of the Secular Modern: Talal Asad and His Interlocutors.* Stanford: Stanford University Press, 2006.

Scott, James. *The Moral Economy of the Peasant.* Princeton, NJ: Princeton University Press, 1976.

Selkirk, James. *Recollections of Ceylon, After a Residence of Thirteen Years.* London: J. Hatchard and Son, 1844.

Seneviratne, H. L. *The Work of Kings: The New Buddhism in Sri Lanka.* Chicago: University of Chicago Press, 1999.

Shastri, Amita. "An Open Economy in a Time of Civil War." In *Economy, Culture, and Civil War in Sri Lanka,* ed. Deborah Winslow and Michael Woost, 73–94. Bloomington: Indiana University Press, 2004.

Shipley-Weaver, Jesse. "Comedians, Pastors, and the Miraculous Agency of Charisma in Ghana." *Cultural Anthropology* 24, no. 3 (2009): 523–52.

Sihlé, Nicolas. "Towards a Comparative Anthropology of the Buddhist Gift (and Other Transfers." *Religion Compass* 9, no. 11 (2015): 352–85.

Silva, Kalinga Tudor. "Identity, Infection, and Fear: A Preliminary Analysis of COVID-19 Drivers and Responses in Sri Lanka." Colombo: International Centre for Ethnic Studies (ICES), 2020.

Simmel, Georg. *The Sociology of Georg Simmel.* Trans. Kurt H. Wolff. New York: Free Press, 1950.

Simpson, Bob. "Possession, Dispossession and the Social Distribution of Knowledge among Sri Lankan Ritual Specialists." *Journal of the Royal Anthropological Institute* 3, no. 1 (1997): 43–59.

Singh, Bhrigupati. "Agonistic Intimacy and Moral Aspiration in Popular Hinduism: A Study in the Political Theology of the Neighbor." *American Ethnologist* 38, no. 3 (2011): 430–50.

Smith, Bardwell L. "The Ideal Social Order as Portrayed in the Chronicles of Ceylon." In *Religion and Legitimation of Power in Sri Lanka*, ed. Bardwell Smith, 48–72. Chambersberg, PA: Anima, 1978.

Somaratna, G. P. V. *Origins of the Pentecostal Mission in Sri Lanka*. Nugegoda, Sri Lanka: Margaya Fellowship, 1996.

Southwold, Martin. *Buddhism in Life: The Anthropological Study of Religion and the Sinhalese Practice of Buddhism*. Manchester: Manchester University Press,1983.

Spencer, Jonathan. *Anthropology, Politics and the State*. Cambridge: Cambridge University Press, 2007.

—. "Collective Violence and Everyday Practice in Sri Lanka." *Modern Asian Studies* 24, no. 3 (1990): 603–23.

—. "A Nationalism Without Politics? The Illiberal Consequences of Liberal Institutions in Sri Lanka." *Third World Quarterly* 29, no. 3 (2008): 611–29.

—. "The Politics of Tolerance: Buddhists and Christians, Truth and Error in Sri Lanka." In *The Pursuit of Certainty*, ed. Wendy James, 195–214. London: Routledge, 2005.

—. *A Sinhala Village in a Time of Trouble*. New York: Oxford University Press, 1990.

—, ed. *Sri Lanka: History and the Roots of Conflict*. London: Routledge, 1990.

Spencer, Jonathan, Shahul Hasbullah, K. Tudor Silva, Jonathan Goodhand, and Bart Klem. *Checkpoint, Temple, Church and Mosque: a Collaborative Ethnography of War and Peace*. London: Pluto Press, 2015.

Spiro, Melford. *Buddhism and Society: A Great Tradition and Its Burmese Vicissitudes*. London: George Allen & Unwin, 1971.

Stirrat, R. L. *Power and Religiosity in a Postcolonial Setting*. Cambridge: Cambridge University Press, 1992.

Stirrat, R. L., and Heiko Henkel. "The Development Gift: The Problem of Reciprocity in the NGO World." *Annals of the American Academy of Political and Social Science* 554 (November 1997): 66–80.

Stokke, Kristian, and Jayadeva Uyangoda, eds. *Liberal Peace in Question: Politics of State and Market Reform in Sri Lanka*. London: Anthem Press, 2011.

Stolow, Jeremy. "Religion and/as Media." *Theory, Culture and Society* 22, no. 4 (2005):119–45.

Strathern, Alan. *Kingship and Conversion in 16th Century Ceylon: Portuguese Imperialism in a Buddhist Land*. Cambridge: Cambridge University Press, 2007.

Strathern, Marilyn. *The Gender of the Gift: Problems with Women and Problems with Society in Melanesia*. Berkeley: University of California Press, 1988.

Sullivan, Winnifred Fallers. *The Impossibility of Religious Freedom*. Princeton, NJ: Princeton University Press, 2005.

Sullivan, Winnifred F., Elizabeth Shakman Hurd, Saba Mahmood, and Peter Danchin. *Politics of Religious Freedom*. Chicago: University of Chicago Press, 2015.

Sykes, Jim. "Sound Studies, Difference, and Global Concept History." In *Remapping Sound Studies*, ed. Gavin Steingo and Jim Sykes, 203–27. Durham, NC: Duke University Press, 2019.

Tambiah, Stanley J. "Buddhism and This-worldly Activity." *Modern Asian Studies* 7, no. 1 (1973): 1–20.

—. *Buddhism Betrayed? Religion, Politics, and Violence in Sri Lanka*. Chicago: University of Chicago Press, 1992.

—. *The Buddhist Saints of the Forest and the Cult of the Amulets.* Cambridge: Cambridge University Press, 1984.

—. *Sri Lanka: Ethnic Fratricide and the Dismantling of Democracy.* Chicago: University of Chicago Press, 1986.

—. *World Conqueror World Renouncer.* Cambridge: Cambridge University Press, 1976.

Taylor, Charles. "Buffered and Porous Selves." The Immanent Frame. September 2, 2008. https://tif.ssrc.org/2008/09/02/buffered-and-porous-selves/.

Thiranagama, Sharika. "Figurations of Menace." The Immanent Frame. April 1, 2020. https://tif.ssrc.org/2020/04/01/figurations-of-menace/.

—. *In My Mother's House: Civil War in Sri Lanka.* Philadelphia: University of Pennsylvania Press, 2011.

Trainor, Kevin. *Relics, Ritual, and Representation in Buddhism: Rematerializing the Sri Lankan Theravada Tradition.* Cambridge: Cambridge University Press, 1997.

Turner, Alicia. *Saving Buddhism: The Impermanence of Religion in Colonial Burma.* Honolulu: University of Hawai'i Press, 2014.

U.S. Department of State. "International Religious Freedom Report, 2019." https://www.state.gov/reports/2019-report-on-international-religious-freedom/sri-lanka/.

Uyangoda, Jayadeva. "Soma Thero: Significance of His Life and Death." In *Religion in Context: Buddhism and Socio-Political Change in Sri Lanka* ed. Jayadeva Uyangoda, 166–71. Colombo: Social Scientists Association, 2007.

van der Veer, Peter. "Syncretism, Multiculturalism, and the Discourse of Tolerance." In *Syncretism/Anti-Syncretism*, ed. Charles Stewart and Rosalind Shaw, 185–200. London: Routledge, 1994.

van Voorhis, Bruce. Foreword to Basil Fernando, *Power vs. Conscience: the Excommunication of Fr. Tissa Balasuriya*, vii–viii. Hong Kong: Asian Legal Resource Centre, Ltd, 1997.

Venugopal, Rajesh. *Nationalism, Development and Ethnic Conflict in Sri Lanka.* Cambridge: Cambridge University Press, 2018.

Viswanath, Rupa. *The Pariah Problem: Caste, Religion, and the Social in Modern India.* New York: Columbia University Press, 2014.

Viswanathan, Gauri. *Outside the Fold: Conversion, Modernity, and Belief.* Princeton, NJ: Princeton University Press, 1998.

Wadley, Susan S. *Struggling with Destiny in Karimpur, 1925–1984.* Berkeley: University of California Press, 1994.

Walters, Jonathan. "Multireligion on the Bus: Beyond 'Influence' and 'Syncretism' in the Study of Religious Meetings." In *Unmaking the Nation*, ed. Pradeep Jeganathan and Qadri Ismail, 34–54. Colombo: Social Scientists' Association, 1995.

Walton, Jeremy F. *Muslim Civil Society and the Politics of Religious Freedom in Turkey.* New York: Oxford University Press, 2017.

Walton, Jeremy F., and Neena Mahadev. "Religious Plurality, Interreligious Pluralism, and Spatial Practices of Religious Difference." *Religion & Society* 10 (2019): 81–91.

Wasserstrom, Steven M. "Nine Theses on the Study of Religion." In *All Religion Is Inter-Religion: Engaging the Work of Steven Wasserstrom*, ed. Kambiz GhaneaBassiri and Paul Robertson, 9–14. London: Bloomsbury Academic, 2019.

Weber, Max. *Economy and Society.* 1922. Ed. Guenther Roth and Claus Wittlich. Berkeley: University of California Press, 1978.

——. *The Protestant Ethic and the Spirit of Capitalism.* 1905. Trans. S. Kalberg. Chicago: Roxburg Publishing, 2001.

——. *Sociology of Religion.* 1922. Boston: Beacon Press, 1993.

Weerasinghe, Jagath. "Art, War, and Politics in Sri Lanka." 2009. https://www.youtube.com /watch?v=6CXioS8K37A.

Whitaker, Mark. *Amiable Incoherence: Manipulating Histories and Modernities in a Batticaloa Tamil Hindu Temple.* Amsterdam: VU University Press, 1999.

Wimalarathana, Bellanwila. "The Privilege of Erring." *Dialogue* 22 (1995): 29-31.

Winslow, Deborah. "A Political Geography of Deities: Space and the Pantheon in Sinhalese Buddhism." *Journal of Asian Studies* 43, no. 2 (1984): 273-91.

Winslow, Deborah, and Michael Woost. "Introduction: Articulations of Economy and Ethnic Conflict in Sri Lanka." In *Economy, Culture, and Civil War in Sri Lanka*, ed. Deborah Winslow and Michael Woost, 1-28. Bloomington: Indiana University Press, 2004.

Woods, Orlando. "Converting Houses into Churches: The Mobility, Fission, and Sacred Networks of Evangelical House Churches in Sri Lanka." *Environment and Planning D: Society and Space* 31, no. 6 (2013): 1062-75.

Young, Richard F. "The Carpenter-Prēta: An Eighteenth-Century Sinhala-Buddhist Folktale about Jesus." *Asian Folklore Studies* 54, no. 1 (1995): 49-68.

Young, Richard F., and G. S. B. Senanayake. *The Carpenter-Heretic: A Collection of Buddhist Stories about Christianity from Eighteenth Century Sri Lanka.* Colombo: Karunaratne & Sons, 1998.

Young, Richard Fox, and G. P. V. Somaratna. *Vain Debates: The Buddhist-Christian Controversies of Nineteenth-Century Ceylon.* Vienna: De Nobili Research Library, 1996.

Zech, Charles. "Understanding Denominational Structures: Churches as Franchise Organizations." *International Journal of the Economics of Business* 10, no. 3 (2003): 323-35.

Zupanov, Ines G. "Conversion, Illness and Possession: Catholic Missionary Healing in Early Modern South Asia." *Purusārtha* 27 (2008): 263-300.

——. "Jesuit Orientalism: Correspondence between Tomas Pereira and Fernão de Queiros," *Tomás Pereira, S.J. (1646–1708) Life, Work and World*, ed. Luís Filipe Barreto, 43-74. Lisbon: Centro Científico e Cultural de Macau, 1996.

Index

Figures are indicated by an italic *f* following the page number.

End of Days (*Antīyama Kālē*), 121. *See also* Last Days

Engelke, Matthew, 29, 272n31

enmity, 42, 47, 53, 66–67, 108, 154, 194, 266, 272n34

eschatology, 12, 27, 30, 69, 73, 103, 118, 192–93, 203, 209, 222, 262, 269n4

ethics in Theravāda Buddhism, 100–104

ethos of pluralism, 32

Eucharist, 67, 119, 137, 164, 168, 170, 178–80, 242

evangelical, defined, 38–40

exorcisms, 55–56, 140, 167–68, 179, 233, 273n11, 278n3, 281n17

face-saving, 237

faith-healing, 56–57, 148–49, 275n5

Fernando, Oshan, 135

feudalism, 64, 134, 275n6, 284n11

Final Judgment, 78, 121, 145

Formations of the Secular (Asad), 1

Francis, Pope, 191

"fraudulent" conversions, 43–47

freedom of conscience, 24–26

Friday Masowe, 29, 272n31

Gajaweera, Nalika, 86

Garland, Robert, 122

geomancy (*vāstu*), 100, 115, 123, 133, 151, 246, 249

Ghanaian Pentecostalism, 27–28, 69–70

gift economy, 111

gift/gifts: *charismata* (gifts of god's grace), 56, 127, 138, 164, 180, 189; *hau* (spirit of the gift), 97–98; patrimonial rationale, 97, 284n10; philanthropy and religious conversion, 57–62. *See also* charity

Girard, René, 271n22

giving, as monastic vocation, 2, 90, 105–10

glossolalia, 10–11, 137, 170, 180

good karma (*puñña karmaya*), 129, 195, 213

Good News (Christian), 6–7, 11, 13, 113–14, 122, 125, 146, 150, 192–93, 241, 243, 259–60, 264

Gotama Buddha, 8, 102, 123, 131, 198, 200, 209, 211, 215, 219–20. *See also* Buddha

grace: born-again Christians and, 224; *charismata* (gifts of god's grace), 56, 127, 138, 164, 169, 180, 189; divine grace in Catholicism, 164, 169; economies of belief, 66–69; in Hinduism, 168, 281n17; Holy Spirit (*Subha Ātmaya*), 28, 231; inter-religion in Sri Lanka, 26–32, 39; karma and, 222, 224, 265; miracles and, 127; Protestant Christianity, 284n4

guardian deities (*deviyō*), 116, 124, 133–34, 205, 216, 252

gurunānsē (ritual specialist), 248–49, 254, 259

Guyer, Jane, 69

habitus, 11, 51, 54, 230–31

Hardy, Robert Spence, 75, 78

Harris, Elizabeth, 87

hau (spirit of the gift), 97–98

Haynes, Naomi, 39

Heim, Maria, 103

Hindus/Hinduism: animal sacrifice, 263; Brahmanical Hinduism, 100, 102, 275n6, 284n11; caste distinctions, 84, 246, 275n6; caste in, 84–85; charity and, 104, 106–9; conversions of, 35, 84, 225–26, 278n33; *dānadharma* (righteous ritual giving), 101; devotions, 183f, 184; grace and, 168, 281n17; "idolatry," 169; Jesuit orientalism and, 270n17; laicization, 282n5; population census, 17; *saṃsāra*, 193, 199, 202, 214, 216, 220–22; spirit possession, 129, 257, 273n11; Tamil people and, 108; televised Ramayana and, 13–14, 269n6

Hobbes, Thomas, 144

Holy Spirit (*Śuddha Ātmaya*): baptism and, 152; believers and, 98; in Eucharist, 179–80; grace through, 28, 231; intercessional immediacy through, 7–8, 10; Jesus Christ through, 193, 238; manifestation of God through, 171, 179; miracles and, 113–16, 125–28, 130, 136–39, 145; readiness to receive, 251; sanctification by, 164; televangelism and, 15